AF622086

2019

How Modi Won India

2019

How Modi Won India

Rajdeep Sardesai

HarperCollins *Publishers* India

First published in hardback in India by
HarperCollins *Publishers* in 2019

HarperCollins Publishers India, Cyber City, Building 10-A, Gurugram,
Haryana-122002, India
www.harpercollins.co.in

First published in paperback in 2020

2 4 6 8 10 9 7 5 3 1

Copyright © Rajdeep Sardesai 2019, 2020

P-ISBN: 978-93-9032-734-8
E-ISBN: 978-93-5357-393-5

The views and opinions expressed in this book are the author's own and the facts are as reported by him, and the publishers are not in any way liable for the same.

Rajdeep Sardesai asserts the moral right
to be identified as the author of this work.

All rights reserved. No part of this publication may be reproduced, stored in a retrieval system, or transmitted, in any form or by any means, electronic, mechanical, photocopying, recording or otherwise, without the prior permission of the publishers.

Without limiting the exclusive rights of any author, contributor or the publisher of this publication, any unauthorized use of this publication to train generative artificial intelligence (AI) technologies is expressly prohibited. HarperCollins also exercise their rights under Article 4(3) of the Digital Single Market Directive 2019/790 and expressly reserve this publication from the text and data-mining exception.

Typeset in 11.5/16 Dante MT Std at
Manipal Technology Ltd, Manipal

Printed and bound at
MicroPrints India, New Delhi

HarperCollins Publishers, Macken House, 39/40 Mayor Street
Upper, Dublin 1, D01 C9W8, Ireland

To

Ishan and Tarini

Contents

PREFACE

Madison Madness

MADISON Square Garden in midtown Manhattan is a global amphitheatre of dreams. From celebrated basketball players to boxers, from musicians to entertainers, some of the biggest performers of our times have taken centre stage in the arena. On 28 September 2014, a very different rock concert was being staged, its lead artiste a bearded gent from Gujarat who, only months before, had been sworn in as India's fourteenth prime minister. As the crowd chanted his name with a frenzy normally reserved for a pop star, Narendra Damodardas Modi must have felt he had arrived as an international celebrity.

It was a bright day in New York. As the city ambled along that late Sunday morning, tourists training their cameras upwards, families shouting for running toddlers, couples strolling arm in arm, an unusual sight was unfolding. A growing crowd of Indians, waving the tricolour, banners and posters, began to flock to the sidewalk outside Madison Square Garden, TV reporters tracking them breathlessly. It was a diverse crowd, mostly young. Women wore bright silk saris as if dressed for an evening out. Long-haired students lounged in groups, taking selfies and whooping 'Modi! Modi!' Sprightly senior citizens sporting jauntily angled caps engaged in animated conversation. Non-resident Indian families that had trekked long distances to be there. A tangible sense of excitement was coursing through the gathering that waited in line as if to watch the latest hit film.

Only a day before, Mr Modi had been a star attraction at New York's Central Park, hobnobbing with Hollywood icon Hugh Jackman before an audience of star-struck youth. In a seven-minute speech in English, Mr Modi spoke like a feel-good guru, ending his address with, 'May the force be with you.' India's prime ministers thus far have been normally formal personages who strictly follow official protocol and would not have shared the stage with a Hollywood star so readily or attempted to engage with him through current lingo. Yet Mr Modi consistently pushes the boundaries of prime-ministerial behaviour and being seen shooting the breeze with a movie star is part of the youth-friendly, pop culture-friendly, with-it image he tries hard to cultivate. As the prime minister held aloft a slightly dazed Jackman's hand, the crowd, many of whom were gawky tattooed American teenagers with limited knowledge of India, cheered the speaker with typical New York rumbustious energy.

By contrast, the multitudes who thronged Madison Square Garden on 28 September were mainly affluent Indian Americans, many of them Gujaratis from across the United States. The US chapter of the Overseas Friends of BJP had organized the event along with local Indian–American groups and tickets had been sold in advance. The hall was packed with more than 19,000 people, representative of the rising power of the Indian diaspora in the country, several of whom wore white Modi T-shirts, others waving posters and banners.

Out on the sidewalk, I wandered over to a group of Gujarati families who had travelled up from New Jersey to catch a glimpse of Mr Modi. They had been living in the US for decades but said they were proud of their heritage and Hindu identity. They looked after the family store and were grateful to be in a country where honest hard work is fulsomely rewarded. Yet they missed home and wished that India would get a leader who could transform it and bring real change. To them, Modi was the man and, as Gujaratis, they were particularly proud that not only was a fellow Gujarati the prime minister but that he was such a popular one. Dressed in sharp suits and colourful saris they argued that Modi was the only Indian prime minister (after Indira Gandhi) who believes in consistently reaching out to people. 'He has a connection with the people and makes sure to keep meeting as many as possible,' they said. 'Other PMs have generally stayed away from too much public contact. Mr Manmohan Singh was respected but he was so shy. Modi is a poor man who has come up the hard way, he is one of us.' There was a combative aggressive edge to them as well as they made it a point to tell me that they did not trust journalists who had tried so hard to 'spoil Modiji's name.' 'You are among those journalists,' said one of the women, half laughing, half accusatory. I sensed that in a crowd where adoration shaded into hysteria and where any endorsement of Modi carried with it a white-hot rage at his detractors, I was not exactly in very friendly company.

Covering the event from the midst of this excited crowd of Modi supporters, the atmosphere seemed a trifle surreal to me. I had known Mr Modi the politician for over two decades but hadn't quite expected the smooth transition he had so rapidly made from a kurta-pyjama–clad neta to a trendsetting, fashionably dressed superstar politician. This, after all, was a leader who had been persona non grata in the US for over a decade, his visa having been cancelled in 2005 in the aftermath of the 2002 Gujarat riots. Those riots have largely defined Mr Modi's persona in the popular imagination, both for those who see him through their prism and for those who vociferously denounce any attempts to do so.

Ironically, the man who had played a role in the visa cancellation was now part of a cheerleading entourage that had travelled to New York ahead of the prime minister's visit. Zafar Sareshwala is an Ahmedabad-based businessman whose offices had been attacked and burnt during the 2002 violence. Sareshwala was living in England at the time and had petitioned the courts and political leaders to ensure that action was taken against Mr Modi.

'I saw him as a villain who was responsible for the attacks on Muslims in Gujarat,' he would later tell me. However, a meeting with Mr Modi in April 2003 at London's upscale St. James' Court Hotel, arranged by editor-news anchor Rajat Sharma, changed his mind. 'The image that I had of a leader who was anti-Muslim was very different from the man I met and spoke to. Mr Modi convinced me that he was keen to ensure that Muslims were rehabilitated and the atmosphere of fear and discrimination removed,' claims Sareshwala.

The bearded businessman returned to India and became Mr Modi's 'Muslim face' brand ambassador on TV debates. His businesses flourished and he was eventually appointed the chancellor of Hyderabad's Maulana Azad National Urdu University. In New York, Sareshwala had the privilege of staying in the same hotel as the prime minister, albeit on a different floor.

Another special guest of the prime minister staying in the luxuriously appointed New York Palace Hotel was business magnate Gautam Adani, whose fortunes had also dramatically transformed in the Modi years in Gujarat. Adani and Sareshwala were among the few who appeared to have unlimited access to the prime minister in New York. 'Look, the PM had a very packed schedule but I think he was happy to have a few familiar people around him on his first big visit to a Western capital. We would sit and occasionally have a meal together, all very simple Gujarati vegetarian food,' recalls Sareshwala.

The large media contingent which was tracking Mr Modi's every move was being kept at arm's length. The traditional practice of allowing journalists to accompany the prime minister on his plane had been stopped – the first sign that Mr Modi was determined to rewrite the rules of engagement with the media and not cede even an inch of space to the Fourth Estate. 'Don't think the prime minister likes you guys too much, you ask too many questions,' a Ministry of External Affairs (MEA) official said, laughing.

For Mr Modi, the euphoric reception he was receiving in New York must have seemed like the ultimate redemption. On stage with him at Madison Square Garden were thirty-odd US officials, including several senators and a governor. He has always been deeply influenced by the US.

In his album of photos, a picture of him with friends outside the White House in the early 1990s takes pride of place. He had spent months in the New Jersey area, home to thousands of Gujarati expatriates, and had once told a close friend that 'America is truly a great country that India should learn from'.

Which is why Washington's decision to ostracize him had haunted him. In 2013, after being named the Bharatiya Janata Party's (BJP) prime-ministerial candidate, he was invited to address the Wharton Business School's India Conference, only to have the invitation withdrawn at the last minute after a group of professors protested. 'These are leftists who have unleashed hatred for Modi,' he had told me at the time in a phone conversation. I didn't respond but could sense the anger in the voice.

Now, faced with the roar of approval as the US officials gave Mr Modi a standing ovation, the rage melted away. The senators though were mere props that afternoon to the main act. A triumphal video of Mr Modi was being played on a giant screen, dwarfing all else around him. It showed Mr Modi's rise from being a humble chaiwallah (tea seller) to becoming the leader of the world's largest democracy. Every time the prime minister's image flashed on the screen, chants of 'Modi, Modi' would erupt with even greater passion.

Outside the main arena, the crowd that had spilled on to the streets was agitated and truculent. Many of them had not been able to enter and were desperate for a glimpse of their hero. Amidst the frenzied atmosphere, a small group was protesting against the 2002 riots while a few were raising the demand for a separate Khalistani state. The New York police had ensured the protesters were kept away from the euphoric Modi contingent that had taken over the sidewalks.

I, however, was caught in the middle of the madness. Literally. We had decided to go 'live' with public reactions to the Modi visit and had set up our live unit on the street. My aim was to get the crowd to respond to what I thought was the obvious question to ask: 'How do you explain this ecstatic reaction to a leader who till only a year ago was denied entry into the US? Do you think the Americans made a mistake in denying Mr Modi a travel visa?' The crowd didn't seem to warm up to the questions. Instead, they were offended. 'How can you talk like this about our elected prime minister?' one of them asked me angrily. 'Aren't you the same guy who covered the Gujarat riots? You people will never learn to appreciate what Modi is. You are here with an agenda,' was another sharp response.

As the crowd began slogan-shouting and came dangerously close to surrounding us, my video-journalist Tahir Chowdhary suggested we move away from the spot. That is when someone kicked at my shins even as another voice called for my family to be packed off to Pakistan. This violent and abusive action was not caught on the video which would be circulated later and go viral on the internet.

Instead, what was caught on tape was what happened next. Someone in the crowd suddenly accused all journalists of being 'bloody news traders'. Something inside me snapped at that moment. The incessant finger-pointing and abuse got to me. Relentlessly targeted by Modi-supporting trolls on social media as 'libtard, sickularist' et al., I had begun to feel hunted by what are called the 'Modi bhakts'. I was on edge, just as the crowd was too. I removed the mike, took off my jacket and got into a scuffle with the abuser – an act of professional stupidity that I would deeply regret. But at that moment, all I felt was trapped in a whirl of angry, abusive voices that were targeting me simply for my reportage of the 2002 riots where I had done, in my reckoning, a journalist's duty. My professionalism was being repeatedly questioned and my family was being viciously insulted – I had to respond.

In hindsight, I was wrong to have reacted in the manner that I did. Dealing with raucous crowds, however ill-behaved, is an occupational hazard and I should have maintained my cool. As my cameraperson dragged me away from the spot, a more sympathetic local voice came up to explain the crowd behaviour that had caught me off guard. 'Sir, I have been watching you for years and I respect your work. Please appreciate that we are here to celebrate Mr Modi's win. For you this may be just another professional assignment, but for us this is a moment to rejoice and be part of history. You can think what you want; for us Narendrabhai is Godlike!'

The young man's words were prescient. Modi was no longer just another successful politician as I had imagined him to be. For his adoring supporters, he was now almost a deity: the cult of Modi was here to stay.

INTRODUCTION

How Modi Won India: 13 Ms, 2 Ws and a GK of success

AN Indian election is like a great mela, a festival of colour and chaos, of magic and madness, which throws up any number of wondrous stories. Here is one that perhaps best exemplifies the dramatic nature of the 2019 verdict. An octogenarian woman voting in a village near Rae Bareli stands in front of the electronic voting machine (EVM) and refuses to vote. The returning officer goes up to her and asks if he can help. 'I don't need your help, you people are all cheats, I am going to report you,' the lady screeches back. The worried officer inquires what the issue is. 'Yeh machine dekho. Kahan hain Modiji ka photo. Main bas Modiji ko vote dene aayi hoon!' (Look at this EVM. Show me where Narendra Modi's picture is on the machine. I have come here only to vote for Modi!) she barks angrily. The officer smiles and dutifully explains to the woman who can't read or write properly that Modi is not contesting from Rae Bareli but that if she wishes to vote for the BJP, she can press the lotus symbol on the EVM. 'Woh sab hum nahin jaante. Hum toh direct Modiji ko hi vote denge!' (Don't know all that, I will directly vote only for Modi!) the lady insists. It takes almost half an hour before order is restored and the woman finally casts her vote.

I experience my own 'Rae Bareli moment' in Phulpur in eastern Uttar Pradesh (UP). The original constituency of India's first prime minister, Jawaharlal Nehru, which he held for over a decade, Phulpur is sometimes called 'Nehru's constituency'. Taking a break from the oppressive campaign trail heat, I am sitting at a roadside dhaba where I meet a group of young men in their early twenties. One of them, Ajay Yadav, says he is a commerce graduate who has been unsuccessfully applying for a job for almost a year. 'Educated unemployed' is a familiar calling card across the country. Ajay admits to feeling a little disappointed with the Modi government's unfulfilled promise of 'rozgaar' (jobs). So, who will you vote for, I ask him. 'Kya option hai, sir, Modiji hi to hai,' he sighs. But why would you vote for Modi if you are jobless, I ask. 'Sir, unhone toh Pakistan ko sabak sikhaya hai!' (He has taught a lesson to Pakistan!) he says firmly, his face suddenly lighting up. But how will teaching Pakistan a lesson get him a job, I persist. 'Sir, woh sab theek hai par pehle toh desh ke baare mein sochna hai. Yeh chunaav desh ko bachane ka hai jo Modi hi kar sakte hain!' (Be that as it may, this election is about the country. It is about saving the country, which only Modi can do!) he remarks pointedly. Ajay then tells me that he is part of a WhatsApp group called 'Hum Desh-Bhakt' from where he claims to get all the news, including 'reports' that 500 terrorists were killed in the air strike in Balakot. In Nehru's bastion, Modi rules unchallenged.

From Rae Bareli to Phulpur, from Nagpur to New Delhi, I heard similar voices on the campaign trail that only confirm my belief that 2019 is best described as the TIMO 'wave' election – There Is Modi Only. An oft-repeated BJP social media campaign slogan perhaps best illustrates this phenomenon: 'Aayega toh Modi hi' (Modi only will come), a feeling of near-inevitability over the final outcome. In a sense, in an election fought across 543 constituencies and in 29 states and 7 union territories, there was only one dominant messenger who was also the overriding message. As a senior BJP leader candidly admits, 'I don't think most people even knew the name of our candidate they were voting for!' Never before in the history of Indian elections has one leader exercised such complete dominance over the voter mindspace. The only two who come to mind are Nehru in the 1950s and Indira Gandhi in the 1971 election. Nehru, of course, was Mahatma Gandhi's anointed heir, the 'people's prince' spurred forward by the idealism of the freedom movement and his own personal charisma. Indira was the archetypal populist nationalist, her rousing 'Garibi hatao' slogan instantly connecting her with the multitudes who saw her as their ultimate 'Indira Amma' or Mother Indira.

Modi's monopolistic politics is clearly more Indira than Jawaharlal: he is, like Indira, a putative political despot, someone whose populist rhetoric invokes awe and fear in equal measure, a divisive figure but also a compelling one. The hard data only confirms the impact that Modi had on the final verdict – an even bigger landslide than the 2014 victory.

- The Lokniti–Centre for the Study of Developing Societies (CSDS) post-poll survey suggests that 32 per cent of those who supported the BJP would not have voted for the party if Modi was not the prime-ministerial candidate. The figure was 27 per cent in 2014. The Axis My India survey claims that Modi was the chief reason for 29 per cent of the voters choosing the BJP. In other words, had Modi not been the party leader, the BJP would not have been anywhere close to a majority.
- In 2014, the BJP won 65.8 per cent of the seats from which it contested. This figure rose to 69.3 per cent in 2019. In 2014, the BJP polled more than 50 per cent of the votes in 136 of the 428 seats it contested which increased to as many as 224 of the 436 seats it contested in 2019 (the BJP's overall vote share increased from 31 per cent in 2014 to 37.4 in 2019 and in 17 states and union territories it won more than 50 per cent of the votes). In nearly 75 per cent of the seats the BJP won, the margins were more than 1 lakh votes while fifteen BJP candidates won by more than 5 lakh votes.
- In 2014, more than 80 per cent of the BJP seats were won in the Hindi heartland and the western states of Gujarat and Maharashtra.

In 2019, the party's geographical footprint spread to Bengal and Odisha in the east, broke barriers in the North-east, swept Karnataka and even made inroads in Telangana.

- During the main campaign period, Modi addressed rallies in 134 constituencies. The BJP won in 99 of them, a very high strike rate of 73 per cent.
- In 2019, as per the Lokniti–CSDS post poll, the BJP vote increased amongst all Hindu castes and communities by 8 per cent from 36 per cent in 2014 to 44 per cent. The Other Backward Castes (OBC) and Dalit vote went up by a striking 10 per cent, the Adivasi vote by 7 per cent, indicating a broad Hindu cross-class, cross-caste sweep.

And yet, while statistics are always useful in measuring the scope and extent of an election 'TsuNamo', they don't reveal the backstory, the key personalities, strategies and turning points hidden behind the number-crunching. Which is what this book seeks to do, almost as a sequel to my previous election book, *2014: The Election That Changed India*.

In 2014, Modi was the challenger, a regional chieftain from Gujarat seeking to conquer Delhi by riding in on a wave of anti-incumbency sentiment against the ruling Manmohan Singh–led United Progressive Alliance (UPA) 2 government. It was quite possibly an easier win since the anger and fatigue against the Congress was palpable and simply needed someone around whom it could crystallize. Modi, with his promise of 'achhe din' (good days) and strong leadership (mazboot neta), became a national alternative by offering a completely polar-opposite persona to that of the incumbent unassuming, 'accidental' prime minister. The 'Hindu hriday samrat' of Gujarat 2002 was now projected as a 'vikas purush', a harbinger of change. To an extent, 2014 was an election where hope and rage coexisted, an election fought against the backdrop of serious corruption charges against Congress leaders, high inflation and a general sense of policy paralysis – it was an easy call to make. In comparison, 2019 was the more difficult election to predict.

Surely, a pro-incumbency wave was more difficult to create than an anti-incumbency one? This is where the 2019 Modi election story becomes fascinating, providing an insight into the rapidly changing nature of electioneering, and even how contemporary India is transforming just as swiftly.

Psephologist-turned-politician Yogendra Yadav describes the BJP as 'the only twenty-first-century-ready' party in the country. Yadav uses four *Ms* to explain the BJP's electoral successes: Modi, Machine, Media and Money. Each of these are examined at different stages in the book but I am going to go a shade 'manic' with my *Ms* by adding nine more contributory factors: Messaging, Marketing, Mobile, Middle Class, Millennials, (anti-)Muslim Majoritarianism, 'Muscular' nationalism, Masood Azhar, Mahagathbandhan (grand alliance); two *Ws* – Welfarism and WhatsApp – and a ubiquitous *GK* for Garib Kisan.

We start with Modi, the pivotal figure around whom the BJP has structured its ascent to political supremacy. After five years in office, Modi was no longer a natural claimant to the 'anti-establishment' identity that he had so assiduously projected in 2014. Then, he was the Vadnagar-born son of a chaiwallah, an allusion that he used effectively to challenge the so-called 'Lutyens elite', a pejorative term for those attached to the Nehru–Gandhi dynasty. Now, he was the sole occupant of 7 Lok Kalyan Marg, a VVIP travelling in his high-end Toyota Land Cruiser SUV, surrounded by a fleet of armoured BMW 7-series luxury sedans. In 2014, he could claim to be a 'victim' of a campaign of calumny against him for failing to stop the 2002 Gujarat riots in which more than 1000 people died: he had even been ostracized in several global capitals. Now, he was criss-crossing the world with a fawning media tracking his every move with breathless excitement. In 2014, Modi could attack the incumbent without being held fully accountable for his own past actions, but now, in 2019, he was the man in charge whose multiple promises would be measured against their on-ground delivery. In 2014, Modi could get away by holding out the hope that if black money in foreign banks was brought back to the country, ₹15 lakh would be deposited in the bank account of every Indian. Then, it was a well-spun dream, now it seemed like a self-confessed 'jumla'.

How, then, did Modi manage to retain a large measure of public trust even while continuing to play dream merchant? This is where his carefully sculpted imagery as the political strongman with an enormous appetite for disruption and risk-taking decisive leadership comes to the fore, as does the undeniable personal connect and communication he has established with the voter. Even a contentious, and potentially disastrous decision like demonetization, was packaged as part of a 'holy war' against corruption being led by a self-styled 'fakir' acting on behalf of the helpless citizenry. Many knowledgeable political observers have pointed to Modi belonging to a global trend of 'elected autocrats', powerful individual leaders who, by sheer force of personality, are able to project themselves as agents of change. Trump, Putin, Erdogan, Orban, Netanyahu, Bolsanaro – Modi has been included in this league of muscular leaders who rule more by diktat than democratic consensus and even subvert democratic processes with impunity. And yet, Modi is distinct because, frankly, India's democracy is sui generis: messy and diverse with a history of a million brewing mutinies. Most of the other nations with strongman leaders have a tradition of dictatorial regimes, while the US is a presidential system where the chief executive in the White House is always the focus. Modi's skill is that he has been able to impose a presidential-style governance model on a parliamentary system and has done it with such chutzpah that it seems he was made for the job. He is, as I suggest in the first chapter, the unquestioned 'Big Boss', a '56-inch-chest', alpha-male leader who 'commands and controls' an increasingly personality-driven political system with a mix of fear and theatre, someone whose penchant for glitzy events gives him a showman-like cult status among his hypnotized followers. That a Rashtriya Swayamsevak Sangh (RSS) pracharak who, until 2002, had not even won an election and held no administrative post till he was made Gujarat chief minister in 2001, should now play such a central role in Indian politics is a riveting story and a core aspect of the book.

But 2019 is not just about Modi's larger-than-life image. In this seminal election, Modi shared the frame, in a sense, with another *M*: the BJP's election 'machine' represented by party president Amit Shah. In 2014, Shah was general secretary in charge of the crucial UP battleground and consequently had an important but more limited role. This time, as party chief, he was presiding over the 'the largest political party in the world': BJP membership numbers may be contested but what is irrefutable is the manner in which the indefatigable political operator has mobilized an immense network that extends all the way to the smallest booth worker, ensuring crucial last-mile feet on the ground. The BJP, as part of the Sangh Parivar, has always been a cadre-based party, but the nature of the involvement of these cadres in the political process has fundamentally changed from workers to 'participants': from 'panna pramukhs' who connect with every voter on each page of an electoral roll to 'labharti sampark pramukhs' who were meant to bond with beneficiaries of government programmes to 'vistaraks' tasked with expanding the party at the grassroots, Shah has constructed a political juggernaut. That the BJP is now building spanking new offices in every district of the country equipped with digital libraries and modern communication facilities is further proof of Shah's vaulting ambitions: this is not just an election machine but, as I detail in the book, a gargantuan ideological and commercial enterprise with tentacles far more widespread than one might imagine, a 'new' BJP that functions like a vast corporation, not just a political party. The BJP president even has a professionally managed personal election consultancy, Association of Billion Minds (ABM), working round the clock for him on key projects. Modi may be the commander and the face of this enterprise, but it is Shah who is the charioteer, and whose boundless energy, organizational aptitude, ideological rigour, caste re-engineering prowess and, yes, ruthless and vengeful edge that give the chariot its invincibility. Together, Modi and Shah have become the 'jodi number one' of Indian politics, both having transformed the image of the traditional, accommodating, non-confrontational politician from Gujarat into a hard-nosed political animal for whom means don't matter, only the ends do (Chapter 2).

But like every grandly built machine, the BJP too needs oil to keep the wheels moving forward effortlessly. Money is the *M* that has always sustained the political ecosystem and 2019 was no different. Former chief election commissioner (CEC) Dr S.Y. Quraishi remarks, 'Money has always played a significant part in our elections, but the scale and influence now is unimaginable.' A Centre for Media Studies report has called the 2019 elections 'the most expensive election ever, anywhere', estimating a total of ₹27,000 crore was spent on the polls, around 45 per cent by the BJP alone. It is difficult to uncover the real amounts involved: digging through the dark, murky world of election financing is beyond the scope of this book, though election watchdogs like the Association for Democratic Reforms routinely expose the symbiotic relationship between cash, crime and politics and warn of the dangers of opaque funding mechanisms like highly secretive election bonds. What I can definitively say from my numerous interactions with netas and their cronies in the business world is that cash is still king at election time and the BJP has a huge fiscal advantage over its competition. Regional parties seem more cash rich, but why the Congress, which ruled India for much of the last seven decades, has been unable to match the BJP's financial muscle is one of the great mysteries of Indian politics: maybe the oft-repeated joke that the 'Congress is a poor party with wealthy individuals' now haunts the grand old party at election time.

But no amount of money can ensure an election triumph unless it is backed by a strong message, our next *M*. In 2019, Modi had a story to tell: 'Sabka saath, sabka vikas', was an inclusive slogan that appealed to a large number of people cutting across castes and classes, even more than the 2014 'Achhe din' message. If the 2014 mandate was about 'hope', at the heart of the 2019 pro-incumbency verdict is the notion of 'trust': central to the messaging is a profound faith in Modi as the ultimate guide to a better future, a promise of 'vikas', of a 'new' corruption-free India, of a 5-trillion-dollar economy, best captured in the song on the third anniversary of the Modi government: 'Mera desh badal raha hai, aage bad raha hai' (My country is changing, is moving forward). Even if 'achhe din' have not quite come for many, the confidence that they will arrive one day sustains the Modi model of governance, almost like a long-term bank deposit which guarantees future returns. The Modi government claims to have launched more than 100 schemes in five years, that is, one nearly every two weeks. Even allowing for political hyperbole and the fact that many of the schemes are UPA ideas which have simply been rebranded and repackaged, the idea of a new project almost every fortnight reveals a government in perpetual campaign mode.

Which brings me to the *W* factor that is intrinsic to the Modi mantra: 'Welfarism', especially for the largest vote bank, *GK*, the 'Garib Kisan' (poor farmer). In every major speech, Modi almost always refers to the 'garib kisan'. Every major transfer and redistribution of wealth promises to create a social safety net for the poor and reduce income inequalities. Even demonetization was sought to be legitimized in the name of the 'garib kisan' versus the 'dhanna seth'. In 2014, Modi was pitched as a feel-good guru and anti-corruption crusader, selling the 'achhe din' dream; in 2019, the dream seller was also the 'mai–baap' benefactor of the poor, promising effective last-mile delivery of basic services like gas connections (Ujwala), toilets (Swachh Bharat), electricity (Saubhagya), bank accounts (Jan Dhan), cheap loans (Mudra), housing (Awas Yojana), health insurance (Ayushman Bharat) and more. It marks Modi's complete transformation from 'suit-boot' business-blessed politician to 'garibon ka neta', a makeover that I believe was essential to his rising popularity graph (Chapter 3). It also reflects the shifting social base of the BJP: from a party once dismissively referred to as a 'Brahmin Bania' party of urban traders, it is now an increasingly 'Mandalized' political force which has made deep inroads into the lower castes/classes and rural hinterland – once the Congress's core vote.

The BJP has claimed that more than 22 crore families benefited from the Modi government's schemes. Let us allow for duplication and exaggerated claims and reduce the number by 30 per cent: it still comes to roughly 15 crore beneficiaries. The BJP won 22.6 crore votes in 2019 as against 17.1 crore votes in 2014, a gain of 5.5 crore votes. Who is to say that these additional votes didn't come from the 'labhartis' or beneficiaries of the government's welfare schemes, especially as the BJP's vote share has risen in rural India and among the poor?

When I posed this question to a senior UPA minister, the response was combative: 'Do you know that more people were lifted out of poverty in the ten years of the Manmohan Singh government than in any other period in our history? So why don't you credit us for a change?' The former minister is not entirely wrong: a UN report states 271 million Indians were lifted out of poverty between 2006 and 2016, the fastest global reduction. And yet, the fact is the UPA was unable to 'sell' its anti-poverty programming like the rural employment guarantee scheme as a 'direct benefit' from the ruling party to the voter. In contrast, one of Modi's successes was marketing the notion of a 'new' post-2014 India which will provide tangible benefits and not just handouts to the masses. 'Marketing' then is the next *M* that Brand Modi has succeeded in by creating a near-total identification between 'leader' and 'beneficiary'. Certainly, no Indian government before this has paid so much attention to the micro-detailing of its glossy campaigns. The 7-crore-plus (the figure at the time of the 2019 elections) Ujwala gas beneficiaries received a personal letter from the prime minister, as if to suggest that the cylinder was a 'gift' from the Supreme Leader. The BJP's 'labharti pramukhs' were given lists of the beneficiaries, asked to visit every one of them, take a picture of them with their cylinder and then post it online. More than 160 call centres were set up across India one year before the elections from where calls, SMSs, WhatsApp messages were sent as reminders of what the Modi government was providing (Chapter 8). Not surprisingly, 71 per cent of those sampled in a Lokniti–CSDS post-poll survey give credit to the Centre for the Ujwala and Jan Dhan schemes, only 14 per cent to the state government. Ayushman Bharat has followed a similar pattern and even been branded in the media as 'Modi-Care'. Nationalist strongmen politicians have often been described as individuals who tap into a powerful sense of national aspiration, irrespective of whether there's actual delivery or not. This aspiration or hunger or the 'Yeh dil maange more!' mood is adeptly made part of Modi's many marketing campaigns. I once jokingly remarked at an editorial meeting with our sales and marketing team: 'Modi could teach you all you need to know about marketing that they won't teach you at business school!'

A key tool in this marketing drive is another *M*: the ubiquitous mobile phone. If there is any growth that has matched the rise of Modi in the last five years it is that of the smartphone (led by Jio boss Mukesh Ambani to keep up with the *M* word!). By April 2019, India had 450 million smartphone users as against 155 million at the election in 2014. Mobile data in India is the cheapest in the world and costs about one-tenth of what it did two years ago. A large amount of the data consumed is through videos and videos on mobiles are now becoming a primary source of information. I was surprised to meet tribal community leaders in a remote Odisha village who had downloaded the NaMo app and were proudly showing me Modi-centric videos on their newly acquired smartphones.

This unchecked spread of mobile phones has enabled the effective use of the other *W*: the 'WhatsApp' revolution which is easily the most commonly used messenger service today. At the start of the 2019 election cycle, the number of WhatsApp users in India was over 300 million and counting. For political parties, WhatsApp is now an integral part of their communication strategy, a cheap, fast and effective way of scaling up their outreach. But here too, the BJP is way ahead of the game. In Bengal alone the party claims to have set up 50,000 WhatsApp groups right down to the booth level, each group being used as a real-time propaganda weapon, especially among the younger demographic. But these groups have a dark side: an alternate narrative is being spread through political WhatsApp groups – dubbed as a WhatsApp university – where young minds are rapidly indoctrinated into a make-believe 'fake news' universe.

Which brings me to the millennials, another *M* which is now a key driver of the Modi cult. Of the 90-crore-plus Indian electorate, around 8.4 crore were first-time voters in the 18–22 age bracket, close to 10 per cent. A Lokniti–CSDS post-poll survey (see appendix) notes that younger voters (18–27) were 9 percentage points more likely to want Modi as prime minister than the older voters in the 56-plus age group. In fact, as many as 51 per cent first-time voters wanted Modi as their prime minister in 2019 as compared to 43 per cent in this same age group in 2014. In effect, there was a clear 8 per cent rise in support for Modi in this important age group. How does one explain the influence that an almost 70-year-old leader wields over an entirely different generation, especially when his prime rival, Rahul Gandhi, is twenty years younger? Could it be his tech-savvy, energetic multimedia presence – he had a combined following of around 110 million on Facebook, Twitter and Instagram in May 2019 and even had viral TikTok videos circulating his dialogues – that gives him an edge? Or is this a lost, rootless generation of teenagers which is simply craving a superhero-like figure, a yearning which Modi satisfies with his promise of dispensing with old elites, his impatience with old ways, and his repeatedly emphasized aim of building a 'new', merit-driven India instead? His willingness to offer exam advice to students, upload yoga and fitness videos is all part of the packaging of Modi as an inspirational modern-day 'guru-neta' who is unchained by the conventional stereotyping of an everyday politician.

The other key demographic that favours Modi is the middle class, an ever-widening group that is slowly cutting through traditional metro-centric classifications. A few weeks before he passed away in August 2019, the late BJP leader Arun Jaitley told me that he was convinced that the political ascendancy of Modi was directly linked to the growing influence of the middle class, not just in terms of setting the narrative but actually playing a decisive role in the final election outcome. 'V.P. Singh was a middle-class hero at one time but even he couldn't build a superman image around the middle class in the way Narendrabhai has,' was Jaitley's contention.

There is no accurate number for the size of this middle class but recent surveys put it at between 300 million and 400 million or almost a third of the population, although there are several income variables within the class itself. 'Narendrabhai is the icon of an aspirational India where those who have a two-wheeler today will push for a car tomorrow,' claimed Jaitley. There is little doubt that the BJP, in a strange way, has been the biggest beneficiary of the economic liberalization initiated by the Congress, capturing the zeitgeist of the age in a manner that its opponents have singularly failed to in recent times. The Congress liberalized the economy, but failed to grasp how economic transformation would change politics. Modi revels in this change and perhaps, more than any other contemporary leader, has consciously and constantly reached out to the 'neo-middle class' and addressed their sense of weariness and impatience with the 'chalta hai' mantra of a slow-moving, corrupt, status quo-ist system. A familiar refrain one heard in middle-class homes on the campaign trail: 'Congress ko humne sattar saal diye hain, Modiji ko dus saal toh dene chahiye.' (We gave the Congress seventy years, we can at least give Modi ten years.)

Modi was also shrewd enough to realize that, largely, the middle class's proclivities tend to go beyond mall-driven consumerism to sharpened religious identity. In particular, the growing anti-Muslim, majoritarian sentiment in Hindu middle-class households was latched upon to create a 'hawa' where a Hindu consolidation, driven by the upper castes but stretching to OBCs and Dalit groups too, was clearly discernible. I was stunned to meet any number of men and women on the campaign trail who didn't think twice before expressing an assertive sense of Hinduness while indicating their voter preferences (except in southern states like Tamil Nadu, Andhra and Kerala where regional identities still offer a fierce challenge to any religious homogenization).

The 'Muslim as enemy' idea has been part of the Sangh Parivar's propaganda machine for decades, but its true political impact is only being felt now. Modi, after all, is a product of the Ram Janmabhoomi movement in the 1990s. That is where he first cut his political teeth as one of the organizers of his mentor L.K. Advani's rath yatra. He is also the Hindutva poster boy of 2002, the 'Hero of Hatred' and 'The Great Divider' as *India Today* magazine covers at the time described him. Modi may not have overtly used typical Hindutva rhetoric in the 2019 campaign but the subliminal messaging was always there. While speaking in Wardha, he attacked Rahul Gandhi's decision to contest from Wayanad in Kerala. 'The Congress insulted Hindus. People have decided to punish the Congress ... That is why they are forced to take refuge in places where the majority is the minority.' (Wayanad has a large Muslim–Christian population). Or indeed, his 'shamshan' (cremation) versus 'kabristan' (burial ground) analogy during the 2017 UP election when accusing his rivals of 'minority appeasement'.

The fact is, Modi has succeeded in 'mainstreaming' Hindu majoritarian politics, pushed the Congress on the defensive by branding it a pro-Muslim party, and thereby ensured the ideological primacy of the saffron brotherhood. At the *India Today* conclave in 2018, Sonia Gandhi admitted as much when she said the BJP had managed to paint the Congress as a 'Muslim party'. The rise of the 'political Hindu', be it a violent cow-vigilante group or a Hindu prelate as chief minister of India's most populous state, is an unmistakable reality that strikes at the heart of a plural, secular India (Chapter 4). Not surprisingly, Muslim support for the BJP remains in single digits – 8 per cent as per the Lokniti–CSDS post-poll survey.

The firming up of a pan-Hindu identity needs a trigger at election time. Which leads me to a potentially defining moment in the 2019 campaign. On 14 February, when a Central Reserve Police Force (CRPF) convoy in Kashmir's Pulwama district was hit by a suicide bomber and 40 jawans were killed, the campaign narrative took a sudden, and arguably, decisive twist. Where the opposition campaign on jobs and agrarian distress may have otherwise gathered some traction, the Indian Air Force (IAF) retaliatory strike on Balakot in Pakistan completely changed the dominant rhetoric. Not only did it make national security and 'nationalism' or 'rashtrawaad' an emotive, unifying talking point, it enhanced Modi's image as the muscular nationalist leader who had taken the audacious risk of entering Pakistani airspace to avenge Indian lives (Chapter 6). The Lokniti–CSDS post-poll survey shows that the National Democratic Alliance (NDA) had a 22 per cent lead over the UPA amongst those who had heard of the Balakot strike compared to just 5 per cent among those who hadn't. Balakot gave Modi the crucial 'X factor' in any marathon election campaign: momentum. The media called this the 'Balakot bump'. It was this booster dose of hyper-nationalism that inextricably linked Modi's persona to a rousing 'Bharat Mata ki Jai' war cry and fervent tricolour-waving, subsuming any potential counter-narrative. No other Indian prime minister on the campaign trail has shown the audacity to publicly declare, in what Hindi news channels called a 'hunkar' (war cry), 'Hum ghar mein ghus ke marenge', as Modi did in 2019. In doing so, he not only echoed and gave voice to mass fury against 'jihadist' terrorists but also stood firm as a prime minister who would do anything to wreak vengeance on the nation's 'enemies'.

To that extent, Modi owes his final surge to another *M*, Masood Azhar, the Jaish-e-Mohammed chief, whose group is widely held responsible for the Pulwama suicide attack. 'Muscular' nationalism thrives on an inexhaustible search for an enemy. In 2002, it was the Godhra Muslim and then Pakistani army chief General Pervez Musharraf (Modi won that first election); in 2019, it was Masood, the Pakistan-based jihadi terror factory and Kashmiri militants. A 'deshbhakt versus deshdrohi' (national versus anti-national) narrative was craftily played on the ground, squeezing the opposition out from the 'national' battleground and leaving it even more vulnerable to attack.

Post-Balakot, Modi as the tough, indomitable neta ('Modi hai toh mumkin hai' was the new catchline) took on the so-called mahagathbandhan or grand alliance that appeared increasingly wobbly and eventually unsustainable. With the BJP making the election deliberately presidential – Modi versus who? – the opposition was trapped into seeking desperate alliances that had little in common except blind anti-Modi-ism. The likes of Mayawati and Mamata (two more *Ms*!) who were pitched as potential 'Mahagathbandhan' prime-ministerial options are emblematic of the opposition's crisis of credibility. Accused of conspicuous self-aggrandizement, Mayawati has been unable to look beyond narrow caste-identity politics which, over time, has become limited to her own Jatav community within UP, and has not even endured as a wider Dalit consolidation any more. Mamata too has been boxed in by her own limitations in providing good governance. Didi is a leader whose instincts when cornered are to resort to her own unique brand of nativist populism, but in the deepening Hindu–Muslim divide in Bengal she too became trapped and almost helpless (Chapter 8).

The ostensible leader of the mahagathbandhan in 2019 was to have been Rahul Gandhi, or so it was expected after the Congress won three state elections in December 2018. Rahul doesn't begin with an *M* but in a way he did contribute to Modi's triumph. The Gandhi family scion is an enigmatic, erratic figure: at one level, propelled by genuine reformist impulses and a democratic fervour but at another level, sorely lacking in sharp political instincts and himself a product of a feudal political culture where lineage matters more than merit. As a fifth-generation dynast of the Nehru–Gandhi family, Rahul was an ideal opponent for Modi to play the kaamdar (worker) versus naamdar (dynast) binary which has proved so effective in the past. Rahul perhaps had a chance to strike by localizing the elections as much as possible, but the relentless 'Chowkidar chor hai' sloganeering made Modi the central figure in the election dynamics and willy-nilly almost played into the BJP's hands. In a presidential-style contest, Rahul, already scarred by the BJP's persistent 'Pappu' propaganda, found himself at a loss in the face of Modi's demagoguery. Rahul was an energetic campaigner but in the end, quite frankly, like in 2014, he never seemed to miss an opportunity to miss an opportunity (Chapters 5 and 8). Five years ago, he could have understandably blamed the UPA government's patchy inheritance for the Congress defeat but this time he can't shift the blame: this was a campaign planned and executed by Team Rahul and it flopped badly.

Crucially, the Congress seems to have gradually vacated the centrist 'nationalist' space. (Its secular credentials were already compromised in the late 1980s and early 1990s over Shah Bano, Ayodhya and much more.) For example, the Congress manifesto makes excellent observations on the economy and agriculture but its proposal to review the Armed Forces Special Powers Act (AFSPA) in J&K sent the wrong signal on national security toughness and was ill-timed in light of the Pulwama terror strike. Lefty undergraduate radicalism is no substitute for firm no-nonsense patriotism, especially at election time. One statistic is sufficient to explain the extent of the Congress debacle: of the 190 seats where there was a one-on-one fight between the BJP and Congress, the BJP won as many as 175 seats with an average margin of a whopping 23 per cent, while, nationwide, two of every five Congress candidates lost their deposits. Clearly, the Congress is facing a profound ideological, leadership and organizational crisis, and the BJP has become the new hegemon of Indian politics. 'Moditva', as I choose to call this hegemonical trend, brings nation (rashtra), religion (dharma) and jan-kalyan (public welfare) onto one massive common platform, almost crowding out the entire opposition.

I have left 'Media' – the final *M* – for the very end because it is the one that I am most intimately connected with and as I write about the role of the media in the 2019 campaign, I find myself wrestling with my own private and professional demons. As a practising journalist for more than thirty years in both print and TV, and having covered elections stretching back to 1989, I have never quite seen an Indian election where the mainstream media narrative, with rare exceptions, was so blatantly and horribly one-sided. The sheer scale of the Modi victory would suggest that the constant media exposure was, at best, only a small contributory factor – Modi and the BJP would probably have won in any case – and yet, the media's role as fawning political cheerleader deserves closer examination (Chapter 7). In the maddeningly competitive world of TV, in particular, TRPs (television rating points) are an all-consuming obsession for nearly every channel. Audience research data shows that Modi was high TRP, his rivals were not. The temptation, as a result, was always to show even more of Modi, and much less of the opposition. As one news editor candidly remarked, 'I don't think we created the Modi wave but we certainly rode on it.' As the adage goes, the media is incapable of making a zero into a hero, but it can push a hero into the bracket of superhero.

I had heard a distinctly similar explanation in 2014 too, only this time the lines between news and propaganda were even more categorically blurred. The uncritical gaze cast on the Modi government meant that there are few platforms left for asking those in power the inconvenient questions. When the government, for example, was accused of fudging crucial economic data on jobs and growth figures, there were just a handful in the media who were willing to challenge the government upfront. Compare this with the manner in which the Manmohan Singh–led UPA 2 government was placed in the dock almost every day during the Anna Hazare anti-corruption movement, leading the wounded Dr Singh to remark, 'History will be kinder to me than the media.' Unlike Team Modi, the UPA government didn't have a media strategy: it simply relinquished the space on all government policies to the prime-time news warriors and thus made itself a sitting duck. The Modi government went the other extreme by ensuring an obsessive control of the media narrative, as well as dollops of intimidation of journalists through aggressive displays of state power.

The rise of the so-called 'nationalist' channels in particular – many of them happily pliable and openly patronized by the government – has divided newsrooms like never before. The sharply polarizing nature of rowdy studio debates has meant that there is less space for dissent or for nuance and context to a story. Anyone who differs even slightly from the government line, let alone disagrees, is immediately branded as being part of an 'anti-national' lobby: be it an opposition leader, a Jawaharlal Nehru University (JNU) student leader like Kanhaiya Kumar, an anti-establishment journalist like Gauri Lankesh, a Nobel laureate like Amartya Sen, or a writer like Arundhati Roy. A young journalist working with one of these channels quit her job within a year. 'My news editor would tell me every morning, let's find some story to nail the opposition. After a while, you realize that what you are doing is not reporting news but pushing agendas,' she laments. What news TV did manage to create in 2019 is a 'mahaul' (ambience) in which Modi was seemingly invincible and the opposition cripplingly inept, especially among urban middle-class TV-watching audiences.

But, significantly, 2019 was not just a media war being fought on a TV screen near you. The rise of social media can be empowering for the citizenry but has also created an alternative platform to spread real-time fake news and vicious misinformation under the guise of 'democratizing' public opinion. This is a brutish ecosystem which can be promoted or controlled by a political force possessing unlimited resources to match their unbridled ambition. What was once an open forum for public debate is now, in large part, harnessed to the almost sinister machinations of resource-saturated political cyber agendas. The number of BJP-affiliated groups and individuals operating online, on Facebook and on Twitter, suggests the emergence of a humongous social media 'army' which is now capable of manipulating the political discourse with zero accountability. News TV also has an incestuous relationship with the social media narrative: a Twitter hashtag or 'trend', for example, can instantly become the subject of a TV debate and vice versa. Farmer suicides or job losses don't trend on Twitter but any issue linked to religion or nationalism often does, thereby shaping the divisive discourse.

In a sense, if the aim of the election game is to capture mindspace, then the BJP has succeeded in 2019 in what is best described as a 'total poll capture': on the ground through its organizational machine and unrestrained executive power, but also backed by the air power of its vastly superior multimedia communication engine. In the process, a consummate political communicator like Modi becomes near-indestructible. He is able to create 'news events' almost at will from New York to Kedarnath: 'politics as spectacle' has been a recurring phenomenon during the Modi years in which shock-and-awe tactics are used to enhance an inexorably narcissistic personality cult and 'invisibilize' any opposition through clever optics and endless photo-ops.

In their 2018 book *How to Rig an Election*, authors Nic Cheeseman and Brian Klaas write about an 'authoritarian toolbox' where autocratic governments use different strategies to manipulate electoral processes. While the book focuses mainly on despotic African regimes, there are signs of a creeping corrosion within India's institutional processes too, with very little pushback in the face of dictatorial behaviour. Maybe we too are a country in 'democratic recession', hostage to the political paradox of frequent, high-voltage elections but eroding democratic values. Is there really a level playing field in Indian elections today is a troubling question which offers even more disquieting answers.

In my three decades as a journalist, I have relished observing the roller coaster of Indian politics, and examining the twists and turns in the country's political dynamics has provided much professional satisfaction. But I must confess to lately feeling disillusioned by the hyper-polarized environment where even newsrooms are neatly divided between 'us' and 'them'; where journalists are favoured if they ingratiate themselves with the regime or systematically targeted and ostracized for telling truth to power. (While writing this book I witnessed first-hand the 'fear factor' at work with a number of people just too scared to come on record and speak freely.) The news universe seems trapped in partisan battles, and the space for a free and independent media that offers democracy its much-needed oxygen is rapidly shrinking. TV studios have begun to resemble courtrooms where news anchors end up playing judge, jury and prosecutor, and where solid reportage loses out to gladiatorial debates.

Today, more than ever, it is essential to chronicle the turbulent times which we live in; to rise above the noise of a 24x7 breaking-news cycle, go beyond the agendas of right and left. In a way, this book is meant to take you on a journey beyond the screaming headlines, into the heart of a momentous election that has defined a 'new' India. I hope you enjoy the ride!

ONE

Big Boss Is Here

BY noon on 23 May 2019 it was apparent that TsuNamo 2.0 had hit the country. What many political pundits had believed would be a long day of twists and turns turned out to be a hopelessly one-sided Indian Political League grand final yet again: Narendra Modi had simply smashed all his opponents out of the park. With the numbers flashing on the screen suggesting that the NDA would cross the 300 mark, the excitement in the studio became palpable. Our pollster Pradeep Gupta of Axis My India had predicted that the NDA would get between 340 and 365 seats. It was a big call to make: common analysis till exit-poll day had indicated that 2019 was not 2014 and the NDA would struggle to cross the halfway mark. 'The real election begins after the counting, all pollsters will have egg on their face,' a senior opposition leader had warned us that morning.

Gupta though was confident of his numbers. A shy, rather unassuming individual, he didn't have the swagger of a smooth-talking news anchor nor did he have a professional background in political forecasting. He ran a printing and consumer research and marketing company in Mumbai that handled electricity, gas and railway ticket billing and product advertising. 'My father was a Gandhian and a freedom fighter and I was always fascinated by politics and media. I guess it is more exciting to know who is winning an election than who is using which toothpaste!' he told me with a glint in his eyes.

I first met Gupta in November 2015 soon after the Bihar elections. Then, he had predicted that the Nitish Kumar–Lalu Prasad combine would sweep the elections with a three-fourths majority and the BJP would be routed. The news channel which had contracted him refused to carry the poll, perhaps fearing a backlash from the Modi government if the numbers were proven wrong. As it turned out, the Axis poll was spot on. I was impressed and suggested that he meet the India Today management to discuss the possibility of doing a poll for us. For the next three years, he worked with our team and built a solid reputation for getting the poll numbers right. Unlike other pollsters, Gupta didn't believe in random sampling but in getting his surveyors to visit every constituency. It seemed like a rather ambitious project but it was clearly working.

We weren't the only ones to spot Gupta's talent. Soon the BJP and other political parties were also seeking his number-crunching expertise. In 2018, he was contracted by BJP president Amit Shah to do polling for the party, a move that bothered me since it suggested a potential conflict of interest. 'Don't worry, I will do the exit poll for you guys but I cannot do an opinion poll now since that would be inappropriate,' was his honest confession. I remained sceptical, especially when he got his book released by Shah with the entire BJP top brass in attendance. On exit-poll day, when Gupta showed us his numbers, my first reaction was: 'You better be right, my friend, because if you get this one wrong, everyone will say that Amit Shah has bought you!'

In the office sweepstakes, I had predicted that the NDA would get between 340 and 350 seats. My assessment was based entirely on my travels across the country during which I had sensed a rising tide of support for Prime Minister Modi. Unlike Gupta, I didn't have a large team of surveyors to back my prediction; the numbers were based on guesswork as much as intuition. Journalists are often clueless while forecasting election results; even while writing a column the previous week hinting at TsuNamo 2.0, I had given sufficient caveats to bail me out in case I was wrong. Gupta didn't have that journalistic luxury.

The 2019 exit poll was on a Sunday evening, the last day of the marathon seven-phase election schedule. The next morning, the markets hit fresh all-time highs. The Sensex climbed more than 1400 points while the Nifty-50 index vaulted 421 points, the biggest single-day gains in a decade. Investor sentiment had been boosted by the prediction that the NDA was heading for an absolute majority. The big gainers included the stocks of Gautam Adani– and Anil Ambani–owned companies, both businessmen considered close to the Modi government. In the TV studios, the opposition cried foul. 'All of you have been bought by the markets and satta bazar,' said a Congress spokesperson. Even an experienced Congress politician like Madhya Pradesh Chief Minister Kamal Nath was dismissive: 'This is not an exit poll but an entertainment poll, you are part of a BJP game to play with the markets!'

Gupta's credibility, that of the India Today news network and of exit polls in general was on the line. After all, exit polls had gone badly wrong in the Brexit referendum, the 2016 US presidential elections, and even in Australia on the very morning of our exit poll. An Indian exit poll is even more difficult to get right because of the sheer expanse of the electorate. For seventy-two hours, we were harangued by angry SMSs and WhatsApp messages accusing us of having 'sold out'. Which is why as the actual numbers began to pour in, our elation at having got the poll numbers right was matched with a sense of relief. The pressure had suddenly been released. For the fifty-year-old pollster it was more than he could handle: he broke down on live TV. In a frenzied, competitive TV news environment, the image of an emotionally exhausted Gupta with tears streaming down his face is now one of the enduring moments of the 2019 election coverage. As I put my arm around him, he whispered into the camera lens, 'We did it!'

While we were going through an emotional roller coaster in the studio, one man though it seems was unconcerned. A typically confident Narendra Modi was reportedly watching the election results unfold from the comfort of his 7 Lok Kalyan Marg residence. Or at least he wasn't displaying any overt signs of nervousness. Only days earlier, he had insisted before the media at the BJP headquarters that he would get more than 300 seats and return to power. Then, it had seemed like a usual political boast before D-day but now the numbers were proving him right. According to his aides, unlike Gupta, Modi did not shed a tear, but there was a smile of quiet satisfaction that lit up his face. During the campaign, he had claimed that however hard his main opponent, Rahul Gandhi or the 'Khan Market gang' (an allusion to the so-called Delhi elite) tried, they would never be able to dismantle his image, which was built on a forty-five-year-long 'tapasya' (ascetic striving). This tapasya had now brought him to the very pinnacle of political power: he would be a ten-year prime minister after all as he had asserted from the very first day of his tenure.

Modi and I first met during the 1990 Ram Janmabhoomi rath yatra and had kept in regular touch since. In the build-up to the 2014 campaign, we would often speak on the phone, our conversations stretching late into the night. And yet, once he occupied the prime minister's chair, our communication ended almost totally: we have exchanged a few cursory greetings on a couple of formal occasions, but little else. Despite the break in our interaction, we still had several common acquaintances from Gujarat and it was to one of these that I sent a congratulatory message on the evening of 23 May. 'I am sure he will be happy to receive it from you. Tum toh purane dost ho!' (You are an old friend), was the prompt reply accompanied by a 'broad smile' emoji.

That night, as I was about to go to sleep after a long counting day in the TV studios, I got another SMS from the same individual: 'My dear Rajdeep, remember, Modi ko harana mushkil hi nahin namumkin hai!' (It is not just difficult but impossible to defeat Modi!) The dialogue from the superhit Hindi film *Don* was perhaps reflective of the buoyant mood in the prime minister's inner circle. Five years after his initial conquest of a national election, the pracharak-politician from the dusty, sleepy town of Vadnagar, Gujarat, was now the unquestioned political boss of India.

A man in a hurry, Narendra Modi flew into Delhi on 22 May 2014 to take over as India's fourteenth prime minister in an Adani Group–owned private jet. It was perhaps a signature style statement designed to send out a political message: he would set his own rules, unfettered by propriety or convention. During the campaign Modi was accused by his rivals of political cronyism and giving land to the Adanis at throwaway prices. Yet here he was, openly, and unapologetically, advertising his links with his Gujarati industrialist friend, literally daring his critics to take him on.

'Susti se kaam ab nahin chalega, action ki zaroorat hai' (Laziness will not do, we need action), he told a senior bureaucrat who had come to greet him at the airport with the traditional bouquet of flowers. 'He kept the flowers aside and told me, "Dost, yeh phool se kuch nahin hoga, mujhe ideas chahiye, action chahiye!"' (Flowers will not accomplish anything, I want ideas and action!) recalls the bureaucrat.

The 'action' that Modi hoped would unfold was defined on swearing-in day itself for which the prime minister had chosen to invite leaders of the South Asian Association for Regional Cooperation (SAARC) region for the ceremony being held in the grand forecourt of Rashtrapati Bhavan. It was the first political showstopper for a prime minister whose event management skills and preference for headline-grabbing 'spectacle' politics would soon become a trademark of his government. The decision to invite heads of SAARC countries for the swearing-in of India's new prime minister was thrillingly unusual. Even opposition politicians like former Jammu and Kashmir (J&K) chief minister Omar Abdullah called the move 'excellent' and hoped it signalled a beginning in a comprehensive dialogue process between India and Pakistan.

The ceremony itself was suitably grand. Despite being nurtured in the austere RSS shakha culture, there is nothing spare about Modi's preference for official grandeur: he likes government events to make as big a splash as possible. 'We were only given 72 hours to prepare, many of us were totally clueless as to what had prompted the sudden decision,' recalls a diplomat involved in making the last-minute arrangements. Despite the fearfully hot May afternoon in Delhi, the show of state power was not dampened. A magnificent red carpet covered the dais and radiated outwards to the audience that included row upon row of richly dressed Bollywood stars, top bureaucrats, celebrities, business tycoons and parliamentarians. For the first time Doordarshan was covering the ceremony with minute-to-minute commentary from an anchor as had only been done previously for Republic Day parades. This was no ordinary swearing-in ceremony; it was one which the entire South Asian neighbourhood was called upon to witness in the style of a grand durbar, an almost royal investiture of a leader crowned with a massive mandate, a ceremonial flourish of an ostentatiously new leadership style. After the oath-taking, leaders of the SAARC countries filed past Modi, offering greetings and a handshake. Dressed in a cream kurta-pyjama and beige waistcoat, Modi bowed low before each of them, exchanging a particularly fond greeting with the then Pakistan prime minister Nawaz Sharif. No surprises, the event was streamed live on YouTube.

The decision to reach out to regional leaders, including Sharif, was the result of an idea floated by a group of retired diplomats and national security officials close to the BJP who felt that Modi needed to send out a strong message to the neighbourhood, showing that he was a prime minister with a difference who was ready to take bold risks. Even the then foreign secretary Sujatha Singh had not been kept in the loop when taking this call. (An appointee of the previous Manmohan Singh government in 2013, Singh would be sacked in January 2015, six months before completing her tenure.) 'I think the idea of an informal SAARC summit at his swearing-in appealed to the prime minister's sense of theatre and his desire to be seen as an international personality, especially after he was ostracized by large parts of the global community post the Gujarat riots. Maybe, he wanted to create a slice of history on day one itself,' former diplomat K.C. Singh tells me. The Indian prime minister being sworn in with the leaders of South Asia in attendance was without precedent. Modi had achieved his primary goal with the ceremony: 'Event-driven' marketing and headline management would coexist with even greater frequency in his government.

Among the retired officials who had endorsed Modi's day-one gambit was practised Pakistan-watcher and former intelligence bureau chief Ajit Doval. During his long career in government, the outwardly nondescript Doval, with a fixed bright gaze behind his glasses, had served as the archetypal secret agent. He had earned a reputation of being a daredevil 007-like 'spymaster'. There is even an apocryphal narrative of his having spent seven years in Pakistan – 'undercover' – as a Muslim. He would often regale his large troop of journalistic admirers over long and loud evenings of drinks with sensational stories of how he had penetrated the Pakistani 'establishment' while risking his cover being blown.

Truth is, Doval served as a high-ranking intelligence official in the Indian high commission in Islamabad for three years in the early 1980s where his 'acquaintances' included a rising young Pakistani politician, Nawaz Sharif. 'When the Indian cricket team under Sunil Gavaskar came to Pakistan in 1982–83, Doval got Sharif to throw a lavish dinner for the team at his farmhouse near Lahore,' recalls a former diplomat.

Doval's reputation as an adventurous Indian equivalent of James Bond was further enhanced during Operation Black Thunder in 1988 – when he reportedly disguised himself as a rickshaw-wallah to infiltrate the Khalistani militant group holed up inside the Golden Temple. 'A courageous, no-nonsense yaaron ka yaar' (best among friends), is how one former colleague describes him. His critics claim he is a politically aligned officer with a 'daroga' (head constable) mindset who lacks strategic vision. 'He thinks like a jailer, whose danda settles everything,' is how a critic describes him. Strategic affairs journalist Nitin Gokhale, who has known Doval for three decades, argues that within the intelligence community, the former intelligence officer retains a certain aura that has helped unite the different government agencies involved in covert operations. 'He has ensured a synergy and integration within the security establishment that was missing in the previous government,' says Gokhale.

From 2009 till 2014, Doval, who retired from government in 2005, was a founding director at the Vivekananda International Foundation (VIF), a think tank populated by retired bureaucrats and diplomats in the national capital. The organization is believed to have strong links with the RSS and generally pushes the BJP–RSS view on national security and global affairs. The Chennai-based RSS ideologue S. Gurumurthy was one of the group's chief benefactors. The VIF also organized a seminar on black money in March 2011, where the attendees included activist Anna Hazare, right to information (RTI) campaigner Arvind Kejriwal and retired police officer Kiran Bedi. Just weeks later, the trio would play a key role in the 2011 anti-corruption campaign that would mark the beginning of the end of the Manmohan Singh government, sparking off speculation about a 'hidden saffron hand' fuelling the protests. 'We at VIF have not funded the Anna agitation,' insisted Doval when quizzed at the time but he also did admit that the 'return of black money locked in Swiss bank accounts' must become a 'national mission'. When the UPA was in power, we would often invite Doval to the studio as a talking head to represent a right-wing viewpoint. I once introduced him as strategic expert close to the BJP only to be promptly admonished, 'I am not close to anyone but have my own independent mind. Please introduce me as director of VIF.'

Doval, in fact, rarely held back in his public statements and editorials, his views on minorities, Kashmir and Bangladeshi immigrants sharp-edged and contentious, often mirroring the BJP–RSS vision of Hindutva nationalism. As far as ideological predilection is concerned, there is no doubt that in his writings Doval appears as a hawkish, right-wing advocate of a strong national security state which must gird its loins to face the looming threat of Islamist terror and spare little time for those concerned with excesses of security forces or human rights of citizens. In a speech in 2010 at a BJP event, Doval maintained that political parties must reject the idea of 'unity in diversity'. 'We cannot base our nation-building on diversity. A nation can't be strengthened by weakening the forces of unity and strengthening the forces of diversity because we have a diverse culture,' he claimed.

In another address he gave in 2010 at an event to mark Universal Brotherhood Day, uploaded on YouTube under the title of 'Ajit Doval on Muslims Mentality' and highlighted in a lengthy *Caravan* profile in September 2017, he says, 'If India stopped preaching universal brotherhood – we have done it for too long, for too many centuries – and if we had been strong enough, probably there would have been a much greater peace. Weakness is the greatest provocation for violence ... Universal brotherhood will be butchered because you are weak ... Dharma will be conquered because you are weak.'

In a TV debate, he told us that the Indian state needed to get tough with Pakistan and 'take out' underworld don Dawood Ibrahim. 'If Israel can conduct cross-border raids, why can't India? Is it because we are a weak state that has allowed infiltrators to compromise our security apparatus?' he thundered.

It was just the kind of strident machismo that probably appealed to Modi who had been assiduously courted by Doval when he was Gujarat chief minister. Doval had helped the Gujarat government set up the Raksha Shakti University in 2009, which offers degree and diploma courses in internal security. He also strongly defended the Gujarat police and intelligence officers charged with extrajudicial killings. 'There are many who feel that there is a higher rationale for such actions in compelling circumstances,' he wrote in 2010.

Not surprisingly, Doval was the new prime minister's first major appointment as national security adviser. The pocket-sized, stern-looking Doval would become arguably the most powerful person in the Modi Prime Minister's Office (PMO): he was the point person for the prime minister on all internal and external security-related issues, had a decisive say on Kashmir, Pakistan, China and the neighbourhood, and even West Asia. Claims one former senior official in the home ministry, 'He was like a super home-cum-foreign-affairs minister. When the minister called we might have got away with not picking up the phone, but when Doval was on the hotline, no one dared not answer!'

Doval's pre-eminent position in the Modi government was not without controversy. His son Shaurya, a successful, smooth-talking investment banker who had worked in New York, London and Singapore, had set up the India Foundation in 2009, a right-wing policy think tank which claimed to look at India from a 'nationalist Indian perspective', and whose board of directors included BJP–RSS leaders like Ram Madhav, and Union ministers Nirmala Sitharaman, M.J. Akbar and Suresh Prabhu, all of whom would later play influential roles in the Modi government. The foundation would often host receptions for visiting heads of state and hold annual conclaves and seminars. I attended an India Foundation reception for a visiting Nepal prime minister which was held at a five-star hotel banquet hall with virtually the entire union cabinet in attendance. 'We have an alignment of interest with the BJP because we come from the same ideological family, but there is no conflict of interest; we weren't lobbying with the ministers for any favours. Many of them have a long-standing relationship with the foundation and were there in their personal capacity,' insists Shaurya.

Clearly though, the highly networked foundation had privileged access to those in power. Its offices too moved from south Delhi's residential colony of Jangpura to the more upscale Lutyens' Delhi address of Hailey Road and the scope of its activities widened considerably after the Modi government came to power. 'Battle me on ideas, not on falsehood. Yes, we get voluntary contributions from corporates, Sangh Parivar outfits and have even sometimes got events co-sponsored with the MEA but we are a non-profit charitable trust that isn't financially dependent on any individual or institution. I have never sought favours by using my father's position. You forget, this isn't a Congress government but a Modi government. These things just don't happen,' is the forty-five-year-old banker's angry response. However, the perception that the India Foundation is 'blessed' by the ruling establishment is hard to ignore. If the Sonia Gandhi–led UPA had patronized Left leaning NGOs, the Modi government was determined to create its own network of right-wing-affiliated groups who would promote their policies.

Doval wasn't the only retired officer joining the Modi administration. Another key appointee was Nripendra Misra, as principal secretary to the prime minister. The elderly, soft-spoken Misra was seen as an archetypal, well-connected bureaucrat from the all-powerful UP cadre, with a firm grip on the political dynamics of the capital. Misra too was linked to the VIF, albeit in a more tenuous manner; he had attended a few seminars at the foundation on the invitation of Doval. He had formidable links across party lines, having worked closely with the Mulayam Singh Yadav and Kalyan Singh governments in UP. He was even accused of informing on Yadav's every move to BJP leaders during the contentious Ayodhya dispute in the early 1990s. After retirement from the Indian Administrative Service (IAS), he served as the chairperson of the Telecom Regulatory Authority of India (TRAI) under the Manmohan Singh government until 2009. 'Misraji has the sharpest political antennae in government, he knows everything there is to know about how the bureaucracy works,' is how one senior official describes his role. (Misra would finally quit the PMO in August 2019.)

Assisting Misra in the PMO was his namesake: the bespectacled, serious-faced P.K. Mishra, who had served as secretary to Modi during his tenure as Gujarat chief minister (2001–04), and was drafted to play a key role in 'managing' the bureaucracy. From transfers and postings to overseeing the Modi government's flagship programmes, Misra and Mishra, along with a tightly knit group of officers, would be the new administration's eyes and ears. 'When either of the Misra–Mishra duo called up, we had to be up and ready, there was no place to hide!' says a former bureaucrat.

P.K. Mishra was just one of several Gujarat cadre officers who would make the shift from Gandhinagar to the national capital. A.K. Sharma, another IAS officer from the state who had helped organize Modi's showpiece Vibrant Gujarat project and worked in the chief minister's office for over a decade, also became part of the inner circle in the PMO and was given the responsibility of monitoring key infrastructure projects. The prime minister's private secretary, Rajeev Topno, was another Gujarat cadre appointee. 'Mr Modi instinctively trusts bureaucrats more than he does politicians. The PM is convinced that most netas are overly ambitious and only looking to serve their personal agendas,' one senior BJP politician tells me.

A more controversial Modi appointment from Gujarat was Indian Police Service (IPS) officer Rakesh Asthana, who would be drafted into the Central Bureau of Investigation (CBI) as a special director. Asthana had led the special investigation team into the Godhra incident in February 2002 in which fifty-nine people, mainly Vishwa Hindu Parishad (VHP) karsevaks on their way back from Ayodhya, died in a fire inside the Sabarmati Express. The horrific act would trigger communal riots across the state.

I had met Asthana in April 2002, soon after he had taken over the investigations into the sensitive case. 'Prima facie it appears to be a spontaneous act triggered by an altercation between the local Muslims living near the station and the karsevaks,' he told me on record. But months later, Asthana appeared to change his mind: the official investigation report claimed that Godhra was a pre-planned conspiracy and an act of terror with cross-border links. The report's findings would form an important element of Modi's 2002 Gujarat campaign as he lashed out at Pakistan-sponsored terror and its 'local' connections. Despite objections raised over his appointment by legal activists, Asthana remained in his CBI post till October 2018 when he was finally shunted out after a bitter and public feud broke out with Alok Verma, the agency's director. 'Asthana was always seen as a Modi man in Gujarat. He was brought to Delhi on the specific instructions of the prime minister who had known him since the Godhra investigation,' claims R.B. Sreekumar, former director general of police, Gujarat, who had posed troubling questions over the Modi government's handling of the 2002 violence.

Asthana may have been a contentious choice but like many prime ministers before him, Modi wanted familiar faces around him, 'troubleshooters' whom he could rely upon. Gujarat, after all, was Modi's original political karmabhoomi and he preferred to work with officers whom he could implicitly trust to do his bidding. Despite having spent a fair amount of time in the capital in the 1990s as a party spokesperson and general secretary, Modi had remained a bit of an 'outsider' in the Byzantine power corridors of Delhi: the city wasn't his comfort zone. 'Tum logon ki tarah hum central hall nahin ghoomte' (I don't hang around Parliament's central hall like all of you), he once told a journalist.

In fact, the entire media team in the PMO was dominated by his old staff from the Gandhinagar chief minister's office. They included, for example, Jagdish Thakkar from the information department of the Gujarat government. Rather than appoint a high-profile media adviser (and there were many BJP-aligned journalists queuing up for the job), Modi preferred to have the quietly efficient and affable Jagdishbhai do what he had done for him for years: ensure government press releases were sent out with clockwork precision. Jagdishbhai wasn't comfortable in Delhi but couldn't get himself to tell 'Saheb' that he wanted to go back to Gandhinagar. 'Soo karoon, Saheb mujhe jaane nahin denge' (What to do, the boss won't let me go), he told me a few months before he passed away in December 2018.

Sanjay Bhavsar, another long-serving aide from Gujarat, was brought in to handle prime-ministerial appointments. Modi's influential social media team, led by Hiren Joshi, a qualified electronics engineer, was also drawn from the pool of young tech-friendly professionals who had worked closely with him during his chief-ministerial tenure. Over the next five years, this relatively 'faceless' group would play a crucial role in building up Brand Modi. 'A hard-working, low-profile team for a high-profile, high-achiever individual,' is how one Modi-watcher sums up the overarching dynamics of Team Modi.

Narendra Modi's Gujarat model was driven by a highly centralized chief minister's office in Gandhinagar and he was determined to bring a similar 'command and control' chief executive–like approach to Delhi. On 4 June 2014, Modi called a meeting of all seventy-seven secretaries to the Government of India and asked them for suggestions: 'Tell me how to run my government, give me out-of-the-box solutions.' At the end of the two-hour-long meeting, Modi gave his phone number, email address and official RAX line to the bureaucrats and advised them to directly contact him if they had any issues in their ministry. 'The message was clear to all of us: this was a prime minister who called the shots and his was the last word on all important matters,' recalls an officer.

Modi was keen to create a sharp contrast with his predecessor Manmohan Singh's PMO where, especially in UPA 2, the prime minister's executive authority was gradually ceded to ministerial colleagues, leading to what was often criticized as 'policy paralysis'. One of the first decisions taken by the Modi-led government was to scrap the various Groups of Ministers (GoMs) constituted by Dr Singh to handle contentious policy issues. In the note issued while distributing portfolios, it was specifically mentioned that 'all important policy issues' were the unquestioned domain of the prime minister.

What it meant was that decision-making could often bypass the cabinet system with the PMO taking the major calls. In an article in November 2014, *India Today* listed several examples of this PMO-centric approach to governance. Commerce and industry minister Nirmala Sitharaman was involved in the 'Make in India' campaign only in the final stage. Make in India was seen as Prime Minister Modi's initiative from the get-go and it was only after senior bureaucrats had worked out the details and the prime minister had cleared the plan that the minister was briefed. In another instance, HRD minister Smriti Irani was chairing a meeting on skill development when a notification was issued stating that the department had been taken off her portfolio and given to the Ministry of Youth Affairs and Sports. When a decision to restructure the Food Corporation of India was taken, food minister Ram Vilas Paswan was not consulted on the details.

Paswan's marginalization is a good example of how the coalition dharma was reworked under an imperious political authority. Having started off as a minister in the V.P. Singh government in 1989, Paswan's survival instincts helped him find a berth in different regimes and work with half a dozen prime ministers. In most governments, he managed to carve out an independent identity but in the Modi cabinet, he was effectively isolated and given limited decision-making powers. When I asked him once to explain the difference he saw between Modi and previous prime ministers, he said, 'Modiji ne sab kuch tight rakha hai!' (Modiji controls everything!) with a wry smile.

In order to keep the netas and their babus 'tight', the prime minister deployed to good use his obsession with digital technology and big data. Loaded on Modi's and his key officials' iPads and computers was a digital platform called E-SamikSha which allowed the PMO to monitor all inter-department file movements and establish direct communication with ministry officials. If any official or minister was sitting on a file, the prime minister could personally intervene and a bright red mark would flash on the officer's screen. 'We called it "pradhan mantri ki teesri aankh"!' (The prime minister's third eye!) laughs a former secretary.

Modi's prime-ministerial intervention didn't end there. Every last Wednesday of the month at 3.30 p.m. sharp, for around 90 minutes, the prime minister and PMO officials would meet the chief secretaries of all the states and secretaries to the Government of India via videoconference to review major projects. The interactive platform was called PRAGATI (Pro-Active Governance and Timely Implementation) by Modi who relishes catchy acronyms. 'It was like the monthly exams we wrote in school, only this time it was the PM who was headmaster,' says one officer. 'We had to be prepared because the prime minister had all the details on a screen in front of him. Once, when a state chief secretary was fumbling, the PM joked, "Come on, you have only a few months to retire, let's get this project finished before that!"'

In the time-worn framework of Indian bureaucracy, technology became a major disruptor and businesslike 'efficiency' became the new buzzword. Bureaucrats were encouraged to make short, snappy PowerPoint presentations and use latest gadgets for real-time communication. Online performance dashboards were introduced to ensure technology-driven, real-time surveillance of development projects. 'Why do we need so many files? Why can't we have a paperless office where we give every minister and bureaucrat a tablet to work with and send their cabinet notes via mail?' Modi once asked an aide. The proposal was mooted but didn't quite take off. 'I guess the prime minister was a man in a hurry but the traditional system of file pushers was not!' remarks a senior government official.

With the prime minister working long hours and often into the weekends, bureaucrats were encouraged to follow suit. Keshav Desiraju, who served as secretary in both the Manmohan Singh and Modi governments, says it's wrong to suggest that senior bureaucrats started working much harder only when the government changed in May 2014. 'This is a complete myth that bureaucrats used to wander off to the Golf Club or Delhi Gymkhana for long lunches earlier and everything changed when Modi took over. We worked just as hard when Dr Singh was PM, the workload on a secretary in today's times is such that you just can't afford to slack off.'

And yet, there was an unmistakable sense of change in the air of Lutyens' Delhi, one where the old order was clearly giving way to the new, where the Congress's system of governance by consensus would now be challenged by the freshly minted Modi model of rule by inflexible diktat. In January 2015, the Modi government suddenly cancelled the membership of twenty-seven serving and retired bureaucrats to the exclusive Delhi Golf Club, a perquisite which they had got under the Ministry of Urban Development quota when Kamal Nath was the Congress minister in charge. 'PM Modi is always looking for an opportunity to show who is the boss, that's just the way he likes to keep the administration under his firm grip,' says a long-serving aide. The tough-talking 'strongman' leader would become Modi's signature style, positioned as his predecessor Manmohan Singh's binary opposite: where a self-effacing Singh had striven for consensus, Modi was the domineering authoritarian who set a spanking pace and brooked no argument.

A typical example of the changed nature of leadership in the Modi era was the prime minister's first annual Independence Day speech. For every Indian prime minister, 15 August is a significant occasion to spell out their agenda and set the political narrative. Nehru's many speeches established his commitment to democratic values and broad secular and socialist principles; Lal Bahadur Shastri gave India the rousing 'Jai Jawan, Jai Kisan' slogan; Indira Gandhi laid out her populist manifesto for 'Garibi hatao'; Dr Singh, the self-confessed accidental politician, chose a safer path – his speeches were little more than a recitation of facts and figures delivered in a low-voiced monologue.

Modi was desperately keen to make a mark on the occasion and use the event to project himself as a leader and prime minister with a difference. He has often emphasized that he is India's first prime minister born after Independence and making a robust break with the past and with prime-ministerial precedent was and still remains his calling card. Only a year earlier, on 15 August 2013, as the Gujarat chief minister, he had openly confronted Dr Singh while delivering what was effectively a campaign speech from the sands of Bhuj in Kutch. In what was an unprecedented challenge from a state chief minister, he declared that his Independence Day address would get more attention than the then prime minister's speech. That same year he had addressed a campaign rally in Chhattisgarh from a stage modelled on the Red Fort. Then, he was the challenger eager to be prime minister. Now, he was the prime minister and the ramparts of the historic Red Fort awaited him. Wearing a cream-coloured, short-sleeved kurta, white pyjama and a flamboyant red Rajasthani safa, Modi laced his hour-long speech with trademark oratorical flourishes and catchy one-liners.

One of his major announcements was the abolition of the Planning Commission. A close Modi aide says that the prime minister's antipathy to Yojana Bhavan was a fallout of his chief-ministerial experience: 'He would often tell us, "Why should an elected chief minister have to come to Delhi and run around non-elected officials to clear expenditure proposals? Why do we need the parallel power centre of so-called experts who have no ground experience?"' Modi didn't like, for example, being questioned on Gujarat's relatively weak social indices at commission meetings, preferring instead to show well-packaged videos highlighting the state's economic progress. In one particular instance, Modi got into a heated argument with commission member and social activist Dr Syeda Hameed when asked why he wasn't implementing an education project for Muslim girls in Gujarat. 'I don't look at education from any religious viewpoint,' he retorted angrily.

Dr Hameed had been a vocal critic of Modi's handling of the 2002 Gujarat riots and the verbal spat only convinced Modi further that the Planning Commission was a 'Congress-era' institution that would undermine his authority. The Planning Commission was set up in 1950 by Jawaharlal Nehru in the high noon of the socialist project of centralized planning; now, by abolishing it, Modi was driving another stake into the legacy of India's first prime minister whom he clearly abhors. The commission would be replaced in early 2015 by the NITI Aayog (National Institution for Transforming India), a policy think tank that functions under the direct supervision of the prime minister. Where the Planning Commission provided a well-defined institutional architecture for funding state governments, the NITI Aayog would become another appendage to the Modi government's publicity machine with no financial allocation powers and limited autonomy. 'Fiscal federalism' was the new axiom, but the reality was a vacuum in procedural arrangements for a meaningful interaction between states and the Centre.

'We were all taken unawares by the sudden announcement,' admits a senior government official, according to whom the basic blueprint for setting up the new body was only initiated after the prime minister made his Independence Day declaration. Former UPA minister Jairam Ramesh, who had previously served in the Planning Commission, is scathing in his criticism of the manner in which such a far-reaching decision was taken, describing it as a 'Tughluqian' move. 'It is in keeping with Modi's mindset: everything must bear his imprint, no matter what is the history and what's the legacy,' he says. A sweeping declaration was made before the nation without consulting the key stakeholders, including chief ministers and policymakers. The messaging was clear yet again: in the new governance paradigm, the only viewpoint that mattered was of the single individual at the top.

Modi's was a highly absolutist one-man-show style of leadership that the rich and powerful in India Inc. all too soon came to terms with. In the Manmohan Singh years, industry bodies like the Confederation of Indian Industry (CII) and Federation of Indian Chambers of Commerce and Industry (FICCI) enjoyed almost unlimited access to the PMO. Business delegations frequently called on the prime minister, a structured government–industry dialogue was forged and Dr Singh routinely attended the annual business meets. With Modi, access was severely curtailed. 'It is no longer a case of flash a visiting card and get an appointment; sometimes we have to wait for months,' a senior business leader tells me. Modi's run-ins with the Delhi-based CII, in fact, date back to 2002 when several of its members, led by industry heavyweight Rahul Bajaj, questioned the chief minister as to whether it was safe to invest in Gujarat in the wake of the riots. 'Yes, I did go subsequently to Gandhinagar and build bridges with Modi,' admits Tarun Das, the then CII director general. 'I don't think he holds past grudges against CII any longer.'

The truth is, Modi doesn't forget or forgive easily. In early 2015, one of corporate India's most respected voices, Deepak Parekh, warned of a growing impatience amongst businessmen who felt that nothing had really changed on the ground in terms of ease of doing business despite the Modi government's lofty claims. Parekh's vocal criticism led to unease in government circles: almost overnight, Parekh, who was on almost every major economic policy committee during Dr Singh's tenure, was persona non grata. 'In any case, in this government, every committee is led by bureaucrats, with almost zero private industry participation. In fact, I was once bluntly told by a high-ranking bureaucrat that we don't really need any of you,' an industry leader affirms.

Modi, in fact, has built his own clique of supporters in industry, many of them again from his days as Gujarat chief minister. Gautam Adani is the most recognizable, often part of the entourage that accompanies the prime minister on foreign trips (he generally travels separately but invariably stays in the same hotel as Modi). Adani's varied businesses grew manifold in the Modi decade in Gujarat and he was among the few business magnates who stood by the chief minister during the 2002 violence, even organizing support under the 'Resurgent Gujarat' banner. When Adani's son got married in 2013, Modi made a special effort to attend the festivities, even travelling to Goa for one of the functions. The Gujarat-based Torrent Group's Sudhir Mehta and Swan Energy's Nikhil Merchant are other industrialists who are part of what one bureaucrat calls 'Modiji ke khaas aadmi!' (Modi's special friends!). An illustration of Merchant's clout was highlighted in the news website The Wire, which claims that the Union revenue secretary was transferred out soon after Modi took over as prime minister allegedly because of raids conducted a few months earlier on Swan Energy in Ahmedabad. What is undeniable is that most of these industrialists benefited from public–private partnerships cemented with the Gujarat government when Modi was chief minister.

The billionaire Ambani brothers too share a special relationship with Prime Minister Modi, one which is rooted in strong Gujarat connections. Anil Ambani was a regular visitor to the Vibrant Gujarat summits and was always effusive in his praise of Modi's administrative qualities. His brother, Mukesh, the country's wealthiest industrialist, has friends in all parties but has made it a point to keep Modi within his close embrace. His key corporate affairs man in Ahmedabad, Parimal Nathwani, is an independent Rajya Sabha Member of Parliament (MP) from Jharkhand, elected with BJP support, and has a long association with the prime minister and BJP president Amit Shah. (Nathwani was also the vice president of the Gujarat Cricket Association [GCA] till he stepped down in September 2019 under the cricket board's new rules, which insist on a 'cooling off' period after two three-year terms in office. The GCA, which is controlled by the Modi–Shah duo, is building the largest cricket stadium in the country in Ahmedabad under Nathwani's supervision.) In October 2014, the prime minister attended the highly publicized inauguration of a Reliance Hospital in Mumbai as Mukesh and Nita Ambani's star attraction amidst the VIP guests assembled in single file to greet him. 'With Modi and industry, it all works on personal relationships – either you have a bond with him or you don't,' a seasoned corporate-watcher tells me.

Not surprisingly, most businessmen today are fearful of coming on record to critique the Modi government's track record on the economy. Indian industry has rarely challenged the ruling party but with the Modi government it's no longer just about having proximity to power: there is a stifling fear factor as well. I sensed this most acutely when, during a planned TV debate on demonetization in 2016, a highly respected industry voice dropped out of my show at the very last moment. 'I don't want to get into any further trouble, you know. I will say something and the PMO may not like it!' was his excuse. Another well-known industrialist recalls a business chamber meeting with the prime minister in Mumbai where no one spoke out against the government's economic policies. 'There were so many issues we wanted to raise but the moment the prime minister arrived in the room and asked if we were unhappy with his government, we just clammed up,' recalls the industrialist. The writing on the wall has been obvious from the very outset: question the political leadership at your peril.

The 2014 win had established Modi as the victorious BJP's numero uno and a panoply of images of the new prime minister dominated prime time in his first year: from sitting on a 'jhoola' (swing) in Ahmedabad with Chinese President Xi Jinping to meeting US president Barack Obama at the Rose Gardens in Washington, Modi was literally everywhere. In his first year alone, Modi made nineteen foreign visits and travelled to thirty-seven countries: official records show that the total expense incurred was around ₹211 crore. A key aspect of these high-profile engagements was

Modi's unique style of public outreach. On a visit to the United Kingdom for example, he addressed a massive crowd of more than 60,000 people, mainly NRIs, at London's Wembley arena. 'This event was totally funded by the local community, we didn't need any state support,' insists Manoj Ladwa, founder and director of the India Inc. Group and chief organizer of the Wembley extravaganza. The go-getter Ladwa had been part of Team Modi during the 2014 election campaign and was now recognized as 'Modi's man in London'. The lines between state power and private lobbying were obscured: 'diaspora diplomacy' was the new buzzword and Modi was the star of the show. In what became a trend, Modi used expertly mounted events on the international stage to build a domestic aura as a conquering hero.

But despite the sudden leap into national and even global pre-eminence, Modi hadn't entirely shaken off his provincial Gujarat roots. In his twelve years as chief minister, he had acquired a reputation for being deeply suspicious of fellow politicians. Modi functions as a peremptory one-man show; formal cabinet meetings in Gandhinagar barely lasted a few minutes and no other minister in his government was given any prominence. This political insecurity would follow Modi to Delhi and reflect in the choice of his first cabinet.

Just two days ahead of the cabinet announcement in May 2014, I went to interview senior BJP leader Arun Shourie, known for his soft voice yet fierce, trenchantly independent views. The conversation centred on the finance ministry and the challenges before the economy: Shourie spoke with the confidence of someone who was certain he would be appointed to the key assignment in North Block. Prominent businessmen close to the new government, including Anil Ambani and Gautam Adani, had called on him, and newly appointed PMO officials were consulting him on matters concerning the finance ministry. Yet, when the list of ministers was officially announced, Shourie's name was missing. We were told that Shourie's name had been withdrawn on the insistence of Arun Jaitley, a long-time confidant of Modi's, who had reportedly told the prime minister that Shourie was not someone to be trusted to work in a team environment. When I asked Jaitley if he had vetoed Shourie's appointment, he just smiled and remarked, 'Well, what do you think!'

Jaitley and Shourie, both sharply astute, well educated, urbane cognoscente politicians, had no love lost for each other, often sniping at one another in party fora and outside. Shourie, a much-admired editor and author who had provided the Indian right wing with much-needed intellectual heft, had entered politics in the BJP's Vajpayee–Advani era, and had become a staunch advocate of Modi's capabilities during his tenure as Gujarat chief minister. He was even part of a small group of advisers who were supporting Modi's push for prime minister and would often meet in Gandhinagar to discuss strategy.

In November 2013, soon after Modi was confirmed as the BJP's prime-ministerial candidate, I attended an investors' conference in Mumbai. Shourie was present too. Both of us spoke on the Modi factor and the emerging political scenario. While we concurred that Modi was the front runner for the 2014 elections, I argued that his autocratic tendencies could become a hindrance in the future. 'You people are too critical of Modi. He is just what India needs at the moment after the weak Manmohan Singh government,' Shourie told me then. By mid-2015, Shourie would become a severe critic of Modi, and for the precise reason I had suggested – that Modi was a putative 'dictator'. 'I was wrong about Modi and got carried away by a superficial understanding of the so-called Gujarat model,' he would confess.

I asked Shourie if he would have had a different opinion had he been made finance minister in 2014. After a pause, he quoted the Dalai Lama, 'Very often not getting what you want is a brilliant stroke of luck!' Then he added, 'Even if I had joined this government, I wouldn't have lasted more than six months. Modi is not large-hearted like Vajpayee was. Vajpayee would bring out the best in people, Modi the worst.' (In a TV interview in May 2015, Shourie described Modi as a 'dark triad' personality: narcissistic, remorseless and Machiavellian. This angry, bitter interview would rupture the Modi–Shourie relationship forever.)

With Shourie out of the picture, Jaitley took charge of both the finance and defence portfolios in the Modi government, an affirmation of his close proximity to the prime minister that stretched back to their Gujarat days. Then, Jaitley had used all his legal and communication skills to defend Modi in the aftermath of the Gujarat riots. He was one of the few BJP politicians whom Modi seemed to trust. After Jaitley rather humiliatingly lost the Amritsar Lok Sabha election to the Congress's Amarinder Singh, he was made the leader of the Rajya Sabha and eventually became Modi's crisis manager in Delhi. 'I think the fact that Jaitley lost the 2014 elections from Amritsar meant that he could never challenge Modi's authority or be seen as a political threat; it was a relationship of mutual benefit,' a veteran BJP leader tells me. 'In the Modi government, either Jaitley or Shourie could have survived – the prime minister chose the person he felt more comfortable with,' he added.

Shourie wasn't the only high-profile absentee from the Modi government. Another BJP veteran who lost out in the new power arrangement was former finance minister Yashwant Sinha. In 2013, Sinha, like Shourie, had endorsed Modi's prime-ministerial credentials and while he hadn't contested the 2014 elections, he had enough reason to believe that the new prime minister would 'reward' him suitably. Instead by 2017, he too had been shown the door. Sinha had led a fact-finding team of prominent civil society representatives to review the situation in the Kashmir valley. When he sought an appointment with Prime Minister Modi to submit a report of their findings, he was denied a meeting despite repeated requests. 'I guess he didn't want to take advice from anyone who might offer an alternative viewpoint,' laments Sinha.

In what was seen as an attempt to assert his dominance, the prime minister decided to keep the entire original 'old guard' of the BJP out of executive decision-making at all levels. That Modi's mentor, L.K. Advani, was kept out was no surprise. Advani had publicly challenged Modi's prime-ministerial nomination in 2013 and the acrimonious battle between guru and shishya had almost permanently broken the relationship. 'When Modi gave Advaniji a ticket to contest from Gandhinagar in the 2014 elections, the latter feared that his election may be sabotaged in Gujarat and wanted to shift to Bhopal as a "safe" seat. It was the RSS who had to step in and assure the veteran leader that no such conspiracy was being planned. Such was the hostility between the two camps at the time,' claims a BJP insider.

When I went to meet Advani soon after Modi was sworn in as prime minister, he had little to say. We spoke about films, books, even cricket, but stayed away from politics. It was only in 2015, on the eve of the thirtieth anniversary of the Emergency, that he let his guard down somewhat. In an interview, he warned of the 'return of the Emergency', saying that 'forces that can crush democracy have become stronger'. I asked him explicitly if he was referring to Modi, but Advani ducked the question.

It wasn't just Advani. Also out of the power elite was former BJP president Dr Murli Manohar Joshi. As a young, rising member of the BJP, Modi had accompanied Dr Joshi on an Ekta Yatra to Kashmir in 1991–92. Unlike Advani, Joshi had been more cautious in challenging the ascent of Modi. Once at one of his traditional Diwali Milans, over chaat and kachori, Dr Joshi became nostalgic. 'You know, Modiji and I used to have long conversations on Hindutva and deshbhakti when he was just coming up in the party; we used to speak so frankly with each other,' he reminisced. Yet, in 2017, when a few RSS leaders suggested Dr Joshi's name as a potential nominee for Rashtrapati Bhavan, Modi cold-shouldered the idea. Clearly, Modi saw no reason to be grateful to his seniors, nor did he regard them as allies in his success. In contrast to most political leaders who tend to acquire a cohort of companions in the course of their rise in public life, Modi's leadership is marked by an intriguing lack of any close party comrades, friendships or old Sangh Parivar associations. It seems as if, for him, the relentless, unblinking streak upwards from pracharak to prime minister has been an entirely solitary journey with almost no one having any major contribution in his achievements. And even if anyone did play a role, such as Advani who actively mentored the energetic, burly, bearded RSS organizer from Gujarat in the early 1990s, Modi is reluctant to share or give credit.

'Modi had just won a big majority but I think he feared that this "old caucus" would conspire against him if they were given even half a chance,' a senior BJP leader tells me. This was now a party which was being shaped with the well-defined identity of Prime Minister Modi and he didn't want anyone else to share the spotlight. In August 2014, a 'marg-darshak' mandal or Group of Mentors was created for those in the BJP above seventy-five, namely the troika of Vajpayee, Advani and Dr Joshi. By then, Vajpayee was too ill, Advani too isolated and Joshi too sceptical for the group to have any meaningful role. It did not meet even once. 'I guess we are not needed,' Dr Joshi later remarked ruefully. The creation of the marg-darshak mandal was another attempt by Modi to bolster his 'young', impatient-with-the-old-order, first-prime-minister-born-after-Independence image. It projected him as a force of newness that was keen to make a complete break with the past – an image designed to appeal to voters frustrated with India's lingering inefficiencies and failures.

One Advani 'loyalist' who just about survived the purge was the late Sushma Swaraj, the feisty and charismatic BJP leader who for years was pitched as a future 'face' of the party. Her outward appearance was one of an unassuming, sari-clad, sindoor-adorned 'bharatiya nari', yet Swaraj was an extremely eloquent and argumentative parliamentarian, the only female MP to be awarded the Outstanding Parliamentarian Award. As leader of the opposition in the Manmohan Singh years, she repeatedly put the UPA government on the mat, treating Parliament to displays of her trademark fluent and folksy Hindi and canny political tactics. During the battle for control of the party in 2013, Swaraj was perceived to have distinctly tilted towards her mentor, Advani, when she refused to join the chorus for Modi's elevation as a possible prime-ministerial candidate, suggesting instead that any such decision be taken only after the winter election results of 2013. Modi had clearly not forgotten the episode and was initially keen to deny Swaraj a prize portfolio. It required last-minute intervention on the part of the RSS to convince Modi not to act in anger. Swaraj was made minister for external affairs.

In June 2015, Swaraj was accused of having given an out-of-turn visa favour to fugitive businessman and former Indian Premier League chief Lalit Modi and of even meeting him at a private dinner in London. It can be reasoned that Swaraj, part of a generation of politicians who cultivated a large network of friends and associates, perhaps gave strict institutional propriety a back seat to grant a favour to an old acquaintance (on humanitarian grounds, as she argued later). Such a 'favour' may have been ignored in a more easy-going era, but in the new Modi-created mahaul [atmosphere] against old-style elite connectedness, the story became explosive. News channels considered close to the government went ballistic in calling for Swaraj to immediately step down. With little attempt being made by the government to come out in her defence, the minister was convinced that the 'Sack Sushma' narrative was being pushed by 'rivals' within the party. Jaitley in particular was seen as a peer group competitor. 'I know there are people in this government who are very powerful today who want me out,' she told an aide. Swaraj managed to weather the controversy but was never the same again. 'She knew at the time that she had two options, either suffer in silence or take on a more rebellious avatar; she chose the former,' a friend of the minister tells me. She would rapidly fade from public view, increasingly eclipsed by younger BJP stars like the lively TV actor-turned-politician Smriti Irani, who would become one of the youngest cabinet ministers in the Modi government.

Indeed Swaraj's dramatic transformation from the roaring, perpetually-on-her-feet opposition leader to timid, ornamental minister on mute mode was a striking illustration of the dominance of Modi. During her five-year tenure in South Block, a dutiful Swaraj did not give a single media interview while maintaining an unusually low profile. Easily one of the most articulate, multilingual leaders of the BJP's modern era, she clammed up almost overnight. At an annual MEA lunch for journalists, when one of the beat reporters asked her for a sound bite on a specific news item, she came back with a sharp 'Arre, enjoy the food "bites", no sound bites here!' Excluded from the prime minister's core circle of advisers and high-profile foreign policy initiatives, she chose instead to play kindly aunt – handling a citizens' helpline on Twitter for those who needed the ministry's urgent intervention – to immense success. The marginalization of Swaraj was a pointer to the changed equations: in this Modi-centric government, no one dared to cross the Supreme Leader.

It was a mantra that Rajnath Singh, another potential rival to Modi's supremacy, had learnt early enough. Sober in tone, measured in his speech and widely regarded as amiable even by the opposition, the dhoti-clad Rajput from UP was BJP president in the run-up to the 2014 elections and was seen in a section of the party as a potential consensus candidate in the event of a hung parliament. But rather than even hint at challenging the new power axis, Singh preferred to stay in the background, not once raising a voice of dissent, not even when, as a newly appointed home minister, he was denied a private secretary of his choice. Singh had proposed the name of IPS officer Alok Singh but it was put on hold by the PMO, citing the individual's association with the previous UPA government. Despite feeling slighted, Singh did not protest. 'Rajnathji ka swabhav takraav ka nahin hai' (Rajnathji does not like confrontation), is how a close aide describes the senior leader's non-combative attitude. Combat was not an option anyway. There was a new chief in town and anyone whose loyalties were suspect was under watch.

The creeping sense of dread and anxiety among the ministers was defined early on in a cabinet meeting. A minister in the Modi government was organizing a lavish wedding for his daughter in the national capital and invites had been sent out. Modi was informed of the extravagant arrangements being made. 'So I hear that a big wedding is being planned … looks like some people have a lot of money to spend,' was the prime minister's casual remark at the cabinet meet. Even this seemingly off-the-cuff remark was loaded with meaning. The message was received, and the function was hastily scaled down.

At another cabinet meet, the prime minister made an oblique reference to reports that a few 'Congress-era lobbyists' had been spotted near a particular minister's office. The minister got the message and assured the PMO that he would be more careful in the future. When told that some ministers were going home for an afternoon siesta and would rarely return to the office post-lunch, the prime minister reportedly said, 'Yeh din mein sone ki aadat sehat ke liye achhi nahin.' (It is not a good habit to sleep in the day.) Ministers were explicitly told that they must reach office no later than 9.30 a.m. Puritanical discipline was the new mantra for the mantris: sloth was a thing of the past, energy and efficiency were to be pushed at all levels. Often, this new, dictatorially imposed rulebook looked uncomfortably like regimentation and control, but it was all of a piece with the Modi vision: strictly enforced order was, after all, how the RSS always got things done. 'Modiji is a very good administrator and a hard taskmaster. To call him a dictator is unfair,' says former minister S.S. Ahluwalia.

Dos and don'ts for ministers were spelt out. All foreign trips, official or private, would require political clearance. The request had to be accompanied by a detailed justification note followed by a post-visit report. When a minister reportedly tried to bypass the system and take off on a foreign tour, he was sent a stern warning and his travel curtailed. Ministers were also expected to have 'active' social media profiles on Twitter and Facebook. One minister recalls being pulled up by Modi for not having enough Facebook followers. 'I didn't dare mention to the prime minister that I didn't have a clue of how social media works!' he laughs.

The prime minister's annual showpiece event – Yoga Diwas – was another 'must attend' on the ministers' official to-do lists. Modi has been obsessed with making yoga a global phenomenon since his Gujarat days and often referred to yoga's 'spiritual' power in his public speeches. On his first time at the United Nations' general assembly in September 2014 as prime minister, he succeeded in getting the UN to declare 21 June as International Yoga Day. An elaborate plan was prepared for the inaugural year in 2015 with ministers being assigned specific locations nationwide where they would lead the yoga celebrations before large live audiences at the crack of dawn. It was yet another made-for-TV extravaganza. Modi himself was at Rajpath at 7 a.m., attired in white with a tricolour scarf. 'Who would have ever thought Rajpath would become Yogpath,' he said while acknowledging the 30,000-plus participants who had gathered there.

Not every minister though was an early riser. When one of them arrived a little late for the Yoga Day event, he was reprimanded with a stern phone call to ensure punctuality in the future. On one occasion, a minister was feeling a little unwell ahead of Yoga Day and was desperate to opt out. When he conveyed this to his secretary, he was advised, 'Sir, I don't think this will go down well, better to attend.' Next morning, the minister was up at 6 a.m. sharp to perform his yoga 'duty'.

As one former junior minister would remark in jest in a private conversation with me, 'At times, when we entered a cabinet meeting, it was like we were entering the Big Boss house – someone was watching us all the time,' referring to the popular reality TV show. It seems Indian politics had found a real-life white-bearded Big Boss, someone who was equally omnipresent. 'It is true that the prime minister gets constant updates on what his ministers are up to from multiple sources, both from within the political system and outside it,' admits an aide.

But the Big Boss approach was hardly benign; it had a vengeful, unforgiving edge to it. That even as an all-powerful prime minister, Modi was someone who saw life and politics as a grudge match was apparent in the manner in which he continued to carry old resentments against those whom he had long left behind in his inexorable rise to the top. In April 2015, for example, posters came up at a few places in the national capital wishing former BJP general secretary Sanjay Joshi a happy birthday. Joshi, once an ebullient party leader from Gujarat and RSS favourite, was Modi's long-time rival. He had served in the state in the 1990s when Modi was the party's chief organizer. Modi was certain that it was Joshi who had conspired with his opponents to have him exiled from Gandhinagar for allegedly fomenting a 'revolt' against the then chief minister, Keshubhai

Patel. The printing of the posters and birthday celebrations were traced to Nitin Sardare, a junior BJP worker who was then employed in the office of Shripad Naik, a five-time MP from Goa. Within hours, instructions were issued from the PMO to the minister's office to dismiss Sardare. A fearful Naik hastily complied. Other leaders who attended Joshi's birthday celebrations were also warned not to be seen in his company ever again. Once again the message rang out loudly: no hint of rebellion in the ranks would be tolerated, nor any 'challengers' in the new firmament where only one star blazed bright.

'Modi may be prime minister today and Joshi just another BJP leader, but in the PM's eyes, Joshi is still a rival who must be shown his place by sidelining him completely,' says a BJP–RSS watcher.

Joshi, in a sense, was a reminder of a dark period in Modi's political career in Gujarat that had scarred him deeply. Not surprisingly, Modi chose to turn to someone who had stood by him during his more difficult days in Gujarat. If Vajpayee, the BJP's long-serving mascot, had Advani, the ideological charioteer, by his side, Modi too would find his alter ego and confidant in fellow-Gujarati Amit Shah. A new political partnership would soon come to define the BJP and the country's politics, and would eventually become a springboard for Mission 2019.

TWO

Gujarat's Jodi Number One

LONG before he became national BJP president and was hailed as a modern-day Chanakya, Amit Shah was better known as the political strongman of Sarkhej, a sprawling constituency on the outskirts of Ahmedabad. Shah, or Amitbhai as he is often referred to, had represented Sarkhej as a Member of the Legislative Assembly (MLA) since 1997 and was virtually unbeatable on his home turf. In 2007, when the Congress put up Shashikant Patel, a relatively powerful candidate, against him, Shah reportedly used his clout in the state government as home minister to reactivate old cases that had been filed by the police against Patel. Local real estate dealers were warned not to offer their premises to the Congressman to set up a temporary party office. 'Shah was going to win in any case since Sarkhej is a BJP bastion but he just wanted to eliminate all competition,' recalls an Ahmedabad-based journalist. Shah would defeat Patel by more than 2.35 lakh votes.

Senior Gujarat journalist Rajiv Shah tells a story that perhaps best epitomizes the darker aspects of the Amit Shah persona. In mid-March 2002, barely weeks after the communal riots in which more than 1,000 people lost their lives, Rajiv bumped into Shah as he was coming out of the chief minister's office in Gandhinagar. Concerned about the spiralling violence, Rajiv opened up an informal conversation. 'Why don't you take the initiative to bring the communities together in Ahmedabad, especially in your Sarkhej constituency?' he asked Shah.

Sarkhej has a large Muslim population, most of which lives in the ghetto-like suburb of Juhapura. A series of mini-riots over the years had created an informal 'border' between the Hindu- and Muslim-dominated areas in the constituency. 'Why are you so concerned over the rioting?' was Shah's sharp response. Rajiv was surprised by the reaction from the public representative but then explained that he had an apartment in Sarkhej and was anxious as violence still simmered in the region. 'If you take the initiative and bring Hindu and Muslim leaders on one platform, I am sure the area will become tension-free,' suggested Rajiv. Shah smiled knowingly and replied: 'Which side of Sarkhej is your house situated, ours or theirs?' When a mystified Rajiv gave the location, Shah responded instantly: 'Don't worry then, nothing will happen to your home. Whatever incidents take place, they will occur on the other side of the border.'

Rajiv was stunned by the insensitivity of the answer. 'Here was my legislator openly referring to the Hindu–Muslim divide in his area as if only one side has to be worried if there is a riot.' And yet, for his many supporters in Sarkhej, Shah's blunt answer would probably have been worthy of applause. The Gujarati Hindu middle class in Ahmedabad often refers to the religious divide in the city as one mirroring the 'Indo-Pak border'; in several localities the two communities coexist on either side of a mutually respected invisible 'border' that neither Hindus nor Muslims venture beyond. With his candid, if tactless, reaction, Shah was only reflecting a mindset in which the concerns of only one community really mattered in Ahmedabad's communally surcharged politics. A politically correct neta might have been more cautious before expressing his controversial views, but Amit Shah has always worn his Hindu majoritarian outlook as a badge of pride.

I recall being seated at a lunch with Shah once. As I took my chair, Shah looked at me and grinned. 'Ah, toh aaj anti-Hindu, communist log bhi hamare saath baith gaye hain!' (It looks like anti-Hindu, communist people are also sitting with us.) I contested the description: as a journalist, I am sceptical of the politics of both left and right. For the next few minutes, we engaged in a heated discussion over 'secularism', at the end of which Shah looked at me disapprovingly. 'Thoda aap secular log Hindu dharma pe kitaab padha karo, yeh angrezi kitaab mein kuch rakha nahin hai!' (You secular people should start reading books on Hindu dharma, instead of English books.) Caricaturing secular, liberal Indians as English-speaking elitists is a commonly held fetish in the Sangh Parivar.

It is this combative, controversial personality who was chosen as the president of the BJP in July 2014, within months of the party's path-breaking Lok Sabha triumph. Key to that victory had been the BJP's remarkable sweep in UP where the party and its allies won as many as 73 of the 80 seats, firmly establishing Shah's reputation as a masterful election organizer. But he was also, at the time, a suspect out on bail who had spent three months in jail after being charged with directing extrajudicial killings in Gujarat as minister of state for home. Within the BJP and RSS, Shah's appointment as president sparked off murmurs of a 'Gujarati takeover' although no one was willing to challenge it publicly. Had Prime Minister Narendra Modi taken a big gamble then by choosing his fellow-traveller from Gujarat to head the party?

When I first heard of Shah's appointment as Modi's right hand my mind went back to an interview I had done with Modi in September 2012 when he was Gujarat chief minister. It was just a few weeks after Shah's bail conditions had been relaxed by the Supreme Court and he was allowed to return to Gujarat after spending almost two years outside his home state. Earlier, the apex court had barred Shah from residing in the state for fear that he might interfere in the investigations into the role of the Gujarat police in the alleged fake encounters. Among the many questions I posed to Modi was one on Shah's immediate political future. The Gujarat elections were scheduled for December 2012 and there was uncertainty over whether a leader out on bail would be given a ticket. 'So, will Amit Shah be contesting the elections? What happens to the case against him?' I asked Modi. The interview, where I was made to sit on the floor of the bus Modi was travelling in and forced to look up at him sitting above me while we spoke, had been a testy encounter and that question was perhaps the last straw. 'Law will take its own course,' was Modi's curt response.

The next day as we were preparing to air the interview, I got a call from the chief minister's office; Modi himself was on the line. 'Can you please edit out the portion where I have spoken on Amitbhai's case?' was the urgent request. In the many years that I had known and interviewed the BJP leader, this was the first time he was asking me to remove something he had said on camera. I was a little surprised but reluctantly agreed to edit out the remark on Shah in an attempt to ensure our fraught personal relationship did not deteriorate further. When I related this incident to a long-time political-watcher in Gujarat, he offered an explanation for Modi's seeming defensiveness: 'Please understand, Modi owes Shah a great deal. When Shah was in jail, the CBI tried to extract a confession out of him to somehow implicate Modi in the murder case in which he was charged. The agency even promised to let him off if he turned approver. Shah refused and from that day onwards, Modi remains obligated to Shah. Now, they are an unshakeable jodi, one soul in two bodies!'

Amit Shah and Narendra Modi first met in 1982 at a meeting organized by the RSS in Ahmedabad's Naranpura area where the Shah family owned a house. An eighteen-year-old Shah had just joined the Akhil Bharatiya Vidyarthi Parishad (ABVP), the student wing affiliated to the RSS, while Modi was a thirty-two-year-old pracharak, criss-crossing Gujarat to spread the Sangh's world view. In a spotless white kurta-pyjama with a jhola (bag) hanging from his shoulder, Modi was already making a mark as an inspirational speaker. University politics in Gujarat, not unlike state politics, was dominated at the time by the Congress-led National Students Union of India (NSUI). In 1985, the Congress, under the leadership of

Madhavsinh Solanki, won as many as 149 of the 182 seats while the BJP won a paltry 11 seats.

The next time Shah and Modi encountered each other was in 1987. Pracharak Modi had been 'loaned' by the Sangh to the BJP as a full-time member and had become the state BJP secretary for Gujarat while Shah had moved on to the BJP's Yuva Morcha. The Ahmedabad municipal election being held that year was the first big political test for the BJP after the 1985 electoral debacle. As election-in-charge, Modi was looking for bright, hard-working karyakartas and instantly struck a rapport with the highly committed and enthusiastic Shah. Criss-crossing the bustling streets of Ahmedabad to organize booth workers, Modi would occasionally ride pillion on Shah's scooter as they led the all-out attempt to oust the Congress from the city. Encouraging greater booth worker participation was a major focus as was the task of carefully choosing candidates based on an area's caste and religious demographics. Independent candidates who might cut Congress votes were propped up – a tactic that would be used successfully in future elections too. 'Narendrabhai was an election micro-manager and I think what impressed him was Amitbhai's capacity to work long hours and dedicate himself completely to the task of building the party,' says Ajay Umat, a senior Ahmedabad-based journalist. With Modi as the architect and Shah as the keen apprentice, Mission Ahmedabad paid off: the BJP won the election. The Modi–Shah duo had scored its first political success.

It was, on the face of it, an unlikely partnership of two individuals from very diverse backgrounds. Although both men had roots in north Gujarat's Mehsana district, Modi was born to a humble OBC family – his father ran a tea stall in Vadnagar – and Shah to a wealthy, landed, upper-caste Vaishnav Vania family and was the great-grandson of the nagar seth (city chief) of Gujarat's Mansa town. Shah did his early schooling in Mehsana, until his family shifted to Ahmedabad, where his father ran a lucrative PVC pipe business. Shah himself would later dabble successfully in the stock markets. A staunch family man, Shah would often be spotted having an evening out with his wife, Sonal, at one of Ahmedabad's colourful street corner markets. 'I do have a weakness for food, especially our Gujarati farsan!' he once told me. Modi, in contrast, left his family at an early age to dedicate his life to the RSS. Where Modi likes to dress stylishly and acquire fancy gadgets, Shah is less indulgent: a simple kurta-pyjama and chappals are his sartorial preferences. What united the two was their commitment to the Sangh Parivar's Hindutva ideology and a fierce attachment to the party organization. 'When it comes to ideology, both Modi and Shah are "kattar"' (tough), says Deepak Rajani, a Gujarat-based journalist.

The late 1980s was a period of intense political and ideological churning as the BJP rediscovered its Hindu roots after a failed flirtation with Gandhian socialism. When the Ram Janmabhoomi movement to build a Ram mandir in Ayodhya was launched, Gujarat became the laboratory for the BJP's Hindutva experiment. Under Solanki's leadership, the Congress had created a seemingly impregnable caste alliance in Gujarat called KHAM (Kshatriya, Harijan, Adivasi, Muslim) which the RSS-led Sangh Parivar decided to counter with its own Hindu consolidation: leading the way was the VHP that aligned itself firmly with Gujarat's influential religious sects which enjoyed cross-caste support. While the Congress soon became tangled in faction fights and anti-reservation violence that eventually forced Solanki out of office, the BJP–VHP combine regrouped under the 'Mandir wahin banayenge' slogan. 'Congress samaaj ko tod rahi thi, hum jod rahe the' (Congress was dividing society, we were uniting it), is how Gujarat VHP leader Praveen Togadia describes the strident mandir campaign. The religion-driven politics appealed to Shah's persona. Every year, Shah, who calls himself a devout Ram bhakt, attends the early morning mangal aarti at the Jagannath mandir in Ahmedabad and claims to have visited all of Hinduism's holy shrines at least once.

Shah's first big break on the national stage came when he was appointed as one of the organizers of BJP president L.K. Advani's Gandhinagar campaign in 1991. Advani had shifted to a 'safe' seat in Gujarat after being challenged in New Delhi by film superstar Rajesh Khanna. While Advani barely scraped through with just over 1,500 votes in the national capital, he comfortably won the Gandhinagar seat by over 1 lakh votes. An eager party activist, the twenty-seven-year-old Shah began to be seen as a young leader of promise. Modi too, was heading in the right direction: just a year earlier, in 1990, as the BJP's point person for the state, he had organized the Gujarat leg of Advani's Ram rath yatra as it wended its way from Somnath to Ayodhya. Neither Modi nor the much junior Shah were mass leaders at the time, but they had acquired a reputation as super-efficient organizers of major elections and events.

The early 1990s saw rapid expansion for the BJP in Gujarat as the party launched a statewide membership drive. Modi tasked Shah with registering new members, a laborious process in a pre-digital age but one which would serve as an important lesson for the future. Shah travelled often with Modi as the party sought to penetrate rural Gujarat's powerful panchayat system and get prominent local leaders who were denied space in the Congress to switch sides. It was an early experience in the art of engineering defections that Shah would perfect over time, weaning away key local opposition leaders just ahead of major elections in other states too. Senior Gujarat Congress leader Shaktisinh Gohil, though, offers a very different explanation for the BJP's electoral success in this period. 'The BJP had a very simple formula: before any election in Gujarat they would create a Hindu–Muslim conflict and divide the voters. The Muslim was the permanent "enemy" and the party would manufacture some small or large incident to communalize the electorate. Once, in a municipal by-election, they even went to the extent of spreading rumours of cattle carcasses being tossed into temples!' he claims.

With the entire Sangh Parivar cadre on its side, the BJP's political 'saffronization' push gathered momentum across Gujarat. The party's seniormost leader in the state was the patriarchal figure of Keshubhai Patel from Saurashtra while the younger, more dynamic Shankarsinh Vaghela was the party president, both popular leaders with strong RSS roots. In 1995, when the BJP finally broke the Congress stranglehold over power in Gujarat with a comprehensive victory in the state, Patel and Vaghela were the BJP's main chief-ministerial contenders. Modi initially sided with Patel who became the state's first BJP chief minister, a move that infuriated Vaghela who rebelled and broke with the BJP, forming his own government with Congress support just a year later. 'Do you know that Narendrabhai used to stay in my house when I was an MP in Delhi? I looked after him and helped him so much and yet he was the one who betrayed me. Modi just wanted to remote control Gujarat which I would have never allowed him to. He only wants power at any cost,' claims Vaghela.

Modi too would become a casualty of infighting in the BJP and be forced into virtual 'exile' from Gujarat in 1996 as part of a 'compromise' struck between the various factions that paved the way for the return of Keshubhai Patel as chief minister. In this difficult period in his political career, Shah was one of the few local leaders who stood by Modi and became his unofficial 'informer' in the state. 'Whenever Modi visited Ahmedabad at the time, very few BJP leaders went and openly met him. Shah was the one person who never hesitated in welcoming Modi to his house and being seen in public with him,' remembers journalist Ajay Umat.

With Modi's encouragement, Shah took his next leap forward. After being elected as an MLA for the first time in a by-election in 1997, he decided two years later to make a bid to 'capture' the Ahmedabad District Co-operative Bank, one of the most cash-rich institutions in the state that was traditionally controlled by the Congress. A source of enormous wealth and power, the bank was struggling with mounting bad loans. Shah weaned away local businessmen close to the Congress, formed his own panel of members, and won the election as president of the bank. His election panel also won directorship seats, which meant the majority of the bank's directors were now BJP loyalists. Subsequently, Shah, with his sharp business acumen, turned around the bank's fortunes. 'Taking over the bank was a breakthrough moment for Shah and the BJP. It not only gave Shah political clout but also gave the BJP a huge resource base,' says senior journalist Uday Mahurkar who has known Shah for years. (Shah's various business dealings over the years have been shrouded in mystery:

his 2019 election affidavit declared assets and income worth ₹38.81 crore, up from ₹11.79 crore in 2012. Typically, most netas are believed to be worth much more than their official assets reveal.) Modi, meanwhile, was plotting his comeback in Gujarat, using his stint as a Delhi-based BJP general secretary to slowly convince the party leadership that he was a better bet for the state's future than the ageing Keshubhai. With Shah's help, he even prepared a dossier on Patel's family members and their involvement in financial corruption, a file which he shared with a few editors in Delhi and Ahmedabad. 'I was surprised that a BJP leader was asking us to do stories against his own chief minister but then that is politics I guess,' admits a senior editor. The internal BJP machinations in Gujarat reveal how personal ambitions coexist uneasily with ideological unity: Modi was a disciplined RSS pracharak but he was also an over-ambitious politician desperate for power.

In October 2001, when Modi finally returned to his home state as chief minister, he was keen to induct Shah in his cabinet. But the BJP old guard, which still exercised considerable clout in Gujarat, blocked Shah's entry. Instead, Modi was forced to accept another rising young politician from Ahmedabad, Haren Pandya, as his revenue minister. Pandya belonged to the Keshubhai Patel camp and was a firm opponent of Modi. VHP leader Praveen Togadia was also an independent power centre in Gujarat at the time, and he ensured that a number of his supporters were made ministers, including Gordhan Zadaphia who was given the crucial home portfolio. 'Modi's first cabinet was a compromise arrangement between the BJP factions; he had very little power to choose the ministers,' Mahurkar tells me.

The BJP's election victory in 2002 – the party won a two-thirds majority – on the heels of the communal violence that tore through Gujarat, dramatically changed the power equation in the state. With his anointment as a 'Hindu hriday samrat', Modi was finally a mass leader who could call the shots. One of his first moves was to instal Shah as his minister of state (MOS) for home in place of Zadaphia. Pandya had not even been given a ticket to contest the elections. As MOS home, Shah controlled the crucial police department where Modi wanted someone he could trust implicitly. 'The rest of us ministers had no role in the Modi government, the only minister who had some autonomy was Shah who would even interfere in our ministries because he knew he enjoyed the complete confidence of the chief minister,' says a former cabinet minister.

Shah's ministerial tenure would sharply polarize political opinion and make him a figure both feared and admired in equal measure. 'Shah is a tough and efficient, no-nonsense administrator who would always get the job done,' is how one senior Gujarat bureaucrat puts it. 'A political bully who was busy settling scores with those who had been critical of Modi,' is a contrary view expressed by a retired IPS officer. Rahul Sharma, an outstanding police officer known for his professionalism, for example, found a series of probes being launched against him only because he had prepared CDs containing call details of certain politicians during the riots and placed them before the Nanavati–Shah commission enquiring into the 2002 violence. Sharma had also been instrumental in preventing the communal violence from spreading to the Saurashtra town of Bhavnagar. 'Instead of being commended, I was targeted by the Modi government for doing my duty as a policeman,' he says. In 2015, a disillusioned Sharma quit the police service to start his own legal practice.

Another police officer cites the case of the noted danseuse Mallika Sarabhai who had been openly critical of Modi's handling of the riots. In 2003, the Gujarat government registered a case against Sarabhai for alleged human trafficking and fraud. 'But we found no evidence against her and dropped the trumped-up charges. When Shah heard about it, he was livid and accused us of failing to do our job,' the officer claims. A few years later, the Gujarat government slapped an FIR against the officer in a twenty-six-year-old encounter case. He was eventually acquitted but sought a transfer out of Gujarat.

Sarabhai's case is just one example. Post the 2002 violence, a 'fear factor' had crept into Gujarat's politics with Modi as the domineering chief minister and Shah his 'hitman' and 'eyes and ears' in the government. Shaktisinh Gohil, who was leader of the opposition between 2007 and

2012, alleges that every senior politician and government official was under surveillance. 'All of us were convinced that our phones were being tapped and our conversations were being recorded. Even ruling party leaders were too scared to speak on the phone,' he claims.

According to Gohil, the murder of rebel BJP leader Haren Pandya while he was out on a morning walk in Ahmedabad in March 2003 was a turning point. 'After that, no one wanted to take any chances,' Gohil insists. (Pandya's case has still not been cracked. All twelve people accused of murdering him were acquitted by the Gujarat High Court in 2011. Who killed Haren Pandya is a question that remains unanswered after more than fifteen years.) However, long-serving Gujarat BJP spokesperson Yamal Vyas says that the Congress has used the Haren Pandya murder case to drag Modi and Shah into a needless controversy. 'We handed the case to the CBI on the very first day. There was a Congress government at the Centre between 2004 and 2014 which controlled the CBI and yet the investigating agency did not find anything to link the Gujarat government to the murder,' says Vyas.

Whether the fear factor was exaggerated or not, the fact is that the plain-speaking Shah had unsettled Gujarat's relatively stable political system. Gandhinagar-based journalist Rajiv Shah relates a story of how the minister once organized a demonstration of an Israeli phone-tapping machine for senior police and home department officials. 'You just have to enter a code and then you can listen to whichever phone conversation you want,' a grinning Shah told the officials. 'I don't know whether the tapping device was eventually bought or not, but the officials were so petrified that many of them started keeping two phones, one official and one personal, disclosing their private number only to a small group,' reveals the veteran journalist.

Matters came to a head when Shah was arrested in July 2010 for his alleged role in the killing of gangster Sohrabuddin Sheikh, his wife, Kausar Bi, and an accomplice, Tulsiram Prajapati. The case against him was built on the oral and written testimonies of several 'witnesses', including policemen. Did Shah 'direct' his senior police officers to gun down the trio in a staged encounter as alleged by the CBI? 'This case is a pure political conspiracy, the Congress government somehow wants to trap me and Modiji,' Shah told me when I spoke to him soon after he was released from jail. In December 2014, after the sudden demise of Judge B.H. Loya, who had been hearing the Sohrabuddin case, a special CBI court judge in Mumbai discharged Shah from the matter, affirming, 'I find substance in the main contention made by the applicant that he was involved in the case by the CBI for political reasons.' The CBI chose not to appeal against the lower court verdict. The Modi government had to come to power six months ago, and Shah, by now, was BJP president.

And yet, the story doesn't quite end there. In November 2017, an investigative report suggested that the Loya family was convinced that the judge had not perished of a heart attack as originally claimed, but in fact, had been murdered. Within weeks of this report being made public, I was in Pune where the Loya family now lived. When I tried to reach out to them, I got no response. I even went to the house where the judge's wife and son were staying. 'No one is here. Please leave and stop harassing the family like this,' a security guard at the gate told me. The very next day, I saw Loya's son, Anuj, address a press conference in Mumbai, claiming that he was no longer suspicious of his father's sudden death and the controversy was unnecessarily being stirred up by vested interests. The hurriedly convened press conference came just two days after four Supreme Court judges, in an unprecedented move, publicly challenged the manner in which Chief Justice Dipak Misra was allotting sensitive cases like the Loya matter to 'select' benches. The apex court eventually dismissed a batch of petitions seeking an independent inquiry into the circumstances leading to Loya's death, while observing that the public interest litigations (PILs) were filed 'to settle political scores and scandalize the judiciary'.

Just days after the apex court verdict, I met Shah in Parliament and asked him whether he was now feeling a little more relaxed. He glared at me and then smiled triumphantly. 'Hum toh always relaxed the. Aap mediawale hi itne jump kar rahe the. Aapko laga ki Amitbhai phas gaye jabki iss matter mein kuch bhi nahin hai!' (I was always relaxed. It was you in the media who were getting excited because you thought that Amit Shah will be 'caught' in this case when actually there is nothing to it.) It was a typical combative response.

Shah was in an expansive mood that day, ordering dhokla and chai for the journalists who had gathered around him in the central hall. He began to speak wistfully of his college days, of going to the movies with his wife, how much he missed taking the family for holidays and his love for film music and cricket. 'Do you know I was a good cricketer? No one could get me out in college matches in Ahmedabad!' he declared. I had no desire to debate Shah's cricket skills and could only nod quietly. (Shah had become president of the GCA in 2014 after Modi moved to Delhi as prime minister while his son Jay was joint secretary, suggesting 'family control' of the state cricket body which was once a Congress fiefdom.)

Shah also spoke of his passion for Guru Dutt's movies and the songs and lyrics penned by Sahir Ludhianvi and Kaifi Azmi. He claimed to have been so fascinated by Sahir's poetic genius in the classic film *Pyaasa* that he even went to Mumbai as a teenager to try and meet him. 'There is a Sahir song in *Pyaasa*, "Jala do jala do … yeh duniya agar mil bhi jaye toh kya hai." I was haunted by the words.' Shah also confessed to being a fan of vocalist Bhimsen Joshi: 'Unki aawaz mein jadoo hai.' (There is magic in his voice.)

As Shah spoke enthusiastically about film songs and cricket, I wondered whether he was play-acting for a captive audience or revealing a softer side to life beyond the harsh gaze of politics. At his home-cum-office in Delhi, taking pride of place on the wall are portraits of the ancient thinker Chanakya, the eighth-century Hindu philosopher Adi Shankaracharya and Hindutva proponent Vinayak Damodar Savarkar: a master political strategist, a Vedanta sage and a Hindutva ideologue comprise the troika that Shah claims has shaped his belief system. Maybe, his manic obsession with politics and robust competitive instincts are such that cricket and music are just trivial distractions. At the end of the day, the tenacious Shah remains a 'total' politician, who practises politics 24x7, much like the leader he has followed faithfully for years. For Shah and Modi, politics is not just a career choice; it's a way of life.

Shah does not possess Modi's natural oratorial skills or charismatic presence. Where he is less flamboyant, he is also less politically correct. On 11 August 2014, as Shah addressed the BJP national council for the first time as party president, he openly called for a 'Congress-mukt' Bharat. It was a controversial remark, one designed to raise the hackles of a demoralized opposition which already feared the motives of the Modi–Shah duo seeking to 'eliminate' all rivals. When I met Shah a few days after his provocative speech, he seemed blissfully unperturbed by the fuss. 'Arre, jab cricket match hota hai, toh hum chahte hain ki fast bowler opposition ko bowled karke sabki wicket le, toh phir chunaav mein opposition ko harane mein kya problem hai?' (When there is a cricket match don't we want the fast bowler to bowl out the opposition? Then what is the problem when we seek to defeat the opposition in an election?), he countered. For Shah, an election was the ultimate take-no-prisoners battle, one where there were no prizes for coming second.

Shah claims to have grown up in politics in the cradle of the anti-Congressism of 1970s' Gujarat. This was the time when the student-led Nav Nirman agitation against the Indira Gandhi government began from Gujarat and would go on to set the tone for the anti-Emergency protests that would follow. During the 1977 elections, a number of Janata Party leaders would stay in his home while campaigning in Ahmedabad. 'I was only thirteen but already inspired to see the likes of Acharya Kripalani come to our house and talk of defeating Indira Gandhi,' he reminisced.

His hostility towards the Congress, and the Nehru–Gandhi family in particular, would only grow as Shah took the political plunge himself. Gujarat is a two-party political state and for a member of the BJP, the Congress has always been the 'natural enemy'. When Shah was arrested and jailed in 2010, he was convinced that Ahmed Patel, a fellow-Gujarati and political secretary to Sonia Gandhi, had orchestrated the move against him. His dislike for the Congress turned into hatred and a desire to seek revenge. In August 2017, in a bitterly contested Rajya Sabha election, which included engineering defections through a variety of inducements, Shah tried to avenge himself on Patel. 'In Shah's imagination, politics is war and no battle is too small. He is a poker player when it comes to taking on rivals, often taking risks that others will hesitate to even contemplate,' a senior Gujarat journalist tells me.

The Gandhi family too remained on his radar. 'Yeh ek parivar kab tak desh chalayega?' (How long will this country be ruled by one family?), was his frequently voiced opinion. He didn't even bother with political niceties when it came to the Congress's 'first family': once when he happened to see Sonia Gandhi walking towards him in Parliament, he quickly turned in another direction to avoid greeting her or making any eye contact. This virulent dislike of the Gandhis perhaps explains why the idea of a 'Congress-mukt' Bharat appealed to him. As prime minister, Modi occasionally needs to reach out to the main opposition party but as BJP president, Shah feels no such compulsion. 'We have seen the Congress for many years in power in Gujarat, we know what it is like to be in the opposition, now let them also suffer,' he told a close aide once.

Shah would get an opportunity to strike at the heart of the Congress within months of taking over as BJP president. Assembly elections were scheduled in J&K, Haryana, Jharkhand and Maharashtra between October and December 2014. The Congress ruled all four states or was a part of power-sharing arrangements. Fresh from his Lok Sabha triumph, Shah scented blood. 'In one of the first meetings after taking over, he told us that we must win all the state elections. When one of us said, "Even Jammu Kashmir, sir?", his reply was immediate, "Why not, did I not say every state?"' recalls a BJP office-bearer.

Maharashtra was a particularly big prize with the second highest number of Lok Sabha seats in the country. The BJP had always been the 'junior' partner in its Hindutva alliance with the Shiv Sena. While the BJP was given primacy in the Lok Sabha polls, the Shiv Sena contested the larger share of seats in the Vidhan Sabha elections. It was a deal which had been struck between Sena chief Bal Thackeray and BJP leader Pramod Mahajan in the late 1980s and had survived the test of time. Mahajan once explained to me how the seat distribution would be worked out. 'I would reach Matoshree [the Thackeray residence in Mumbai] with a chit of paper and a few numbers. Balasaheb would crumple the paper and ask, "Pramod, do you really want so many seats?" After which he would smile: "All this is fine as long as we agree that the chief minister will be from the Sena," to which I would just nod and shake hands.' A 'fixed' formula was soon arrived at: the Sena would contest 171 seats and the BJP 117 in the 288-member state assembly. (Nine was the lucky number of the Thackeray family and the numbers on both sides added up to nine!)

But now, neither Balasaheb nor Mahajan were alive, and Shah, true to his hard-nosed style of functioning, wasn't content to live in the past. The BJP had won more seats than the Sena from Maharashtra in the 2014 Lok Sabha polls and a post-poll survey commissioned by Shah showed that similar results could be expected in the state assembly polls too. Significantly, the poll also showed that one in three voters had chosen the alliance only because of Modi's leadership. 'They need us now more than we need them,' was his conclusion. Not surprisingly, a plain-speaking Shah's late-night meeting in Mumbai with the soft-spoken Uddhav Thackeray, Balasaheb's son and heir, in early September 2014 was very different from the easy warmth which had marked the previous equation. Recalls Shiv Sena MP Sanjay Raut, 'Shah came to the meeting as if he had already made up his mind to break the alliance. His approach was "take it or leave it". Naturally, we were offended and felt our asmita [self-respect] was at stake.'

Linguistic pride and Maharashtrian asmita are integral to the Sena's identity as Maharashtra's regional force. Having a Gujarati dictate terms added to the simmering antagonism. 'There was a feeling amongst us that who is a Gujarati to issue diktats to Maharashtrians,' admits Raut. This 'feeling' is not a new one. In 1956, the Samyukta Maharashtra movement had begun to push for the creation of a separate Marathi-speaking state, until, in 1960, Old Bombay was split into Maharashtra and Gujarat. (Later, during the campaign, Uddhav Thackeray would go a step further and liken the Shah–Modi duo to Afzal Khan's 'invading army'.)

Shah though seemed unconcerned. Within hours of his meeting with Uddhav, he returned to Delhi, met Prime Minister Modi and sought his permission to break the twenty-five-year-old alliance with the Sena. Once he had the go-ahead, Shah called a meeting of senior BJP leaders from Maharashtra and asked them to prepare to fight the elections without their long-standing ally. 'Don't say anything in public just yet, but start all the groundwork. We must retain the element of surprise,' he told the team. Away from the media glare, candidates' lists were readied, propaganda material commissioned, district-level workshops held, resources such as GPS-enabled video vans for each region pumped in, and Prime Minister Modi's campaign schedule chalked out. Finally, on 25 September, two days before the last date for filing nominations, the break-up was formally announced. 'We are fighting this election under Modiji's name and we will win in his name,' was Shah's unequivocal message to the BJP cadre.

It was a big gamble. In Maharashtra, a state traditionally dominated by the Congress, the BJP had never even come close to crossing the three-figure mark on its own. It had shared power once with the Shiv Sena in 1995 but that Sena-led government could only be formed with the support of independents. 'There were as many as 160 seats in the state which we had never even contested in the past, but Amitbhai was confident that the anti-incumbency against the Congress and the Modi wave in the Lok Sabha would continue into a state election too. His confidence gave us the hope that we could break new ground,' claims Madhav Bhandari, Maharashtra BJP spokesperson.

A month later, Shah's high-risk, go-for-broke strategy paid off. With 122 seats, the BJP emerged as the single largest party by a significant margin. The Shiv Sena was next with just 63 seats, and the Congress and the Nationalist Congress Party (NCP) brought up the rear with 42 and 41 seats respectively. But Shah wasn't done with his strategizing just yet. As the Sena prevaricated over joining a BJP-led government, a whisper campaign was initiated to suggest that the BJP would not be averse to a post-poll deal with Sharad Pawar's NCP. A desperate Sena leadership had no choice but to fall in line. In choosing the first BJP chief minister for the state, the Modi–Shah duo decided to break with tradition by plumping for the forty-four-year-old, fresh-faced Devendra Fadnavis ahead of the party's 'old guard'. In the Maratha-dominated politics of the state, the risk-taking new BJP leadership chose a Brahmin from Vidarbha. 'The messaging was clear: in contemporary India with a young, aspirational electorate, performance matters more than caste,' says Vinay Sahasrabuddhe, BJP MP and national vice president. Ironically, Shah fancies himself a master of caste arithmetic and, at election time, requires his aides to provide him a detailed caste-wise break-up of each constituency before deciding on candidates and strategy.

The Maharashtra approach was repeated in Haryana too. Here too, buoyed by the 2014 Lok Sabha results, where the BJP had won seven of the ten seats in the state, Shah decided to break the three-year-old alliance with the Haryana Janhit Congress founded by Kuldeep Bishnoi, son of former state chief minister Bhajan Lal, just ahead of the elections. With Modi as the party's mascot once again, Shah crafted an alliance of non-Jat communities, convinced that the BJP could win the state on its own. Bishnoi was furious at being ditched at the last minute. 'After being promised an equal share in seats and the chief ministership, true to its nature of "use and throw" the BJP misused my popularity to build itself in the state. I was brazenly betrayed by the BJP. Amit Shah as the chief puppeteer was central to it all.'

Shah's calculated risk paid off in Haryana too: the BJP won and the Congress was routed. For the state's first BJP chief minister, Modi and Shah made an interesting choice: the low-profile Manohar Lal Khattar, a first-time MLA who had been an RSS pracharak for much of his political life. Modi and Khattar knew each other from their days as Sangh activists and the latter enjoyed the prime minister's full support. Haryana had traditionally been governed by Jat chief ministers but Modi and Shah agreed now that a non-Jat was best suited to lead the state and, breaking with stereotypes, opted for the Punjabi Khattar. 'There were a number of claimants for the post and one senior BJP leader even warned Amitbhai that Khattar would not be able to control the faction fighting in the state. Do you know what Shah's response was? "There is only one faction in the BJP now and it is led by Narendra Modi!"' a BJP leader tells me.

Shah was right. The Modi-led BJP was on a roll. The electoral successes in Maharashtra and Haryana would be followed by a BJP government being formed in Jharkhand and a strong showing in J&K (where in March 2015, the BJP would enter a 'historic' power-sharing arrangement with the Valley-based Peoples Democratic Party [PDP]).

When Shah had taken over the BJP, the party was in power in seven states; three years into his tenure, the BJP was in government in as many as nineteen states. The Congress footprint was on a steady decline. Shah's vision of a 'Congress-mukt' Bharat no longer seemed like a pipe dream. The energetic karyakarta who would wake up at dawn to stick party posters on the walls of his Naranpura neighbourhood in Ahmedabad was now the Midas-touch strategist spearheading his party's 'Golden Age.'

As the BJP moved from one electoral success to another, the question one heard most often was: Is there a Modi–Shah school of election management? 'There is no magic formula, just a clear political and ideological mission based on firm goals, a focus on team-building and perfect coordination at all levels,' claims Bhupendra Yadav, Rajya Sabha MP and BJP general secretary, and a key member of Shah's inner circle. Shah's political opponents are less charitable. Gujarat Congress leader Shaktisinh Gohil calls Shah's methods a mix of 'saam, daam, dand, bhed' (reason, rent, pressure, intrigue). 'Forget everything else, just look at the money power that has been used to win elections at all costs,' says Gohil.

The Congress leader cites numerous instances where Shah allegedly 'sponsored' independent candidates so as to cut into the opposition's votes. For example, according to Gohil, in the 2009 Lok Sabha elections,

Shah reportedly put up two Muslim candidates as independents against Modi's arch-rival, Shankarsinh Vaghela: the two candidates mopped up 32,000 votes between them and Vaghela lost the election by just over 2,000 votes. Former Gujarat Congress president Arjun Modhwadia claims that in the 2017 assembly elections, an independent candidate who was his namesake was drafted to contest the Porbandar seat only to confuse the voters. The candidate even reportedly 'stole' Modhwadia's campaign song. When a police complaint was filed, the local BJP unit turned up in large numbers at the station to protest. 'The independent candidate along with a Bahujan Samaj Party (BSP) nominee were both sponsored by Shah's men only to defeat me,' alleges Modhwadia. The strategy worked. The independent got 1200 votes and the BSP candidate over 5000 votes while Modhwadia lost by just 1800 votes.

Shah's admirers in the BJP, though, insist that their leader is simply an astute practitioner of election realpolitik. 'Those who lose are always making excuses,' claims Gujarat BJP spokesperson Bharat Pandya. In the 2012 assembly elections in Gujarat, for example, Shah was contesting from his home bastion of Naranpura in Ahmedabad. It was his first election since being jailed in 2010 and then banished from Gujarat and he had a point to prove. During the campaign, he asked his supporters to put up posters of his Congress rival, Jeetubhai Patel. When a mystified party worker asked him for an explanation, Shah responded: 'Look, my opponent seems to have given up. But we need to put up at least some of his posters, so our voters know that there is a contest on and come in large numbers on polling day, else they may be tempted to stay at home, thinking that the battle is over!' Shah eventually won by 63,000 votes.

In understanding the enigmatic persona of Shah, the truth, as often is the case, could lie somewhere in between deifying him as the ultimate election guru and demonizing him as a roguish villain. In one of his early meetings with party office bearers after taking over as BJP president, Shah warned his team not to get carried away by the 2014 Lok Sabha victory. 'This is only the beginning; we must not stop until the BJP has expanded to every corner of the country from Kerala to Kashmir. Kabhi rukna nahin, bas sochiye ki haan, hum kar sakte hai' (Never stop, just think, yes, we can do it), was his morale-boosting speech. 'You know, people laughed when Amitbhai claimed our goal was to ensure that the BJP ruled the country for the next thirty years but that's exactly what he sees as his mission,' says BJP national secretary Sunil Deodhar.

And he should know. A Mumbai-based RSS pracharak, Deodhar spent much of the 1990s disseminating Sangh ideology in the North-east. He later took charge of the NGO My Home India whose goal was to connect the youth of the region to the rest of India. In 2014, Shah sent Deodhar to Agartala with just one goal: wrest power from the left in Tripura.

Mission Tripura, in a sense, best exemplifies the audacity of the ambition of the Modi–Shah duo. Here was a state which sent just two members to the Lok Sabha, where the BJP had never won even a Vidhan Sabha seat, where it had no presence at the panchayat level and where the left and the Congress had dominated politics for years. In fact, Tripura was a 'red' bastion. The Communist Party of India (Marxist) (CPI[M])-led government under Chief Minister Manik Sarkar had ruled the state since 1998. It seemed, at the outset, a hopeless task. 'I remember when we first held meetings in 2015, barely a few hundred people attended, often out of curiosity. But Amitbhai was never discouraged, he kept telling us to work harder, enrol more members, set up more booth committees. Every month, he would personally review the progress we had made and by mid-2017 we had covered every village in the state,' Deodhar tells me.

It was an expansion process riddled with conflict, bloodshed and nasty political plots. Nearly a dozen BJP workers were killed in the political 'war' with left activists, who in turn accused the BJP of inciting political violence. When a BJP leader was killed after village council elections in December 2016, the party organized a shanti yagna and took out shaheed raths or martyr processions across the sixty constituencies of the state in honour of the party workers 'martyred' in the cause. 'It was like a civil disobedience movement, a "jail bharo andolan" of a kind that Tripura had never seen and it became a symbol of public anger against the ruling party. The Congress had been a silent opposition to the left, we were vocal,' explains Deodhar.

In 2017, six Trinamool Congress (TMC) MLAs in Tripura switched over to the BJP after voting for the party in the presidential elections. There were accusations that the BJP had lured the MLAs over with large amounts of cash. Some local BJP leaders even opposed taking in the defectors. 'But Amitbhai was very clear: whoever wanted to join was welcome. Our aim was to ensure that the BJP became the sole opposition to the left. If that meant finishing the Congress and the TMC, then so be it,' declares Deodhar. The strategy bore fruit: in March 2018, the BJP won thirty-six of the sixty seats in the state assembly, a stunning victory for a party that had been non-existent in Tripura before then.

Yet for Shah election victories are not the only parameter by which he judges the success of his 'mission'. As an archetypal sangathan (organization) man, he is equally obsessed with ideological spread. 'We must have a full-fledged party office in every district of the country with a digital library where all the reading material of our ideological beliefs is readily available,' he told his core team in an early interaction as party president. By mid-2019, land had been acquired in the majority of the country's 725 districts and the construction of modern, well-equipped BJP offices was underway across India. A sprawling three-storey central party headquarters in the national capital, spread over 1.7 lakh square feet, was built in eighteen months and inaugurated in February 2018. Where is the money for this large-scale construction coming from, I asked a BJP office-bearer. 'Come on, please! We are the world's largest political party, surely we can raise enough resources for a proper office premises,' was the response. (The buzz within the BJP is that despite easy access to monetary resources, Shah can be notoriously tight-fisted with money and drives a hard bargain when it comes to contractual negotiations.)

As part of this phase of rapid expansion, an ambitious membership drive was launched soon after Shah took over as party chief. You could become a BJP member by giving a missed call to a designated mobile number or by enrolling online. Under the amended rules, every active party member had to induct at least 100 new members into the party fold. The goal was to establish the BJP as the world's largest political party. 'When I began my presidentship, we had roughly 2 crore members. Now the BJP has over 9.2 crore registered members, a 400 per cent increase in membership. Which other party can claim such growth?' Shah told me in 2018. (By the time the general elections took place in 2019, the BJP claimed its membership numbers were close to 11 crore. However, the actual membership numbers are contested and are believed to be far lower than the claims.) Call centres were set up in every state to verify the antecedents of the freshly enrolled members. These call centres would later transform into an even bigger outreach programme ahead of the 2019 elections. Each member's personal details, including their voter ID card number, mobile number and address were entered into a giant database, accessible to the party leadership at any time. When some of the new members were found to be fictitious, Shah personally rang up the person who had prepared the list and warned them not to subvert the system. The BJP even sought the help of private mobile telephone companies to obtain personal data of as many as 4 crore phone users whom the party machinery had been unable to track down. Sharing such data is illegal but the private companies obliged: no one, it seems, was willing to defy the ruling party leadership. 'We claim to hate the communists but we have created our very own Soviet style of a highly regimented, tightly controlled party structure. Not all of us are comfortable with it but I guess it works,' confesses a veteran BJP leader.

Having created such a large and exhaustive membership database, Shah turned his attention to reaping its electoral benefits using a scaled-up technological software system. 'With one SMS at election time, I can now connect to lakhs of party workers instantly,' he often asserts. Unlike Modi, Shah is not much of a tech enthusiast, preferring to rely on the human element for political feedback. But like his leader, he too quickly realized that big data and information technology are crucial enablers in spreading the party's message nationwide. In every workers' meeting,

Shah would stress the need to heighten awareness of social media and mobile technology amongst the karyakartas. Thousands of WhatsApp groups were set up to ensure targeted messaging and the constant flow of information between party members. Training camps were organized at the district level to encourage workers to embrace new technological innovations. 'Under Amitji's leadership, we have institutionalized technology as part of the organization's DNA,' affirms Amit Malviya, the BJP's IT and social media head.

The booth management process was streamlined too. As a cadre-based party, the BJP believes the booth worker is key to its organizational strength at election time. It is the highly motivated booth worker who tips the scales in your favour in a tightly fought election. By April 2019, the BJP claims to have set up booth committees of around fifteen to twenty members each in 8.63 lakh of the total 10.32 lakh booths in the country. (The ones left out were largely in 'minority-dominated' areas where traditionally the party had virtually no voter base.) A cluster of five to six booths makes up a Shakti Kendra which reports into the district-level mandals. Within each booth, panna pramukhs, or page incharges, are assigned a page of the electoral roll (approximately sixty voters, with around thirty on either side of a page), and asked to stay in touch with the voters on their list as a first point of contact. The panna pramukh reports to the booth prabhari, or the booth incharge. A twenty-three-point plan of action for the booth workers was prepared two years in advance of the 2019 elections: the tasks ranged from verifying voter lists to enrolling fifty new members per booth to connecting with eminent citizens in the area. Door-to-door campaigning has always been integral to any election in India, and Shah ensured that the outreach was systemized and monitored through a year-round feedback mechanism. 'If we are the world's biggest political army, the lakhs of booth workers are our soldiers and a weapon that no other party can match,' says Ram Lal, the BJP's former national organizational secretary.

To energize the booth workers, Shah launched an innovative nationwide Vistarak Yojana in 2017, where party supporters were encouraged to become vistaraks, or part-time political workers, and dedicate anywhere from a few weeks to six months to two years, to spread the BJP's ideological message (the word 'vistarak' literally means 'expansionist'). These vistaraks, mostly under the age of forty, were encouraged to travel across the country and interact with booth workers, spend a few days in their homes and create a sense of 'brotherhood', integral to the Sangh's original concept of the 'party as parivar'. Nearly 3 lakh vistaraks participated in the first phase of this highly systematic and intensive booth contact programme. On the eve of the 2019 elections, the BJP had over 3000 vistaraks – one for each assembly segment and two per Lok Sabha constituency – many of whom had spent two years in the field acting as a connect between the booth workers and party leaders. 'Do you know that the vistaraks only returned home more than two months after the elections were over when I wrote to tell them that their task was done – such is their commitment to the cause,' boasts Shah.

A detailed plan was initiated to hold at least five to six events every year at the booth level to mark important milestones, be it Syama Prasad Mukherjee Balidan Diwas (Martyrdom Day), or Deendayal Upadhyaya's birth anniversary. It is mandatory for senior party functionaries to attend these public functions. 'We were always an ideology-driven party but under adhyakshji's [president] guidance, we took the process of constant "sampark" [connectedness] with party cadres to a new level, not just during election time but right across the year,' says general secretary Bhupendra Yadav while describing the party's booth-centric approach.

Shah led from the front in this Sampark Abhiyan by travelling continuously to participate in and organize party programmes across the country. In their book, *Amit Shah and the March of BJP,* authors Anirban Ganguly and Shiwanand Dwivedi claim that Shah travelled more than 7,90,000 kilometres between August 2014 and September 2018, an average of 519 kilometres per day, as part of the BJP's outreach programmes. The trips would often be short two- to three-day visits to a particular state, sometimes including at least one meal at the home of a local BJP worker. 'We have always had a tradition of pravaas [travel] and yatra in the Sangh and the BJP, but I don't think any previous party president has matched the sheer energy of Amitbhai in this regard,' an office-bearer tells me.

Shah's indefatigable stamina is similar to Modi's; both the supreme leader and his deputy appear to be workaholics. In fact, this perception of a 'neta who never rests or sleeps' has been artfully used to enhance a 'karma yogi' image. Modi's supporters will tell you how the prime minister barely sleeps for a few hours and always prefers to travel at night for his long-haul flights so that he doesn't waste even a moment of daylight meant for official engagements. Shah too is portrayed in similar terms as a leader who is always on the job. Union minister Ravi Shankar Prasad relates how Shah called him up at midnight once and asked him to travel early next morning to Varanasi during the 2017 UP elections. '"Rahul Gandhi and Akhilesh Yadav are holding a press conference at 10.30 a.m. tomorrow, I want you to be there to rebut them," is what he told me. Then, at 2 a.m., Amitbhai calls me again to say, "Don't worry, Ravi, you don't have to go now, the presser is cancelled." Now, tell me, how many leaders do you know who will get into such late-night micro-management in an election campaign?' asks Prasad.

I had an opportunity to observe Shah's long working hours once while travelling to Lucknow. I was on a 6.40 a.m. flight to the city, bleary-eyed and dishevelled, struggling to get going so early in the morning, when Shah entered the plane in his crisply ironed kurta-pyjama, sharp-eyed and bustling. He had just returned well past midnight from Kolkata and here he was, barely six hours later, on the road again. While I chomped on the airline breakfast of idli-sambar, Shah declined any food. 'I am fasting today, only water,' he told the air hostess. He had a series of political engagements in Lucknow; I was attending a seminar. As it turned out, we were staying in the same hotel, on the same floor. A little after 11 p.m., in the middle of watching the final overs of an exciting IPL game on TV, I heard a commotion in the corridor. Shah had arrived in the hotel along with a posse of security personnel, having finished his public meetings. Party leaders were queued up to speak to him. These meetings extended well past midnight. Next morning, I woke up around 7 a.m. and decided to knock on Shah's door. I was told he had already left for Delhi by the early morning flight. It was, I guessed, just another day in the life of arguably the country's second most powerful politician.

The politically savvy Himanta Biswa Sarma, the Assam minister who switched to the BJP from the Congress in 2015 to emerge as Shah's point person for the North-east, has experienced both the BJP and Congress leadership's style of functioning from close quarters. For the battle-hardened Sarma, Shah's success formula lies in his ability to combine ideological and organizational vigour with political realism. 'In the Congress, we were always in danger of losing seats because we had to accommodate various factions while distributing tickets. In the BJP, Shah is not there to placate any individual or group. He only demands poll victory. At election meetings, he will listen to all of us but in the end, he has his own strong feedback system made up of multiple sources, be it booth workers or large voter surveys he commissions himself so no one can bluff him,' emphasizes Sarma.

Shah's critics, though, suggest there is a darker, more fearsome side to the way the BJP president has built the party into a well-oiled election machine. 'If you are part of Shah's inner coterie, you will survive and even flourish. But if you dare question his judgement, then he will cast you aside in no time. The party is now run like a police state in the name of discipline,' says a former BJP office-bearer who claims he was removed from his post only because of his proximity to the Advani household. Another BJP leader, now out of favour, recalls how a newly elected Rajya Sabha MP was reprimanded by Shah in front of his colleagues in Parliament. Shah was reportedly upset that the MP hadn't publicized his planned visit to the MP's home state sufficiently. 'Can't you even organize proper hoardings and ensure stories and advertising in the newspapers and on TV? Why did we make you an MP?' Shah berated the junior member. When a veteran BJP leader who had been with the party since its Jana Sangh days approached Shah for a ticket from Mumbai or Thane for the 2019 elections, he was dismissively told that he lacked the 'resources' to win the election. 'I was shocked and, yes, a little hurt, but then in this new order in the BJP, ideology matters less than winnability at election time,' says the old-timer.

Former BJP MP and newspaper editor Dr Chandan Mitra says that the most significant difference between the Vajpayee–Advani period and the Modi–Shah era is the lack of 'openness' within the party now. 'Earlier, during parliamentary party meetings, Vajpayeeji and Advaniji would encourage us to speak freely, like an open house. Now, no one dare raise their voice for fear of retribution,' says Dr Mitra, who left the BJP for the TMC in 2018, claiming that he was feeling 'suffocated' in the party.

Bharat Singh, a BJP MP from Ballia, once took the 'bold' step of questioning the leadership at a parliamentary party meeting, saying it wasn't as easy to 'sell' the Modi government's achievements to the people as it was made out to be. 'Please come to my constituency and see the state of the roads,' he reportedly complained. The MP was immediately silenced by those around him. Afterwards, he was asked to come to the party headquarters where he was given a dressing-down by a senior BJP official. When the 2019 election list was announced, Singh's name was omitted. 'I don't know why I was not given a ticket,' he tells me. 'Please ask the party leadership. Maybe they didn't like me speaking out.'

A more high-profile MP to find himself in Shah's cross hairs was Varun Gandhi, the BJP's Nehru–Gandhi family face. An MP at just twenty-nine, Varun was appointed party general secretary in 2012 when Rajnath Singh was BJP chief. The moment Shah took over in 2014, Varun was dropped from his team. 'Bahut bolta hai, apne aap ko bahut bada samajhta hai, party discipline nahi jaanta' (He talks too much, thinks no end of himself, doesn't understand party discipline), Shah told an aide. Ahead of the 2017 UP assembly elections, a group of MPs met the party chief and suggested that Varun be named as the BJP's chief-ministerial candidate. 'Bhaiyaji is very popular,' they claimed. Shah was incensed. 'Yeh pressure tactic nahi chalenge!' (These pressure tactics won't work!) he said firmly. Not a single candidate recommended by Varun was given a ticket and he was kept out of the party's 'star' campaigner list. 'Shah prefers quiet, hard-working individuals. He is suspicious of these ambitious, English-speaking types!'

a BJP leader tells me. In Shah's 'war' against the so-called Lutyens' elite, a privileged family background and an elite education are, in fact, major disadvantages.

Shah remains unfazed by those who criticize his authoritarian streak. What drives you, I asked the BJP president once at a party function. 'Sangathan aur vichardhara. Hamari ladai vichardhara ki hai. Yeh Hindutva aur deshbhakti ki ladai hai' (Organization and ideology. Ours is an ideological fight for Hindutva and nationalism), was his stout reply. His steely gaze suggested that neither controversy nor criticism would quell the missionary zeal to succeed. In the remorseless and relentless pursuit of his goals, he would not bow down to any opponent. As party general and organizer-in-chief, Shah was determined to spread the message of Hindu nationalism far and wide: election victories, I sensed, were only a means to achieving the ultimate ambition of a modern-day 'Hindu' India.

The series of BJP's election victories in 2014 had convinced most political observers that the Modi–Shah juggernaut was unstoppable. But notions of political invincibility, like illusions of human immortality, are often transient as Gujarat's 'jodi number one' was about to find out.

THREE

From 'Suit Boot' to 'Garibon ka Neta'

IN a city where shopping is a way of life, the rise of Jade Blue as one of Ahmedabad's premier retail stores for men's fashion mirrors the transition of Narendra Modi from Gujarat's regional satrap to style icon for the 'new India' generation. On an early summer evening when neon lights sparkle across the city's upscale malls, Jade Blue's flagship showroom in the heart of Ahmedabad's bustling C.G. Road is bursting with people. It is wedding season in Gujarat and there is a mad scramble for finely stitched suits and colourfully embroidered sherwanis. But the hottest selling item remains the shop's branded Modi kurtas and jackets. 'Yes, even now the first thing that my customers ask for is the latest kurta or jacket worn by Prime Minister Modi,' says Jitendra 'Jitubhai' Chauhan who, along with brother Bipin Chauhan, co-owns the retail chain.

If Modi takes justifiable pride in his long and successful journey from Vadnagar to 7 Lok Kalyan Marg, the Chauhans too are a symbol of unbridled Gujarati enterprise and upward mobility. The family's early years were spent living in a chawl in the dust and squalor of the old walled city. Their father was a master tailor who decided one day to give up his profession and embark on a spiritual quest, leaving the family in virtual penury. A benevolent uncle and the boys' maternal grandfather took the teenage Jitu and Bipin under their wing and taught them the craft over long hours after school. In 1981, they took a loan of ₹1.5 lakh and bought a 250-square-foot shop in Ahmedabad's congested cloth market in Ratanpole; today, the ₹265-crore Jade Blue empire stretches across twenty-two stores, including three in Ahmedabad and fourteen in Gujarat alone. 'I guess Narendrabhai is our lucky charm,' says a cheerful-looking Jitubhai. 'He became our client in 1989 and since then we have never looked back.' The brothers were looking for influential people in Ahmedabad who would endorse their shop and the rising star of the BJP in Gujarat fitted their need. Today, Jade Blue's long list of VIP patrons includes business magnate Gautam Adani and powerful Congress leader Ahmed Patel. 'We don't discriminate between parties and individuals, we want everyone to wear our clothes,' laughs Jitubhai.

Modi, in a sense, is the ideal brand ambassador for a tailoring enterprise. Keenly conscious of his appearance, he is always well dressed and nattily accessorized. The RSS pracharak-turned-politician has defied the stereotype of the traditional swayamsevak for whom trendy dressing is not an ideological priority. Gujarat, in particular, had been deeply influenced by Gandhian habits of simplicity and austerity and the white, khadi kurta-pyjama–clad politician was always the dominant image, one that cut across party lines. Even in his pracharak years, Modi would dress in a spotlessly clean, well-starched, white kurta-pyjama; hair well combed, the trimmed beard never looking frayed or untidy. A pocket comb was a permanent accessory. 'Amongst RSS leaders, Modi was distinctive, I don't think we have ever seen him, right from the very beginning of his political career, in clothes that were creased or crumpled in any manner,' recalls senior Ahmedabad-based journalist Darshan Desai. Modi's brother Pankaj tells me that his sibling's desire to dress well started early. 'Narendrabhai was always well groomed even when in school – it came naturally to him,' he says.

A senior BJP leader from Gujarat remembers how once, in the early 1990s, Modi, then party secretary for the state, was unusually late for a function in Surat because he had taken a long car journey which had left him looking a little dishevelled. 'He insisted on first going to the local hotel, having a bath, changing his clothes and then attending the event even if it meant keeping the audience waiting,' claims the leader.

Modi's sartorial options were limited in those early years. The more old-fashioned white kurta with long sleeves and pyjama was gradually replaced by the well-stitched half-kurta, with a chosen few colours and patterns for variety. The sleeves were cut in a manner so that the length was just a little longer than his upper arm and the kurta designed so that Modi could display a certain broad-chested muscularity. A fastidious Modi would personally supervise the smallest details while giving his measurements to the tailors. 'The half-sleeve kurta idea was entirely Narendrabhai's and he was very clear that it should not be too loose but should be comfortable enough for him to stretch his arms easily,' Jitendra Chauhan tells me. (Modi himself has claimed in an interview to actor Akshay Kumar that he devised the half-sleeve kurta in his nomadic years as a pracharak so that he would have less material to wash and the smaller-sized kurta would fit easily into his tiny jhola!)

When Modi became Gujarat chief minister, the half-kurta slowly gave way to a jacket for official engagements, this time more formal in appearance but again with a distinct edge. 'The Modi jacket is not like a Nehru jacket which is more in the nature of a bandhgala [closed neck] in design. The Modi jacket is wider along the neck, a bit longer and much more comfortable, especially for the summers. The earlier formal jackets were in the usual black or cream colours. Narendrabhai likes more colourful jackets, he wants us to experiment with a variety of colours. That is his USP,' claims Jitubhai.

The relationship between Jade Blue and Modi has continued even after he moved to Delhi as prime minister. 'Every few months, my brother Bipin goes to Delhi to the prime minister's residence to take measurements for any new clothes we are stitching for Narendrabhai,' Jitubhai tells me. So how many jacket-kurtas do you make for him annually and who pays for them, I ask. 'It is difficult to put a number to the clothes we have designed exclusively for Modiji but on an average, we make five to six kurtas and two to three jackets every two months for him. As for who pays the bills, the fact is, that there are many friends and admirers of the prime minister who come to us with the raw fabric and ask us to stitch jackets and kurtas which they want to gift him. It is their love for Modiji which brings them to us!' he remarks.

However, it was a gift from one such fanatical Modi follower that placed the prime minister squarely in the eye of the proverbial storm. Ramesh Bhikabhai, a Gujarati NRI businessman and diamond manufacturer, presented the prime minister with a bandhgala-style suit with the name Narendra Damodardas Modi embroidered on it in a pinstripe pattern. 'I have been a part of the Vibrant Gujarat events over the years and have been a big supporter of Modiji. I wanted the prime minister to attend the wedding [of Bhikabhai's son] and thought the suit was the perfect surprise gift,' he tells me. 'We only did the tailoring and dispatched the suit to the prime minister's residence,' claims Jitubhai.

As it turned out, Modi couldn't attend the wedding because he was preoccupied with weightier matters of state. US President Barack Obama was in the national capital, the first American president to attend Republic Day celebrations as the official state guest. 'It was a big moment for the prime minister and India. Don't forget, this is the same country which had ostracized Modi when he was Gujarat chief minister, so naturally this was seen in South Block as a diplomatic coup of sorts,' is how a senior diplomat puts it. From the moment the Obamas landed in Delhi, Modi seemed determined to create a favourable impression on them. Breaking with protocol, he even rushed to the airport to receive them with a warm bear hug. It would become a familiar sight every time a major foreign dignitary came visiting.

The real stir was created when Modi met with President Obama for official bilateral talks at Hyderabad House after the parade had concluded. The two leaders zoomed in through the heavily fortified gates in their armoured black BMW 7-series luxury cars, walked across the well-manicured lawns and settled down for a cup of tea. As TV cameras tracked the two leaders' every move, close-up shots revealed thin golden stripes on the prime minister's suit. When the camera lens zoomed in further, the prime minister's full name could be seen clearly embroidered in shimmering gold. For a few hours, diplomatic niceties were forgotten as social media and even TV channels buzzed with pictures of the prime minister's rather odd choice of clothing: Ramesh Bhikabhai's wedding gift was now a national debating point. 'Forget the retired Indian Foreign Service [IFS] officers, let's get a fashion designer into the studio,' I recall telling my guest relations team. The verdict in the studio and outside was near-unanimous: the prime minister had exhibited a narcissistic streak by choosing a formal occasion like a US presidential visit to wear a suit with his own name embroidered on it. For once, even frenzied Modi fans on social media were on the back foot, unable to hide their astonishment at what appeared to be a prime-ministerial gaffe.

So why did Modi decide to wear that suit? Critics suggest it is a sign of personal vanity, heightened by rapid and remarkable political success. A possible sociological explanation could lie in Modi's formative years in a small town, his belonging to a low-income family, his desire to break away from memories of a childhood spent in poverty and his transition into a life of VIP privilege. Right through his career in public life, Modi has consciously used his wardrobe as a power statement and for deft image-building. His simple but well-starched kurtas set him apart during his pracharak days; now the smartly cut jackets were designed to distinguish him from the surging crowds around him. Flashing Mont Blanc fountain pens and branded Swiss Luxury watches and sporting designer spectacle frames, the aim of the Modi persona is to show that he is an exceptional figure, unchained by political convention.

If the khadi kurta-pyjama represented austerity in the Gandhian age, the Modi jacket-kurta with the branded accessories are symbols of a new acquisitive, aspirational society. This, after all, was a leader who, during his tenure as Gujarat chief minister, had once worn a Texan hat, a cowboy jacket, jeans and shoes during the Kutch winter festival to make a style statement. 'When you have Amitabh Bachchan as your Gujarat tourism brand ambassador, you don't want to feel left out, do you?' says a former Gandhinagar-based government official.

Yet this time, by parading a monogrammed suit with such nonchalance, Modi had perhaps misread the public mood and handed his opponents a lifeline. The timing couldn't have been worse. In December 2014, the Modi government had issued a land acquisition ordinance that would make it easier for companies to acquire agricultural land, leading to the opposition charging the prime minister of 'selling out' to corporate India (the ordinance was withdrawn in August 2015 after sustained protests). Congress leader Rahul Gandhi who had been mum since the crushing 2014 Lok Sabha defeat suddenly found his voice and accused the Modi government of being a 'suit-boot ki sarkar'. It was a stinging critique, one which would force the prime minister to get into damage control mode and eventually auction the controversial suit for charity. But the damage was done: right through 2015, the image of 'suit-boot ki sarkar' would stick to Brand Modi. Ironically, it wasn't the Gandhi scion but another more politically savvy opposition leader who would grab the opportunity the prime minister had presented while scoring a sartorial self-goal.

Arvind Kejriwal was brooding, seemingly depressed after the 2014 Lok Sabha debacle, when I met him a few weeks after the general elections. The Aam Aadmi Party (AAP) leader had resigned as chief minister of Delhi in February 2014 and had since watched his hopes of becoming a national alternative also slowly evaporate in the face of the Modi wave. He had taken on the BJP's prime-ministerial face in Varanasi, a David versus Goliath battle which he had fought valiantly but lost. Significantly, the fledgling AAP had lost all seven Lok Sabha seats in Delhi, the city-state which had propelled Kejriwal to national prominence just months earlier, to the BJP. 'We made a mistake in trying too much too soon,' he admitted.

The meteoric political rise of the slightly built, white shirt, black trousers and chappal-wearing Kejriwal had intrigued me: an IIT-educated, Indian Revenue Service official who had gone from being anti-corruption activist to chief minister of Delhi in just over twenty-four months. AAP had emerged at the time of the Anna Hazare–led 'India Against Corruption' street protests of 2011, pitching itself as a force of change and promising to sweep away the dust of corruption from Indian politics. With the broom as its election symbol and the Gandhi topi as its signature image, AAP was riding the growing public anger against the power elite. In its debut assembly election in December 2013 in Delhi, AAP put both the BJP and the Congress on notice, winning as many as twenty-eight of the seventy seats in the national capital. The romantic idealism of a new anti-establishment force was hugely attractive for the national media which projected Kejriwal as a middle-class hero who would challenge everything that was bad and unsavoury about India's political culture. Even when he resigned within weeks of taking over as Delhi chief minister after promising to initiate criminal charges against some of the country's top corporates and politicians, he retained a measure of public goodwill.

But the 2014 general elections proved a bridge too far and AAP's unsuccessful campaign exposed the limitations of the political start-up. Suddenly, Kejriwal fell off the map: the funds dried up, a few colleagues started questioning his leadership credentials and bored TV cameras looked away. Failure can be lonely and the future seemed bleak for an embryonic political force. Kejriwal knew he had just one last shot at redemption: the Delhi elections of February 2015. As the gloom slowly lifted with the passage of time, Kejriwal threw himself into the election battle months ahead of voting day. A systematic mass contact programme was launched with Kejriwal himself campaigning in each of Delhi's seventy constituencies to re-establish a personal connect. AAP had limited funds but a large volunteer base. Mohalla prabharis were appointed for every street in the city – AAP's version the BJP's tried-and-tested panna pramukhs who were responsible for the last-mile door-to-door campaigning. AAP also had a small but highly committed social media army, ready to challenge the BJP's better-equipped internet warriors. The innovative campaign also led to the setting up of Delhi Dialogue, a unique initiative aimed at creating a crowdsourced manifesto for the city.

While AAP was in overdrive in a make-or-break election, the BJP was relaxed, complacent, almost overconfident. After all, the Modi wave had triumphed in major state elections in Maharashtra, Haryana and Jharkhand; why would a relatively small city-state like Delhi be any different? 'I think that's where the BJP made a big mistake. Delhi was different because AAP was seen as a genuine alternative to the traditional politics of the city just as the BJP under Modi was able to tap into a similar sentiment at the national level,' says Ashutosh, the journalist who was convenor of AAP's Delhi unit at the time. He had contested the 2014 elections on an AAP ticket from Delhi's Chandni Chowk constituency and lost. 'I recall voters telling me at the time that we will vote for Modiji at the Centre but when there are Vidhan Sabha elections, we will vote for Kejriwal and AAP,' he claims. AAP plastered the city's autorickshaws and street corners with posters calling for 'Paanch Saal Kejriwal', their take on the BJP's 2014 battle cry: 'Abki baar Modi sarkar'. 'We took on the BJP by taking a leaf from their own campaign playbook by making the elections presidential,' remarks Ashutosh.

In the second week of January 2015, just weeks ahead of voting day, the BJP finally sat up and took notice of the trouble looming. Party president Amit Shah commissioned a poll which showed that Kejriwal was, by some distance, the preferred choice for chief minister. The BJP just didn't have a credible local face to challenge the AAP leader. The party's best bet, the mild-mannered Dr Harsh Vardhan had already lost out in the 2013 elections. 'We thought we would make the battle "Modi versus who" without realizing that the rules of a state election are different at times to a national election,' admits a senior BJP leader. A desperate Shah convened a meeting with Arun Jaitley, then finance minister in the Modi government and someone closely associated with the capital's politics. 'Let's try and defeat Kejriwal at his own game: if he claims to be an anti-corruption crusader, we will also opt for one!' Jaitley reportedly suggested.

The BJP chose Dr Kiran Bedi as a last-minute, out-of-the-box gambit. The country's first woman IPS officer, Bedi had been an integral part of the India Against Corruption movement along with Kejriwal before they had a bitter falling out. 'Arvind committed a breach of trust by forming a political party when Anna wanted our movement to remain apolitical. He used Anna for his personal ambitions,' she claims. Now, the BJP was offering the police officer-turned-activist a chance to settle scores with her former comrade. Dr Bedi confirms that it was Jaitley who persuaded her to take the plunge. 'There had been offers in the past also to join politics but I had resisted them. This time I was tempted when Jaitley promised me that I could focus on governance issues while the party leadership would handle the political aspects. I have served Delhi all my life and I saw this as another opportunity to do so. And yes, the fact that Arvind was on the other side also influenced my decision since I wanted him to be exposed,' she tells me.

It would prove to be a bad call. The livewire Bedi had been a combative police administrator with a reputation for being an argumentative and uncompromising public servant who often sparred with her seniors and political bosses. Hers wasn't the ideal temperament for the minefield that is Delhi politics. A deeply factionalized BJP state unit saw her as an 'outsider' and her sudden entry only served to widen the rift within. She was ill at ease with the cut and thrust of electioneering. Following Dr Bedi on the campaign trail, I noticed how uncomfortable she became when eager party workers surged forward to meet her on the road. 'Peechhe hato, thoda toh discipline rakho' (Stay back, maintain some discipline), she admonished them. This tough, no-nonsense approach might have worked while in uniform, but flopped in electoral politics where the rules of engagement are very different. By contrast, the sharp-eyed Kejriwal was proving to be a consummate practitioner of vote-bank politics, having already gained a firm foothold amongst Delhi's teeming slum pockets with a promise of free water and slashed power tariffs. In the battle between the two Magsaysay awardees, there could be only one winner. 'I guess we got into the race too late, I just couldn't compete with Arvind's brand of populist politics,' Dr Bedi admits.

When the election results were announced on 10 February 2015, AAP had won sixty-seven of the seventy seats. While the victory had been predicted by most exit pollsters, it was the scale of the triumph that was stunning. In a state which the BJP had swept just months before in the Lok Sabha polls, the party had suffered a near wipe-out. Just days after strutting across the capital in his now infamous suit, Modi had been defeated by a relatively inexperienced politician who had made a class war against Delhi's 'VVIP' culture his calling card. If the 'suit-boot' of the prime minister had been lampooned as a symbol of the privileged elite, Kejriwal's Gandhi topi was positioned as an emblem of simplicity. 'Sir, khaas aadmi jo hawa mein rehte hain unko asli aam aadmi ne aaj haraya hai' (The VIP who lives in the air has been defeated by the common man on the ground), exulted the tea boy who was serving us in the TV studio when the results filtered in. The reference was perhaps as much to the prime minister's frequent foreign trips as to his extravagant dress sense. Clearly, the aura of invincibility that surrounded the Modi persona and Shah's election management prowess had been dramatically breached.

The BJP leadership's political ego had been punctured but they tried hard to mask it. A day after the party's Delhi debacle, Shah hosted a reception for his son's wedding in the national capital. The political toughie was playing gregarious host, insisting that every guest partake in the vast spread of delicious Old Delhi street food that had been laid out. Still, the journalist in me couldn't help asking the BJP president for a reaction to the election defeat. Shah's broad smile thinned for a moment and he coolly answered, 'Aaj rajneeti nahin.' (No politics today.) But as I was leaving the stage after wishing the bridal couple, the pugnacious Shah couldn't resist having the last word: 'Delhi toh ek hi chunaav hai, abhi toh Bihar iss saal baaki hai!' (Delhi is only one election, Bihar is still left this year). It was yet another blunt reminder that unlike cynical journalists the experienced neta always views the glass as half full.

What commerce is to Gujarat, politics is to Bihar. Across Bihar's dusty tracks and paan-stained streets, people having animated conversations on politics is a familiar sight. In August 2015, just three months ahead of the state elections, Bihar found a new talking point: Nitish Kumar and Lalu Prasad Yadav, friends turned foes, announced their decision to forge an electoral alliance. It was the latest chapter in a political saga that had stretched over a quarter-century and seen many twists and turns. Student activists in the 1970s, Kumar and Lalu Prasad had emerged on Bihar's political landscape during the anti-Emergency JP movement and the rise of backward caste Mandal politics. If Lalu Prasad was the flamboyant mass leader who challenged the upper-caste monopoly on power, Nitish was the low-key administrator who made good governance his mantra. In time their personal ambitions drove them apart and led to acrimonious public sparring, but between them, they had dominated Bihar's power pyramid since 1990. Now, however, an ever-intensifying Modi wave was poised to sweep them both aside.

Kumar's Janata Dal (United) (JD[U]) had broken away from the NDA in June 2013 when it became clear that Modi would be the prime-ministerial face of the BJP. For Kumar, Modi symbolized Hindu extremist politics which he wanted to distance himself from. Lalu Prasad was the original Modi adversary, having built his career on an unflinching opposition to the Sangh Parivar's Hindutva politics. Both, though, were on the wrong side of the 2014 election results: Prasad's Rashtriya Janata Dal (RJD) won just four seats, the JD(U) two, while the BJP-led alliance won thirty-one of the forty seats. Hours after the results, where the list of vanquished included Rabri Devi and Misa Bharti, wife and daughter of Lalu Prasad, Kumar dialled his one-time partner and offered a word of sympathy: 'Chunaav mein yeh sab hota hai, aage bahut kuch karna hai!' (These things happen in elections, there is much still to be done!) It was the first step towards a political reconciliation of the bitter rivals. 'The Lalu–Nitish tie-up was basically about survival, they came together because they realized that Modi was now the bigger enemy who would finish them both,' says Manish Kumar, senior Patna-based journalist.

The 'mahagathbandhan' of Bihar's two premier backward caste leaders with the Congress was the first post-2014 broad-based anti-Modi alliance to be forged. Not only did the coming together of Nitish Kumar and Lalu Prasad create a powerful backward caste coalition, it also revived the 'Mandal versus Kamandal' narrative of the 1990s (the BJP was branded as a 'Kamandal' party because of its links with the sant-sadhu samaj). Kumar even 'stole' one of Modi's back-room strategists to work on his side. The bespectacled Prashant Kishor had been an integral part of Modi's 2014 'Mission 272' campaign, operating out of the then Gujarat chief minister's office in Gandhinagar. In 2013, he had set up an outfit, Citizens for Accountable Governance (CAG) which effectively functioned as the marketing and strategic arm of the 'Modi for PM' campaign. The 'Chai pe Charcha' events had been one of the many innovative programmes devised by Kishor to package Brand Modi to the voter. But once Modi became prime minister and shifted to Delhi, Kishor found himself being slowly sidelined. The buzz in Delhi was that Kishor, who had attempted to create a US presidential campaign–style strategy for an Indian parliamentary system, wanted a greater role for himself as a White House-esque 'chief of staff' in the Modi PMO. 'Amit Shah didn't like Prashant's proximity to Modi and saw him as a rival who was trying to make his CAG organization bigger than the BJP sangathan,' a BJP leader tells me. Kishor dismisses reports of any turf wars. 'I wanted to institutionalize the CAG into a new governance model which would encourage thousands of professionals to make a lateral entry into public life, from the panchayat to the PMO; there was no question of competing with the BJP's party structure,' he asserts.

Kishor's idea though didn't find enough traction and by the end of 2014, he was looking for options. That is when he met Nitish Kumar and offered to manage his Bihar election campaign. 'People think that I joined hands with Nitishji to take revenge on the Modi–Shah combine. Nothing could be further from the truth. I had built a full team of several hundred young people at CAG and we needed a fresh opportunity to prove ourselves as political activists. It was a question of our survival,' is Kishor's explanation.

The Kumar–Kishor equation turned out to be the perfect fit. An old-style politician, Kumar had never really focused on election marketing and management techniques, relying instead on 'jod-tod' statecraft and his personal image as a 'sushasan babu' (good governance leader) to win elections. The 2014 Modi blitz had left him nonplussed and he desperately needed professional help. For Kishor too, working in Bihar was a homecoming of sorts. His family hailed from Samastipur and in a previous avatar as a public health professional with the UN, he had worked on the successful polio programme in the state. 'My relationship with Nitishji is not just professional but also personal,' he tells me. (In September 2018, Kishor would officially join the JD[U].)

The first piece of advice Kishor gave his new patron was that he should return as Bihar chief minister. Kumar had resigned within days of the 2014 election debacle, owning moral responsibility, and appointed his party colleague Jitan Ram Manjhi as chief minister. Manjhi was a Mahadalit, and Kumar had hoped that his elevation would widen the JD(U)'s caste base. The experiment was a disaster as Manjhi began to assert his independence and hobnob with the BJP. 'My message to Nitishji was simple: you can only win an election in Bihar when you are the chief-ministerial face, not through a proxy,' says Kishor. It took three months to persuade Kumar to take back the reins of power in February 2015. Manjhi was ousted after a series of dramatic and rapid realignments within the JD(U).

With Kumar back in the chief minister's saddle, Kishor got to work. CAG was rechristened I-PAC, and the strategist who had once lived in Modi's home in Gandhinagar now moved in with the prime minister's arch-rival in Patna. The highly successful Chai pe Charcha of the Modi campaign was now replicated in a Har Ghar Dastak outreach programme aimed at getting the chief minister's message to voters through a door-to-door volunteer-driven exercise. A massive publicity campaign was launched around Kumar. Every poster had larger-than-life images of a smiling Nitish: 'Bihar mein bahaar hai, Nitish se Kumar hai' was the new slogan. Before the BJP could react, the JD(U) had captured every major hoarding space in the state. When Modi questioned Kumar's political DNA, pointing out his frequent changes in party allegiances, Kumar hit back by suggesting that the prime minister was insulting the people of Bihar. 'Bihari versus Bahari' (Locals versus Outsiders) became the new rallying cry; Kumar was pitched as a local hero ranged against the Modi–Shah duo. 'It is my firm belief that Indian elections are presidential, even at the state level. We were pitching Nitishji as a credible face of Bihar while the BJP was relying on Modi's national popularity,' says Kishor who would later run similarly successful 'presidential'-style campaigns for the Congress's Captain Amarinder Singh in Punjab and the Yuvajana Sramika Rythu (YSR) Congress's Jagan Mohan Reddy in Andhra Pradesh.

While Kumar was the chief-ministerial face, Lalu Prasad provided the cadre muscle and a substantial Yadav–Muslim support base. Under his 'simple man' exterior lurked remarkably sharp political intuition. When a group of Muslims came to see him at his Patna residence during the campaign, he cautioned them, 'Dekho, BJP iss chunaav ko Hindu–Muslim karna chahti hai. Aap khamosh rahiye, chunaav ke din ghar se nikalna!' (BJP wants to make this election a Hindu–Muslim debate. Stay quiet now, only come out on polling day!) Just a few weeks ahead of the elections, interestingly enough, the RSS handed Nitish and Lalu Prasad a political advantage. In an interview to the Sangh Parivar magazine, *Organiser*, RSS chief Mohan Bhagwat suddenly pitched for a review of the caste reservation policy. Lalu Prasad was the first to react. 'The BJP wants to do away with reservations,' he thundered, consciously stirring a 'backward versus forward' caste divide. 'Bhagwat ne BJP ka bantadhar kar diya' (Bhagwat has ruined the BJP), he laughed when I asked him for an election prediction. The colour was back on his cheeks and there was a spring in the step of the charismatic mass politician. Lalu Prasad, original master of caste politics, sensed a change in the offing.

Shah though didn't seem overly affected by the changing dynamics in Bihar or the caste arithmetic advantage his opponents had gained. He had spent months on the campaign, criss-crossing the state, working on his own caste equations and micro-detailing the BJP's booth-level strategy. 'Modiji ki chemistry inke gathbandhan se kahin zyada maayne rakhti hai' (Modji's chemistry is far more powerful than this alliance), he told an aide. Every BJP poster had life-size images of Modi and Shah: the local Bihar leadership was mostly missing. The BJP president was convinced that it was the leadership of Modi that was responsible for the 2014 Lok Sabha win in Bihar, and 2015 would be no different. When some of us journalists asked him about his poll reading, he grinned. 'Minimum 180, usse zyada bhi aa sakte hain.' (A minimum of 180 seats, maybe more.) When I suggested that the TV polls were now predicting a tight race, he chuckled. 'Opinion poll aur journalist toh BJP ko hamesha harate hain.' (Opinion polls and journalists always show the BJP losing.)

When the results came out on 8 November 2015, Shah's forecast seemed like empty bluster. Backward caste consolidation had trumped all else; the 'mahagathbandhan' had won an impressive 178 of the 243 seats. The BJP-led alliance came away with only 58 seats. For the second time in a year, the Modi bubble had been decisively pricked and Shah's election management and leadership style was now under the scanner. Within days, the knives were out: the old guard led by L.K. Advani, Yashwant Sinha and Murli Manohar Joshi issued a statement claiming, 'the party has been emasculated and is being forced to kow-tow to a handful', while calling for a complete review of the results. 'We have learnt nothing from the crushing defeat in Delhi,' the statement added. Suddenly, 2014 was forgotten; all anyone could talk about was 2015, *annus horribilis* in election terms for Gujarat's 'jodi number one'. Modi and Shah knew they had to do something drastic and soon to arrest the slide. The 'suit-boot ki sarkar' was in need of a political course correction.

From the time he first became a contender for prime minister in 2013, Narendra Modi had often spoken of his 'humble origins' in the north Gujarat town of Vadnagar – something he rarely did as Gujarat chief minister for more than a decade. It was as if, overnight, the 'chaiwallah' (tea boy) persona had become an essential part of the Modi life story, even when his critics questioned whether he had really sold tea at the local railway station as he claimed. The imagery of having risen out of poverty was meant to remind the voters that this was a leader who understood the pain of the poor from personal experience, unlike his political rivals. Modi was the 'kaamdar' (working class) who was fighting the 'naamdars' (dynasts).

One story that Modi often relates to audiences is how his mother, Heerabehn, would struggle with the smoke from cooking on firewood or cow dung. 'I would hear my mother cough all day and wonder what could be done to ensure that neither she nor any other woman in the neighbourhood would have to go through this ordeal ever again.' When he met with senior PMO officials and a few union ministers soon after he took office, he reportedly asked them, 'What is the point in being prime minister if you can't serve the poor?' The group was told to return with a blueprint of how the prime minister's dream would be translated into action.

A few weeks later, Nripendra Misra, principal secretary to the prime minister, met Modi along with Dharmendra Pradhan, the petroleum minister. A detailed presentation was made on the ministry's plans to distribute 5 crore free gas connections to families below the poverty line over the next five years. Modi was initially hesitant to give the connections free of cost, claiming that it would only encourage a 'freebie' culture among the electorate. A compromise was arrived at: while the first LPG cylinder connection would be free, the refill would have to be bought at subsidized market rates. 'The prime minister's message to us was clear: we have to embrace this scheme with a "missionary-like" zeal, and scale it up so that it becomes a mass movement,' says Pradhan, a Rajya Sabha MP from Odisha, one of the country's poorer states. 'Scale' is a word that prime minister Modi likes to use often: 'bada karo' (make it big) is a frequent instruction to his ministers. As a first step, the prime minister made a personal appeal to well-to-do citizens to voluntarily surrender their LPG subsidies. An artful message, the 'Give It Up' campaign, was aimed at stirring a conscientious spirit of sacrifice among the citizenry.

On 1 May 2016, the Pradhan Mantri Ujwala Yojana (PMUY) was launched from the socio-economically backward Ballia district in eastern UP, the state which returns the highest number of MPs and which was going to assembly polls in less than a year. Dressed in a simple white kurta-pyjama, Modi was seen bending graciously towards a sari-clad rural homemaker on stage, handing her the first free LPG connection. The project, bringing much-needed relief to impoverished households, had a clear political significance: a personalized letter from the prime minister with his photograph would accompany the 'gifting' of the one-time grant of ₹1,600 per family. Every petrol station across the country began to carry an Ujwala hoarding with a picture of the beaming prime minister. The identification of Ujwala with Modi was complete and deliberate. 'We wanted to emphasize that this wasn't just another government scheme; it was a project which was personally being driven by Prime Minister Modi,' a senior official explains.

If the National Rural Employment Guarantee Act (NREGA) had been the previous UPA government's definitive pro-poor project, Ujwala was now the Modi government's big-ticket response. The difference is where NREGA claimed to draw inspiration from the ideals of Mahatma Gandhi and was named after him, Ujwala was completely identified with Prime Minister Modi. An important step had been taken in erasing the 'suit-boot' image and replacing it with the more humble 'garibon ka neta' (leader of the poor) idea.

Ujwala wasn't the only large-scale programme on the prime minister's agenda. During his first Independence Day speech on 15 August 2014, Modi announced a 'Swachh Bharat' (Clean India) campaign to provide toilet access to every rural household, in honour of Mahatma Gandhi's memory. For the first time, an Indian prime minister had used the platform of the Independence Day speech to make a nationwide appeal to put public hygiene and sanitation on top of the political agenda. Modi had reportedly mooted the idea in 2013 itself when, in a conversation with his aides in Gandhinagar, he spoke of the need to pay homage to Gandhi. 'Narendrabhai wasn't even prime minister then but he told us that he wanted to start a project that would be a remembrance to the Mahatma when the nation celebrated his 150th birth anniversary in October 2019!' remembers the aide.

The Swachh Bharat campaign was replete with Gandhian symbolism. With the logo – the words 'Swachh Bharat' enclosed within the spherical frames of the Mahatma's spectacles – Modi found a way to link his prime ministership to the greatest Indian of the modern era. 'We crowdsourced the logo by inviting ideas from the public but, trust me, when the final design was conceptualized, it was the prime minister who picked one of the most enduring images of Gandhi,' a PMO official tells me.

For decades, the RSS, where Modi cut his political teeth, had struggled to shake off the taint of the Mahatma's assassination. Now, with a high-profile Swachh Bharat campaign that was formally launched at New Delhi's Rajpath on 2 October 2014 by Prime Minister Modi, flanked by senior party members all holding brooms, the appropriation of the Mahatma's legacy by the Sangh Parivar took off. Over the next five years, the Swachh Bharat Mission would become the flagship scheme of the Modi government; the aggressive marketing blitz that followed would firmly and indelibly associate the project with the prime minister (and assure a rich haul of votes come election time).

At a media event in December 2014, Jairam Ramesh, who had held the sanitation portfolio in the Manmohan Singh government, pointed out that the UPA had initiated a cleanliness project named Nirmal Bharat but had failed to advertise it as expertly as Modi. 'I guess Mr Modi just borrowed our idea, changed the name and marketed it better!' bemoaned Ramesh. In fact, in 2012, Ramesh had asserted 'mandir se bhi pavitra hai shauchalya' (toilets are even purer than temples) – a remark he was ferociously targeted for by the BJP – so, possibly, a toilet-building campaign was not an entirely new idea. But Parameswaran Iyer, the UP cadre IAS officer who has led the Swachh Bharat Mission from February 2016, insists there is a difference of 'day and night' between the two projects because of the way the prime minister himself threw his weight behind the Swachh Bharat campaign. 'Just look at the manner in which the prime minister embraced the idea of toilet-building, invested his political capital in making it a national mission and, yes, became our communicator-in-chief,' he points out. Iyer was a well-considered choice for the task. He had taken voluntary retirement from the government in 2009 to lead the World Bank's water and sanitation projects, before being recalled to become secretary in the drinking water and sanitation department. 'I guess most senior government officers saw this ministry as unattractive. I saw it as an opportunity to do something constructive,' he says.

Official figures show that Swachh Bharat has been a major success. Nearly 9.6 crore toilets have been built in the five years since October 2014, and 5.7 lakh out of 6 lakh villages were declared open defecation free by May 2019. Rural sanitation coverage touched almost every village. 'This isn't just another project, it's become a mass movement with the prime minister as its face,' says Iyer. In the India Today Mood of the Nation poll in January 2019 voters rated the campaign as the number one achievement of the Modi government. For over a decade, the prime minister had tried to shake off the legacy of having presided over the bloody 2002 Gujarat riots. Now, the carefully choreographed image of the prime minister, broom in hand, outside a Valmiki colony in the national capital, would be his way of sweeping away the past. He was now reinventing himself as a modern-day leader imbued with Gandhian values – without abandoning his RSS origins. The streets would be cleansed, so would his past. Clean toilets, clean slate.

Over the next three years, the Swachh Bharat Mission and the Ujwala campaign would play a crucial role in enhancing the prime minister's personal standing among the poor, especially rural women. On a visit to UP ahead of the 2019 elections, several women from a village near Agra described the gas connection and toilets as having transformed their lives. 'Shauchalaya hamare liye izzat ghar hai aur gas cylinder ek diya' (The toilet has given us self-respect and the LPG cylinder is a light), one woman told me. By the time the 2019 elections rolled by, the government claimed to have given 6 crore free gas connections through direct cash transfers to genuine beneficiaries, nearly half of them to Dalit and Adivasi homes.

It wasn't just limited to toilets and gas connections: a slew of state-funded welfarist schemes were launched to woo the poor. The Pradhan Mantri Jan Dhan Yojana – launched simultaneously in seventy-six centres and with a gala function in Delhi's plush Vigyan Bhavan where Modi handed out bank accounts to rural women on stage – set out to expand financial inclusion with universal banking as a focus. There were others as well: the Pradhan Mantri Mudra Scheme aimed to extend affordable credit to microenterprises, the Pradhan Mantri Awas Yojana to provide low-cost housing, and the Ayushman Bharat Yojana to provide free health treatment to 10 crore poor families. All these programmes aimed at recasting the prime minister as a messiah of the poor and not the jet-setting 'suit-boot' leader flying in and out of global capitals. 'We were able to create a sense of hope amongst a neo-aspirational class: if my neighbour has a house in the village through the Awas Yojana, one day I will get one too,' is how a PMO official describes the overarching philosophy.

Many of these welfare schemes had existed in the UPA years as well. As had delivery models like Aadhaar, the biometric identification system, created and built by global tech services giant Infosys co-founder Nandan Nilekani when he was made the chairperson of the Unique Identification Authority of India (UIDAI) with cabinet rank in the Manmohan Singh government. Nilekani fought the 2014 elections from south Bangalore and lost on a Congress ticket, but post-defeat, the Congress had little time for the tech genius. Nilekani was packing his bags and preparing to vacate his government bungalow in Delhi in June 2014 when he sought and obtained an appointment with Prime Minister Modi. 'I made it clear that I was meeting him in the national public interest, and not as a politician,' Nilekani points out.

During the bitter election campaign, Modi had repeatedly questioned Aadhaar's value, even dismissively dubbing it a 'white elephant'. But when they met, Modi was so impressed with Nilekani's sharp-skilled defence of the UIDAI project that, barely a week later, the then finance minister, Arun Jaitley, increased the budgetary allocation for Aadhaar. A UPA-birthed scheme was now fully identified with the Modi sarkar.

Take also the direct benefit transfers or DBT – first rolled out in January 2013, when the UPA was in power, to ensure greater efficiency and transparency in transferring cash benefits to the poor while reducing the vast number of illegitimate beneficiaries under government welfare programmes. Within a year of taking over, the Modi government had taken full ownership by transferring the DBT project to the Cabinet Secretariat in 2015. As is his wont, Modi even coined a catchy acronym – 'JAM': J for Jan Dhan, A for Aadhaar and M for mobile – to explain to the common citizen in simple terms the benefits of linking Jan Dhan accounts with their Aadhaar and mobile numbers. Fixing greater accountability of local bureaucracies by big-data analysis and real-time e-monitoring of each department's progress – most welfare schemes are tracked on dashboards in various nodal ministries at the Centre – would contribute to what Team Modi likes to depict as 'mission-mode' method for better delivery of benefits. Amitabh Kant, CEO of NITI Aayog, who relishes throwing numbers as a sales pitch, tells me, 'Since 2015, DBT Bharat has enabled the total transfers of more than ₹7.6 lakh crore across 439 schemes, thus saving the exchequer more than ₹1.4 lakh crore. We have eliminated brokers and middlemen and are fuelling a billion aspirations.'

Shorn of the hype, in pure political terms, the messaging was clear: the Modi government was making the successful last-mile distribution of benefits to the poor and needy its USP. In the build-up to the 2019 elections, this would become the BJP's biggest electoral weapon. Beneficiaries were consciously targeted in every political communication as a potentially large vote bank that cut across traditional caste divides (the BJP claims that at the time of the 2019 elections there were as many as 22 crore beneficiaries of various government programmes). 'The base may have been laid out in the UPA years but the pyramid of welfarism was built by the Modi government – even our worst critics can't deny this,' senior minister Nitin Gadkari tells me.

At the core of every scheme's outreach was the prime minister's flamboyant persona. Where the self-effacing Dr Manmohan Singh was always almost reluctant to take credit for governmental achievements, Modi is the polar opposite: every milestone and anniversary is shared across media – be it the prime minister's social media sites, the NaMo app or his monthly 'Mann ki Baat' radio programmes. Innovative citizen engagement was created through digital platforms like the PMO-driven MyGov site and when it came to organizing public events around these prize schemes, not a single opportunity was missed. For example, when the Jan Dhan Yojana was recognized by the Guinness Book of World Records for opening the most bank accounts in a single week, the announcement was followed by a carpet-bombing of high-profile celebrations led by the prime minister himself. 'Yes, there was a band, baaja, baarat echo effect,' admits a senior government official, 'but at the end of the day, what is wrong if a government tom-toms its report card and accomplishments.'

Lost in the astutely choreographed cacophony were some hard facts: for example, over 23 per cent of the 33.5 crore Jan Dhan accounts opened till December 2018 were inoperative in that calendar year; non-performing assets (NPAs) under the Mudra loan scheme doubled in 2018–19 to over ₹16,400 crore while only one in every five beneficiaries started a new business; Ayushman Bharat awareness was barely 20 per cent in states like Bihar and Haryana while a number of hospitals were found defrauding the scheme. And yet, the intent and campaign pitch of the Modi government was unmistakable. This was first and foremost a 'garib–kisan ki sarkar' (a government of the poor and farmers). 'We've broken the urban-centric image of the BJP once and for all by giving wings to the great rural India dream,' enthused Jaitley. The minister was not wrong. The BJP's social base was steadily moving from its upper-caste origins to a more plebeian foundation.

While the well-marketed welfare programmes were effective in gradually shifting the narrative away from the 'suit-boot' jibe, Modi wasn't content with the impact. The prime minister felt the need for an even bigger buzz if he was to truly bury the ghosts of the monogrammed suit and be embedded in popular imagination as a 'revolutionary' change agent. It was time for Modi-style shock-and-awe muscular-'nationalist' decision-making.

8 November 2016. It was never going to be an ordinary news day. The US was going to vote after a long and rather spiteful presidential campaign between Democratic nominee Hillary Clinton and her arch Republican rival, Donald Trump. With his rumbustious unconventional behaviour, Trump had intrigued the world and the US election was on everyone's mind. Most Indian news channels usually rely on the world news agencies for footage, but this time the presence of the highly tele-conscious Trump ensured that almost every news channel had planned extensive news coverage of the elections. I had travelled to Washington in the lead-up to the elections and now, back in the studio, was looking forward to an exciting election night. Just two days earlier, I had attended the BJP's annual Diwali Milan, one of the rare occasions when the prime minister briefly interacts with journalists. As he went around shaking hands with the mediapersons crowding around him, the prime minister spotted me in the distance and asked: 'Arre, tum kab America se wapas aaye, chunaav hone tak ruke nahin?' (When did you come back from America? Why didn't you stay till the elections were over?) I was a little taken aback that the prime minister seemed to be aware of my travels and muttered somewhat incoherently, 'Sir, US mein Trump hai, yahan toh aap newsmaker hain!' (In the US, there is Trump, here you are the newsmaker!) It was meant to be a humorous riposte but I am not sure the prime minister saw the lighter side; he grimaced slightly before moving away to greet more valued guests.

In a strange way, my wisecrack would prove prophetic.

Around 7.30 p.m. in the evening, even as I was preparing for the 9 p.m. show with special guests on the American presidential elections from the US and India, there was a news alert that the prime minister would be addressing the nation around 8 p.m. The newsroom was galvanized into action. Earlier in the day, the prime minister had held a meeting with the service chiefs. Could the prime minister be making a major announcement on action against Pakistan? After all, just weeks earlier, there had been a cross-border 'surgical strike' against terror camps inside Pakistan. Could the Modi government now be going a step further and declaring war? A newsroom is a manic place in a big breaking-news situation where the mind gets caught in the frenzied atmosphere and the lines between information and speculation are often blurred. I must confess going on air and in an act of pure guesswork, babbling on about a possible escalating conflict with Pakistan. Defence and strategic affairs experts were hastily lined up to prepare for reactions to any prime-ministerial announcement.

A few minutes after 8 p.m., Prime Minister Modi, clad in a white kurta-pyjama and beige sleeveless jacket, appeared on Doordarshan, the national broadcaster. The tricolour stretched in the background, the Ashok Chakra was conspicuously emblazoned on the prime-ministerial podium. The setting was big, it was national. The excitement in the newsroom was now even more palpable, as we prepared ourselves for a declaration of war.

But within seconds it was obvious that a very different kind of 'war' was on the prime minister's mind. There wasn't a word in the opening remarks on Pakistan, Kashmir or the terror threat. Instead, the prime minister was speaking on the more prosaic issue of the economy and repeatedly referring to 'garibi' (poverty). The hot sense of anticipation in the newsroom began to wind down.

As the prime minister began to list out a series of welfare schemes for the 'gaon, garib, kisan' (village, poor, farmer) from Jan Dhan to Ujwala to the Pradhan Mantri Fasal Bima Yojana (crop insurance scheme), it seemed as if Modi was blandly reciting a report card of the government. Midway, the prime minister changed tack. In a slightly theatrical tone with the hand movements too now marked by aggressive finger-pointing, he began speaking about black money and corruption. The newsroom remained unimpressed. Another lecture on the parallel economy, not quite the headline-grabbing news story we had imagined. We were already over ten minutes into the prime minister's speech. Maybe we should stick to our original plan of focusing on the US presidential elections, I told my 9 p.m. news show producers. After all, the prime minister had routinely spoken out on these issues.

And then it hit. Around fifteen minutes into the prime minister's speech came the dramatic announcement: 'Behnon aur bhaiyon, desh ko bhrashtachar aur kale dhan ke deemak se uthane ke liye ek aur sakht kadam uthane ke liye zaroori ho gaya hai. Aaj madhya ratri, yaani 8 November 2016 ki raatri ko barah baje se, vartaman se jaari 500 rupay aur 1,000 rupay currency ke note legal tender nahin rahenge.' (Brothers and sisters, it has become necessary to take yet another tough step to save the country from the disease of corruption and black money. From midnight on this day, 8 November 2016, all 500- and 1,000-rupee notes in circulation will no longer be legal tender.) For a moment, there was stunned silence in the newsroom. Had we got this right? Had the prime minister just declared that all 500- and 1,000-rupee notes were now illegal? A colleague with better knowledge of finance and economics burst out: 'Bloody hell, he has just demonetized more than 80 per cent of the currency in circulation!'

Trump and the US presidential elections quickly faded to distant memory. My guest relations assistant turned to me with a quick question: 'Should I try and get guests on the economy now?' Yes, yes, I nodded in a daze, still not clear of the full implications of the prime-ministerial announcement. I looked around the newsroom and saw that excitement had been replaced by palpable anxiety. My gaze shifted uneasily from the buzzing TV screen to my wallet: hadn't I withdrawn ₹25,000 in cash from the bank only this morning in crisp 500- and 1,000-rupee notes for the monthly household expenses? Had the prime minister just cleaned out my pocket? 'Don't worry, you have till the end of December to deposit your old notes in the bank,' a colleague informed me with a half-smile. I gathered my wits as fast as I could. It was almost 9 p.m., there was a show to be done and the prime minister was still speaking, making the same points in English, insisting that the 'war' on black money was a 'war on terrorists' who had bought weaponry from cash transactions.

Mr Modi's landmark address to the nation ended just a little after 9 p.m., sixty-three minutes after it had begun. As the nation counted its notes, early next morning, there was more breaking news: Trump had just defied the pollsters to become the next US president. My mind, however, was preoccupied with a more mundane thought than the next White House occupant: Should I queue up at the bank now or in a few hours?

The Modi government's demonetization plan had been in the making for nearly a year. The idea was first floated in February 2016 at a high-level meeting of Prime Minister Modi with then finance minister, Arun Jaitley, select officers of the PMO and the finance ministry, and Reserve Bank of India (RBI) governor Raghuram Rajan. An unimpressed, even concerned, Rajan reportedly told the prime minister that demonetization was not the answer to resolving the vexed black money problem and kept urging caution. 'It won't work, sir, but if you still decide to go ahead with it, please do not touch the 500-rupee note which is now commonly transacted currency and please prepare to do it with military-style precision and planning,' he advised Modi. The RBI even prepared a detailed note outlining the potential costs and benefits of demonetization, as well as the alternatives that could achieve similar goals. 'Yes, I have said this before, I tried to persuade every level of the government that it was a bad idea,' Rajan tells me.

Highly regarded in the financial world, a former IIT Delhi and IIM Ahmedabad alumnus and professor of economics at Chicago University, Rajan became the youngest chief economist of the International Monetary Fund at the age of forty. He was one of the few who foresaw the great crash of 2008, and repeatedly warned of the fundamental stresses in the American and global economies that led in the end to the financial meltdown. In 2012, he was appointed as the chief economic adviser by the

Manmohan Singh government, and became RBI governor the following year. His academic credentials were impressive as was his intent to overhaul a creaking banking system. His imposing stature, photogenic good looks and refined demeanour had the media swooning: 'Rockstar Rajan' was the 'Bond of Mint Street'.

And yet, from early 2016, Rajan found himself at the receiving end of a vicious and unprovoked attack from Dr Subramanian Swamy, the maverick politician who had become a nominated Rajya Sabha MP. The fire-spitting Dr Swamy, who has strong links with the Sangh Parivar, repeatedly accused Rajan of mismanaging the economy and even questioned his patriotism by saying 'he is not fully Indian'. It was a terribly unfair and venomous allegation, one that should have attracted immediate censure from the Modi government. Instead, the sniping continued unchecked for months. Finally, on 27 June 2016, the prime minister spoke up in Rajan's defence in an interview – a week *after* Rajan announced his decision to quit the RBI governor's post. It almost seemed as if Modi had chosen a politically convenient time to speak up, once the reputational damage had been done. When I asked Rajan at his book release event in 2017 whether the malicious public campaign against him was responsible for his decision to step down, he tried to duck the question: 'I thought this interview was about my book!' But it was clear from his face that the 'anti-national' jibe had affected him deeply.

Did Rajan's opposition to demonetization spark off an orchestrated campaign against him? Had his consistent refusal to play cheerleader to Modi's 'Make in India' campaign caused his downfall? Had his references to Hitler in one of his public speeches on democracy and another reference to the Indian economy being a 'one-eyed king in the land of the blind' offended the leadership? When I posed these questions to Rajan, his email response was: 'Why the troll army took up the name "Hitler" or my suggestion of "making in India for India" and thought of it as criticism of their leader beats me. There clearly was an agenda to make me out to be part of a fifth column – no matter that I raised interest rates three times during the Manmohan Singh government and cut them six or seven times during the Modi government and that we succeeded in our goal of bringing down inflation. Who drove the agenda, I will not speculate but I am sure you can see patterns.'

Indeed, the pattern does seem clear. Modi's self-image as Supreme Leader meant that he would brook no dissent and was more than happy to see the back of a credible and charismatic RBI governor striving to retain the autonomy of the institution he led. The Western world may admire Rajan's knowledge but Prime Minister Modi, whose educational qualifications have been questioned by critics, appears to be insecure, even contemptuous of fine academic minds from a broadly secular and liberal tradition. When Nobel laureate Amartya Sen described demonetization as a 'despotic action', Modi hit back with 'hard work is more powerful than Harvard'. In India's elite policy environment, once dominated by anglicized Ivy Leaguers and Oxbridge intellectuals, Modi, with his prized 'chaiwallah' vernacular credentials, tends to lash out at those who he feels lack his grassroots connect and practical political experience.

Maybe, Dr Swamy was a pawn in this political game of chess designed to checkmate Rajan or perhaps he was typically relishing a well-publicized joust. The fiercely ambitious Dr Swamy had been quite vocal about his desire to be the finance minister and harboured a visceral dislike for the incumbent, Arun Jaitley. By striking at Rajan, he was effectively undermining Jaitley's stewardship in the North Block. Either way, the prime minister's conspicuous silence suggests that Rajan's leadership of the RBI had become politically inconvenient for many vested interests. Especially, the list of influential bank defaulters against whom the RBI governor had urged the PMO to launch a 'coordinated investigation' in a detailed letter written to the PMO in February 2015.

With Rajan out of the way, the prime minister could proceed with his demonetization plan without any serious internal opposition. Soon after the initial meeting in February, a small core group was put in place to implement the decision. Its members included Arun Jaitley, economic affairs secretary Shaktikanta Das (who would be appointed RBI governor in December 2018), PMO officials Nripendra Misra and P.K. Mishra and a deputy governor in the RBI in charge of currency operations. The group began meeting regularly to discuss the modalities of demonetization in the utmost secrecy. 'In one of our first meetings in June, we decided the shape and form of the new 2000- and 500-rupee notes but we had to make sure that no one had a clue of what was going on. It was a top-secret, highly sensitive operation,' claimed Jaitley. Even the finance minister's own secretary and senior officials in the ministry, including the then chief economic adviser, Arvind Subramanian, were kept in the dark.

By end October, the nuts and bolts were more or less in place although there were still a few lingering doubts about the automated currency printing presses' ability to replenish the system with sufficient high-value notes. There were some fears too that the government plan might have been leaked: a Hindi newspaper had published an article indicating that a new note may soon be in circulation. 'We realized that the more we delayed, the more there was a danger of something going wrong,' admits a senior government official. Peak Diwali shopping was likely to be over by 8 November, the team concluded. That would be D-day.

When the cabinet meeting was called that Tuesday evening around 6 p.m., the agenda suggested that it was a routine one. Ministers were asked to leave their mobile phones outside in what has now become standard practice and the doors were firmly locked. The prime minister then informed his colleagues of what was about to unfold in the next few hours, and asked Jaitley to further explain the details of the move. 'We were all a bit shocked but were also too scared to really raise a doubt,' confesses a union minister. One or two ministers finally summoned up the courage to ask just how the government proposed to ensure there wasn't any sudden currency shortage only to be firmly told, 'All is taken care of.'

Modi had already recorded his Doordarshan speech just ahead of the cabinet meeting. Key security and intelligence officials had also been informed just hours earlier. The RBI under its new governor, Urjit Patel, had called an emergency board meeting at 5.30 p.m. and given the green signal to the proposal after expressing some reservations. 'It [demonetization] is a commendable measure but will have a short-term negative impact on GDP for the current year,' read the minutes of the meeting. Bank chiefs were apprised via videoconferencing and told to prepare for a long week ahead. No one was quite sure of what was in store. Only one man seemed supremely confident. When a cabinet colleague presented a slightly worried look, the prime minister smiled. 'Sab theek hoga, yeh to game-changer hai!' (All will be well, this is a game-changer!)

'Tell me, why did the Modi government do this demonetization?' asked Dr Manmohan Singh in his typically soft, halting voice. I had gone to meet the former prime minister soon after the government announced demonetization, hoping to get a reaction from him. The Oxbridge-educated economist and former prime minister had famously and dramatically liberalized India's economy as finance minister in 1991. Known to be a liberal reformer, Singh had always operated within rational, recognized consensus-based norms. As usual, he was reluctant to speak on camera, insisting that he wasn't meant for the TV age. But the economist in him had been stirred by recent events and he seemed agitated. 'It's a bad call, you don't disrupt a growing economy like this overnight!' he said. A few days later, Dr Singh spoke in the Rajya Sabha on the issue, warning that the implementation of demonetization was a case of 'organized loot and legalized plunder' and a 'monumental disaster' that would hit the poor the hardest and could lead to the GDP declining by around two percentage points. For a man of few words, that is perhaps the sharpest attack he has ever made in his long career in public life.

On the face of it, Dr Singh was spot on. In the days that followed the radical announcement, the country was gripped by economic chaos. The serpentine queues outside banks were symbolic of a financial structure that was clearly ill-prepared and ill-equipped to handle the shock treatment that Prime Minister Modi had chosen to inject into the system. After all, the 500- and 1000-rupee notes constituted around 86 per cent of the total currency in circulation. ATM machines began to run dry, the quantity of new notes being printed was insufficient compared to the demand, people were collapsing in the long wait outside banks and a sense of panic had spread, especially amongst those working in the vast informal sector who were heavily dependent on cash exchanges.

And yet, as I travelled across the country to report on the impact of demonetization on the aam aadmi, I was also struck by how the majority of those queueing up in bank lines seemed pleased with the prime minister's action. Were they suffering? Yes. Had life become tougher? Yes. Had Modi done the wrong thing? No. 'Note-bandi se Modiji ne bade aadmi ko achha sabak sikhaya hai, sir' (Modi has taught the rich a good lesson with demonetization), was the dominant sentiment. A poll conducted by the C-Voter agency less than a fortnight after demonetization suggested that a whopping 80–86 per cent of those surveyed felt that the inconvenience caused was worth the effort of combating black money. Modi, in fact, made a jibe at journalists like me while addressing a large rally near the national capital. 'Kuch patrakar line mein khade logon se jaakar baar baar poochh rahe hain ki aapko kaisa lagta hai, aapko takleef hai ki nahin ... log unko jawab de rahe hain, ki hum Modiji aur desh ke saath hain' (Some journalists are asking people in bank queues again and again if they are inconvenienced, but people are saying they are firmly with Modi and the nation), he told the adoring crowds.

The prime minister had positioned demonetization or 'note-bandi' as a sort of 'dharmayudh' or holy war he was waging against the country's corrupt elite. In characteristically melodramatic style, he told a gathering in Goa to bear the pain of demonetization for just fifty days, after which they could punish him on the streets if he was proven wrong. 'Maine sirf pachas din maange hain ... 30 December tak mujhe mauka dijiye ... Agar 30 December ke baad koi kami reh jaaye, koi meri galti nikal aaye, koi mera galat irada nikal jaye, aap jis chaurahe mein mujhe khada karenge, main khada hokar desh jo saza karega wo saza bhugatne ke liye taiyyar hoon ...' (I have only asked for fifty days. Give me time till 30 December. After that, if any fault is found in my intentions or actions, I am willing to suffer any punishment given by the country.) This was classic Modi-style political theatre: dramatic and emotional dialogues that would resonate with a public craving for a strong and persuasive leader whom they could trust. By communicating directly with the people at all times, Modi, with his scorching oratory, was claiming that demonetization was a collective crusade towards the larger goal of nation-building, a 'war' where 'kaala dhan' (black money) was the common enemy.

The truth is, for all its hype, demonetization did not meet any of its professed goals. Terrorism, especially in the Kashmir valley, showed no signs of abating. Within two years, the total cash in circulation had surpassed pre-demonetization levels. Official statistics also show that 99 per cent of the demonetized currency notes returned to the banking system. Growth in digital payments, after an initial spurt, slowly subsided to pre-demonetization levels. While the tax to GDP ratio increased initially and there was a swell in people filing tax returns for the first time, these trends too have not sustained. The cash crunch disrupted economic activity terribly. Micro and small industries were the worst-hit. Job losses mounted. The pre-demonetization, growing at over 8 per cent, high-growth economy began to stall, sputtering at around a 6 per cent quarterly growth rate two years later, and down to 5 per cent by mid-2019. Dr Singh's warning proved prophetic.

So, why did Modi initiate an economically contentious move like demonetization? The opposition is convinced that the move was driven by pure politics. 'Look, the prime minister wanted to bankrupt the opposition parties ahead of the crucial UP elections, especially the regional outfits that are almost completely dependent on cash,' a senior Samajwadi Party (SP) leader claims. Lawyer-turned-Congress politician Kapil Sibal insists that demonetization was a financial 'scam' which allowed senior BJP functionaries in the know to exchange large amounts of cash and perform real estate transactions that went unnoticed. 'It was one big money-laundering exercise that was designed to enrich one party,' he insists.

In April 2019, just ahead of the general elections, Sibal released hidden camera footage which purportedly showed currencies being exchanged for a commission post-demonetization. 'It is sad that no media saw it fit to investigate the scam,' he laments. While the money-laundering allegations were never confirmed, there have been persistent reports about commission centres in Mumbai, Surat and Ahmedabad where old notes could be exchanged for new on a 70–30 commission (for every ₹100 note exchanged, ₹30 was paid as commission).

The BJP, however, rubbishes these charges. Instead, the ruling party insists that 'kaala dhan' was an obsession with the prime minister even during his tenure as Gujarat chief minister. 'Modiji often spoke about it in public gatherings and even attended seminars on the issue,' Jaitley tells me. In November 2013, Anil Bokil, a Pune-based self-styled 'economic revolutionary' met Modi in Gandhinagar to present him with a blueprint for tackling the black money problem. 'My appointment was for ten minutes, our meeting lasted almost two hours,' he tells me. Bokil, who runs the NGO Artha-kranti, has been pushing for a phase-wise elimination of all high-value currency since 1999, canvassing his ideas with politicians across party lines. 'I do not have any Hindutva leanings, but yes, the RSS was amongst the first organizations to support my views and the likes of Baba Ramdev openly endorsed my campaign,' he says. Whether Bokil and his supporters ultimately influenced Modi to experiment with demonetization is unclear but a number of the prime minister's close associates, including national security adviser Doval, did offer him unqualified support. Bokil himself argues though that he wouldn't have demonetized so much currency in one go. 'Modi did demonetization like an open-heart surgery without providing any anaesthesia to the common man,' he counters.

And yet, it was that very common man who was cheering the abrupt, massive intervention by the state in citizens' right to their own money, and applauding Modi personally. Maybe the prime minister had picked his moment well. He was exactly halfway through his five-year prime-ministerial tenure and realized that it was time to dispel any creeping anti-incumbency by taking a drastic new step that would firmly shift the narrative away from all other vexed issues of governance and foreground a 'war on the corrupt' as his campaign pitch. During the 2014 election campaign, Modi had claimed that if black money stashed abroad was brought back to the country, ₹15 lakh would be deposited in every citizen's bank account. The opposition had used this as a talking point to embarrass the Modi government, especially when BJP president Shah admitted that the 15-lakh remark was just an election 'jumla'. In his 2014 Independence Day address, Modi had thundered, 'Na khaoonga, na khane doonga' (Won't take a bribe, nor allow anyone to take one), a vow that seemed like an empty boast at the time. Large-scale corruption had been a key reason for the downfall of the Manmohan Singh government. Now, demonetization, howsoever flawed and chaotic, was the Modi government's response to those who were questioning his anti-corruption credentials, one that affirmed his position as a risk-taking political strongman who does not shy away from taking bold decisions.

The biannual India Today Mood of the Nation poll in January 2017 confirmed this. Weeks after demonetization, the poll showed a surge in Modi's popularity, with 65 per cent – 15 per cent more than the previous poll in August 2015 – of those surveyed endorsing his leadership. The poll claimed that if elections were held right away, Modi would win a whopping 360 Lok Sabha seats, up again by 56 seats from the August data. It was clear that the poor in particular were rooting for demonetization and Modi, and his transition from 'suit-boot' neta to a Robin Hood–like champion of the downtrodden was near-complete. As one Maharashtra MP tellingly pointed out to me, 'You know, the poor farmer won't mind if his bullock cart is stuck so long as he believes that the Mercedes on the road also has a punctured tyre. That's how demonetization is working.' With the rural and urban poor on his side, the prime minister had not only 'stolen' his main rival the Congress's core vote bank, he had now carved one for himself.

Maybe, 'De-mo' was Modi's 'Eureka' moment, not unlike the one that motivated Indira Gandhi decades ago to execute her lightning strike for the poor by nationalizing major banks. But would the prevailing mood translate into votes? The UP elections were just weeks away in February–March 2017; the most populous and politically significant state would decide the immediate fate of Prime Minister Modi's 'game-changer'.

FOUR

The Rise of the 'Political' Hindu

THERE is no Indian state election quite like UP's. A Bihar election is politically more robust; elections south of the Vindhyas are infinitely more colourful; and a Bengal election is now bloodier. But the complexity of an election in India's most populous state is unmatched. The intricacies of Indian politics are in full play across vast tracts of the Gangetic heartland; caste and community forming complicated mathematical equations and sometimes combustible chemistry. With a population of over 23 crore, UP's sheer size – it is larger than every country in Africa, Europe and South America – makes predicting an election here hazardous. I covered my first UP election in 1993 at the peak of the 'Ram wave', just months after the Babri Masjid was demolished. Swayed by the euphoria of the 'saffron' Hindu political mobilization, my first instinct was to write of a possible BJP sweep. As it turned out, the nascent alliance between the SP and the BSP edged ahead: Mandal had trumped Mandir, caste equations had scored over religious identity.

The 2017 election too was being fought under a similar shadow of uncertainty and chaos. The political churning that had begun in the state in the early 1990s had still not fully settled. The larger plot of pitting caste against community remained the same, only the characters were different. Mulayam Singh Yadav's son Akhilesh Yadav now led UP. The son bore a striking physical resemblance to his father but didn't really have the latter's appetite or skill to navigate the cut-throat world of UP politics.

Mulayam had started life as a teacher in a small district college in western UP. He was also the village wrestling champion, a qualification that would prove most useful as he transited into UP's political 'dangal'. A follower of Ram Manohar Lohia's socialism, Mulayam was always 'Netaji', a pugnacious battler who had clawed his way to power with grit and raw energy. Akhilesh, by contrast, was a gen-next neta, suave and urbane, with a degree in environmental engineering from the University of Sydney. He enjoyed a game of tennis and liked to take his family for holidays to London and Dubai. His soft-spoken, charming wife, Dimple, was also an MP, and his English-speaking children were learning horse-riding. The sprawling gym in the chief minister's bungalow in Lucknow was equipped with the latest equipment and there was even a floodlit mini-football field in the garden. 'I cannot be Netaji but I intend to take his legacy forward,' he told me once.

But that legacy was in danger ahead of the 2017 elections. Mulayam had visibly aged and was in and out of hospital. With the patriarch of the SP missing in action, a fractious family battle broke out within the vast Yadav parivar which dominated the party's top leadership. Akhilesh's uncle, Shivpal, a senior minister in his cabinet, kept sniping at his nephew and questioned the younger Yadav's credentials to lead the party. Shivpal had a firm grip on the party organization but also a dodgy reputation of being hand in glove with a clique of corrupt bureaucrats and contractors. The Public Works Department (PWD) minister in the Akhilesh cabinet, he was once caught on camera telling local officials to 'steal a little but don't loot'. The story ran on a loop on the channel and I got a threatening call from one of Shivpal's aides. 'Mantriji is very angry with the story. Beware, we can switch off the channel at any time!'

Another uncle, Ram Gopal Yadav, a more thoughtful and cultured Rajya Sabha MP, chose to back Akhilesh even as other relatives began to take sides. This family soap opera would eventually undermine the SP's capacity to be truly battle-ready at election time. When I met Mulayam at his bungalow in Lucknow, he cut a lonely and forlorn figure. 'Aaj kal hum thoda bimaar rehte hain par sab jaldi theek hoga' (I am a little unwell but I am sure all will be well soon), he mumbled, almost oblivious to the family squabble that was tearing apart the edifice that he had built with so much effort. The once rock-solid SP was now a bit like a private family business in complete disarray.

The BSP, the other powerful regional force of UP, was also facing a crisis of its own making. Its founder, Kanshi Ram, a towering figure who had worked tirelessly to mobilize Dalit groups under the banner of Ambedkarism, had passed away in 2006, handing over the baton to his chosen successor, Mayawati. Unlike her mentor, four-time chief minister Mayawati was not driven by organization-building impulses as much as an insatiable ambition to capture power at all costs. Kanshi Ram, with his unkempt hair, crumpled white bush shirt and trousers, looked like, and was, an old-fashioned political revolutionary. In contrast Mayawati, attired in a tailored salwar-kameez, with expensive diamonds and luxury bags as preferred accessories, struck a very different note as a leader. As chief minister, she had even spent money from the public exchequer to build statues of herself, forcing the Supreme Court to intervene and ask her to reimburse the state treasury. She owned several large properties in Delhi and Lucknow and was facing charges in a disproportionate assets case. Just ahead of the 2017 elections, an income tax report claimed that Mayawati's brother Anand Kumar was being probed for owning a slew of companies and unaccounted assets worth over ₹1,300 crore. When I managed to catch up with Mayawati at an election rally, she was curt and bad-tempered. 'Dekhiye, main kisi ko interview nahin doongi, aap aise camera ko bina ijazat ke yahan nahin la sakte' (Look here, I will not give an interview to anyone, you cannot bring your camera here without permission), she said grumpily. Her brusque response was disconnected from reality given that in the 2014 Lok Sabha polls the BSP had failed to win a single seat.

At least the SP and the BSP had a social and political base they could still count on. For the Congress, UP had become a large, unending desert with no oasis in sight. The party that had monopolized power in UP in the first decades after Independence was now a marginal player, not having exerted any influence in the state since 1989. There was a time when the party would regularly get nearly 50 per cent of the vote share and comfortable majorities in UP in both the state and national elections. Now, the Congress was struggling to get a double-digit vote share and had barely a handful of MLAs in the assembly. In fact, UP was crucially important for Congress vice president Rahul Gandhi's own political future. 'The SP and BSP are temporary forces who will eventually fade away, you will soon see a resurgence of the Congress in UP,' he told us journalists at an impromptu media gathering ahead of the 2012 UP elections.

The recovery hadn't happened then and now, five years later, Gandhi was still hoping for another miraculous shift in fortunes. Less than twelve months before the elections, in April 2016, the Congress brought former Modi strategist Prashant Kishor on board to guide their UP campaign. Fresh from his triumph in Bihar, Kishor was suddenly the man with the golden election touch. Priyanka Gandhi Vadra, in particular, was impressed with Kishor's political management skills and recommended him to Rahul. Kishor's preliminary suggestion was a radical one: 'Let us make Priyanka the Congress nominee for UP chief ministership.' He would later tell me, 'Yes, I did pitch for Priyanka because I do believe every election in this country is now presidential and you need a credible chief-ministerial candidate to compete. Priyanka as a young charismatic face was ideally suited for the challenge.'

Reportedly, Priyanka initially agreed to take up the gauntlet only to back out a few months later. A UP Congress leader privy to the discussions revealed that her brother was on board but their mother, Sonia Gandhi, was not. 'Sonia felt that making Priyanka the UP chief-ministerial candidate would undermine Rahul's leadership and his future as the next Congress president.' Unfazed, Kishor made another attempt. 'Let's at least make Priyanka the chief campaigner, and we will find some credible face to be the candidate,' he told the Congress camp. Veteran politician and former Delhi chief minister the late Sheila Dikshit was now pitched as a surprise choice for the post. 'Dikshit was a Brahmin so she could attract the Congress's traditional upper-caste vote, had experience in administration and was generally well regarded,' is Kishor's explanation. Rahul Gandhi, meanwhile, had embarked on a kisan yatra, a month-long roadshow across UP meant to reach out to farmers and marginalized communities with the promise of a farm loan waiver. The enthusiastic crowds along the 2,500 kilometre roadshow from Deoria to Delhi hinted at the possibility of a Congress revival. The Congress slogan – 'Sataees saal, UP behaal' (Twenty-seven years, UP in a mess) – was a direct attack on the SP and BSP leadership who had mostly ruled the state since 1990. 'We really thought the force was with us and people saw us as an alternative,' says Raj Babbar, the film-star-turned-politician who had just been appointed the UP Congress president.

And yet, just weeks later, the Congress executed a drastic U-turn in strategy. Akhilesh Yadav, beleaguered by the family internecine warfare, signalled that he was open to forming an election alliance with the Congress. Led by its long-serving general secretary and MP, Ghulam Nabi Azad, the Congress's old guard jumped at the prospect of a tie-up. 'Look, we don't have the resources on the ground to fight this election on our own, a tie-up is a win–win for all,' was Azad's advice. Frantic negotiations began over seat-sharing that continued for several weeks before the alliance was officially cemented. The Congress now had a new catchline on its posters – 'UP ko yeh saath pasand hai' (UP likes this partnership) – along with photos of Rahul and Akhilesh. The same party which had been attacked for messing up the state was now the Congress's formal ally. The idea of 'Sheila for CM' was junked and Priyanka too was held back from leading the campaign. 'I guess with all the twists and turns, it was a bit crazy,' admits Kishor, 'but then that is the Congress party for you, too many power centres.'

A confused Congress, an imploding SP and a troubled BSP leadership: the political arena in UP was opening up for the BJP to take full advantage. The party, under the Modi–Shah combine, was primed to capture power in India's most politically crucial state and make it the base camp for their continuing conquest of the country.

For BJP president Amit Shah, 'Mission UP 2017' began where the battle for the Centre in 2014 had ended. Barely had the dust settled on the BJP's unprecedented majority in Parliament that Shah began plotting the party's strategy for the prize that was Lucknow. Just weeks after the May 2014 verdict, Shah telephoned Sunil Bansal, a rising star within the Sangh Parivar, who had worked closely with Shah on the 2014 UP campaign where the BJP won a stunning seventy-three out of eighty seats. Bansal was the national joint general secretary of the ABVP in Delhi when he was deputed by the RSS to assist Shah ahead of the 2014 Lok Sabha elections. Together the two men had charted the party's campaign in the state, from booth management to constituency-level supervision. Bansal was on a short post-election break in his original home state of Rajasthan when Shah sent him a missive: 'I need you to go back to UP and plan for the 2017 elections.' As a loyal Sangh pracharak, Bansal did not ask too many questions. He was being 'rewarded' for the BJP's performance in the 2014 Lok Sabha elections in UP by being made the sangathan mahamantri, or organizational general secretary, a crucial post in which he would directly report into the BJP president.

The first challenge for Bansal was to chalk out the BJP's campaign for the 2015 UP panchayat elections. Despite the massive 2014 mandate, the general impression was that the party had benefited in UP from the nationwide Modi wave, when in fact its organization in the state was still lagging behind the locally entrenched cadres of the SP and the BSP. Using their extended spells in power in Lucknow to distribute patronage, the SP and the BSP had created a vast network of party workers across the state. In contrast, the BJP's core members were confined to urban and semi-urban pockets and in the 2012 assembly elections the party had finished a poor third. The panchayats, as Shah had learnt in his early days in politics in Gujarat, held the key to the BJP's political revival. UP has more than 58,000 panchayats with more than 7 lakh gram panchayat members across the state, thus success in panchayat polls necessitated a large-scale operation. 'I want you to enrol at least one crore new members into the BJP in UP in the next thirty days,' Shah told Bansal at a meeting in November 2014. The BJP had just around 14 lakh members in UP at the time, and the party chief was asking for the figure to be multiplied several times over. Bansal wasn't sure if it was possible but he didn't bother arguing. 'With Amitbhai, once he sets a target, you learn not to say no, he is a very hard taskmaster,' Bansal tells me.

The BJP had recently launched an ambitious nationwide membership drive, encouraging people to join the party by giving a missed call to a designated number, thus enabling the party to reach out to many young volunteers during the 2014 Lok Sabha campaign. Bansal decided that the only way out was to increase booth-level participation in the membership drive. UP has more than 1.6 lakh booths, another huge number that requires a massive ground-level presence. Around 1.2 lakh booths were identified and all the BJP booth committees were told to enrol at least 100 new members each in their area. A mammoth door-to-door exercise began in late 2014 and culminated in early 2015 with 80 lakh new members, just short of the target set by Shah. A round-the-clock call centre in Lucknow was verifying and connecting with the new members. 'The membership drive was the first important step in building our party structure at the grassroots. Until then, we were only an urban party in UP, now by strongly contesting the panchayat elections, we created our own rural leadership,' claims Bansal. Each of the booth-level groups was encouraged to create its own WhatsApp communities to ensure constant and real-time interaction with members: in the run-up to the UP elections, the BJP had created nearly 15,000 such groups to spread the party's message. (The number would increase to more than 35,000 ahead of the 2019 Lok Sabha polls.) This ravenous hunger for political success radiated from the very top, all the way down to the ranks of the gathered electoral army. The message was clear: go forth, multiply and win at all costs.

A key element of this rapid political expansion was a conscious social engineering strategy that targeted the non-Yadav OBCs and non-Jatav Dalits, communities which had the numbers but didn't have the matching political clout. Shah had carefully studied the caste dynamics of UP and concluded that the best hope for the BJP was to go beyond the party's traditional upper-caste base and enrol local leaders from backward caste and Dalit groups who were denied their due by the SP and the BSP. As a predominantly Yadav-led party the SP had cemented a Yadav–Muslim alliance but Yadavs were just around 9 per cent of the state's population. The remaining non-Yadav OBCs, scattered across the state, constituted as much as 36 per cent of UP's population and were increasingly feeling left out in the 'Yadav Raj'. 'They are the vote bank we need to get on our side and then no one can stop us,' was Shah's clear-cut message. Another key target group were the non-Jatav Dalits who comprised nearly half of the state's 21 per cent Dalit population but were firmly kept out of Mayawati's Jatav-dominated BSP.

In early 2015, the BJP launched a 'Swasparshi' campaign, aimed to unite Hindus across castes. Around 800 party workers from the OBC and Dalit communities were identified and dispatched to places within the state which had a high concentration of members of their own castes. A mass mobilization drive began: the BJP held Scheduled Caste (SC) and OBC sammelans in each of UP's 403 constituencies, right down to meetings for specific caste groups like Rajbhars, Mauryas, Valmikis, Sonkars and dozens of other scattered sub-castes. By 31 March 2015, the BJP had a verified data bank of 1.13 crore newly registered members in UP, well in excess of the target set by Shah, 40 lakh of whom were directly involved in party work. 'We now had a "fauj" [army] on the ground to match the SP's and the BSP's clout,' enthuses Bansal.

Over the next twelve months, Bansal would criss-cross UP, often travelling four to five days in a week before returning to the party headquarters in Lucknow for a review. Like his party chief, he too had inexhaustible energy, often taking meetings till late into the night, usually sleeping in a small room allotted to him above the party office, and then setting off the next morning for another long day of pravaas (travel). 'I guess I am a karyakarta first, then a leader, so my first instinct is to get as much feedback from workers as possible,' he claims. Clearly, the energy of the RSS karyakarta in the field hasn't abated since the organization's beginnings in the 1920s. Tireless, sleepless, suffused with ideological zeal, the almost invisible saffron karyakarta travels light, travels fast and travels extensively, intent on converting as many as possible to his cause.

This time in UP, Modi and Shah were taking no chances. The successive defeats in Delhi and Bihar had worried them; another failure was out of the question. From early 2016, Shah decided to personally monitor the UP campaign. He would spend at least a week every month in the state, addressing party meetings and booth volunteer camps. Modi even advised the BJP president to set up his own professional election strategy consulting unit. Thus was ABM created.

The genesis of ABM offers a fascinating insight into how the Modi–Shah-led BJP was transformed from a political party into an election machine with tentacles that stretched right across society. In 2013, Prashant Kishor, Modi's election strategist at the time, proposed setting up a women's empowerment NGO, the Sarvani Foundation, as part of its extensive voter outreach programme. The NGO would not be directly connected to Kishor or Modi but was meant, over time, to build an influential support group for the Modi campaign. 'We were told that we would initially work amongst acid attack survivors to build credibility and then slowly create a wider platform to attract voters,' a former Kishor aide tells me. A Huffington Post investigation in April 2019 reveals that the Sarvani Foundation was registered in Ahmedabad in August 2013 with a former Jet Airways flight attendant and a former sales support specialist for Adobe listed as owners. One owner was the wife and the other was a sister of one of Kishor's employees. The Foundation, though, never took off as Modi and Kishor parted ways after the 2014 elections and Shah took over as BJP chief.

In 2016, the Modi–Shah duo decided to revive the Foundation and rename it the Association of Billion Minds. Ahmedabad-based businessman Deepak Patel was tasked with assembling a crack team similar to Kishor's CAG which had created innovative themes like Chai pe Charcha for Modi's 2014 campaign. K. Sunil, an NYU graduate who had also worked earlier with CAG, was brought on board to lead a young team that comprised of IIT engineers, lawyers and business management professionals. (In 2018, Sunil would switch to the Dravida Munnetra Kazhagam (DMK) campaign. He was replaced at ABM by another ex-CAG man, Himanshu Singh, who had worked as a McKinsey management consultant.) 'We were around a 180-member team, many of us in our mid-twenties and early thirties. Some had worked with Prashant on the 2014 campaign earlier. We weren't being paid big bucks, but it was a fresh challenge and there was always the excitement of working on a big political campaign. It wasn't as if we were BJP members or had any firm ideological alignment, but yes, there was a broad admiration for Modi's decisive leadership style,' a former ABM employee tells me.

ABM's mandate for UP was to work as an 'end-to-end in-house specialized election management agency'. Its assignments included preparing detailed ground-level reports for the BJP president, using big-data analysis to provide constant constituency-level feedback, organizing 'kamal melas' (lotus fests), bike rallies, youth meets and 'mahila camps' for key target groups such as the women beneficiaries of government programmes like Ujwala, handling social media engagement across platforms like Facebook and Twitter, even providing background notes on potential candidates. 'We were not a substitute for the party organization but were only offering professional management back-end services as a value addition to the BJP's existing systems,' is how a former ABM team leader puts it. (ABM would play a role in the 2019 campaign as well while organizing the BJP's 'Bharat ke Mann ki Baat' manifesto outreach and handling Facebook pages like 'Nation with NaMo'.)

At the top of this well-oiled election management pyramid was Modi himself. Ever since he had decided to contest the 2014 elections from Varanasi, the BJP's prime-ministerial candidate had gone from being a Gujarati regional chieftain to a charismatic national leader with roots in the Gangetic heartland. The moment he stepped on UP's soil, Modi was repackaged as a 'vikas purush', 'Hindu hriday samrat' and, crucially, an OBC leader all rolled into one. He launched his Varanasi campaign with a one liner: 'Maa Ganga ne bulaya hai.' The regional chieftain from Gandhinagar was now a son of UP's soil who was promising to alter the state's landscape. 'Unlike the local [of UP], Modiji has a cross-class, cross-caste appeal; frankly, he was a bigger draw for us than even Vajpayeeji in UP since Atalji was essentially a Brahmin, an upper-caste leader,' a senior UP BJP leader remarks.

By January 2017, while the country was still coming to terms with demonetization, Modi plunged into the UP campaign with characteristic vigour. Just three days before demonetization, on 5 November 2016, the BJP had launched a Parivartan Yatra from four different corners of the state. Even as its opponents were battling their internal crises, the BJP hit the road with the usual frenetic ground-level activity, organizing party rallies in every constituency. 'Our aim was simple, capture the narrative as early as possible with Modiji as our mascot for change,' is how Bansal explains the strategy.

If in the lead-up to the 2014 election Modi had trained his guns squarely on the alleged scams in the Manmohan Singh–led UPA government, this time it was his UP-based adversaries – Akhilesh Yadav and Mayawati – who were on his radar. I attended Modi's Parivartan Yatra 'mega-show' in Agra, held soon after demonetization, where he addressed a raucous crowd of supporters with demagogic fervour. In a nearly forty-minute speech, the prime minister used the word 'garib' more than fifty times, 'madhyam vargiya' (middle class) just a little less. Arms flailing, fists clenched, screeching and hectoring by turn, he seemed like a man possessed, belting out his defence of note-bandi as a 'war against corruption': 'Bhaiyon, behnon, kya kisi garib ya madhyam-vargiya ke paas kaala dhan hota hai ... Kuch logon ne desh ki puri economy ko barbaad kiya hai aur garib ko loota hai ... Main jaanta hoon paanch sau aur hazaar ke noton ko band karne se aapko toh asuvidha hui hai lekin kuch beimaan logon ki zindagi tabah ho jaaye aisa dand unko Modi ne diya hai ...' (Brothers, sisters, does any poor or middle-class person have black money? Some people have destroyed the economy, looted the poor ... I know that banning 500- and 1000-rupee notes has inconvenienced you but the lives of the corrupt have been destroyed by my one step ...)

Towards the end of his speech, Modi had succeeded in stirring his audience into a near-frenzy, asking them to join him in this 'holy war' against the 'beimaan' (corrupt). He didn't mention his political rivals by name but spoke often enough of those in power who had 'looted' the state exchequer, all the while contrasting them with his government's pro-poor schemes. He concluded his speech with a rousing battle cry – 'Bharat Mata ki Jai' – one that was echoed by the multitudes who had gathered there. It was a theatrical performance yet again, but it had struck a chord with the voters. The narrative for UP 2017 had been set: demonetization was a class war, a battle between rich and poor, as well as a moral crusade of good versus evil; a purge even. Modi positioned himself as a desi Robin Hood standing up for the country's deprived masses, a righteous leader ready to sacrifice his very office to wage the good fight for social and economic justice. In a state where more than a quarter of its residents lived below the poverty line, Modi's words would resonate far and wide.

Wending our way from the rally, I encountered a group of potato farmers outside Agra. There had been newspaper reports of how severely demonetization had affected small farmers. The entire chain of cash exchanges at the local mandis had been disrupted by the sudden withdrawal of currency notes. As we struck up a conversation, the farmers admitted being in grave financial trouble. 'Haan, dikkat toh bahut hai' (Yes, it is very difficult), they told me. So, will you vote for the BJP, I asked. 'Sir, hum toh SaPa ke voter hain, par iss baar Modiji ko vote denge'

(We are SP voters, but this time we will vote for BJP), said one. Why, I asked? 'Modiji kaale dhan ke khilaaf ladai lad rahe hain, ab kuch to achha hoga!' (Modiji is fighting against black money, something good will surely come of it!) And then I popped the inevitable 'UP question': Which caste do you belong to? 'Hum toh Yadav hain, sir!' (We are Yadavs!) one of them stoutly replied. If in the potato-growing Yadav heartland, farmers were being swayed by Modi's appeal, then clearly the winds of change were blowing far more swiftly than one had earlier imagined.

There was another unspoken factor working to the BJP's advantage: the party in power at the Centre had far more access to monetary resources post-demonetization than its opponents. Parties like the SP and BSP, which ran their political engine on disproportionate cash transactions, suddenly found their resources precariously stretched. The BJP, on the other hand, appeared to have no shortage of funds: the party had even given brand-new bikes and mobile phones to several of their booth workers engaged in last-mile propaganda. On the campaign trail with Akhilesh Yadav, I asked him how demonetization had affected the cash flow in electioneering. 'Yeh sawaal mujhe nahin, Amit Shah ko poochho!' (Don't ask me this question, ask it to Amit Shah!) he laughed. At one location, our chopper was not allowed to take off for almost half an hour because the air traffic control refused permission. 'Forget the money, see how they have grounded us here also!' was his wry observation.

It was evident during the campaign period that the BJP was riding on the tailwinds of significant popular approval and had gained momentum. Yet when the final UP results were declared on 11 March 2017, the sheer scale of the BJP's victory was staggering. The BJP won a record 312 of the 403 seats in the state assembly. The SP won just 47, the BSP was a poor third with 19 seats, and the Congress had been decimated once again and left with only 7 seats. The Akhilesh–Rahul alliance had failed; Mayawati's limitations had been exposed. The BJP, however, had scored its first majority win in UP since 1991 when the Ram Janmabhoomi wave had swept the state and heralded the beginning of the Advani–Vajpayee era in Indian politics. Now, Modi was the warrior-king and Shah his charioteer: after the failures in Delhi and Bihar, Gujarat's 'jodi number one' was firmly back on track and had proven that 2014 was no fluke. The lotus was blooming in a land where once the elephant and cycle had steamed ahead.

The next day, Modi and Shah led the BJP celebrations at the party headquarters in the national capital in what would become a familiar ritual after every major success. The prime minister even staged a mini roadshow along Ashoka Road, where he had once lived a more anonymous life as a general secretary. This time, flanked by Special Protection Group (SPG) commandos, a fleet of cars, and jubilant supporters showering him with rose petals, he was exulting in his biggest moment in the political sun since his 2014 triumph. 'This is a golden moment in the BJP's history and an opportunity to work for the poor and downtrodden ... We have seen many dreams being promised to win elections. But my dream is to take this "new India" forward in the seventy-fifth year of our independence. I am not someone who thinks in terms of elections ... What these results have done is empower my ambition for 2022, to fulfil the aspirations of every Indian, to take India to newer heights. When we mark seventy-five years of freedom in 2022, we should have made a "new India" that will make Gandhi, Sardar Patel and Dr Ambedkar proud,' he proclaimed to the cheering party workers.

That speech marked the launch of Modi's 2019 campaign more than two years in advance. Once again there was a strong emphasis on 'garib', 'gaon' and 'kisan'. The policy framework for his government's potential re-election had been established: pro-poor schemes would squarely remain the focus and 'new India' a fresh buzzword after the 'Achhe din' slogan of 2014. As Shah said in his address, 'In demonetization, the poor are united with the prime minister and the government. Today, for the first time after Independence, we have a prime minister who has ignited a hope for the future among the poor.'

The election results were a final stamp of approval, in a sense, for the most risky decision of the Modi-led BJP yet: that elections would be fought for, and won on, what was previously the preserve of a left-leaning Congress – a pro-poor, anti-rich pitch. The prime minister's strategy had clearly been overwhelmingly endorsed by UP's voters. 'We can argue on the economic fallout of demonetization, but let's be clear, politically it was a resounding success,' Arun Jaitley would later tell me.

I too was secretly pleased that for once my prediction of a UP election result hadn't gone awry. But as the BJP parliamentary board met to decide on its chief-ministerial options, not even the most perceptive political observer could have anticipated just who was about to ascend to Lucknow's top job.

Yogi Adityanath, the saffron-robed Gorakhpur MP, had finished his day's work and settled down to rest in the spacious Gorakhnath mutt when he got a call late in the evening. It was the BJP president. 'The prime minister and I need to meet you first thing tomorrow morning,' Shah said in clipped tones. A slightly dazed Adityanath pointed out that he was in Gorakhpur and with the last train to Delhi having already left it would be tough for him to reach in time. 'Don't worry, we will send a chartered plane tomorrow morning to have you picked up, be ready,' was the sharp response. Next morning, an anxious Adityanath found himself on his way to the prime minister's residence with mounting curiosity. Just a few days earlier, he had sent his passport to the PMO for approval to be part of a parliamentary delegation that was travelling to the US, only to be informed by the then external affairs minister, Sushma Swaraj, that he was to 'stay put' in India. It was the first sign that something was brewing.

A few hours after his meeting with the prime minister and the BJP–RSS top brass, Adityanath was again airborne, this time travelling to Lucknow. On board with him was Venkaiah Naidu, the central BJP observer for UP and Keshav Prasad Maurya, the affable state BJP president and a potential contender for the chief minister's post. Adityanath's nervousness at being summoned to Delhi had now been replaced by quiet elation: the prime minister had just informed him that he would be the next chief minister of

UP. The formal announcement was made nearly a week after the election results were declared. 'UP mein rehna hoga, toh Yogi Yogi kehna hoga!' (If you want to live in UP, you will have to say Yogi, Yogi!) Adityanath's supporters chanted vociferously.

And yet, for many both within the BJP and outside, this was not quite the coronation they had expected. The rabble-rousing Adityanath had, after all, always been a controversial figure, an 'outsider' within the BJP's established UP leadership. Just ahead of the 2017 elections there had been persistent reports that Adityanath was pressurizing the BJP leadership to give tickets to members of his Hindu Yuva Vahini (HYV), a notorious 'saffron army' which he had formed in 2002 almost as a parallel power centre in his eastern UP bastion. The HYV's predominantly young cadres were accused of goondaism, mostly directed at Muslims, and had several cases of arson, rioting, even murder, filed against them. Writes journalist Dhirendra Jha in his book *Shadow Armies*: 'Communal riots became unusually frequent in Gorakhpur and its neighbourhood after the formation of HYV in March 2002. It has either been involved directly or indirectly in virtually each of these incidents. What begins as a conflict between individuals from two communities turns into a communal flare-up only when Adityanath or other HYV leaders jump in.'

It wasn't just his inflammatory anti-minority speeches that had got Adityanath into trouble. In February 1999, he was charged with the murder of Satyaprakash Yadav, a gunman affiliated to local SP leader Talat Aziz. Yadav was shot in broad daylight and Yogi Adityanath's name was at the top of the list of the accused in the police FIR. Yet he was allowed to get away scot-free after the home ministry at the Centre, headed by L.K. Advani at the time, intervened. 'Yogi is both feared and admired in this region, feared because of the muscle power of his supporters and admired because he is, after all, the head of the much-revered Gorakhnath mutt,' says Shafi Azmi, a senior Gorakhpur-based journalist.

I first met Adityanath in 1998, soon after he became one of the youngest MPs in the country at the age of twenty-six. In his flowing saffron garments, gold earring, pale orange socks (he wears socks round the year) and rubber sandals, he always cut a distinctive figure in Parliament. While he was a conscientious MP who often raised questions and introduced private members' bill in the Lok Sabha – mostly connected to religious issues like cow-slaughter and constituency-level problems – the five-time MP also seemed a bit of a loner, sitting quietly in Parliament's central hall, oblivious to the chatter around him. Once when we got talking, I asked him about his usage of the divisive term 'love jihad' to describe the marriage of a Muslim man with a Hindu woman. The HYV cadres had been accused of beating up such couples on several occasions. Adityanath justified his campaign in his deceptively gentle tone: 'Dekhiye, yeh desh Hinduon ka hai, yeh Hindu rashtra hai. Hamein koi Musalamanon se dushmani nahin par agar woh hamari betiyon ko zabardasti le jayenge, toh hum chup nahin rahenge!' (Look, this country belongs to Hindus, this is a Hindu rashtra. We don't have any enmity towards Muslims but if they forcibly take away our daughters, you can't expect us to stay silent!) I was disturbed by his unapologetic bigotry but chose not to argue. A woman journalist colleague had informed me how, when she was tracking Adityanath on the campaign trail, she was politely told not to sit in the same car as him. 'Yogiji mahilaon ke saath akele nahin baithenge,' (Yogiji will not sit alone with women), was the clear instruction.

This then was the monk-turned-politician whom the BJP leadership had chosen to spearhead its 'new India' vision in the country's most populous state. It was an intriguing choice, which reports suggested had not been the prime minister's first one. Modi was reportedly keen on Ghazipur MP Manoj Sinha, the quintessential 'Modi-man' oozing the can-do attitude that the prime minister is partial to. Sinha was a minister in the Union government at the time and had earned a reputation for being an efficient administrator. Just days before the announcement on the UP chief minister was to be made, Sinha had been spotted in Parliament, grinning broadly and effusively greeting his fellow MPs, his body language suggesting that he was a likely nominee. When he travelled to Varanasi, a larger-than-normal posse of lal-batti escort cars was waiting for him at the airport – another indication that the ever-alert UP bureaucracy was scenting a power shift. 'It is completely untrue that I was sounded out for the chief minister's job. I went to Varanasi to condole with the family of a party worker who had passed away and then went to take darshan at Baba Vishwanath mandir. I do it every time I am in Varanasi, so there is nothing unusual in what was happening,' Sinha tells me.

While Modi was mulling chief-ministerial options, Shah and the RSS leadership were fixated on Adityanath. Six months ahead of the UP elections, Shah had asked union home minister Rajnath Singh if he would be open to moving to Lucknow only to be politely rebuffed. Interestingly, a survey conducted among party workers had shown that Adityanath was the preferred choice as chief minister if the BJP formed the government. Shah was reportedly impressed with Adityanath's loyal following across castes (even though the head priest of the Gorakhnath mutt is a Thakur, the religious order has a sizeable following among backward castes), but it was one incident in particular that swung it for Adityanath in the party president's eyes.

In 2013, while travelling through Gorakhpur, Shah, then the BJP general secretary, was suddenly set upon by angry protesters. Still new to UP's conflict-ridden politics, Shah did not have any security personnel with him at the time and urgently dialled Adityanath for assistance. Though Yogi was not in town, within minutes many young volunteers of the HYV roared in on their bikes and took the situation in hand. Says Shantanu Gupta, a biographer of Adityanath, 'Shah realized that day that Yogi was a doer, someone who not only controlled a large and influential Mutt but was also a tough leader who could always be counted on to handle a crisis situation.'

The RSS too had had a long relationship with the Gorakhnath mutt, especially given the monastic establishment's active role in the politics of eastern UP and the Ram Janmabhoomi movement in particular. Mahant Avaidyanath, Adityanath's mentor and his predecessor as chief priest at the mutt, was a driving force in the late 1980s in mobilizing support among the sant-sadhu samaj and political leaders for the construction of a Ram mandir in Ayodhya. A four-time MP himself, first with the Hindu Mahasabha and later the BJP, the mahant was carrying forward the tradition of the highly politically active Gorakhnath monastic order in its pursuit of religious aims through political mobilization. The 'liberation' of Hindu sacred places had always been a key campaign point for the mutt's priest-politicians. Adityanath had first come to Gorakhpur in 1993 as twenty-one-year-old Ajay Singh Bisht to research the mutt's customs and folklore. He was soon drawn into a life of monasticism by Avaidyanath and became determined to take forward his guru's legacy as a vocal advocate of building a Ram mandir on the disputed site in Ayodhya. 'After Yogi took charge of the mutt in 1996, it was he, along with the VHP, who sustained and popularized the Ram Janmabhoomi movement in his areas of influence in eastern UP when other BJP leaders appeared to lose interest,' claims Vijay Trivedi, another Yogi biographer.

Not surprisingly then, RSS sarsanghchalak Mohan Bhagwat was among those who actively pitched for Adityanath as chief minister. Given the strong majority which the BJP now enjoyed at the Centre, Bhagwat and the RSS hierarchy were convinced that the time was opportune to push the party's core Hindutva ideological agenda in which building a Ram mandir in Ayodhya was a deeply cherished ambition. 'Earlier BJP-led governments in Delhi and Lucknow were constrained by coalition pressures. Now, we had no pressure whatsoever, so making Yogi chief minister would send out the right signal to our cadres and supporters that the Sangh Parivar was fully committed to the Ram mandir,' a senior RSS functionary tells me. A phone conversation between Prime Minister Modi and the RSS chief reportedly clinched the decision to anoint Adityanath as chief minister. The appointment of Adityanath became another demonstration of the BJP's increasingly unapologetic politics of religious nationalism to advance the cause of Hindu majoritarianism. The aggressive Modi–Shah-led BJP doesn't see Hinduism as the spiritual calling of the renunciate, but as a political weapon in their bid to seize power and capture the state.

That's why, even though not his first choice, in a strange way, the unprecedented ascent of a Hindu priest as chief minister of an Indian state suited Modi too. Despite positioning himself as a global leader and hi-tech governance guru, Modi's roots were firmly embedded in Hindutva politics. For the pracharak-politician, the shift from 'Hindu hriday samrat' to a 'Sabka Saath, Sabka Vikas' statesmanlike leader was primarily strategic: as prime minister, he had to be seen as rising above the din of communally polarized politics. But ever so often, Modi would offer a reminder of his previous avatar as a believer in Hindu political assertion. For example, ahead of the fourth phase of polling in the 2017 UP polls, he announced at a rally in Fatehpur, 'If you create a kabristan [graveyard] in a village, then a shamshaan [cremation ground] should also be created. If electricity is given uninterrupted in Ramzan, then it should be given in Diwali without a break too. Bhedbhaav nahin hona chahiye.' (There should be no discrimination.)

The high-pitched rhetoric was aimed to contrast a Modi-led BJP with the Akhilesh Yadav government which was accused of 'Muslim appeasement'. But now, with Yogi in charge in Lucknow, Modi could afford to outsource the potentially more incendiary and divisive agenda to someone for whom it was second nature. Modi would continue to push his 'sabka saath', 'good governance' messaging but without compromising on his core religio-political beliefs ingrained from his many years spent in the saffron brotherhood. The RSS's first full-time pracharak prime minister is always a pracharak first.

It was a distinction that a Delhi-based group of Muslim political activists learnt soon after Modi took over as prime minister. The group was keen to invite him for their annual Eid iftaar function. After some effort, they managed to get an appointment with the prime minister. While Modi obliged them with the customary photo-op, the moment they asked him to join them for the iftaar celebrations, he politely refused. 'We realized that the prime minister would happily participate in the Ganga Aarti ritual in Varanasi but he would not take part in any Muslim community festivity,' a member of the delegation later told me.

Zafar Sareshwala, the Ahmedabad-based Bohri Muslim businessman-friend of the prime minister, said he once tried to persuade Modi to attend an iftaar party in Gujarat in 2012. 'Modiji's response was very explicit: "Zafarbhai, I have my navratra fast like you observe roza in Ramzan which is the ultimate form of purity and spiritual faith, but these iftaars are like a political tamasha which I do not wish to be a part of,"' Sareshwala recalls.

In a state like UP, where 19 per cent of the population is Muslim, the political messaging of having a Hindu religious monk as chief minister was unambiguous: there would now be a fundamental change in intercommunity power equations. In the Akhilesh years and in the Mayawati regime before, Muslims were seen to be disproportionately represented in government. The BJP, however, did not give a single ticket to a Muslim in the 2017 UP elections, a clear sign of growing political exclusion. I brought this up with the minority affairs minister, Mukhtar Abbas Naqvi, who had become the most prominent 'Muslim face' in the Modi cabinet at the Centre. 'You see, at election time, we look at a variety of factors, but "winnability" is most important. We want to give Muslims tickets but then we must also be confident that they can win the seat,' was his blunt response. That not a single Muslim was considered capable of attracting voters to the BJP in a 403-member state assembly was perhaps a reflection of how sharply divisive the BJP was perceived to be and how polarized the political class had become between Hindus on the one side and Muslims on the other.

Interestingly, Naqvi also participated in a heated TV debate I hosted where he was pitted against Hyderabad MP Asaduddin Owaisi on the contentious issue of a complete ban on the sale of cattle meat in some BJP states. 'Those who are dying without eating beef can go to Pakistan or Arab countries or any other part of the world where it is available ... even Muslims are against it,' he contended. Owaisi immediately countered by asking whether the BJP would impose a ban on beef across India, including states with large beef-eating populations like Goa and those in the North-east where it was in power. 'The problem is beef is "mummy" for you in UP and "yummy" in the North-east and Goa,' was Owaisi's clever riposte. For once, the amiable Naqvi was noticeably furious and stumped for an answer.

One of the promises on the UP BJP election manifesto was the shutdown of all 'illegal' slaughterhouses and the imposition of a blanket ban on all mechanized slaughterhouses. Within days of coming to power, the Yogi government's first major decision was to order police officials to prepare an action plan for the closure of slaughterhouses across the state. Raids were conducted in many parts, with officials peremptorily forcing meat-processing units to close down without even serving a notice. 'It was a hasty decision which was taken entirely for political reasons without any planning,' admits a senior UP government official.

A ₹22,000-crore trade in which more than 6.5 lakh people, the majority of them Muslims and Dalits, were directly involved was now on the brink of collapse. Fauzan Alavi, a spokesperson for the All India Meat and Livestock Exporters Association, insists that the entire debate on the ban on slaughtering cattle has been wrongly framed. 'Firstly, the meat we export is buffalo meat, not cow. Secondly, it is not just Muslims, but non-Muslims too who are involved in the business. Thirdly, the so-called illegal slaughterhouses are not privately run but are supposed to be maintained by municipal bodies. Fourthly, the income generated benefits lakhs of farmers who sell their livestock. And don't forget ancillary businesses like tanneries which are also dependent on the trade. You can't destroy so many lives like this on someone's whim,' he says angrily.

A few weeks after the Yogi government's firman, I travelled along the dusty tracks near the Ghaziabad–Hapur highway where many of the slaughterhouses had proliferated in recent years for a spot check. Most of them had been forcibly closed down, including some run by legitimate buffalo-meat exporters. 'There is a total sense of panic that has gripped us, everyone is too scared to speak out. When we tell the officials that we have a licence to export buffalo meat, they say they will take samples for forensic examination. If you argue with them, they say that these are orders from Maharaj!' one meat exporter told me. Another small-unit owner appeared traumatized while describing how the police raiding authorities were openly seeking bribes to allow the slaughterhouse to function. 'We need so many permissions to carry on, with every permission a bribe has to be paid to someone,' I was told. As is usual in India, state diktats breed corruption at every level; when livelihoods and industries are banned, open honest trade is further driven into the squalid underground.

And yet, not everyone in the Hapur area appeared to be as troubled by the overnight crackdown. In the Hindu-dominated neighbourhoods, Yogi's decision was met with near-universal approval. The abattoirs were allegedly run in terribly unhygienic conditions and the residents had often complained of animal waste being thrown into municipal drains and streets, emitting a stench that would remain for days. 'At last we have a government that cares for Hindu feelings,' a thrilled local BJP leader told me. 'Yogiji ki sarkar mein ab yeh sab nahin chalega!' (All this [slaughter] won't be allowed in Yogiji's government!)

If Hapur was a mirror for the rest of UP, and indeed, the country, then Yogi-style 'cow' politics was clearly working on the ground: creeping Hindu–Muslim religious polarization was economically ruinous but politically beneficial. The BJP leadership at the Centre too seemed to realize and thrill to the impact of Adityanath's strident appeal to religious sentiments. Suddenly, the UP chief minister was pitched as the party's star campaigner in every major state election, a crowd-puller wherever he went, especially in areas with a large minority population. Paradoxically, in UP, Adityanath was undergoing an image makeover. Bureaucrats confessed to be pleasantly surprised by the chief minister's zero tolerance for corruption, enormous capacity for hard work and focus on administrative issues that went beyond identity politics. 'He is a good listener who will take copious notes at meetings and doesn't engage in loose talk. And yes, the usual political fixers don't hang around him,' a senior IAS officer claims.

But the moment Adityanath hit the campaign trail, he appeared to once again transform into the original firebrand demagogue, almost as if he had been 'liberated' from the constraints of office by the excitable crowds he was addressing. Whether he was raking up the love jihad issue in Kerala and Karnataka or threatening Muslim migrants in Bengal, Adityanath on the road was the great polarizer, always a hit with a boisterous crowd. I attended one such rally in the picturesque town of Sirsi in coastal Karnataka, a region with a substantial Muslim population where he accused the Congress government of protecting 'jihadi' forces that were killing innocent Hindus. 'The Congress is not concerned about protecting cows or the nation. They will protect the jihadi terrorists like Yasin Bhatkal ...' he warned. He also spoke of the BJP's commitment to 'sushasan' (good governance) but it was his more provocative sloganeering on issues ranging from 'jihadi' crime to the 'exploding' Muslim population that drew the maximum applause.

The results of the 2018 Karnataka elections were a thumbs-up for the outspoken cleric. The BJP won in most of the constituencies where Adityanath had campaigned. 'He may be a controversial figure for our opponents but he is a match winner for us,' enthused a BJP campaign manager. Once again, I did not dispute, but silently asked myself: Yes, Adityanath's clamorous rhetoric was drawing in the votes but at what cost? And whose?

Around 50 kilometres from the national capital, the gleaming six-lane Noida–Greater Noida Expressway dotted with well-manicured trees, large MNC office complexes and residential skyscrapers suddenly gives way to chaotic roundabouts, small factory units, green paddy fields and dusty tracks. This is Bisada, a tiny village in Dadri town, where 'new India' collides with the 'old'. A number of farmers here have had their fertile land acquired by successive UP governments which claim to have paid them handsomely for the land acquisition. Young men on flashy motorbikes, wearing bright Benetton and Adidas T-shirts, guide us to the village whose entrance is marked by a life-size statue of Rana Pratap, a reminder that I'm entering a Rajput-dominated panchayat. As I dodge a herd of cows and buffaloes, the irony is inescapable: this is the village where, on the night of 28 September 2015, a man was brutally lynched to death because his attackers allegedly suspected him of slaughtering cattle and eating beef, a horrific slaying that catapulted Bisada from a nondescript address to the centre stage of national politics.

Mohammad Akhlaq was a fifty-two-year-old resident of Bisada, a local 'lohar' (blacksmith) who helped repair agricultural and household equipment. He had a large family and worked hard to lift his children out of poverty and illiteracy; one of his sons, Sartaj, had got a good job as a technician in the Indian Air Force. On Bakra Eid, as was often done as part of the festive ritual, Akhlaq invited a few of his Thakur neighbours for a meal. Everything seemed fine, until a day later when the rumour that a calf had been killed in the village and the meat that Akhlaq had served his guests was beef began making the rounds. At about 10.20 p.m., the local temple priest made an announcement asking people to assemble near Akhlaq's house. More than 1,500 people gathered, broke open Akhlaq's wooden front door, entered the courtyard, insisted on seeing what was stored in his refrigerator and, convinced that the meat in the fridge was beef, attacked the man. Akhlaq and his other son Danish were brutally beaten with lathis and sticks. By the time the police arrived, more than an hour later, the frail Akhlaq had collapsed and his son was bleeding heavily. Akhlaq died on the way to the hospital; Danish, beaten unconscious, underwent two brain surgeries. Eighteen people, all belonging to the majority Thakur community, were arrested. Many of them were teenagers.

If the murderous assault on Akhlaq was not shocking enough, the political power play that followed was horrifying and sickening. Various Hindu extremist outfits bellowed about their right to protect 'gau mata', insisting that anyone who dared to slaughter a cow would meet a similar fate, and called for the immediate release of all those arrested. Muslim leaders from UP also descended on Bisada and immediately made large cash offerings to Akhlaq's family. While one of them, the SP's Azam Khan, a loud-mouthed minister in the Akhilesh government, was literally chased away from the village, another UP politician, the BSP's Nasimuddin Siddiqui (who later joined the Congress), was accused of crass posturing when waving currency notes at TV cameras. A string of politicians from Rahul Gandhi to the CPI(M)'s Brinda Karat and Hyderabad MP Asaduddin Owaisi made their way to Bisada to condole with the victim's family.

The local BJP MP, Dr Mahesh Sharma, the culture and tourism minister in the Modi government, also queued up at the village, only to play a rather disconcerting role. Although he promised the law would be upheld, instead of outrightly condemning the lynching as the savage crime that it was, he described it as an 'accident'. 'Momentary hai,' said the minister. 'Gaay ke maas par hum logon ka ... Andar se atma hilne lagti hai [When it comes to beef ... our soul starts shaking]. You can kill other animals, people don't react ... We have linked the cow with our mother.' Here was a government minister, sworn to uphold the civil liberties focused Constitution of India, almost rationalizing the bloody violence that had been unleashed in the name of religious sentiments. Not surprisingly, Sharma, who runs a chain of hospitals in the area, came a year later for the funeral of one of the accused who had died in jail. The villagers had draped the coffin with the Indian flag, seeking apparently to ascribe a sense of 'heroism', however false and unwarranted, on someone who had been jailed for murder. Their claim was that the accused was now a 'martyr' to the cause of upholding 'Hindu values'. When some of us journalists buttonholed the minister in Parliament's corridors and asked for an explanation, his answer stunned us. 'You see, yeh maamla logon ke sentiments se juda hua hai' (This matter is connected with people's sentiments), he said. The implication was ominous: as long as they were linked to the majority community's religious identity, crimes like lynching in the name of 'Hindu sentiments' would be ignored by high officials in the Modi government.

Sharma's effete and intentionally vague responses emanated from the tangled web of local politics; but what of Prime Minister Modi who had called for a ten-year moratorium on caste and communal violence in his first Independence Day speech in August 2014? Would he not condemn this heinous attack? Modi finally broke his silence eight long days after the Dadri lynching, that too a day after the then president, Pranab Mukherjee, had expressed his anguish. Making an oblique reference to the incident, Modi said at a rally in Bihar's Nawada, 'I have said this earlier too, Hindus should decide whether to fight Muslims or poverty, Muslims have to decide whether to fight Hindus or poverty. The country has to stay united, only communal harmony and brotherhood will take the nation forward ...' Couched in banal generalities, the remark was far from outright condemnation and revealed a calculating political mind that wasn't willing to directly confront militant Hinduism. When questioned on the prime minister's prolonged silence during one of the many raucous prime-time debates that followed Akhlaq's death, the BJP's TV face Dr Sambit Patra hit back with unbridled aggression: 'Why should the prime minister be expected to speak out every time? Isn't law and order a state subject, why don't you question the minority appeasing Akhilesh government in UP instead of being obsessed with Mr Modi?'

The prime minister's failure to respond effectively to the Dadri lynching was challenged not so much by his political opposition but by a group of public intellectuals – writers, artists, activists – who expressed their horror and anger at what they saw as 'rising communal intolerance' in the country. When author Nayantara Sahgal, a niece of Jawaharlal Nehru's, led a spirited campaign to return government-sponsored literary awards, she and other artists were immediately labelled the 'award wapsi' gang. G.V.L. Narasimha Rao, another of the BJP's prominent tele-hawks, became apoplectic on camera, accusing the group of 'conspiring' against the Modi government. 'Why do these people only speak up now? Where were they when Sikhs were killed in 1984, or when Kashmiri Pandits were driven out of the Valley in 1990?' he fumed. I had to remind Rao politely that Ms Sahgal, a lifelong civil liberties campaigner, had indeed spoken out on various other issues in the past too, be it the Emergency imposed by her cousin Indira Gandhi, or indeed, the grisly 1984 anti-Sikh riots.

The truth is, Akhlaq's death was not an isolated incident. Although the National Crime Research Bureau does not track lynchings or hate crimes separately, Hate Crime Watch, a database maintained by the portal Factchecker.in, recorded 296 hate crimes motivated by religious bias in the decade since 2009, which resulted in 100 deaths and left 737 people injured. Muslims, 14 per cent of the population, were victims in 59 per cent of the cases, and Hindus, nearly 80 per cent of the population, were victims in 14 per cent of the cases. UP, especially the communally fraught western region, witnessed the most such crimes. Of the 296 hate crimes, 30 per cent were under the pretext of cow protection, Muslims and Dalits being the primary victims. The data journalism site IndiaSpend claimed that as many as 97 per cent of the post-2010 bovine-related attacks were reported after 2014 when the Modi government took over and that more than half the attacks were based on rumours. In many cases, the attackers were mobs or groups linked to the VHP, Bajrang Dal and local gau-rakshak samitis. What was just as troubling was the manner in which so many of the lynchings were brazenly videographed by the attackers as proud moments of religious triumphalism. As human rights activist Harsh Mander wrote in a powerful op-ed in *The Hindu*, 'The message that such performative lynching communicates is stark and unambiguous. That if you are of a targeted community, you are no longer safe. In no place, and at no time. You can be attacked in your home: a mob can enter it and check what meat is cooking and bludgeon you to death claiming that it is cow meat. For being visibly Muslim you can be lynched on a train, while walking down the road, at your workplace or a park. This fear, assiduously encouraged by the ruling establishment, is the most shameful marker of these five years.'

Mander is one of the most vocal critics of the Modi government, and has inevitably been accused by the BJP of a partisan intervention. But on the ground it is clear that his words are chillingly accurate: rising hate speech by politicians has taken a terrible toll on the daily lives of citizens, caused inordinate suffering and had disastrous implications on local community relations. I had travelled to Bisada in 2015, soon after Akhlaq was killed, in a crowd of TV crews from Delhi, but we were all denied entry into the village by an angry mob. 'Aap TV wale hamare gaon ko badnaam kar rahe hain' (You TV people have defamed our village), one of the mob leaders told me then.

Four years later, in July 2019, I returned to Bisada, quietly and in a far less surcharged atmosphere. Through the village's narrow winding lanes, littered with dung and smelling of ordure, I came to Akhlaq's doomed home, now abandoned and sealed by the police. His family left Bisada long ago; his widow and children have now moved in with Sartaj to an IAF colony in Delhi. Bisada has a population of nearly 20,000, with thirty to forty Muslim homes. Near the local village mosque, I met Imran (name changed on request), a thin, middle-aged bearded man. His family has lived in Bisada for generations, his son works as a labourer in the cement factory in Dadri. I asked him how life had changed after Akhlaq's murder. 'Galat hua, sir, lekin zyada sochne se koi phayda nahin. Hamein kisi se koi jhagda nahin karna' (It was wrong, but best not to think too much about it. We don't want to fight with anyone), he said in hushed tones. There was, I sensed, an air of karmic resignation, an acutely distressing realization of his minority status in the village.

At a gaushala on the main village road, amidst a large herd of cows and buffaloes, I met Sanjay Rana, a fifty-year-old sturdy-looking farmer with a pot belly and thick neck. Rana was Akhlaq's neighbour and his twenty-three-year-old son Vishal had been arrested in 2015 in the lynching case. Vishal was now out on bail, like all the other accused, and the trial was yet to begin. 'Yeh sab police ki saazish hai, galat logon ko pakda unhone' (This is a police conspiracy, the wrong people were arrested), he bristled. Rana, dressed in a bright saffron kurta, insisted that he was not a BJP leader although he admitted to having paid ₹5 to become a party member more than a decade ago. An affluent landowning Thakur, he claimed to have regularly donated money for marriages and religious festivities in the village. 'I had given cash to Akhlaq too for Eid. All this Hindu–Muslim enmity is only created by the media,' he insisted.

Why was Akhlaq killed then, I asked. 'Dekhiye, jab koi kriya hoti hai, toh uski pratikriya bhi toh hogi. Akhlaq ne hamari gau mata ki hatya karke apradh kiya, uska response toh swabhavik hai.' (When there is an action, there will be a reaction. Akhlaq committed the crime of killing a cow, there was bound to be a response), he argued. I reminded him that conflicting UP government and forensic reports had not conclusively proven that the meat was beef. Rana was unmoved. 'Gau maas hi tha' (It was definitely beef), he asserted. 'So are you telling me the life of a cow matters more than that of a human being?' I pointedly asked. Rana stared at me unblinkingly with his bright bigoted eyes. 'Yeh aap patrakar log nahin samjhoge!' (You journalists will not understand this!)

By now, a small group of people had gathered and begun to mill around, including the village pradhan (chief), also a Thakur. Pepsi was served all around in small plastic cups. I pressed on, determined to understand how cow politics worked here on ground zero of hate crimes. 'So tell me, who did you vote for in the Lok Sabha elections,' I asked. 'Hamare gaon mein sabhi ne BJP ko vote diya' (In our village, everyone voted for BJP), was the prompt reply. Why, I asked. 'Dekhiye, hamein koi Mahesh Sharma se lagaav nahin. Hamne vote Modiji aur Yogiji ke naam pe diya. Modiji deshbhakt hain aur Yogiji toh devta hain. Wohi ek neta hain jo jaante hain ki Hindu dharm mein gaay ka kya mahatva hai, kitni shraddha hai' (Look, we have no great attraction for Mahesh Sharma, the local MP. We voted for Modiji and Yogiji. Modiji is a patriot and Yogiji is the one politician who realizes the importance and devotion for the cow in Hindu religion), was Rana's emphatic answer. I later remembered that Adityanath had come to Bisada to launch the BJP's 2019 election campaign in the Greater Noida area where lynching accused Vishal Rana was spotted cheering from the front row, a symbolic juxtaposition that appeared designed to send out an unmistakable message of the Yogi government's political solidarity with the gau-rakshak Hindu militias.

What do you think then of the Rahul Gandhis, Mayawatis and Akhileshs, I asked as a parting shot. 'Bhaisaab, woh sab Muslim premi aur Hindu virodhi hain' (They are pro-Muslim and anti-Hindu), said

Rana angrily. And then, he landed a final punch: 'Bahut ho gaya yeh Musalmanon ka prem, yeh sab cow smuggling karte hain, hamein apne samaj ko bachana hai!' (Enough of this love for Muslims, they are all cow smugglers. We have to save our society!) A menacing, almost crazed look had come into the faces around me, perhaps not too dissimilar from the faces that must have confronted Akhlaq just before he had his life beaten out of him. This time, mercifully, there were no lathis; only words coming at me with the force of blows.

In the run-up to the 2019 elections, I would hear similarly belligerent voices on social media and in daily conversation, often in the most unlikely places, including, at times, elite middle-class homes. The Nehruvian idea of a plural, multi-faith India was under assault as never before, Muslims and minorities were routinely demonized and the political vocabulary of hate 'normalized'. Could an ideologically spineless and organizationally weakened Congress with an untested and uninspiring leadership rise up to the challenge of political Hindutva? The answer was blowing in the suffocatingly hot winds scorching through the Hindi heartland and beyond.

FIVE

An Enigma Called Rahul Gandhi

IN July 2017, Manish Tiwari, the suave Congress leader who likes to wear the hat of a policy wonk, hosted a lunch in the leafy colonial-era surroundings of Delhi's genteel Gymkhana Club in honour of a visiting foreign delegation from an American think tank. Among the gathered talking heads, politicians, journalists and sundry other big noises of Delhi, was one rather important guest who arrived a little late: a kurta-clad, rather sheepishly smiling Rahul Gandhi. No sooner had he entered than journalists made a beeline for the then Congress vice president to fire questions and draw him into an all-too-rare candid conversation.

Speculation had been swirling for months about the Gandhi family scion taking over as Congress president and the natural question on every news-hungry journalist's mind was when he would actually take the plunge. As obsequious politicians clustered around to ingratiate themselves with Rahul, the young leader didn't seem too bothered by the media scrutiny, holding forth expansively on his political beliefs instead.

Yet as the chatter progressed and journalists badgered him about his plans, Rahul Gandhi became impatient. 'Why don't you all tell me,' he demanded angrily, 'where Narendra Modi was at my age and what he was doing in his forties?'

When I chose to raise the tricky question of his elevation to presidentship, Rahul became visibly discomfited. 'You media fellows need to get your spine back and ask the right questions of the Modi government. The Congress party will handle itself just fine!' he shot back.

Even as liveried waiters bustled around serving delicious chicken tikka and fish fingers, Rahul had provided us some food for thought. Where indeed was Modi at forty-seven, the age of the Congress heir apparent at the time?

In 1997, the forty-seven-year-old Modi was a BJP general secretary, handling states like Haryana, Himachal Pradesh and J&K. He wasn't in the Gujarat chief ministerial race, much less a potential prime minister of the future. The subtext of Rahul's message to us was clear that day: he wasn't a man in a hurry, he had age on his side, was willing to bide his time and wait for the Modi government to slip.

When I shared my experience with a senior Congress leader, he didn't seem surprised at all. 'Look, you must understand, Rahul is not your normal politician. For him, politics must be seen with a long-term view, not only in terms of the next election,' he said. Yet Rahul's was the romanticized world view of a political dreamer. Several members of the grand old party were increasingly exasperated, wondering whether Gandhi was truly cut out for competitive 24x7 politics. As a Congress veteran tells me, 'Rahul needs to realize that Modi isn't Morarji Desai who will just bend and keel over. If you keep playing the waiting game, the party will soon be over!' The Congress party is defined by access to power and having lost a series of elections after the 2014 debacle, party leaders were beginning to wonder, albeit in private, if their leader possessed the ability to challenge Modi's dominant persona. The 2014 Lok Sabha defeat was a bitter pill to swallow. Rahul was reportedly furious at being made the fall guy for the Congress's worst ever performance. At a Congress Working Committee (CWC) meeting held at the party's 24 Akbar Road headquarters to review the disastrous showing, no leaders were willing to put up their hand and accept responsibility for the loss. Instead, their gaze would invariably turn to Rahul every time a question was posed on where the strategy had misfired. Coming out of the meeting, a livid Rahul told a friend: 'Why the hell should I be responsible for a mandate against a UPA government which I wasn't even a part of?' For Rahul, it was the 'old guard' around his mother, Congress president Sonia Gandhi, which ought to be held accountable. They, after all, controlled the levers of power while he had chosen to focus on working with youth organizations like the Youth Congress and the NSUI. He saw himself as the angry young change-maker, up against an entrenched coterie which was preventing him from galvanizing the Congress.

Annoyed with his comatose party and with his mother for not defending him more vigorously at the CWC meeting, Rahul took off for his annual midsummer vacation abroad. When, in June 2014, soon after the poll defeat, the idea was mooted of him taking over as the Congress party leader in the Lok Sabha, a bad-tempered Rahul rejected the offer. 'Sorry, I am not interested in any position in Parliament,' was his curt response. The Congress would eventually nominate old Karnataka warhorse and prominent Dalit face Mallikarjun Kharge as its Lok Sabha leader. In any case, with just forty-four seats, the Congress could not stake claim to the post of leader of the opposition. Not for the first time in a political career that had begun in 2004 had Gandhi chosen not to take up a position of responsibility even though many in his generation like Sachin Pilot and Jyotiraditya Scindia had already served as ministers. (Rahul would remain a peripheral figure in Parliament in the sixteenth Lok Sabha, participating in just twelve debates, not asking a single question-hour question, and registering only 51 per cent attendance.)

The silent tug-of-war between Rahul and the old guard around Sonia continued for almost two years between 2014 and 2016, leaving the party rudderless and struggling to halt the electoral march of the BJP in state election after election.

An early victim of the war within the party was ambitious Assam leader Himanta Biswa Sarma. The Congress's defeat in the Lok Sabha elections of 2014 opened a window of opportunity for Sarma to challenge the veteran three-term chief minister Tarun Gogoi, then eighty years old. Sarma was in his mid-forties, an energetic, locally influential doer, who also ran a successful TV news network in Assam. 'You have to effect a generation change in the Congress if you want to win the next election in Assam,' Sarma bluntly told Sonia Gandhi and her political secretary, Ahmed Patel. The party leadership agreed to send Kharge as an observer to Guwahati to verify Sarma's claim that he enjoyed the support of a majority of the MLAs. Kharge's report confirmed that Sarma was backed by fifty-two of the seventy-eight MLAs. 'I was assured by Soniaji and Ahmed Patel that it was only a matter of time before I was made chief minister,' claims Sarma.

Yet, when Rahul returned to India after his midsummer break in July 2014, he immediately red-flagged Sarma's elevation. 'No way, I will not accept the removal of Mr Gogoi in this manner,' was his explicit message. Unwilling to confront Rahul, the Congress high command decided to put the Assam leadership issue on hold. Left out in the cold, Sarma resigned as minister in the Gogoi cabinet to step up the pressure on the party high command. 'I was angry and felt betrayed but didn't want to leave a party I had been part of since 1993,' he declares. Sarma had other issues to deal with too at the time: his name had cropped up in the multi-crore Saradha chit fund scam.

After being granted a respite by the courts, in early 2015, Sarma decided to try his luck again, shuttling between Delhi and Guwahati to convince the party leadership that he was their man for the top job in Assam. In every meeting, despite support for Sarma from senior leaders like Patel and Ghulam Nabi Azad, Rahul would veto any change of guard. A final meeting was held at Rahul's Tughlaq Road residence in March 2015 with Gogoi, Sarma and Assam Congress president Anjan Dutta in attendance. Sarma claims that five minutes into the conversation, Rahul seemed to lose interest. 'Look, you can do what you want, I am not concerned, please deal with C.P. Joshi [the Congress general secretary in charge of Assam], he will solve all your issues. Don't come to me again,' he burst out angrily. Political leaders setting out to rebuild their party do not, generally, have the luxury of tantrums, yet Rahul the entitled heir often came in the way of Rahul the politician.

Sarma's story then takes another bizarre twist: he insists that Rahul then began to play with his pet dog, Pidi, a cute black-and-white puppy, and feeding him biscuits from the plate on the table. 'Just imagine,' says Sarma heatedly, 'we were being asked to share biscuits from the same plate that Rahul was feeding his dog. What could be more humiliating?' A Rahul aide tells me that Sarma deliberately 'planted' the Pidi story to make his planned exit from the Congress look like principled indignation. 'He was already negotiating with the BJP so where is the question of Rahul "humiliating" him. We had even agreed to accommodate six of his people in the ministry and asked him to bide his time before being made chief minister but he was a man in a hurry,' is the counterargument.

Either way, the Pidi story went viral and Sarma was through with the Congress. When he sought an appointment with Sonia Gandhi a few days later, he was asked to come through the back gate of 10 Janpath. 'I had been meeting Soniaji for years, this is the first time ever that I was asked not to come through the front door. When I asked Madam why, she told me, "You also are a father and a parent, Himanta. You understand that as a mother, I can't go against the wishes of my son, don't you?" I knew that day that my time was up in the Congress,' says Sarma. The matriarch's 'helplessness' against her son and heir is an oft-repeated tale in Delhi's power circles. Sonia Gandhi may be the longest-serving Congress president who has led the party to two electoral successes, yet reportedly tries to never cross her chosen successor. In August 2015, Sarma finally joined the BJP. He admits to having been in talks with Ram Madhav, BJP general secretary for Assam at the time, for several months before a final meeting with BJP president Amit Shah clinched the deal. When Gandhi was told that Sarma was switching sides, he reportedly frantically tried to contact him. After several missed calls, when the two finally spoke, Sarma kept the conversation brief: 'Sorry Rahulji, I have already committed to Amit Shahji. It is too late now.' Less than a year later, Sarma would play a major role in the BJP winning an absolute majority for the first time in Assam, ending fifteen years of uninterrupted Congress rule. He would also go on to become a key player in the BJP's North-east push, helping to cement ties with regional parties. 'At the end of the day, what happens, happens for the best. I guess Rahul just didn't like my face for some reason. I am very grateful to him because had he not behaved in the way he did, maybe I would still be in the Congress and would have lost the opportunity to serve the BJP and the people of Assam,' says Sarma with a mischievous smile. Where the BJP leadership immediately spotted political talent, the Congress high command turned its back on it, or recognized it too late.

While it can be argued that Sarma's exit from the Congress may not entirely have been due to Rahul's intransigent attitude, yet the manner in which the episode played out does reflect poorly on the Congress leader's political judgement. Here was a relatively young, go-getter politician with the kind of drive and determination the Congress so desperately needed to make a comeback after the 2014 fiasco – 'A real political animal,' is how former Madhya Pradesh chief minister Digvijaya Singh describes Sarma – and yet the party did little to retain him. Perhaps it was his reputation for being a slightly grubby leader who cut corners to get ahead that was his undoing, or maybe it was, as Sarma claims, his equations with the older generation of Congress leaders that got him tangled in an internal power struggle. Either way, contemporary politics is not a morality play and Rahul Gandhi's fierce likes and dislikes proved counterproductive in a political milieu where personal adjustment, deft compromise and, let's face it, a willingness to get one's hands a little dirty, are often necessary ingredients for success.

Nor is Sarma's an isolated case. In Goa, the Congress's failure to strike a 'deal' with Vijai Sardesai's Goa Forward party in the 2017 assembly elections probably cost them power in the coastal state. Like Sarma, Sardesai too was an ambitious young politician who had previously been Youth Congress president in Goa. In 2012, he quit the party when he was denied a ticket. He then contested as an independent and was elected to the state assembly. Appealing to Goan pride, he formed his own Goa

Forward party ahead of the 2017 elections. When he approached the Congress for an alliance, Digvijaya Singh, then Congress general secretary for Goa, indicated he was open to the tie-up and asked Sardesai to come to Delhi for a final stamp of approval from Rahul Gandhi. 'I waited in Delhi for a week but Rahul refused to meet me. It was clear that he didn't want an alliance with us for whatever reason,' claims Sardesai. Digvijaya Singh, though, assured Sardesai that the Congress would not put up a candidate against him. Yet, just hours before the nomination process was to end, a Congress candidate was chosen to fight him. 'How can one trust such a party which says one thing and does something quite different?' argues Sardesai.

The pushy, determined politician would soon have his 'revenge'. When the Goa results were declared, the Congress had won seventeen seats in the forty-member Goa assembly and emerged as the single largest party; they were within striking distance of a majority. It was, however, the Goa Forward party, with its three seats, which would be the king-maker. On the night of the results, I rang up Sardesai (a distant relative) to congratulate him and, more crucially, find out what his next move would be. Sardesai was with Digvijaya Singh in a Panaji hotel, negotiating a 'deal' to form the government. 'It is all more or less agreed upon, we will give Vijai whatever ministry he wants,' Digvijaya told me during the same phone conversation. But Sardesai wanted to know who would be the Congress's chief-ministerial choice. 'When I spoke to Rahul past midnight, he told me that the chief minister will be the choice of the party legislators and refused to make any commitment,' claims Sardesai. The next morning, when Digvijaya Singh tried to contact Sardesai, his phone was switched off. A few hours later, the Goa Forward leader announced an alliance with the BJP and marched to the governor's house with then defence minister Manohar Parikkar to lay claim to form a government. A ponderous and slow-moving leadership cost the Congress the Goa government at the last minute.

'Your relative has betrayed us,' lamented Digvijaya Singh. I listened quietly, determined not to get entangled in a messy power game. There were reports of how BJP union minister Nitin Gadkari had flown in, on a private charter late at night, and clinched the deal, as well as allegations of financial dealings. 'No money changed hands. I switched to the BJP because I trusted Parikkar and had no faith in Rahul to give me a fair deal,' counters Sardesai.

Yet it is perhaps unfair to pin the blame for the Congress's failures in Goa and Assam on Rahul alone. He had, after all, relied on his two general secretaries, Digvijaya Singh and C.P. Joshi, and they had failed to deliver. But both episodes also raised questions over Rahul's political intuition, or rather the lack of it. 'The problem is Rahul doesn't think like a politician, he doesn't have the political instincts to tackle a crisis situation nor does he have experienced political hands around to guide him. In fact, he has a certain contempt for the old-style political operators who know how to "manage" the system,' says Rasheed Kidwai, senior journalist and long-time Congress-watcher. Kidwai, author of a biography of Sonia Gandhi, draws an interesting contrast between the styles of functioning of mother and son. 'Sonia knew her political limitations and used people like Ahmed Patel, Ghulam Nabi who were more practiced, rooted "desi" politicians to resolve tricky situations. Rahul prefers to have white-collar, anglicized people around him with little or no political experience. You can't run a party like the Congress by relying only on people from a similar social background,' points out Kidwai.

Indeed, a roll call of Rahul's inner circle confirms Kidwai's point. Almost all his close advisers conform to a stereotype of well-born, English-speaking, well-educated (in several instances with foreign degrees), ideologically sharply left young men with strong NGO affiliations, but lacking the political bandwidth that comes only after years in the field. Rahul's personal aide, the affable Kaushal Vidyarthee, for instance, is a studious young man with a doctorate in social policy from Oxford where he wrote his thesis on incorporating Dalits into the Indian business economy. Another personal assistant, Alankar Sawai, who left a private bank to join the back-room team, is also deeply influenced by Dalit–Bahujan politics. Sandeep Singh, a former JNU student, was Rahul's Hindi speech-writer: he was part of the All India Students Association (AISA), the student wing of the far-left Communist Party of India (Marxist–Leninist), and had once reportedly waved black flags at Dr Manmohan Singh during a student rally (Sandeep now works as part of Priyanka Gandhi Vadra's team). The soft-spoken and slender Kanishka Singh, who has been with Rahul for more than a decade, quit his job with a New York-based merchant bank to assist the Congress leader on a variety of issues, from finance to legal matters to overseas visits. Singh's father, S.K. Singh, was a former foreign secretary with strong ties to the Gandhi family. Another investment banker to join Rahul's core team was the Wharton-educated Praveen Chakravarty, who would play a key role in election planning as head of the Congress's data analytics team. Nikhil Alva, son of veteran Congress leader Margaret Alva, would lead Rahul's media outreach: Nikhil had been a successful TV producer and was also a class senior of Rahul's at St. Stephen's College. K.B. Byju, a former SPG officer, handled Rahul's security detail and tour programmes while K. Raju, a Telangana IAS officer who quit the service to head the Congress's scheduled caste cell, was his chief of staff.

'Tell me now, where is the Ahmed Patel–Ghulam Nabi-like politically shrewd back-room manager in this group whom Rahul can turn to for expert advice?' asks Kidwai.

Rahul, though, seemed comfortable with his chosen ideological fellow-travellers even if they had limited political experience. For example, Sachin Rao, a graduate in corporate strategy from a University of Michigan business school, was picked up by Rahul to assist him in training members of the Youth Congress and NSUI. Upon his return in 2005, Rao went on a journey of self-discovery through rural India and slum areas that led him to quit his corporate lifestyle and work instead in the 'poverty and development' space. Spotted first by Congress leader Jairam Ramesh, Rao was soon drafted into Rahul's youth-centric think tank and in February 2019 was appointed secretary in charge of training. 'Rahul's brief to me was clear from day one. He wanted to open up new spaces in politics for the young by making the organization more inclusive and decentralized,' says Rao, who now runs a four-day monthly session in Gandhian values for party workers at Sevagram Ashram in Wardha, a measure of his unswerving commitment to the pursuit of value-based politics.

But how would this ideals-driven, NGO-style team fit into a political milieu where politics has ceased to become a battle of ideas, and where rank careerism has replaced perfectionistic politics? 'Rahul wants to change the Congress culture, make it more pro-people rather than just lusting for power,' says Girish Chodankar, who worked closely with Rao to restructure the party's student wing, NSUI. Chodankar, who would later become state Congress president for Goa, claims that the aim of 'Team Rahul' was to truly 'reform' the party by encouraging fresh talent. 'We even organized, for the first time, direct elections to all youth organization posts by setting up our very own election commission. Rahul wanted to "democratize" the party which was not liked by those within the Congress who feared losing their powers,' he tells me. Whether it was an ideological or generational clash, the Congress was clearly struggling to come to terms with what one senior leader describes as 'Rahul's fantasy life in a bubble'. Gandhi's earnest yet bookish moves did not win too much enthusiastic party support, particularly as his own vote-drawing abilities remained under a cloud.

Perhaps Rahul Gandhi's long-term 'vision' for the Congress would have been more acceptable to the rest of the party if it had delivered real electoral success on the ground. The fact is, the Congress was hurtling from one defeat to another while the list of political miscalculations only grew. In 2016, for example, the party tied up with the Left Front in Bengal to take on former Congresswoman and chief minister Mamata Banerjee. The Congress–Left Front alliance was routed as the TMC swept the polls. On the day of the results, the TMC chief was scathing in her indictment of Rahul Gandhi's politics. 'He is a kid who is the biggest USP for Narendra Modi!' she thundered. Once a staunch Rajiv Gandhi loyalist, Mamata reportedly pronounced in private: 'The boy has no future.'

A member of Team Rahul later justified the tie-up with the left in Bengal as a consequence of the Congress leader's unshakeable belief that the Indian left was morally superior to other political parties in the fight against communal forces. Rahul felt a 'comradeship' with the likes of CPI(M) general secretary Sitaram Yechury that he didn't even with his own party persons. This might partly explain Rahul's decision in February 2016 to suddenly come out in vocal support of Kanhaiya Kumar, JNU students' union leader, who was charged with sedition and arrested by the Delhi police after a video surfaced of some people in JNU chanting anti-India and pro-Kashmir 'azaadi' slogans. The CPI student wing leader claimed that he was being framed by the rival BJP-backed ABVP and alleged that the videos were doctored. Almost overnight, the charismatic Kanhaiya with his pungent oratory became a poster boy for the anti-Modi forces. Rahul too joined the chorus, even choosing to attend a solidarity meeting at the JNU campus. It was possibly an instinctive decision, one that was driven by his growing ideological affinity to the left. But it also gave the BJP another opportunity to question Rahul's 'Indianness' with Kanhaiya and his supporters being branded as 'anti-nationals'. 'A leader like Indira Gandhi would never be seen openly aligning with JNU student leaders in this manner. You may be attracted by someone's anti-establishment stand but remember, you are not in a college campus, you are leading a mainstream political party like the Congress which cannot afford to vacate the centrist, nationalist space,' a senior Congress leader remarks. Kanhaiya's core constituency was swayed by his spirited interrogation of Hindutva politics but the murky world of Indian electoral politics is far removed from the dreamy and theory-based idealism of a JNU campus. The air of undergraduate radicalism that hangs about Rahul, often seen in public unshaven and in blue jeans, prevents him from standing forth strongly as a pragmatic, centrist politician of gravitas.

Haryana is yet another glaring instance of the chasm that existed between Rahul's dream project of 'reforming' the Congress and ground reality. Just ahead of the 2014 elections, Gandhi appointed thirty-seven-year-old Ashok Tanwar as president of the state Congress in Haryana. One of Rahul's 'boys', Tanwar had been a Youth Congress and NSUI president but had no mass appeal in Haryana's Jat-dominated polity. The party's two-time chief minister Bhupinder Singh Hooda felt he was being sidelined and the faction fighting between the 'old' guard and the 'new' only intensified. 'Hooda did everything he could to finish the party; he runs his own parallel "Hooda Congress" in Haryana and refuses to accept anyone else as leader,' an angry Tanwar insists. So, why didn't Rahul step in to end the bitter feud, I asked Tanwar. 'You please ask him that. I think he tried his best, but it is not easy in a party like the Congress where there are many wheels within wheels,' is the exasperated response. (Tanwar would quit the Congress in October 2019 just ahead of the Haryana state elections.) In the Sonia-led Congress, the well-networked Hooda was a powerful state chieftain and a major fundraiser for the party. The wrangling has had its adverse fallout: in a state which the Congress ruled for a decade from 2004, not only has the party lost a string of local elections to the BJP but the party organization has also weakened. 'Do you know, we don't even have a single proper Congress district or block committee today in the state! How do you expect to fight the BJP?' a grumpy Hooda bemoans. In fact, a senior CWC member reveals that the party doesn't have proper functioning units or offices in nearly 250 districts across the country, a telling indictment of the rot and atrophy in the party organization.

The Congress's organizational crisis had been building up since the early 1990s so again it would be unfair to hold Rahul alone responsible for the party's predicament. But his complex, enigmatic persona was hardly helping matters. His friends insist that Rahul is a good listener, sincere and thoughtful, open to new ideas and genuinely keen to find solutions to vital issues like agrarian distress and job scarcity, not quite the 'Pappu' (idiot) his opponents have so deliberately and strategically made him out to be. But at public events, he appears easily distracted, often playing with his mobile or staring expressionlessly into the distance. 'Rahul is a genuine idealist who has lived a sheltered life. He preaches the right values of love and harmony, is committed to taking on the RSS's Hindu nationalism and defending the idea of a plural India but the reality is that politics today is driven by divisive issues like caste and religion which he can't quite fathom,' explains Kumar Ketkar, veteran journalist-turned-Congress MP.

A strange inaccessibility even while dealing with colleagues has been another concern. One former Congress chief minister claims that he had to wait for weeks for an appointment with Rahul. Another senior Congress leader from Maharashtra shares a story that perhaps exemplifies the problem of Rahul's disconnect with the relentless demands of running a political party. 'I tried to meet with Rahulji for five years to apprise him of the ground realities in the state and yet each time his office would promise to fix a meeting which would never materialize. Finally, I buttonholed Rahulji at a party function and asked him for his mobile number. He just smiled and redirected me to his office. People who were with the Youth Congress could access him easily and those of us who have spent a lifetime in the party were cast aside. It's a crazy way for a party to function,' argues the senior leader. Team Rahul, however, dismisses the inaccessibility charge: 'Surely, you don't expect Rahul to give his personal mobile number to every party functionary. Does Modi do it?'

But nothing was quite as bizarre as Rahul's decision to suddenly take off in the midst of a hectic budget session in February 2015 just a week after the Congress had been wiped out in the Delhi assembly elections. Without informing even senior party leaders, Rahul flew off on a two-month 'sabbatical' to four South East Asian countries – Myanmar, Cambodia, Vietnam, Thailand – for what a close friend describes as 'time to reflect and meditate'. Rahul spent three weeks in Myanmar attending a vipassana programme, apart from visiting Buddhist heritage centres in the other countries. With him was Sameer Sharma, son of former union minister Captain Satish Sharma who was a close family friend of the Gandhis and had been a core member of Rajiv Gandhi's coterie.

For the ruling BJP, the Congress leader's 'vacation' only provided more ammunition to target the Gandhi scion as a 'non-serious' politician. Even Congress MPs were at their wits' end to explain their leader's absence. 'When we need him to lead from the front, he goes missing in action,' was a familiar lament in Parliament. The backstory gleaned from multiple sources is that Rahul was angry with Sonia's reluctance to give him a free hand to ease out the older generation of leaders around her. In late 2014 Rahul had met dozens of party workers and leaders to prepare a blueprint for the Congress's revival. The proposals included virtually dismantling the party's omnipotent 'high command' culture and ensuring, for example, that ticket distribution at election time was not handled by Congress general secretaries but decided by conducting US-style 'primaries' where workers would have a say in their choice of candidates. A cautious Sonia didn't want to rock the boat. A petulant Rahul had an outburst and, acting on impulse, left town. Or so the story went within Congress circles. 'Rahul is a bit of a nihilist, he wants to reform the Congress by dismantling its structures, but he doesn't realize that in a grand old party, you have to be more patient in effecting change,' a senior Congress leader points out.

In the way she steers the Congress, Sonia Gandhi is ever the dutiful, self-denying bahu, a proxy of the Nehru–Gandhi ancestors, who hesitates to openly use or demonstrate her own power or personality. She's clear about her position: she's holding the seat for the bloodline she is honoured to represent, and demands respect for the family she herself has loyally served all her adult life. Preserving the old Congress, thus, is not just political strategy but also family duty, and Sonia Gandhi could never radically overturn what she must always protect. Rahul has no such compunctions and is eager to disrupt, but lacking his mother's stature or popularity, is unable to properly implement any of his plans on his own. His sudden unannounced holiday was part frustrated rebellion, part time off.

Sam Pitroda, the founding chairman of India's erstwhile Telecom Commission and a close friend of the Gandhi family, defends Rahul's decision to take an unexpected break. 'Look, all over the world, a politician has a private life, his own interests. Rahul is a kind, sensitive, very intelligent young man whom the BJP is unfairly and wrongly abusing as a "Pappu". If he wants to spend some time away from the noise, what's wrong with it?'

Rahul's desire for privacy may have been perfectly justified if he was not the 'face' of India's oldest national party, if he was not indeed being groomed to take over the legacy of a family that has given the country three prime ministers. In Indian politics, the lines between the personal and the political are blurred, there is no place to escape from the unending whirl of public engagements or, indeed go into a sulk when you don't get your way. By simply choosing to take off on a holiday with his buddies in the middle of a Parliament session, Rahul came off once again as an entitled dynast, soaked in privilege, someone who enjoyed great power without equal responsibility. He might have got away with this impetuous act if he was a leader who was delivering votes to the Congress. But he wasn't doing that either. When the party leader can't get votes, when the commander shies away from combat, the troops down the line fall into disarray. 'Only two things unite the Congress: the Gandhi family and the scent of power. Rahul has inherited the family name but he hasn't got us power,' remarks a CWC member ruefully.

With Modi and the BJP on a roll, Rahul seemed to be running out of both time and excuses. By mid-2017, it was apparent that the waiting game wasn't working either. Ironically, it would be in the janmabhoomi of Prime Minister Modi that Rahul would discover his political mojo.

Rajya Sabha elections in the country are comparatively tame affairs, devoid of the intense competition of a direct election. Gujarat, in particular, is a state where politics normally works through conciliation, a two-party state where the ideological fault lines between the BJP and Congress are not quite so sharply drawn. The August 2017 Rajya Sabha elections in Gujarat, though, were unique. Suddenly, a friendly fight was transformed into a fierce battle between Amit Shah and Ahmed Patel, two political heavyweights pitted against each other. The BJP president was convinced that Patel, loyal political secretary to Sonia Gandhi, was the brain behind the move to jail him in 2010 and force him out of Gujarat in the Sohrabuddin fake encounter case. 'Yeh Soniaji ke aadmiyon ki saazish hai' (This is a plot by Sonia Gandhi's people), he would reiterate. The Gujarat Rajya Sabha elections were Shah's opportunity to take revenge. Three seats in the upper house were at stake; the BJP was more or less guaranteed two (Shah, making his parliamentary debut, and Smriti Irani) but the third seat was up for grabs. The mild-mannered, amiable yet sharp-eyed Patel, the quintessential back-room manager, had been a permanent fixture in the upper house since 1991. Now he was facing a fight for political survival.

Just ahead of the polls, six Congress MLAs suddenly resigned, further reducing Congress numbers in the assembly. Senior Congress leader Shankarsinh Vaghela also indicated his willingness to switch sides with his supporters: Vaghela, a former state BJP president, was reportedly promised a governor's post. A day before the nominations were to be filed came an even bigger blow: Patel's right-hand man and chief whip of the Congress in the assembly, Balvantsinh Rajput filed his nomination as an independent candidate to take on his mentor. Rajput, who had started life as a tea seller before going on to manage a ₹250-crore edible oil business, was offered lucrative perks to defect. (He would later become chairman of the state-owned Gujarat Industrial Development Corporation.) Police officers were keeping tabs on the movements of Congress MLAs and calling up their relatives to intensify the pressure on them. Two NCP MLAs were also contacted and the party's central leadership was even allegedly offered ministerial berths in the Modi government for voting against Patel. 'Saam, daam, dand, bhed – the BJP was using the entire official machinery with a single-point agenda to defeat me,' claims Patel. The BJP under Amit Shah follows scorched-earth tactics and the take-no-prisoners style of politics. Every contest is a do-or-die battle, executed on a whatever-it-takes strategy designed to stun the enemy into inaction.

In desperation, the Congress moved forty-four of its MLAs to a resort near Bengaluru, owned by a relative of local Congress leader

D.K. Shivakumar. They would return to Gandhinagar the day before polling. Managing the campaign for Patel was senior Gujarat Congress leader Shaktisinh Gohil who was literally herding the legislators from one high-security zone to another. Gohil, an experienced hand, knew that this fight would go down to the wire. Sitting in the polling booth as Patel's agent, he was keeping a watchful eye on every vote being cast and had a Plan B in place in case things got really tough. It was a simple but clever plan: Gohil advised two Congress MLAs, who were planning to vote for the BJP, to show their vote to Shah who was also seated in the same room. The two gullible MLAs didn't realize this was a violation of the Rajya Sabha elections' secret ballot rules. As soon as the two rebel MLAs gormlessly displayed their ballots to Shah, Gohil sprang into action, insisting their votes be cancelled forthwith. This sparked off a major controversy. The BJP protested, taking the matter to the Election Commission (EC) in Delhi. Well past midnight the EC's decision was finally declared: the commission ruled in favour of the Congress and the two MLAs' votes were indeed annulled. Patel had won the election by just one vote! When the result was announced, Gohil screamed in delight and, turning to a crestfallen Shah, uttered an uncharacteristic expletive. 'Yes, I got a bit carried away,' he admits with a laugh.

For the Congress, the verdict brought relief and hope: not only had their long-serving Congress MP won, but, crucially, Shah's invincibility had been challenged in his home ground. Suddenly, the Congress had a spring in its step ahead of the December 2017 Gujarat assembly elections. A crack team led by Ashok Gehlot, former Rajasthan chief minister and a veteran organization man, was put in place to manage the elections. The team included retired police officers who were tasked with last-mile booth management, perhaps the first time the Congress 'outsourced' this crucial task to professionals. Many of these officers had been targeted under the Modi–Shah regime in the state and were ready for payback. The Congress even put an innovative social media plan in place under the direction of Rohan Gupta, a young Ahmedabad-based businessman who was heading the party's IT cell. 'We were actually ahead of the BJP in the social media game in Gujarat. Our "Vikas gaando thayo che" [Development has gone crazy] campaign catchline trended for days,' claims Gupta.

A bold move was made to expand the party's base by wooing young anti-Modi leaders, including the pugnacious Hardik Patel, the crafty Alpesh Thakor and firebrand Jignesh Mevani. United by a fierce anti-Modiism, all three were pushing for greater space for themselves in Gujarat's Hindutva-driven political laboratory. All three men belonged to influential caste groups: Thakor was an OBC leader who was fighting on the reservation plank; Mevani, a Dalit activist with a rebellious streak who had briefly been part of AAP before striking out on his own; and Patel, a local Patidar who was attracting huge crowds after spearheading a violent agitation in favour of reservation. Of the trio, Patel's political trajectory is perhaps the most fascinating. While interviewing him at his home in Ahmedabad, I was struck by the many portraits of Shiv Sena supremo Bal Thackeray, that adorned his walls. 'Yes, he is my hero. I admire his fighting spirit,' Hardik Patel told me. That a poster boy for the Congress was a fanboy of the anti-Congress stalwart Thackeray and revered his hero from the opposite side of the fence was another illustration of the many leaps and swings of Indian politics which never cease to amaze.

What was also startling was Rahul Gandhi's transformation. As I tracked him on the Gujarat campaign trail, it seemed for the first time that he was actually relishing the political combat, holding three to four meetings every day for almost a month. He even started visiting temples, including the much revered Somnath mandir which holds a salient place in the Hindutva political psychology. Here Rahul was attempting to take a leaf out of his grandmother Indira Gandhi's political playbook. The senior Mrs G stands accused of playing 'Hindu' politics long before the BJP, of starting the trend in Indian politics of using religious symbolism for political ends. The Somnath visit sparked off a controversy, with the BJP accusing Rahul of registering as a 'non-Hindu' in the temple diary. It was a fake story – no such entry existed – but it pushed the Congress to affirm Rahul's Hindu credentials with chief party spokesperson Randeep Singh Surjewala asserting, 'Not only is Rahul Gandhiji a Hindu, he is a janeu-dhari [thread-wearing Brahmin] Hindu.' I asked Surjewala later if the BJP campaign had forced the Congress on the defensive. 'Not at all, we were only demolishing a fake narrative that was being maliciously spread,' he maintains.

Temple-hopping would, in fact, become an essential part of Rahul's strategy in future state elections, a clear sign of the Congress finally realizing that it could not afford to vacate the 'political Hindu' space entirely to the BJP. Journalist-turned-MP Ketkar insists that Gandhi's temple visits were not prompted by electoral compulsions but his religious beliefs. 'Look, I have had a long conversation with him on religion and spirituality in which Rahul told me he was a Shiva bhakt who had undertaken a long trek to Kedarnath, and was reading extensively on ancient Hindu scriptures. So visiting temples was not a photo op but came naturally to him,' claims Ketkar.

Whether out of conviction or compulsion, the fact is Rahul was finally beginning to play the election game, even wholeheartedly embracing social media sites like Twitter and Facebook which he had previously, almost disdainfully, shunned. Aggressive and confrontational – there was a discernible air of confidence in his public speeches which had been missing till then. He even launched a stinging personal attack on BJP president Amit Shah over an investigative report in the news website The Wire that claimed that a company owned by Shah's son Jay had multiplied its revenues several times over since 2014. The no-holds-barred attack seemed to lift the Congress from its defensive mindset. 'Rahul removed the fear of Modi–Shah from the minds of the average Congress worker,' affirms Pawan Khera, the spirited Congress spokesperson. As Rahul raised pressing issues like job scarcity and falling incomes from agriculture, the audiences seemed to warm up to him. His Hindi had improved by leaps and bounds as had his ability to land the occasional punch with sharp, if slightly irreverent, one-liners, the most catchy of which was his renaming of the goods and services tax (GST) as the 'Gabbar Singh Tax'. 'He was challenging Modi at his own acronyms game,' enthuses Khera.

GST was one important reason why the Congress felt it had half a chance in Gujarat. In a state with a large and dominant business community, the sudden imposition of a nationwide indirect tax with multiple slabs was viewed with mounting scepticism, even anger. Ensuring tax compliance has been a challenge for every government, a reflection of a commercial ethos which has thrived on tax avoidance. Much like demonetization, GST was a politically risky decision with an uncertain economic fallout, but one which the Modi-led government was determined to enforce. Hasmukh Adhia, the then union revenue secretary and another trusted Gujarat cadre officer in Team Modi, reveals that several high-ranking BJP leaders were against any tax introduction before the state elections. The self-effacing bureaucrat who was entrusted with planning the GST roll-out says that it was Modi and finance minister Jaitley who held firm in the face of numerous objections. 'Without their support it would have been impossible to have GST in place so quickly. They were behind us all the way,' he avers. Disruptive, risk-taking decisions, it seems, are built into the Modi government's DNA.

Modi introduced the tax in June 2017, just months ahead of the Gujarat elections, with typical fanfare. At a special midnight session of Parliament, Modi enthusiastically projected the arrival of the GST as his own 'Tryst with Destiny' moment. Only he wasn't invoking Nehru but another son of Gujarat: 'GST marks the economic integration of India just like what Sardar Patel did decades back by unifying our princely states,' he thundered with a rhetorical flourish. His diehard critic Arun Shourie remarked in a TV interview: 'To announce a *tax* with such fanfare in Parliament is just vulgar.'

Far away from Modi's rhetoric, the mood was very different in the land of Sardar. Already struggling with the fallout of demonetization, GST's complex tax structure was seen as another blow to many small businesses in the informal sector. In the mercantile town of Surat, for example, traders went on an indefinite strike, storming the city's main textile market with black flags. In other parts of the state too, there were visible signs of fury, with many shops downing their shutters in protest against the forcible imposition of GST. 'This Modi government thinks we are tax chors, we will also teach them a lesson,' was a common complaint. Drought-hit Saurashtra echoed with the cries of cotton farmers on the warpath. After having ruled Gujarat for more than two decades, anti-incumbency pushed the BJP on the back foot for the first time. As Shah would later confess to a senior journalist, 'Of all the elections I have fought in Gujarat, this 2017 election was the toughest.'

Yet the BJP in Gujarat is an extremely well-established force with spanking party offices embedded in towns and districts across the state. Shah had the advantage of having built a much stronger organization than the Congress in Gujarat. Huge numbers of locally connected Sangh Parivar cadres stood at the ready as Shah's tried-and-tested ground force. 'We just made sure that we mobilized many more feet on the ground in the crucial close contest seats, Congress created a "hawa" but they didn't have the ground network to build on it,' says Gujarat BJP spokesperson Bharat Pandya. When it came down to the final stretch, the BJP pulled out two other familiar weapons: the entrenched Hindu–Muslim divide and Modi's larger-than-life persona. For example, just weeks ahead of polling, posters appeared mysteriously in towns like Surat claiming that Ahmed Patel would be chief minister if Congress won the elections. Taking the cue, Modi warned voters at a public meeting that a Pakistani military officer had appealed for Patel to be made the chief minister. It was an all too recognizable game plan, one which had echoes of the strikingly communal 2002 campaign when Patel was constantly referred to as Mian Ahmedbhai. 'Look, whenever the BJP is in trouble in Gujarat, they unfailingly play the Pakistan–Muslim card in desperation,' says Congress spokesperson Rohan Gupta. At a rally in Mehsana, Modi made another stunning claim. Virtually accusing former prime minister Manmohan Singh of complicity with Pakistan, he wondered aloud why Singh had attended a dinner party with Pakistani guests at the home of senior Congress leader Mani Shankar Aiyar. A prime minister accusing his predecessor of possible treason was low even by the tawdry standards of political discourse in India. But it worked with the crowd. Open prejudice and stoking of belligerent religious and nationalist impulses were cunningly and effectively deployed by a cornered BJP leadership, calculated to raise passions among the highly Islamophobic Gujarat voter.

This wasn't the only occasion when Modi artfully shifted the narrative in Gujarat to his advantage. The garrulous and sharp-tongued Aiyar came in his line of fire once again when he called Modi a 'neech kisam ka aadmi' (small-minded person) in the midst of a heated campaign. Aiyar was responding to Modi's criticism that the Congress had betrayed Dr Bhimrao Ambedkar, and Rahul Gandhi was too busy chasing 'Baba Bholenath' in temples to worry about Babasaheb. Aiyar, whose 'chaiwallah' reference was cleverly used by Modi ahead of the 2014 elections to create emotional capital about his humble origins, was now accused of hurling a casteist slur. The phrase 'neech kisam ka aadmi' was wickedly twisted to 'neech jaati' (low caste) – and the prime minister declared that the Congress was against the poor and backward classes in the country. Modi as 'victim of elitist disdain' or the 'poor outsider at the mercy of abuse from the privileged class': these are themes the prime minister has perfected over time. Worried about the political fallout, the Congress immediately suspended Aiyar from the party without even seeking an explanation from him. It seemed a rather hasty step to take against an old family loyalist but it was one designed to stave off further political embarrassment. Unlike his mother, Rahul didn't have any particular affection for the old Rajiv Gandhi–era stalwart. The manner in which Aiyar was suspended was cold and ruthless. Despite repeated attempts by Aiyar to meet him, Rahul did not oblige even once. 'I am bewildered by the party leadership's attitude towards me. I often ask my colleagues in the party, at least let me know, am I an ass, or an asset!' says Aiyar with characteristic pungent sarcasm. (His suspension was revoked nine months later in August 2018, on the eve of Rajiv Gandhi's birth anniversary.)

Modi had one final card to play on the last day of the Gujarat campaign. I remember being woken up late at night – I was in Ahmedabad that day – by a BJP spokesperson who excitedly told me, 'Kaale Sabarmati riverbank zaroor aao jo [Do come to the Sabarmati riverbank tomorrow].

Something big is going to happen!' The 'big' news was the prime minister would be taking a ride in a seaplane from the Sabarmati riverfront in Ahmedabad to visit the Ambaji temple in his home district of Mehsana. Although there were genuine security concerns – no person with Z-plus security is allowed to fly in a single-engine aircraft because of the risks the small plane poses – it didn't really seem to matter at the time: an election was to be won and Modi-style 'shock-and-awe' campaigning was literally in the air. It was an archetypal made-for-live-TV Modi event, another political spectacle choreographed with typical razzmatazz: Modi waving to the cheering crowds assembled along the spruced-up riverfront (his showpiece 'development' project when he was chief minister), and posing next to the plane just long enough for the cameras to take a flurry of shots. As he took off in the blue and white aircraft, skimming over gushing, foaming waters and then lifting off, the crowds went delirious, almost as if Modi was a 'flying Superman'. For Amdavadis, who often complain about there not being enough water in the river, the sight of a seaplane had novelty, holding out a well-packaged dream of a 'new' tourist adventure. 'The seaplane had a great connect with the youth and women in particular and showed once again why Modi is so popular in Gujarat – he embodies middle-class aspirations,' says Ajay Umat, a senior Ahmedabad-based journalist. Modi's seaplane ride had clearly muddied the waters for the opposition.

A few days later when the results were declared, it was apparent that the last-stretch surge and harking to hard nationalistic and religious emotions had delivered. The BJP scraped home with 99 seats in the 182-member assembly, its lowest tally since first capturing power in Gujarat in 1995, while the Congress ended up with 77 seats. The two cities of Ahmedabad and Surat made all the difference, with the BJP winning the bulk of the seats there. I asked one of the Surat traders how the BJP managed to sweep the city despite the anger over GST. His answer was interesting: 'GST is badly implemented and yes, we are still angry about it, but when it comes to voting, we have to think of Hindutva also!' The Congress knew it was a missed opportunity. 'It was just a matter of ten to twelve seats. It was really very close, and with slightly better election management, we could have won,' bemoaned Congress leader Ahmed Patel. For the BJP though, the victory marked a remarkable feat: its sixth consecutive win in Gujarat. 'The Congress threw everything at us, GST, caste politics, farmers, jobs, and yet we won. It shows how Amitbhai's organization and Narendrabhai's appeal cannot be matched in Gujarat,' gushes Bharat Pandya.

For Rahul Gandhi, the Gujarat results were a mixed bag. He had lost yet another election battle, but this time he had at least shown the will to take the fight to his opponents' door. The Congress was content to claim a 'moral victory' – a strange term to use since there are no prizes for runners-up in electoral politics. Just forty-eight hours before the Gujarat results were announced, Rahul was formally appointed Congress president at the party headquarters. Unlike the BJP's well-planned events, Rahul's appointment was made amidst the customary Congress chaos and disorganized last-minute pandemonium: passes being distributed at the eleventh hour, obsequious partymen jostling to catch the eye of the Gandhi family and even a mild stampede at the gate. On the dais, things seemed smoother as Rahul Gandhi was handed over a certificate of 'election' in the presence of his mother and former prime minister Dr Singh. The election had been a formality since no one else had stood against him. As he kissed his mother on the forehead, with sister Priyanka beaming in the background, the family portrait was complete. Sonia's nineteen-year reign as the longest-serving party president was over but the Congress remained in the firm grip of the Gandhi–Nehru family. 'I want to assure all the Congress workers and leaders that you are all my family. I want to tell the youth of this country that Congress is often referred to as the grand old party but going forth we are going to make it the grand old young party,' Rahul told his supporters. His elevation was a stark reminder to political observers how his parachuting to the party's top post has always been shot through with a deep paradox: can someone who wants to fundamentally change the Congress party also at the same time assume that his own birthright-based status in the party will remain unchallenged? Can a leader who is ostensibly committed to glasnost remain a constant representative of the status quo?

At the 'coronation' there was a sense of relief more than elation, a certain lack of spontaneity in applause amongst the crowd, many of whom were youth and farmers, packed into their Scorpios and trucks and brought in from neighbouring Haryana and Outer Delhi. At forty-seven, Rahul had arrived, but not quite: yes, he had become party president at an age when Modi was only a BJP general secretary, but his ascent was still being seen as dynastical succession, a reflection of the Congress's failure to find strong leadership outside of a family. Rahul had put up a resolute, spirited fight in Gujarat, but he still needed a major political victory and, indeed, a clear narrative before he could be considered a future leader of substance.

Rahul Gandhi was barely seventeen when the Bofors gun scandal erupted in 1987, hobbling the then Rajiv Gandhi government and eventually becoming a major reason for its fall in 1989. He was perhaps too young to decipher the minutiae of the deal, but old enough to realize that it was the allegations of kickbacks that severely and fatally dented his father's 'Mr Clean' image. Rahul never referred to Bofors in his public interactions but it is possible that the scars hadn't healed. 'Of course, the family was affected. Anyone would be if you keep calling people thieves and corrupt without proving the charges,' says Sam Pitroda, who was part of Rajiv's back-room team.

If Rahul was subconsciously waiting for an opportunity to hit back, he would get it in the guise of the multi-crore Rafale aircraft deal signed by the Modi government in April 2015 during a prime-ministerial visit to France. As with Bofors, there were no questions about the quality of the aircraft being purchased. There were, however, whispers of how the existing defence procurement procedures had been violated by suddenly setting aside an almost finalized 126-aicraft deal between Hindustan Aeronautics and French manufacturer Dassault Aviation, and striking instead an intergovernmental agreement for the purchase of 36 off-the-shelf Rafale fighters for ₹58,000 crore or Euro 7.8 billion. Businessman Anil Ambani, who had almost zero experience in the defence sector, was one of the prime beneficiaries of a lucrative offset clause in the contract, further raising eyebrows. Defence journalist Ajai Shukla recalls meeting Ambani at the Bengaluru Aero Show in February 2015. 'It was apparent that he was lobbying for contracts, especially with the French and the Russians, and using his political connections to project himself as Modi's man,' recalls Shukla.

It was this contentious Modi–Ambani connection that the Congress was seeking to take advantage of, in the hope that the allegations of favouritism, nepotism and crony capitalism would stick. The 'suit-boot ki sarkar' jibe was back, only now there was a story to illustrate it. Or so the Congress believed. 'Look, prima facie, there is nothing in the Rafale deal that is above board, from price escalation to sweetheart deals, it looks like a straight case of crony corruption,' Congress's feisty chief spokesperson Surjewala insists.

Surjewala was part of a core group of Congress leaders who began digging deeper into the Rafale documents. There are indications that some defence ministry bureaucrats and potential aircraft competitors had also leaked the documents, some of which were shared with Rahul Gandhi. 'I think Rahul was immediately convinced that this was a case of corruption that involved no less than the prime minister and he was keen to take it up in a big way,' claims Surjewala.

For eighteen months in the build-up to the 2019 elections, Rafale became almost synonymous with Rahul Gandhi. Once seen as a reluctant speaker, he would now use any and every opportunity to hammer home the point of an alleged Modi–Ambani nexus. Every time there was a news break on Rafale, reporters on the Congress beat would rush to the party headquarters where Rahul himself would address a 'special' press conference. He addressed nearly ten such hurriedly put together interactions on Rafale during which his body language seemed designed to reposition himself as an unflinching anti-corruption crusader: rolling up his sleeves, thumping the table, stabbing fingers at the camera, this was the Congress president in a new avatar as the 'angry young man'. A suited-booted PM obliging his millionaire crony was the Congress's pitch, one they hoped would stir anti-rich fervour and also help deflect Modi's constant harping on the Gandhis' inherited privileges, by pointing to the PM's own VIP friends. 'PM ne chori kar Ambani ko paise diye!' (The PM has robbed and given money to Ambani!) The finer details of the complicated Rafale contract were avoided. For example, was it true that dozens of companies, and not just Ambani, were in line to benefit from offset contracts worth around ₹30,000 crore? This was clearly a battle between perception and fact and the Congress leadership was hopeful that the Modi–Ambani proximity would be enough to prove their culpability in the public domain. From Rahul's own finger-wagging outrage on Rafale, it was evident that the Congress chief not only fully and genuinely believed that the deal stank, but that Rafale 'corruption' would resonate widely amongst the voters.

Initially, the Modi government's response was to ignore Rahul's diatribe. I recall meeting the then defence minister, the late Manohar Parikkar, soon after the allegations of corruption and procedural impropriety first surfaced. Parikkar, who was at the time slowly finding his feet in Delhi, was a fellow-Goan, and we would occasionally meet to discuss developments in our home state and chat on a range of topics from military matters to even the price of his favourite fish. One day, I raised the issue of Rafale pricing and asked if he would speak to me in detail on record about it. 'You should direct all these questions to the PMO, not to me. I would prefer not to speak on this,' was the normally garrulous politician's terse response. Parikkar's reluctance to open up on Rafale intrigued me. The distinct impression I got was that he didn't want to be drawn into the raging controversy over aircraft pricing since he was not part of the final negotiations and was informed of the deal just before the prime minister left for France in early April 2015. In fact, Parikkar was not even in France when the contract was announced but instead was on a weekend sojourn to his favourite Goa. This was Modi's preferred form of lightning action: the all-in-all strongman of his government, he determined the course of action, and would act himself, preferably alone, and never mind the concerned ministers.

In March 2017, Parikkar returned to Goa as chief minister, and Nirmala Sitharaman took over as the country's first full-time woman defence minister. It was a surprise choice. No one had anticipated such a dramatic career leap for a first-time Rajya Sabha MP. Indeed, her rise is a textbook case in eye-catching political mobility. I was first introduced to Sitharaman sometime in 2010 by my guest relations team. We were struggling to get a BJP spokesperson for a studio debate when my guest coordinator helpfully suggested that we invite this 'new lady' whom he had just seen on another channel. 'She is very articulate with good English, sir,' he said. An English-speaking BJP guest was like gold dust: the party's array of spokespersons was mostly dominated by Hindi speakers. The slightly stern-looking Sitharaman had no mass base and had never contested an election. A relatively recent entrant into the BJP, she was suddenly a much-sought-after figure on national TV as a party spokesperson. An educated English-speaking woman, formerly of JNU and Price Waterhouse, as calm and expert a speaker as any of India's patrician, well-spoken civil servants. Sitharaman did not let us down. Elegantly and simply dressed, she came to the studio well prepared and spoke with firmness and confidence, without sounding shrill or irritable. We had 'discovered' a new face. Nor were we the only ones impressed: Prime Minister Modi too noticed her talent and drafted her into his cabinet, first as commerce minister and then in the crucial defence portfolio before she became the country's first woman full-time finance minister in Modi 2.0. Sitharaman's meteoric rise reflects the abysmal lack of technocratic experience in the saffron ranks.

Unlike Parikkar, who kept his Rafale interjections to the minimum, Sitharaman decided that attack was the best form of defence. In a staunch justification of the deal, she hit back at Rahul in Parliament: 'Their strategy is to spit and run. Defence ministry has run without dalals in the last five years. Bofors was a scam, Rafale is not. Bofors sank Congress,

Rafale will bring Modi back to power.' As she stared down the opposition benches, the prime minister appeared relieved to have found his own strike weapon: Sitharaman versus Rahul was one of the more engaging face-offs of the sixteenth Lok Sabha.

But Rahul wasn't backing off just yet. The orders to Surjewala and his team were clear: keep the heat on Rafale. With less than a year to go for the 2019 elections, the Congress decided to hold 100 press conferences in two phases across the country in August 2018. 'The instructions were to carpet-bomb the country with Rafale so that it stayed top of the mind,' says Khera. And yet, when we at India Today commissioned an Axis My India political tracker barely a month later, it suggested that more than 75 per cent of the voters in the assembly election–bound states had not even heard of Rafale. Clearly, the Congress campaign on Rafale wasn't having the desired effect. 'When you don't have a case, you can't just manufacture one by throwing allegations,' contends BJP spokesperson G.V.L. Narasimha Rao.

Interestingly, Surjewala admits that many senior leaders within the Congress were not in sync with the party leadership on Rafale. Apparently, the party's media and research department prepared detailed dockets on Rafale which they circulated among all the state Congress units, MPs, MLAs, chief ministers and other important party functionaries. 'And yet, in the end, we didn't get the kind of support we wanted from other opposition leaders and even those within our party. You can't expect Rahul to do it all on his own,' reasons Surjewala.

Why did Rahul Gandhi in 2019 fail to become the V.P. Singh of 1989, a magnet for opposition unity? Why did Rafale not become a twenty-first-century Bofors? It's a question I posed to veteran journalist N. Ram, who had played an important role in exposing the Bofors kickbacks and also written several front-page stories on Rafale in *The Hindu*. 'Non-transparency in decision-making is a defining feature in both Bofors and Rafale but the key difference is that no money trail has been discovered in the aircraft deal so far, whereas the Bofors investigation began with the discovery of the pay-offs. Also, V.P. Singh and his supporters had at least two years to campaign on Bofors ahead of the 1989 elections while Rahul and the opposition had a much shorter time to work up Rafale as a campaign issue,' is Ram's explanation.

I believe Rahul failed to land a knockout blow on Rafale not only because the so-called money trail was never fully uncovered, but also because he was not really in a position to become a credible mascot for a nationwide anti-corruption campaign. As Congress president, he had inherited the legacy of the party's reputation for having tolerated and benefited from political corruption in previous decades. Anna Hazare's anti-corruption agitation in 2011 in particular had done irreparable damage to the Congress's image and by raking up Rafale, Rahul wasn't going to erase public memory so soon. V.P. Singh succeeded in 1989 because he portrayed himself as the quintessential political 'outsider' who was promising to clean up politics; Rahul, in comparison, was still perceived as the ultimate 'insider' within the Congress, someone who owed his privileged position to his surname. A political dynast, carrying the baggage of the decadent ancient regime, levelling shrill charges against the 'common man' PM and that too without clear evidence of graft, became, in many quarters, another cause for the jeering derision against Rahul. Moreover, the Indian public, and indeed the media, was still enjoying an extended honeymoon with Modi and was unwilling to fully interrogate him. In the end, it boiled down to plain and simple credibility quotient: the prime minister was trusted, Rahul was not. Rafale gave Rahul a narrative to take to the voters, but he simply did not possess the necessary political authority to convince people that his was a believable story. Somehow, he still didn't look and sound like a serious politician: Rahul wasn't quite 'Pappu' any more but the BJP's relentless campaign to destroy his image had worked effectively. He just wasn't considered a seasoned leader who could be a viable alternative to Modi.

The most obvious example of this 'non-serious' politics was the now famous hug–wink episode during a no-confidence debate in Parliament in July 2018 when Rahul suddenly decided to hop across the aisle to Modi and embrace him. If Modi was caught by surprise, as he evidently was, he pretended not to show it, staying in his seat and patting Rahul on his head like an indulgent elder. I was sitting in the Parliament gallery and like many others around me was completely flummoxed; nobody was quite sure what was going on. We had barely digested the drama unfolding in front of our eyes when Rahul literally caught the eye of the camera again: this time, he was seen winking at his colleague Jyotiraditya Scindia who was seated next to him. A hug and a wink – Rahul was making all the headlines, but was also showing a flippant disregard for parliamentary etiquette and revealing a rather juvenile attitude towards the grave business of the house. Parliament after all was not an extension of his family home nor a place for teenage antics. When I asked a Rahul aide if the drama was pre-scripted, the response I got was, 'No, not at all, Rahul just wants to show he loves his political rivals too and carries no hatred for Modi personally.' I couldn't quite fathom the love–hate psychobabble. It all seemed a trifle immature and wholly unnecessary: politics wasn't a place for love gurus or for 'jadoo ki jhappis'. The hug–wink moment may have briefly lit up TV screens, but the overall impression one got was of an unserious kid who treated Parliament as a playground.

The talk of 'loving the enemy' and 'Congress ka pyaar vs BJP ki nafrat' seemed even more out of place when, just a few months later, Rahul began to target Modi with the confrontational and bellicose slogan: 'Chowkidar chor hai'. Modi often referred to himself as the 'desh ka chowkidar' who was guarding the nation's interests. Rahul first unleashed the slogan at an election rally in Rajasthan in September 2018, probably hoping that it would become the modern version of the popular refrain during the Bofors controversy: 'Gali gali mein shor hai, Rajiv Gandhi chor hai.' The Rahul camp believed that Rafale had provided them sufficient ammunition to bring down this carefully sculpted anti-corruption image of the prime minister. And not just Rafale: when the Nirav Modi–Mehul Choksi money-laundering scam broke out in early 2018, the Congress felt that it could draw a link to the prime minister since both fugitive businessmen were Gujaratis who had fled the country before the enforcement agencies could get to them. 'The chowkidar has failed to guard the wealth of the nation – it was the perfect analogy to use,' maintains a Rahul aide. Apparently, it was left activist Sandeep Singh, one of Rahul's speech-writers, who coined the 'Chowkidar chor hai' phrase, the same person who had conceptualized GST as 'Gabbar Singh Tax'.

And yet, it was a war cry that backfired badly. Hard on the heels of 'Chowkidar chor hai', the prime minister's team hit back with their own impactful 'Main bhi chowkidar' campaign. As a senior Congress leader admits, 'When you use words like "chor" against the prime minister, and a popular figure like Modi at that, you must base it on hard facts, not just on innuendo.' A slogan not only needs to be clever, it needs to grow organically from the persona of the slogan's main face. When Indira Gandhi screamed 'Garibi Hatao', she stood forth as the people's princess rebelling on behalf of the poorest against feudal Congress overlords. When Obama bellowed 'Yes, we can', it was the cry of an African-American man, drawn from the depths of America's long quest for racial and social justice. Soon, 'Chowkidar chor hai' began to sound like the personal grudge of a frustrated political aristocrat who was taking on a populist demagogue with mass support. An agenda of anti-Modi abuse and negativism without a clear-cut vision for the future was always likely to be subject to diminishing returns. Time was running out for Rahul and the Congress in their efforts to debunk Modi's image as an incorruptible politician.

State elections ahead of a big general election year are usually seen as crucial in building momentum for the major political parties. However, the 2018 assembly election battles weren't just about energizing the party cadres for the Congress; it was literally make-or-break time for the grand old party. At the start of the year, the Congress was in power in just three states – Punjab, Karnataka and Mizoram – and the union territory of Puducherry. Two of these states, Karnataka and Mizoram, were among the six going to the assembly polls, as were the large Hindi-belt states of Rajasthan, Madhya Pradesh and Chhattisgarh, and the southern state of

Telangana. The Congress desperately needed to win at least three of these combats, especially those with the BJP in the Hindi heartland. 'We knew that if we lost these elections we might as well give up the 2019 war,' a member of Rahul's team tells me.

The Congress by now was frantic. Nervousness and anxiety prevailed at all levels and the party even considered hiring a foreign political consultant, Steve Jarding, a well-regarded Harvard University professor, to manage its campaign. Rahul had met Jarding along with Sam Pitroda in London in August 2018, and was impressed enough to ask him to get in touch with the party's think tank. In an email (seen by this author), Jarding speaks of how he is 'very keen' to work with the Congress but that the party must take a decision soon because 'time is very short' and a 'large campaign needs to be mounted'. 'We didn't go ahead with it in the end because Jarding was asking for too much money,' claims a senior Congress leader. (A fee upwards of 1 million USD was reportedly asked for.) That Jarding was even being spoken to with just six months left for the elections suggests a vote of no-confidence in the existing election management team, and confusion and lack of resolve in planning and strategy on the part of the Congress.

It wasn't just Jarding. Just a year earlier, in July 2017, Cambridge Analytica (CA), a British political consulting firm which combined data mining and analysis with strategic communication, met Rahul in Delhi and offered a multi-million dollar proposal to handle the Congress campaign. A three-member CA team headed by CEO Alexander Nix was asked to meet Jairam Ramesh and take the discussions forward. Once again, the Congress hesitated because of a funds crunch. In early 2018, the organization found itself embroiled in a global political scandal when it was revealed that CA had harvested the personal data of millions of Facebook profiles without their consent and used it for political advertising in the 2015 US senate elections and 2016 Trump presidential campaign. Nix was suspended from CA in March 2018 after undercover video footage showed him claiming his company was using honey traps, bribery stings and prostitutes, among other tactics, to influence more than

200 elections for clients across the world. 'I guess we just got lucky in the end that we didn't sign with CA, else a fresh scandal would have broken out,' concedes a Congress leader.

With no foreign help, the Congress would now have to rely on its own resources in the Indian election war. Karnataka was the first battle, scheduled for May 2018 – the only Congress state government south of the Vindhyas and a crucial source of revenue generation ahead of the general elections. Once again, like in Gujarat, Rahul began early, embarking on a bus yatra and anointing then chief minister Siddaramaiah as the party's face. Siddaramaiah was a doughty old hand, one of the Congress's last remaining regional chieftains, almost inaudible in English but in his native Kannada, a colourful speaker who didn't pull punches and engaged his audiences with sharp wit and humour. His rival from the BJP, B.S. Yeddyurappa was very similar in nature: another local leader who had successfully carved his own base. And then there was the old warhorse, former prime minister H.D. Deve Gowda, who ran the Janata Dal (Secular) like a family proprietary firm with son H.D. Kumaraswamy. The sharp caste and subregional variations in this three-way battle made predicting the Karnataka election a bit of a nightmare. It was one outcome which even star pollster Pradeep Gupta of Axis My India would get wrong. He predicted a Congress win but the final results threw up a hung assembly with the BJP as the number one party, though tantalizingly short of the halfway mark.

For once, the Congress showed more hunger and street-smartness than the BJP, and moved in with unusual swiftness. Overnight the much-derided back-room boys from the 'old guard' took charge. Even before the results were announced, senior leaders Ghulam Nabi Azad and Ashok Gehlot flew to Bengaluru to start negotiations with Deve Gowda and his son. The Gowda–Kumaraswamy duo was typically keeping all options open. During the campaign, Rahul had taunted the father–son combine as the BJP's 'B' team and Gowda wasn't going to forgive or forget easily. 'I want to speak to Soniaji, not Rahul,' he made it clear to the Congress interlocutors. A call from Sonia was duly arranged, and the alliance forged.

The Congress managed to cling on to power in Karnataka, but only after it conceded the chief minister's chair to Kumaraswamy, winner of only 37 seats in a 224-member assembly. When I met the new chief minister at Bengaluru's Taj West End, where he had set up base in a luxurious cottage, Kumaraswamy seemed mighty chuffed at having wrested another shot at the top job. 'You know, I met Rahulji in Delhi. He is a nice person even if he spoke against us in the campaign. He has accepted all our demands, very decent and innocent boy,' he said. That even after becoming Congress president, Rahul was not seen as a first among equals by other opposition leaders was confirmed at Kumaraswamy's swearing-in. A host of opposition leaders, from Mayawati and Akhilesh Yadav to Mamata Banerjee and Chandrababu Naidu, descended on Bengaluru in May 2018 for the swearing-in of the Karnataka chief minister. It was a signal moment for opposition unity against Modi as they assembled on stage – a galaxy of regional satraps, all smiles and laughs, holding each other's hands aloft, like a procession of jolly potentates. Rahul was there, along with Sonia, but he was just another face in the line-up, just another politician jostling for space in an emerging anti-BJP, anti-Modi 'mahagathbandhan'.

In Telangana, a state which the Congress had created in 2014, the party struck an alliance with Chandrababu Naidu's Telugu Desam Party (TDP). Naidu had left the NDA in April 2018 in an acrimonious break-up with the Modi government and was looking to shore up his party's depleting support. Team Rahul was pleased to have someone who had parted ways with Modi now extol Rahul's leadership qualities. Moreover, Naidu had the financial muscle which the Congress was still lacking. An internal party poll survey also seemed to indicate that a Congress–TDP alliance would have the numbers to take on the ruling Telangana Rashtra Samiti (TRS). This turned out to be another serious error of judgement on the part of Team Rahul. In Telangana, Naidu was seen as an Andhra leader who had tried to prevent the formation of a separate state. The alliance also exposed Rahul to a fierce attack from Chief Minister K. Chandrashekhar Rao, or KCR, the TRS chief. 'Rahul

Gandhi is the biggest buffoon,' he said angrily. When I asked him if he had overreacted, KCR was unapologetic: 'Arre, this boy hugs and winks in Parliament, who will take him seriously?' The Congress–TDP alliance or 'mahakutumi' bombed at the political box office as the Telangana electorate contemptuously dismissed this ill-conceived alliance of erstwhile enemies. Another state was lost.

Now the three Hindi-speaking states were the Congress's last hope. Although all three states were BJP-ruled, the saffron party was up against decades-old anti-incumbency. Here, whether by design or default, Rahul seemed to get it right. In Chhattisgarh, Raman Singh had been in power for fifteen years, and signs of fatigue and anti-incumbency were visible all over. In 2013, Naxalites attacked a convoy of the Congress's senior state leaders on their way back from a political rally, killing several people and grievously injuring others. After this bloody massacre of almost its entire leadership, the party had slowly rebuilt itself under combative state Congress president Bhupesh Baghel. In a state with a large tribal and Dalit population, most struggling with grinding poverty, Rahul intelligently chose to focus less on Rafale and more on local issues, promising a farm loan waiver, cutting power bills by half and increasing the minimum support price for paddy. 'We were very clear from day one, this is not a national election but a localized battle,' points out Baghel.

Neighbouring Madhya Pradesh was a little more complicated. Here, the Congress was suffering from its all-too-familiar malaise of being a party with too many leaders but hardly any ground workers. Rahul had to decide who would lead the party's campaign in MP: veteran smart operator Kamal Nath or the youthful, assertive Jyotiraditya Scindia. For months, Rahul dithered. His core team was initially not keen on Nath, a nine-time MP who had made his political debut way back in 1980 as a Sanjay Gandhi acolyte, and represented the has-been oldies who were long past their heyday. Or so Team Rahul believed. In contrast, the young Scindia had the advantage of being a charismatic leader and compelling orator. The canny Nath, though, had one major plus: he was a well-networked, wealthy neta who could not just lead but also possibly 'sponsor' the entire Congress campaign. By the time Rahul finally plumped for Nath as state Congress president, it was already May 2018 and there were just six months left for the polls. Nath, a practiced hand, rose to the challenge, immediately fixing the nuts and bolts of the party machinery and making it battle-ready. 'I know the BJP inside out like no one else does,' he boasted. The BJP too was facing factionalism with the then chief minister, Shivraj Singh Chauhan, on the back foot after thirteen years in office. The party's caste equations in the state had gone awry. In 2018, the Supreme Court's 'dilution' of the Scheduled Caste and Scheduled Tribes (Prevention of Atrocities) Act, preventing automatic arrests in crimes against Dalits, sparked wildfire protests among the Dalit community. Fearing the loss of SC/ST votes, the Modi government quickly brought in an amendment restoring the Act to its old form, only to now alienate the upper castes who took up the cudgels against the BJP. The government thus faced the wrath of both upper-caste and SC/ST voters in the state.

Rajasthan was, on the surface, the easiest battle. The state had a reputation for alternately voting out governments every five years, so logically it was now the turn of the Congress to benefit from the anti-incumbency against the Vasundhara Raje-led BJP government. But here too, the party was faced with a leadership tangle. The popular, young and energetic Sachin Pilot had been specifically sent by Rahul to become the Rajasthan Congress president in 2014, one of the first major decisions taken by him independently of his mother. But with weeks to go for the 2018 election, pleasant-mannered, two-time chief minister Ashok Gehlot, who had been drafted into Rahul's Delhi team as general secretary (organization), insisted on going back to Rajasthan to contest the elections. Rahul reluctantly agreed. Pilot was incensed. He and Gehlot were at daggers drawn and didn't try to hide their antipathy towards each other even in public. 'He wants to destroy me politically at every stage and is putting up his own rebel candidates against our nominees,' complained Pilot to the party leadership. The poker-faced Gehlot denied sabotaging the election. Rahul played peacemaker: 'We will decide who becomes chief minister after the elections, for now we must all fight together.' A fragile, temporary peace was bought.

Counting day, 11 December 2018, turned out to be one of the longest in Indian state elections in recent times. By noon, it was clear that the Congress was sweeping Chhattisgarh. By 2 p.m., the Congress had inched closer to the majority mark in Rajasthan but was nowhere near the two-thirds majority predicted: clearly, the Pilot–Gehlot tussle had left its impact on a tight contest. But the most fraught battle was being fought in Madhya Pradesh where the lead changed hands between the Congress and the BJP every few minutes. With recounts and cross-checking going on in several constituencies, it was almost midnight before the Congress edged ahead: 114 seats to the BJP's 109 seats, just one seat short of the halfway mark. Within hours, the quick-thinking Nath had already stitched up deals with the independents and smaller parties. The newspaper headline the next morning said it all: 'Congress 3 BJP nil'.

The mood in the Congress headquarters was ecstatic. Crackers were burst, banners were waved and cheers went up. Boxes of mithai were passed around. After a very long time, there was reason for Rahul to feel elated; exactly a year after being chosen Congress president, he was finally savouring a genuine election triumph, one which he had contributed to in no small measure. *India Today* ran its cover story on the man of the moment: 'The Evolution of Rahul Gandhi' read the headline, with a photo of Rahul in a white kurta-pyjama, matched with his customary sleeveless windbreaker, his hand raised in a smiling half-salute. Rahul was named the 2018 'Newsmaker of the Year' by *India Today* magazine and the lead story tracked his journey from political novice to political challenger: 'Defeating the BJP in 2019 will be an uphill task. And Rahul knows he has to climb many more mountains to achieve it. But in 2018, he has shown that he has the mettle to take on the might of the Modi–Shah combine. He has engineered a Congress revival and emerged as the prime challenger to Modi in the next general election,' the article claimed.

I still had nagging doubts. Was this 2018 victory really an indicator of the possible outcome of a Rahul-versus-Modi presidential-style battle in 2019, or was this verdict driven almost entirely by local factors? After all, on the campaign trail in Rajasthan, we often heard the slogan, 'Vasundhara teri khair nahin, Modi tujh se bair nahin' (We don't care for you Vasundhara but we have no differences with Modi). I had a hunch that these results were by no means a reflection on Modi's popularity, and that the generalizations about Modi's weakness were being made in haste. But Rahul himself appeared to have no self-doubt any more. When a Congress leader went to congratulate him on the assembly election wins but reminded him of the bigger battle that lay ahead, Rahul brushed aside all concerns. 'Look, whatever happens in 2019, Modi is history. It is clear now that he will not be prime minister again, that is a possibility we can safely rule out,' declared a confident Rahul.

Not for the first time, the Congress leadership would make the fatal mistake of underestimating the Modi factor. Previously, in mid-2018, Rahul had made a rare appearance in Parliament's central hall where MPs meet each other informally, making it a point to tell us journalists that he was certain that the BJP would not get more than 220 seats in the Lok Sabha elections. 'Take it from me, Modi isn't getting a majority and he isn't going to get enough allies either to return as prime minister,' he emphasized even as his mother Sonia sitting next to him urged caution. We listened without argument.

Bravado is a politician's second nature, but the line between swagger and overconfidence is a thin one as Rahul and his team were about to find out.

SIX

The Balakot Effect: 'Bharat Mata ki Jai'

ASTUTE politician that he is, Amit Shah's facial expressions rarely give away too much. When he is not looking stern, he tends to look impassive. If the 2018 winter assembly election results had upset the BJP calculations, Shah wasn't telling. At a media conclave just days after the BJP defeat in three key states, Shah was brimming with confidence. 'So sir, are you looking at a hung parliament scenario now in 2019?' asked the suitably deferential anchor. Shah responded expressionlessly: 'Hamein spasht bahumat milegi, clear majority.' The polite anchor sought re-affirmation: 'You mean BJP will once again repeat its 2014 performance?' Shah sounded momentarily irritated: '2014 se kai zyada seeten aayengi, aap iski chinta na karein.' (We will get many more seats than 2014, please don't worry.) There were no counter questions: generally journalists hardly ever cross the BJP president. Was this sheer political bombast or did Shah know something that most pundits did not? Apparently, the self-assuredness stemmed from the findings of a comprehensive nationwide survey. Commissioned by the BJP in August–September 2018, just a few months ahead of the assembly elections, the poll showed the party getting an impressive 297 to 303 seats on its own, more than the 282 seats it had obtained in 2014. In addition, the poll positioned Modi as the most popular leader in the country by some distance with high endorsement for government schemes like Swachh Bharat and Ujwala. The extensive survey involved as many as 5.4 lakh face-to-face interviews across the country, a much larger sample size than what most news organizations can afford. (A professionally conducted survey can cost upwards of ₹200 per sample, so clearly the total expense here ran into several crore.) The survey was supervised by BJP union minister Piyush Goyal, the well-groomed, smooth-talking chartered accountant-turned-neta, who prided himself on his number-crunching skills. Goyal had rapidly emerged as the Modi government's man for all seasons, temporarily substituting as finance minister for the BJP's original go-to man, Arun Jaitley, whose serious health problems had led to frequent bouts of hospitalization. The nattily dressed Goyal walked with a swagger, often carrying multiple mobile phones in his pocket. Well networked into Mumbai's industrial elite, he was the BJP's fund manager and now part of Shah's inner circle. 'Look, we are getting a clear majority and steaming ahead under Modiji's leadership. The survey is very clear, 300 plus to us,' he prophesied. When I asked him where the extra numbers were coming from, he didn't give too much away. 'They are coming from all over the country. Why are you worried? We will surprise all of you once again!'

Goyal's buoyancy was a trifle unsettling for most political observers. Our ground reports as we entered the big election year suggested that the BJP still had some work to do to repeat its 2014 success. The unemployment figures released by the Centre for Monitoring Indian Economy (CMIE) in January 2019 showed a worrying upward movement: CMIE's assessment was the country had lost 1.1 crore jobs in the previous year. The National Sample Survey Office (NSSO) official survey had more bad news: it claimed that the unemployment rate had hit a forty-five-year high of 6.1 per cent in 2017. The government was quick to dismiss the statistic, with NITI Aayog vice chairperson Rajiv Kumar first claiming that it was a draft report, then asking how the country could grow at 7 per cent without generating employment. The news from the crucial farming sector was just as troubling. Incomes from agriculture were declining sharply: average wholesale rates in mandis in October–November 2018 were lower than the government's minimum support price for practically every agricultural commodity except jowar and cotton. The January 2019 India Today Mood of the Nation survey set job creation and farm distress as the Modi government's two biggest challenges: the poll claimed that if general elections were held immediately, the NDA tally would drop by nearly 100 seats – from the 336 seats it got in the 2014 elections to 237 – 35 short of a majority. It was the first time since 2014 that the biannual survey forecast a hung parliament.

Within the capital's political circles and in Mumbai's corporate corridors, there was even a buzz around union minister Nitin Gadkari being projected as a 'Plan B' compromise candidate in case the NDA didn't get a majority on its own. The affable Gadkari enjoyed warm relations with many opposition leaders and business tycoons, always an advantage in any future coalition arrangement. The Nagpur MP's strong connect with the RSS leadership was no secret either. Soon after the BJP's defeat in the December 2018 state elections, Gadkari remarked at a public gathering in Pune, 'Leadership should own up to failures. Success has many fathers but failure is an orphan; leadership should have the vrutti [attitude] to own up to failure and defeat.' The comments were seen to be politically loaded, a jibe aimed at the Modi–Shah leadership. When I met him soon after, Gadkari insisted that his remarks made in Marathi had been twisted out of context. 'So you are not in the PM race?' I asked. 'Arre, tum mere dost ho ya dushman!' (Are you my friend or enemy!) he countered. Clearly, no minister wanted to openly challenge the BJP's leadership just yet, not at least in the run-up to the general elections.

Typically, the Modi–Shah duo was unfazed by all the speculation: rather than rely on external reports to gauge voter mood, they instead got their own detailed internal assessment done of the 2018 assembly results. The setback in Madhya Pradesh was particularly worrying: the state was traditionally a BJP bastion where the party had lost in some of its strongholds, including urban pockets. Feedback from the ground indicated that the BJP's core upper-caste vote had deserted the party in the wake of the Modi government's flip-flop on the SC/ST (Prevention of Atrocities) Act Infuriated by the 'appeasement' of the 'lower orders', the state's Brahmin–Bania voters had decided to teach the party a lesson. The other finding was just as perturbing: Rahul Gandhi's loan waiver promises were resonating with rural voters and influencing the electorate as was the promise of a minimum income for the poor. When Prakash Singh Badal, a former Punjab chief minister and veteran Akali Dal leader, met the prime minister, he offered a simple solution: 'Pradhan Mantriji, bas kisano ko minimum support price [MSP] badhakar khush kar dijiye.' (Prime Minister, keep the farmer happy by raising the MSP.) Another Akali leader was more direct: 'Chunaav ke pehle tijori kholne ka time aa gaya hai!' (The time has come to open the treasury before the elections!)

In his first few years in office, Modi had steadfastly opposed any overt handouts or hiking the MSP for farmers. He had been vociferously and publicly critical of the Manmohan Singh government's farm policies, describing them as inflationary and populist. However, he knew that he couldn't afford to not offer concessions to farmers in a general election year. The message to acting finance minister Goyal was clear: make sure the budget makes everyone feel happy, but especially the kisan. Budgets presented by governments ahead of general elections are usually an end-of-term statement of accounts, or interim budgets. But the Modi government is impatient with such precedence and norms, and the budget presented ahead of the general elections of 2019 was much more than a mere accounting exercise. Instead, a big-ticket policy announcement was made. On 1 February 2019, the government introduced the Pradhan Mantri Kisan Samman Nidhi Yojana that would provide ₹6,000 per year (in three equal instalments) to an estimated 12 crore small and marginal farmers, a total outlay of around ₹75,000 crore. The first tranche would be distributed by the first week of March itself before the election code kicked in. The government machinery sprang into action. 'This is where the last-mile connectivity through direct benefit transfers helped. We could ensure that the money actually reached the intended beneficiaries ahead of the deadline,' a senior bureaucrat tells me. More than 3.1 crore farmers got the first instalment according to official data, mainly in BJP-ruled states. 'We now had a fresh talking point to counter the Congress's loan waiver and minimum income promise,' a BJP leader points out.

It didn't stop there. In a bid to woo back the salaried middle class, Goyal broke with convention to announce a tax cut, a rebate for taxpayers with a taxable income of less than ₹5 lakh who would now, in effect, pay no income tax. Workers in the unorganized sector would be eligible for a reworked pension scheme which would yield an income of ₹3000 per month on maturity. When I bumped into Goyal in Parliament, I asked if he was under pressure to announce the sops because of the impending elections. His answer was as combative as ever: 'Why do you keep thinking we are under pressure when I keep saying we are winning the elections easily!'

The truth is, the Modi government was now moving fast on various fronts with an eye squarely on potential electoral benefits. In the first week of January 2019, the government approved 10 per cent reservation in jobs and higher education for 'economically backward' sections in the general category, hurriedly pushing through a constitutional amendment in Parliament. This 10 per cent reservation for the Economically Weaker Sections would take the total reservations to 60 per cent, well above the 50 per cent prescribed by the Supreme Court. It may have been legally contentious, but Modi knew no party could be seen to be openly opposing reservations in an election year. Clearly, the 2018 election defeat had spurred the Modi government into acting with a renewed sense of urgency.

The Congress leadership, in contrast, seemed to think that since its 'Chowkidar chor hai' slogan and 'pro-kisan' strategy had worked so well in the December assembly elections, all it needed was one final push and it would topple the Modi government. The party strategists were convinced that the poll narrative had changed decisively and Rahul was now the most credible and favoured face as prime-ministerial challenger to Modi. When, in January 2019, M.K. Stalin, the DMK chief, proposed the Congress president as his choice for prime minister, Team Rahul was delighted. 'Until the December elections, we might have baulked at someone projecting Rahul as the person to take on Modi, but now we felt that he was not just the first among equals but actually the only person with the guts and gumption to take on the prime minister,' a Congress leader observes.

Not everyone in the opposition, though, was as gung-ho about the idea of Rahul as the prime-ministerial candidate. Mamata Banerjee for one was still keen to be seen as a magnet for any potential non-BJP coalition. In mid-January 2019, she organized a massive 'United India' rally at Kolkata's Parade Ground, inviting dozens of opposition leaders in a show of strength. She played the perfect host to the opposition, laying out a veritable spread for their delectation, from Bihari litti chokha to south Indian masala dosa, in addition to a range of Bengali items like luchi and aloo'r dom and nolen gur'r patishapta. In a widely circulated photo she was seen personally serving food to her guests as if to establish herself as one of the rallying points for the anti-Modi front. Didi would not just feed, she would also lead! Later, at the rally, insisting that the Modi government had reached its expiry date, she roared, 'Badal do badal do, Delhi ka sarkar badal do.' (Change the government at the Centre.) The rabble-rousing sloganeering was typical Mamata: a feisty regional potentate who was now eyeing Delhi. She wasn't alone.

Buoyed by his success in the Telangana elections, Chief Minister K. Chandrashekhar Rao was also watching the unfolding political drama intently. 'I believe the Telangana model of governance should be replicated across the country,' he told me in an interview. The ambitious leader had reportedly even promised to fund a potential non-BJP, non-Congress front. The rise of regional leaders with national ambitions, and the coalescing of various regional fronts, has been a recurring feature in Indian politics since the early 1990s when the Congress's decline across states created a political vacuum that led to a series of fractured mandates and hung parliaments.

Rahul did not attend Mamata's jamboree, sending Mallikarjun Kharge, the Congress's Lok Sabha leader at the time, instead. His noticeable absence was a pointer to the convoluted nature of anti-Modi opposition politics. Modi was the prime enemy of both Rahul and Mamata but on the ground in Bengal, TMC and Congress workers simply couldn't see eye to eye. KCR too didn't attend Mamata's rally; he refused to share a stage with his Andhra counterpart, Chandrababu Naidu, or indeed the Congress, his sworn local rivals. The left too was not to be seen on the same platform as Didi, given the bitterness in their relations in Bengal (Mamata had sent an invite to the CPI[M] Kerala chief minister Pinarayi Vijayan). Naveen Patnaik, the inscrutable Odisha chief minister, was just as cautious in joining any opposition front, politely declining the invite to attend the rally. 'We were a gathbandhan but certainly not a "maha" gathbandhan. It was really a case of each one for himself,' a TMC leader pointedly remarks. With each party keen to monopolize their own market share, an all-India trade pact became difficult.

It was precisely this confusion in the opposition ranks that the Modi government sought to exploit. At its national council meeting in Delhi in January, the party took up the rallying cry: 'Phir ek baar Modi sarkar' (Once again Modi's government), a slight twist on its 2014 slogan. Addressing the large gathering of party faithful, Modi pitched the battle as one between a 'mazboot' (strong) and a 'majboor' (helpless) government. 'Yeh mahagathbandhan nahin, maha-milawati hai' (This is not a grand alliance but a grand adulteration), he declaimed. It was again a catchy Modi one-liner, one that would be frequently used on the campaign trail to position the election as a quasi-presidential battle: 'Modi versus who?'

The no-holds-barred Modi offensive on the opposition came just a day after a potential game-changer alliance was sealed in UP. Arch adversaries for twenty-five years, the SP and the BSP announced a formal tie-up for the 2019 elections. The setting for the Akhilesh Yadav–Mayawati joint press conference was the luxurious Taj Hotel in Lucknow. The air was crackling with anticipation. First to enter was Akhilesh Yadav, neatly dressed in a kurta-pyjama and black waistcoat, red Samajwadi cap firmly in place. Mayawati, clad in a beige salwar-kameez and brown coat, walked in commandingly a few minutes later, underlining her senior status. Akhilesh seemed happy to let Mayawati do the talking.

'We are holding a joint press conference that will give Modi–Shah, the guru–chela duo, plenty of sleepless nights,' warned the BSP chief in her characteristic straight-talking style. Sitting next to her, Akhilesh smiled gently. After all, it was he who had initiated the seat-sharing talks a few months earlier, soon after winning three by-elections with BSP support in UP in May 2018.

'Yes, I made the first move by going to meet Mayawati at her home to thank her for the support,' revealed Akhilesh. Twenty-four years ago, Mayawati had narrowly escaped being grievously assaulted by SP workers and MLAs at the state guest house in Lucknow – the notorious Guest House incident – after a split in their ruling alliance. She had never forgiven Mulayam Singh Yadav, who she was convinced was behind that dangerous attack on her. Now, the amiable Akhilesh was extending an olive branch. Mayawati, who hadn't won a single Lok Sabha seat in 2014, jumped at the offer, but with one condition. She would have the last word on seat-sharing. Akhilesh, certain that this was a winning alliance, agreed. Of the eighty seats in UP, the BSP and SP would contest thirty-eight seats each, leaving just four to be shared by Ajit Singh's Rashtriya Lok Dal and the Congress. When Congress negotiators suggested that they be given at least ten seats, Mayawati firmly slammed the door in their face. 'Akhilesh was ready, but Behenji was firm in rejecting our demand; she wouldn't even meet us,' a Congress leader from UP says.

So, why did Mayawati not agree to a broader, potentially decisive 'grand' alliance in UP that would include the Congress? When I popped this question to Mayawati's trusted aide and BSP Rajya Sabha MP Satish Mishra, he claimed that the BSP supremo didn't trust the Congress to play fair. 'You see, Behenji instantly gave support to the Congress government in Madhya Pradesh but instead of treating us with respect, they were breaking our party in the state,' he points out. The Congress has another explanation for Mayawati's intransigence: the BSP leader, the Congress believes, was under pressure from the taxman. Her brother had been raided by the Income Tax Department and the Enforcement Directorate (ED) had summoned him for repeated questioning. 'The message from the BJP government to her was clear: you form an alliance with the Congress nationally and we go after you,' claims a senior Congress leader. Mishra refutes this but what is undeniable is that the eventual SP–BSP alliance was less than perfect: not having the Congress on its side would only split the anti-BJP vote.

Team Rahul though didn't seem too concerned by Mayawati's inflexibility. In fact, a section of the Congress was convinced that the party fighting UP on its own could strategically divide the BJP's upper-caste vote to the advantage of the anti-Modi forces. An increasingly self-assured Rahul was just as positive. 'We're going to fight this election on the front foot in UP,' he told his team, a stand he would later reiterate before the media. On 23 January 2019, at around noon, we realized what Rahul's 'front foot' play involved. A terse one-page communiqué issued by the All India Congress Committee (AICC) office read: 'Honourable Congress president has also appointed Smt Priyanka Gandhi Vadra as AICC general secretary for Uttar Pradesh East. She will be taking charge with effect from the first week of February 2019.'

It was a bolt from the blue. Even though Priyanka's public involvement was largely limited to managing her brother's and mother's campaigns in Amethi and Rae Bareli every five years, there had been feverish speculation for some time about her joining politics; periodically, posters would appear at the Congress headquarters urging Priyanka to take the plunge. It was known within Congress circles that Priyanka too relished the political arc lights and, unlike her brother, she was quite comfortable with the prying camera, often offering sharp sound bites and camera-friendly moments. Rajiv Shukla, journalist-Congressman, recalls interviewing Rajiv Gandhi in 1986 and asking him which of his children was keen on politics. 'He told me very clearly that it was Priyanka who was the more interested,' recollects Shukla.

Yet now, when the sudden announcement of Priyanka's entry was made, there were predictably more questions than answers. Why was Priyanka being thrown into the ring now, just two months before the general elections? Why was she diving into the deep end of eastern UP where the Congress base had shrunk and where the party had meagre single-digit support outside the Rae Bareli–Amethi belt? Why only eastern UP when Ghulam Nabi Azad had been general secretary for the entire state? (In another surprise move, Jyotiraditya Scindia was appointed in charge of western UP, an area he had little connect with.)

Frankly, the timing couldn't have been worse: just two days earlier, the Rajasthan High Court had asked Priyanka's husband, Robert Vadra, and his mother to appear before the ED in connection with a land deal case. The ED also wanted to question him on a money-laundering charge involving the alleged purchase of property in London. Ironically, Priyanka herself was in America on a private visit when the statement of her appointment was released. A Congress leader from UP remarks, 'We wanted to celebrate but the person we wanted to meet and greet wasn't even there!' The optics of an absentee Priyanka were only reinforced.

So, what is the story behind Priyanka's selection for the post so late in the election cycle? No Congressperson seems to have a definite explanation. The official account given by Rahul was that the decision had been in the pipeline for a while. 'I have been having a discussion with my sister about her joining politics for years and her pushback to me was that her children were very young and she needed to spend time looking after them,' was Rahul's version. I might have bought it but having known of Priyanka's inclination to enter the fray ahead of the 2017 UP elections itself, this two-year wait seemed inexplicable. My own reasoning is that Priyanka's entry was eventually facilitated by the complicated nature of family politics. In 2016–17, Sonia vetoed Priyanka's attempt to enter politics because she felt that it would undercut Rahul's stature within the Congress even though brother and sister enjoy a close personal bond. But now that Rahul was firmly in place as party chief and had just led the Congress to victory in three states, Sonia's concerns over a dual power centre emerging within the party were assuaged. 'In the end, every major decision regarding Rahul and Priyanka must be approved by Sonia,' a close Gandhi family associate tells me.

For the BJP, Priyanka's elevation provided a fresh talking point and line of attack. 'This is the final confirmation that Rahul Gandhi has failed as leader,' claimed the BJP's man for every sound bite, party spokesperson Sambit Patra. 'Power is "parivar" [family] for the Congress,' came another punchline. The clash of polar opposites, the Modi-led struggle against the 'naamdar' (dynast) by the humble 'kaamdar' (meritocrat) was well and truly revived. Above all, the Vadra connection was played up relentlessly by the BJP. When I introduced her as Priyanka Gandhi on my TV show, the dogged Patra made it a point to remind me: 'Not Priyanka Gandhi; Priyanka Gandhi Vadra.'

Interestingly, upon her return from her US sojourn, Priyanka sent out a strong message of solidarity with her beleaguered husband: ahead of a Congress meeting at the party office in Delhi, she very publicly accompanied Robert to the ED headquarters where he was to be questioned. The couple arrived together in a white Toyota Land Cruiser accompanied by a posse of SPG personnel. Priyanka dropped her husband off at the ED office and then proceeded to take charge of her new assignment. If Priyanka was trying to evoke memories of her grandmother Indira – there is a striking facial resemblance – who had used her post-Emergency incarceration to take the battle to her political opponents, then maybe she had partly succeeded. 'Make no mistake, Priyanka is a fighter,' gushes Shukla.

But succeeding in the harsh political terrain of eastern UP would need more than just fighting spirit. This became apparent when Priyanka finally landed in her 'karmabhoomi' – Lucknow – accompanied by Rahul and Jyotiraditya, the other UP general secretary. The state Congress had planned a roadshow, all the way from Lucknow's Amausi airport to Jawahar Bhawan, the party office, in the heart of the city, a 25-kilometre-long route. Congress posters and flags fluttered along the course, workers with rose petals were planted at vantage points, but it was apparent that, despite their best efforts, the enfeebled UP Congress unit was unable to enthuse the Lucknow populace. Long stretches of the route stood empty on either side, with hardly any crowds to greet the Congress first family. At a number of places, the leaders atop the bus had to duck under overhead electric wires. They also had to shift to an open jeep halfway through the journey because of security constraints. 'It was very badly planned,' says Maushumi Singh, *India Today*'s intrepid journalist on the Congress beat. 'They should have made it a shorter roadshow to attract more people.' The contrast with Modi's masterfully planned and executed roadshows, for example the choreographed spectacle of the PM filing his nomination in Varanasi in April, could not have been more stark. Even so, the Congress had captured precious TV time for an entire day, with Priyanka as the star attraction.

That evening, at the end of the roadshow, Rahul addressed a group of enthusiastic Congress workers on the lawns of Jawahar Bhavan even as Priyanka and Jyotiraditya gave the occasional wave from the stage. 'Chowkidar chor hai!' Rahul exhorted the crowd to repeat after him as he delivered his Rafale-centric speech. 'Why isn't Priyanka speaking, isn't this her big moment?' Maushumi asked party workers. 'Priyanka will speak to you later, not now,' she was told by the Congress media team. For the next two days, Priyanka stayed put mostly at Jawahar Bhavan, meeting party workers late into the night, finishing only around 4 a.m. 'Why don't you go and get some sleep, I will surely speak to you later,' she promised the journalists who were tracking her every move.

On 14 February, Priyanka's media liaison person informed the increasingly impatient journalists that she would hold her first formal press conference that evening at around 7 p.m. 'We will cut live to it and stay with the story, let's get plenty of guests in the studio too to analyse Priyanka's debut performance,' was our news editor's brief to an excited newsroom. I hadn't seen such interest in a Congress leader's press interaction in a long while.

It was time for another dramatic, and in this instance arguably decisive, twist in the roller-coaster journey that the 2019 election was turning out to be.

Looming snow-capped mountains surround the dilapidated hamlets and curving streams of Pulwama district in J&K. Tiny huts and farmsteads hug the slopes along the road. The 271-kilometre-long Jammu–Srinagar highway winds its way through rough, mountainous terrain, the Himalayas in the distance. As one enters the Kashmir valley in spring, nature's varied hues reflect the glory of a land once described by Emperor Jahangir as paradise on earth. In Pulwama, about 40 kilometres from Srinagar, the rich orangish-golden glow of saffron fields and the tall chinar trees provide an impressive backdrop. But spring was still several weeks away when on Thursday, 14 February 2019, an army convoy of seventy-eight vehicles, transporting 2,547 CRPF jawans left Jammu transit camp at 3.30 a.m. It had been a harsh winter and the landscape wore a barren look. The jawans had been stranded in Jammu because of heavy snowfall since 4 February and the convoy strength had been increased to clear the pile-up. The CRPF has sixty-one battalions in the region, forty-eight in Kashmir and thirteen in Jammu, with a total strength of over 60,000. The vehicles were just about an hour away from their destination when, at around 3.10 p.m. in Lethpora in Pulwama district, an explosives-laden vehicle suddenly veered into the Jammu–Srinagar highway from the left by-lane. It overtook the buses at speed, then rammed into the fifth bus in the convoy, and exploded. The bus was blown to bits; the sixth bus too was impacted by the blast. Forty jawans were killed and several injured. Over 80 kilograms of explosives had been used.

Sitting in his sprawling office at the CRPF headquarters in Srinagar, Zulfiqar Hassan, Inspector General (Operations), was hoping for a quiet afternoon. A 1988 Bengal cadre IPS officer, the battle-hardened Hassan, a history graduate from St. Stephen's College, has served in some of the toughest parts of the country, having spent three years handling Naxal operations in Chhattisgarh and two years in the Valley at the time of the attack. 'Shock and then mounting anger,' is how the grey-haired officer describes his initial emotions. Fighting terror in the Valley has always been a major challenge but now there was a new threat: the suicide bomber had come to Kashmir. And for the first time a police convoy had been targeted on a busy highway. In 2003, after the then J&K government alleged that civilians were being inconvenienced by restrictions when army convoys were travelling, the rules were changed to ensure that civilian vehicles were not stopped even during troop movement. Private cars were allowed to overtake and even drive between convoy vehicles. 'We had followed all the standard operating procedures with the Road Opening Party securing this particular stretch of a road by sanitizing it from mines and bombs. What we could not have anticipated was a suicide bomber would hit the convoy like this,' observes Hassan.

It had been a relatively low-key news afternoon in the newsroom as well. Late afternoons are usually slow, a lull before the prime-time storm. The news menu for the day was dominated by preparations for Priyanka's press conference scheduled for that evening and we had lined up our guests and OB vans accordingly. I was walking into the office around 4 p.m. when I saw the breaking news flashes on the screen: 'Blast in Kashmir, several jawans injured.' A blast in Kashmir is unfortunately hardly unusual and the news coming from the ground still seemed sketchy. But by around 5 p.m., it was clear that this wasn't just another terror attack in the Valley. The news flash now reflected greater urgency: 'At least ten jawans feared dead in attack on CRPF convoy.' As the first pictures from the site were broadcast, it became apparent that this was one of the deadlier terror strikes to have taken place in the Valley. An entire bus had been blown to smithereens. A video released by the Jaish-e-Mohammad claimed responsibility and identified Adil Ahmad Dar as the suicide bomber. In the video, Dar, a resident of Gundibagh village of Pulwama, is seen standing in front of Jaish banners and brandishing rifles.

The newsroom was now buzzing. Phones were furiously ringing in South Block too. National Security Adviser Ajit Doval had been alerted and the entire security establishment was called in for an emergency meeting. The prime minister though was not in Delhi: he was away in the forests of Corbett Park, shooting for a Discovery Channel documentary, and was not informed of the terror attack for some time. 'We were not sure of the scale of what had happened so didn't want to create unnecessary panic. The PM's shoot was already over well before 3 p.m.,' insists a PMO official when questioned about the opposition's criticism that the prime minister kept filming while jawans lay dead. The optics though were terrible: a prime minister on a wildlife shoot for a private TV channel while a national security crisis was unfolding showed a howling, dreadful disconnect between ground realities and high officialdom. 'A prime minister out on a picnic while the nation is bleeding,' was the sharp Congress attack. For once, Modi's media machine was on the defensive, forced to provide a minute-by-minute account of the PM's day out in Uttarakhand.

For Prime Minister Modi, the Pulwama attack posed a serious question over his government's handling of the violence-prone Valley and its Pakistan policy. Kashmir had been one of the items on top of the PM's agenda when he took over in 2014, as was Pakistan. The J&K elections in December 2014 had thrown up a hung assembly; the BJP was in a position to bargain with the two Valley-based parties, the National Conference and the PDP, for a power-sharing arrangement. Led by veteran politician Mufti Mohammad Sayeed, the PDP had secured the maximum seats and was the obvious front runner in the alliance game. A tie-up between the PDP and the BJP was never going to be easy given their vastly different ideological positions, but the idea of a Muslim-dominated party breaking bread with a Hindutva force seemed to appeal to both Mufti and Modi, a chance to exorcize the demons of a fraught past. 'I felt that we could create history and break the religious divide once and for all,' Mufti would later tell me. 'What better way was there for Modi to demonstrate his peaceful intentions than by allying with us?'

BJP general secretary Ram Madhav was made the party's point person to kick-start the dialogue while the PDP made its erudite, newly elected MLA, Haseeb Drabu its emissary. 'You won't believe this but we first met in a Sahara Star airport hotel room in Mumbai in January 2015 so that we could avoid the media glare,' reveals Madhav. Soon, the meetings became more frequent and the duo were even christened the 'Ram–Rahim jodi' within political circles. By end February, a blueprint for a common minimum programme of governance was ready. There were two contentious issues, Article 370 and a dialogue with all stakeholders, including the separatist Hurriyat Conference, that took days to resolve. The BJP agreed to keep their ideological stand regarding the abolishment of Article 370 on the back burner and even accepted the PDP's demand to facilitate a dialogue with the separatists. When the draft was finally readied, it was taken to the then finance minister, Arun Jaitley, for his approval. Jaitley, however, was in the midst of budget preparations and couldn't meet the Madhav–Drabu duo inside North Block for security reasons. 'It was almost midnight when Jaitleyji came out and met us on the road outside the finance ministry from where he rang up the prime minister to get the final nod and seal the deal,' discloses Madhav. His counterpart, Drabu, describes it as a 'partnership forged in a spirit of positive intent'.

In March 2015, when Mufti was sworn in as chief minister in Jammu's flower-bedecked General Zorawar Singh Auditorium, it was a piquant political moment which looked outwardly like a clash of civilizations. Kurta-clad Hindutva politicians of the BJP, some sporting orange safas, lined up on stage with the Kashmiri Muslim politicians of the PDP, some of the men in suits, one of the women members in fashionable stiletto heels, another sharply dressed PDP member in a hat, and Sajjad Lone in a pathan suit. Cries of 'Jai Shri Ram' alternated with 'I swear in the name of Allah' during the oath-taking. The alliance was full of unknown possibilities, it seemed as if a new beginning in political coexistence was being incubated. For Modi, in particular, the alliance was a bold gamble, a statesman-like move that would prove to his critics that he was more than just a narrow-minded Hindutva leader. 'Naya Kashmir banana hai' (A new Kashmir has to be built), he told sceptical colleagues. But in January 2016, barely nine months into power, an ailing Mufti suddenly passed away and the romantic illusion of a grand Hindu–Muslim political compact was thrown into chaos. Mufti's daughter, Mehbooba, was a very different politician from her father. Where he was cerebral, she was mercurial; where he was introspective, she was impulsive; where he was a strategist, she was a street fighter. 'With Mehbooba, the comfort factor we had with Mufti saab was gone; she was too caught up in her own politics of appeasing local militant groups,' argues Madhav.

The troubled relationship faced its first big test when Burhan Wani, a young Hizbul Mujahideen terrorist, was killed by security forces in July 2016. Wani had emerged as a popular figure for a dangerous form of violent Islamic radicalism which was simmering under the surface. His death sparked off protests across the Valley. 'Wani's killing was a trigger for the pent-up anger of Kashmiris, especially the youth, who felt betrayed by the ruling PDP. He became a symbolic figure of rebellion against misuse of state power,' says Muzamil Jaleel, a senior journalist who has covered Kashmir for years.

As the violence spread, ninety-six people were killed and several thousands injured. The summer of 2016 was a bloody one in the Valley, another turning point in a conflict that had torn Kashmir apart for over two decades. Until then, Mehbooba had been pushing the Centre to build bridges with the militants and announce a unilateral ceasefire. The violent aftermath of Wani's killing marked the end of the peacemaking efforts as a hard-nosed Doval took over decision-making on Kashmir from Rajnath Singh's home ministry. The security forces launched Operation All Out, with clear instructions that there was to be no let-up in the anti-terror ops. In 2017, 213 militants were killed but terrorism also spiked with 342 terrorist strikes claiming the lives of forty civilians and eighty security forces personnel. The 'Doval doctrine' of 'offensive defence' was now given full play, a strategy devised by the prime minister's national security adviser to keep the enemy constantly on the run, one that was hitting hard at terrorists but also raising concerns over mounting civilian casualties.

By early 2018, the Mehbooba–BJP equation had completely broken down. The BJP accused her of hobnobbing with militants; she in turn blamed the BJP for fanning protests against her government when she acted sternly against the culprits in the horrific Kathua rape and murder case. 'This alliance with the BJP is like drinking poison,' she claimed, giving voice to the simmering discontent. 'The real issue is that Mehbooba had little experience in governance. Her father was a negotiator who tried to build an alliance out of conviction, while she is a bargainer who just couldn't get down to the business of governing a complex state,' says Drabu, who was sacked as state finance minister in March 2018. In June, the BJP formally broke the alliance, ending a three-year experiment, allegedly without even informing Mehbooba of their decision. 'I came to know of it from the media,' she asserts.

That the BJP chose to finally end its J&K alliance just nine months before the 2019 elections reveals how political objectives were slowly shifting, not just in the Valley but also in the rest of the country. For the BJP's core support base, Mehbooba was always the 'enemy', an 'anti-national' figure who had a soft spot for stone-pelting youth. On the other hand, the macho nationalism of the BJP was always at odds with Mehbooba's professed politics of a 'healing touch': if she saw the stone-pelters as 'misguided' youth, the BJP viewed them as hand in glove with jihadi groups. This uneasy relationship had endured till 2018 because, more often than not, power is the glue that binds antagonistic forces seeking benefits, albeit temporary. But the realpolitik of a national election meant that Mehbooba was now eminently dispensable, providing the BJP with an opportunity to re-emphasize its 'nationalistic' credentials. 'I guess it was a doomed alliance in the circumstances,' admits Madhav.

What was also doomed was the knotty India–Pakistan equation, with its yo-yo-like swings. Modi had created a stir with his bold invitation to Nawaz Sharif to attend his swearing-in ceremony. But just three months later, in August 2014, the government cancelled foreign secretary–level talks to protest the invitation extended by the Pakistan high commissioner to separatist Hurriyat leaders to meet them for consultations. Less than a year later, in July 2015, Modi and Sharif were happily posing for the cameras and holding a one-on-one meeting in the Russian city of Ufa. T.C.A. Raghavan, former Indian high commissioner to Pakistan, notes, 'Our diplomatic ties with Islamabad are consciously inconsistent, you just can't do it any other way given the instability inside Pakistan.' Raghavan should know. He was India's man in Islamabad when Modi, in a characteristic headline-grabbing move, dropped in unannounced on Sharif in Lahore while on his way back from Russia via Afghanistan – the first Indian prime minister to visit Pakistan in a decade. It was Christmas Day in 2015 and Modi, it seems, was in a mood to play Santa Claus. He was flown in a chopper to Sharif's palatial residence in Raiwind near Lahore where the Pakistan premier's granddaughter was getting married. It was also Sharif's sixty-sixth birthday, another reason to celebrate. 'None of us were prepared for it. There had been some back-channel talk to restart the dialogue but nothing to suggest that the Indian prime minister would drop in to meet Sharif in such a cagey manner,' admits a former diplomat. But the ability to surprise, to take the odd risk, to stage a spectacular 'event' is Modi's USP, only this time he was dealing with a hostile neighbour whose military establishment calls the shots and isn't used to accommodating any bombshells from the civilian leadership.

Barely a week after Modi and Sharif engaged in their own diplomatic love-fest, on 2 January 2016, six terrorists, heavily armed with explosives and assault weapons struck at the air force station in Pathankot. Once again, this attack starkly revealed that tangling with Pakistan would never be just a smooth exchange of birthday party visits. Seven security personnel were killed in a gun battle that lasted more than seventeen hours; the entire operation stretched over three days. New Delhi and Mumbai were placed on high alert. Two months after the attack, in a break with the past, India even allowed a Pakistani investigation team to visit the airbase and remain for three days, to collect evidence and conduct interviews with witnesses and survivors. 'We wanted to call Islamabad's bluff that they would act against terror groups like the Jaish based on evidence provided to them,' is how a security official describes the controversial move.

Far from the terror groups being reined in, the violence only intensified in that blood-spattered summer in the Kashmir valley in 2016. The deadliest attack occurred on 18 September 2016 at an army camp in Uri in Baramulla district. As many as nineteen soldiers were killed when four terrorists from the Jaish stormed the camp in a predawn ambush, lobbing seventeen grenades in three minutes and catching sleeping soldiers off guard. It was a well-planned terror operation, exposing the gaping holes in a highly fortified security ring around the army base. By now India's most secure targets – an air force and an army camp – had been badly hit. For the Modi government, Uri was the last straw. The prime minister was realizing, as several of his predecessors had, that terror and talks could not coexist. When in the opposition, Modi would often lampoon the Manmohan Singh government for its failure to act decisively against Pak-based terror groups. Now, he was in the hot seat, with no effective results to show for his actions. 'Look, I really think few Indian prime ministers in the last thirty years have tried as hard as Modi to break the impasse with Pakistan. It's just that it isn't easy dealing with an antagonistic neighbour whose army needs to keep the Kashmir pot boiling for its own survival,' remarks Raghavan.

It wasn't just the prime minister whose credibility was on the line. National Security Adviser Doval's own judgement was being called into question. It was Doval who would supervise the entire plan to 'avenge' the Uri attack once he was given the go-ahead by the prime minister. For years, he had been advocating the right of hot pursuit across the Line of Control (LoC); now, he had a chance to translate his words into action. A mini war room was established in the South Block with Doval conducting regular briefings with a small team of officers. After intelligence inputs established the exact location of the launch pads, the army moved in a crack commando team to the LoC on the Indo-Pak border. Armed with M4 assault rifles, under-barrel grenade launchers and night-vision devices, around twenty-five commandos crossed over the LoC and carried out the operations inside Pakistan-Occupied Kashmir (POK) in the early hours of 29 September, barely ten days after the Uri attack. As part of their gear, the troops were carrying helmet-mounted cameras to record the operation. By noon, the MEA and the Ministry of Defence issued a joint statement claiming that, 'During counter-terrorism operations, significant casualties have been caused to the terrorists and those who are trying to support them. We have no plans for continuation of further operations.'

By evening, almost every major news channel had converted their studios into war rooms, with breathless news anchors in army fatigues lending a theatrical touch to the 'surgical strikes'. While Pakistan insisted that there had been no cross-LoC strike, the Modi government maintained that it had gone much further than any previous administration in responding to these terror attacks. No details of the exact number of casualties were officially provided but 'sources' claimed that four terrorist launch pads were destroyed and close to forty terrorists were killed. The narrative was set even before the story could fully unfold: Modi was the 'bold warrior' who had taught Pakistan a 'lesson'. The doctrine of strategic restraint as a political construct guiding previous governments was effectively done away with as soon as the surgical strikes were announced to the world: a new line was drawn in the shifting sands of Indo-Pak engagement.

A few days after the surgical strikes were executed in 2016, I went to meet former prime minister, Dr Singh and asked him for his response to the strikes. Not surprisingly, the camera-shy leader was unwilling to do a TV interview, but gently told me, 'You know, when we were in government, we also undertook similar anti-terror operations, only we didn't publicize it like this.' Dr Singh preferred to keep his counsel on the sensitive issue but his party leader Rahul Gandhi was less restrained, describing the Modi government's actions as 'khoon ki dalali', a rather crude remark which the BJP could easily exploit as indicative of an insensitive approach to the sacrifices of our soldiers.

Truth is, the Modi government *did* 'market' the 2016 surgical strikes with great precision. Within twenty-four hours of the news breaking, local BJP units put up posters in different parts of the country, especially in poll-bound UP, hailing the prime minister's 'achievement'. BJP spokespersons were all over TV screens, exulting over what was being described as a Kargil-like 'triumph' over the 'enemy country'. A few weeks after the surgical strikes, Modi appeared on stage at the Aishbagh Ram Leela Ground in Lucknow, posing with a fake sudarshan chakra, being lauded as the 'avenger of Uri'. Social media – the ultimate echo chamber – was splashed with euphoric hashtags: '56 inch ka seena' (56-inch chest), a reference to Modi's broad-chested political boast. Interestingly, it was only two years later, in June 2018 (and later in September of the same year), as the countdown to the general elections kick-started, that the government released select videos of the strikes. The footage, some of it shot from drone cameras, reveals hazy images of the army opening fire, dramatic enough to convince the TV viewer that sufficient damage was inflicted on Pakistan. Even if the specific loss to terrorists could not be quantified, the perception 'war' in the media had been well and truly won.

I realized the impact of this media frenzy when I went to see the film *Uri: The Surgical Strike* in January 2019. The film which, despite its disclaimers, is an obvious take-off from the 2016 surgical strike operation – even the main political characters are made to resemble Modi and Doval – clearly struck a chord with the audience in the packed hall. Every time the lead actor, Vicky Kaushal, playing the role of the commanding officer, asked his fellow commandos 'How's the josh?', the response in the auditorium was near-hysterical. 'How's the josh?' the viewing public chanted and cheered. As we were leaving the cinema hall, a young man in a bright red T-shirt seemed to recognize me and shouted, 'Bharat Mata ki Jai'! 'People like you on TV must show more deshbhakti instead of criticizing the government all the time,' he remarked pointedly.

Just months ahead of the 2019 elections, the mood of hyper-nationalism was set, especially among the film-crazy urban middle classes. Uri would go on to become one of the blockbuster films of the year and the prime minister and his cabinet ministers often resorted to its popular line 'How's the josh?' in their public interactions. The film would also win four national awards, including best director and actor. The timing of its release was just perfect, almost designed to elevate the Uri strikes into the ultimate act of military heroism at a time when the Modi government was also glorifying the strikes as one of its triumphs (in September 2018, the government organized a 'Parakram Parv', a three-day event across India to celebrate the valour of the soldiers).

'Look, if you think that this is a case of the tail wagging the dog and that we timed this film to suit the Modi government's political agenda, you are completely mistaken,' film producer Ronnie Screwvala tells me. 'I wanted to make a great war film, loved the script shown to me by Aditya [Aditya Dhar is the first-time director of *Uri*] and just decided to back it in 2017 itself. Even the army was initially hesitant to support us which is why we ended up shooting the commando sequences in Serbia. Yes, Mr Doval did encourage us but only by sharing information, most of which is already in the public domain.'

Whether by accident or otherwise, while *Uri* scored at the box office, Team Modi would reap its benefits in the election stakes. Uri though was only a trailer; post-Pulwama, an even bigger strike was in the offing, one that would play out on a much larger stage: the 90-crore-plus Indian electorate.

Narendra Modi arrived in the national capital well past 7 p.m. on 14 February as late winter darkness enveloped the city. It had already been a long day which had begun early morning with a trip to the forests of Uttarakhand for the Discovery Channel shoot. The Pulwama attack meant that the prime minister could scarcely afford to even think of his jungle adventure. A crisis meeting was already on at the national security secretariat, with Doval once again taking charge of the rapidly developing situation. The prime minister was given a full briefing on the nature of the strike. As the death toll rose, it became apparent that the suicide attack had shaken the country. On TV, angry political voices were baying for blood: 'Khoon ka badla khoon' (Blood for blood), screamed a retired major-general. J&K governor Satya Pal Malik was heard admitting to an intelligence failure, a point emphasized by opposition leaders like the Congress's Digvijaya Singh. With the general election announcement less than a month away, time was not on the side of the government. The 2016 surgical strikes had set the template: Team Modi realized that it couldn't afford to sit back and wait for the situation to gradually unravel.

The first step was to ensure that the government, and not the opposition, controlled the narrative. Before the 'intelligence failure' chorus could gather any further momentum, the spirit of martyrdom was invoked. When the bodies of the forty slain CRPF jawans reached Palam air force area in a special Indian Air Force plane the next evening, the prime minister was there to pay homage. With a thick black shawl wrapped around his shoulders, hands folded and head bowed, Modi walked slowly around each of the forty coffins draped in the tricolour. It was a solemn moment, one which opposition leaders, including Rahul Gandhi, were also part of. In a time of national mourning, any talk of 'intelligence failure' seemed jarring. The prime minister also directed all his ministers and BJP MPs to attend the funerals of the jawans who had belonged to their respective states. Funeral processions were organized through the towns and villages of the martyrs: twelve of the jawans were from UP. The mood was one of grief and remembrance, and slowly building up into anger and revenge.

The TV studio was back to being transformed into a high-decibel war room as news channels competed with each other to capture the rage of a wounded nation. Incendiary hashtags like #PakWill Pay and #IndiaWantsRevenge were stamped on the screen. 'Pakistan must be taught a lesson they will never forget, bahut ho chuka,' an angry relative was heard shouting on TV. War-game strategies were being feverishly discussed, including the possibility of targeted missile attacks inside Pakistan. 'So what if there is a threat of a nuclear war, we can meet any challenge,' a general known for his strident views blared on TV.

Inside Pakistan, the mood was more sombre, a reflection of a troubled nation caught in the cross hairs of a crumbling economy and well-entrenched terror infrastructure, with a new leadership at the helm. Imran Khan had been elected prime minister in August 2018, marking the culmination of a remarkable journey from World Cup–winning captain to the country's chief executive. Imran was charismatic and courageous, but where his cricket had dazzled, his political inclinations were viewed with suspicion: he was sometimes referred to as 'Taliban' Khan for his alleged support to the Afghan Taliban militias. Others saw him as a 'puppet' of the army, a leader being propped up by the men in uniform who wanted greater control over the civilian leadership. I knew Imran reasonably well: a strong cricket connection was our common bond and during the 2011 World Cup, Imran had even spent a month with us in the studios as a cricket analyst. Soon after he took over as prime minister, I asked him for an interview, only to receive a stern message via WhatsApp: 'The Indian media has not been kind to me. I can't believe they sided with that crook Nawaz Sharif. I will speak to you, but not now.'

Imran, in fact, enjoyed a peculiar love–hate relationship with India. No other Pakistan prime minister had visited India so often or had so many friends among the country's rich and famous, and yet he was also a politician whose firm views on contentious issues like Kashmir attracted furious responses. In December 2015, Imran was in India to attend Aaj Tak's annual conclave: the Indian high commission in Islamabad offered to facilitate a meeting with Prime Minister Modi. 'What's Mr Modi like?' he asked me. 'I am sure you will find out for yourself soon,' was my prompt response. Imran, then an opposition leader, spent forty-five minutes in conversation with Modi. He returned, clearly bowled over by the Indian prime minister. 'He seems a really nice guy, not at all how the media portrays him!' he gushed. Imran's special assistant, Naeem-ul-Haq, who was also at the meeting, recalls Prime Minister Modi telling Imran that Pakistan should import tea from India. 'It was all very cordial and warm,' says Haq.

In his initial remarks after taking over as prime minister, Imran seemed keen to reciprocate that warmth. 'If India takes one step, we will take two,' promised Imran in his inaugural address to the nation. A month later, in September 2018, reality struck. India called off foreign minister–level talks on the sidelines of the UN General Assembly meet in New York, citing the continuing violence in Kashmir as the reason. 'I am disappointed with the Modi government, I don't understand this behaviour. Surely leaders must look beyond elections,' was his response when I repeated my request for an interview which he once again politely declined.

In November 2018, peace was back on the agenda. India and Pakistan announced that they would develop the Kartarpur Corridor: a 2.5-kilometre corridor that would link two holy Sikh shrines across the border to facilitate the visa-free movement of Sikh pilgrims who wished to visit Gurdwara Darbar Sahib – the final resting place of Guru Nanak Dev – in Pakistan's Kartarpur. The announcement had come on the back of a much-publicized 'hug' between the Pakistan army chief, General Qamar Javed Bajwa, and the Punjab Congress cricketer-turned-politician Navjot Singh Sidhu, during Imran's swearing-in ceremony. 'I am a goodwill ambassador,' exulted Sidhu, brushing aside criticism of his actions, and revelling in his new-found stardom across the border. The hug may have been genuine but suspicion remained that the Pakistan army was using Kartarpur to deflect attention from its continuing support to terror groups operating in the Kashmir valley.

I was, in fact, part of a group of Indian journalists invited to witness the foundation stone–laying ceremony in Pakistan. I jumped at the offer, hoping to once again establish contact with Imran and push for an interview. The visit though was a security nightmare: at almost every step, we were tracked by burly Pakistani Rangers. The domineering presence of the army was suffocating and gave us little chance to move about freely. When Imran finally arrived for a press meet, he mouthed the usual platitudes. 'How many times will you ask me the same questions, we must look ahead, not in the past, else we will get nowhere,' was his tetchy response when I asked him why Pakistan had not taken any action against 1993 Mumbai blast mastermind Dawood Ibrahim and 26/11 accused Hafiz Saeed of the terror outfit Lashkar-e-Taiba. As he was leaving, I reminded him of the promised interview. 'Yes, yes, we will do it, let's first at least resume the dialogue,' he reiterated.

Now, just three months after the jhappiyan-pappiyan (hugs and kisses) of Kartarpur, the massacre in Pulwama came as a wake-up call. The dark side of Pak-based terror groups was bared once again, leaving

New Delhi with few options but to strike back. 'Is India really going to war?' a worried Pakistani journalist friend asked me. I didn't respond but an escalating conflict appeared inevitable. Prime Minister Modi was pretty clear right from the outset: he would not go in for a 'soft' option. 'Previous governments may have chosen the diplomatic route but this prime minister wanted an offensive option that would end Pakistan's 'nuclear blackmail' once and for all,' says a senior official. In 2001, when Parliament was attacked, then Prime Minister Vajpayee had reportedly considered an air strike on Pak-based terror camps but abandoned the idea for fear of the situation spiralling out of control. Instead, a ten-month-long deployment of armed forces along the border under Operation Parakram was the preferred choice. When terrorists struck in Mumbai in 2008, the Manmohan Singh government too had reportedly weighed the options of an air strike before eventually choosing coercive diplomacy as a more effective response. 'I do not know what the air force was telling itself but that [an air strike] is not the message the political leadership heard from the three chiefs who briefed Dr Singh's government. I heard no fear of escalation but only a clear calculation of likely outcomes and which would be better for India,' explains Shiv Shankar Menon, former foreign secretary and national security adviser to the UPA government.

Modi though was unwavering in his belief that the 'strategic restraint' script needed to be rewritten, even if it meant taking an audacious risk before a general election. The message to Doval and the armed forces chiefs was unambiguous: there must be 'visible' action against the terror groups and their handlers embedded in the Pakistani state. The focus needed to be on the terror training camps; collateral damage to civilian and military targets was to be avoided at all costs. In effect, India's response needed to be proportionate to what Pakistan had done and within range of what the international community would view as 'reasonable' action. Says *India Today* editorial director Raj Chengappa, 'The idea was not to prevent escalation but to get the escalation threshold just right.' It was a risk, but one which, in the circumstances, was seen as one well worth taking.

The inside story of the air strikes reveals careful planning and a daring yet simple strategy. Intelligence agencies reportedly chose fifteen places run by different terror groups in Pakistan as potential strike targets. Three specific camps of the Jaish, the organization widely held responsible for Pulwama, were identified: one was in Bahawalpur in Pakistan's Punjab province, the others in Sawai Nallah near Muzaffarabad in Pak-Occupied Kashmir and Balakot in the Khyber-Pakhtunkhwa Province (KPK). The Bahawalpur complex was ruled out because any strike on it might incur civilian casualties: the complex was located within a fairly densely populated area. Sawai Nallah was perhaps the easiest to hit since it was closest to the border but any attack in POK might be seen only as yet another surgical strike. 'Given what had happened in Pulwama, we wanted to make a much bigger noise this time, one that would echo through the country and the world,' admits a government official.

The Jaish camp in Balakot fit all the criteria set by the prime minister: it was located in a relatively isolated area on the crest of a ridge called Jaba Top. Spread over a sprawling six acres, the camp consisted of ten buildings conducting training activities for terrorists. The camp was run by Masood Azhar's brother-in-law Yusuf Azhar, who lived in an abandoned school complex on the campus. It was estimated that over 200 terror recruits were staying in the camp. A fresh group was to join on 25 February, taking the total number to over 300, making it the ideal period to inflict maximum damage. High-resolution satellite imagery was used to determine the lay of the land. On 19 February, Prime Minister Modi gave the go-ahead to the core team led by Doval. The actual strike plan was left to Air Chief Birender Singh Dhanoa to execute. The flying ace and Kargil air operations hero had a reputation of being a no-nonsense man in uniform. 'We were always ready and waiting for this moment for a very long time,' the fighter pilot chief would later tell journalists.

Operation Bandar was carried out around 3 a.m. on 26 February under the cover of darkness by a squadron of a dozen Mirage 2000 aircraft equipped with Israeli built SPICE (Smart Precise Impact and Cost Effective) bombs and aided by a sophisticated guidance system that could hit with precision at an intended target 60 kilometres away. The Mirages were accompanied by four Sukhoi 30s to provide air cover. Two surveillance aircraft and two IL 76s were also deployed for mid-air refuelling. As the aircraft flew into Pakistani airspace, one lot flew towards Bahawalpur, misleading the Pakistan air defence system into believing that the Jaish camp in the Punjab region was the target. As Pakistani fighters scrambled to take on the Indian jets, the low-flying Mirage 2000s headed for Balakot. By the time the Pakistani radar detected them, they were already 150 kilometres away. Five bombs reportedly struck the targets, three of them hitting the buildings where the Jaish recruits were staying. The actual bombing lasted for just thirteen minutes, between 3.40 a.m. and 3.53 a.m.; by the early hours of 26 February, the jets were back in India, mission accomplished.

The 7 a.m. news report was buzzing with the big breaking news: 'Pulwama Avenged' with fireballs spewing out from different corners of the TV set. Shedding any notion of journalistic objectivity, news anchors were congratulating the Modi government for 'teaching Pakistan a lesson'. There was bedlam on social media too: at one stage, all the top ten trends in the country on Twitter were linked to Balakot.

For Prime Minister Modi, the forty-eight hours leading up to the air strikes had been business as usual. On 24 February, he had travelled to Gorakhpur in eastern UP, where the BJP would battle the Akhilesh–Mayawati combine, to launch the Kisan Samman Nidhi Yojana, where the first instalment of the ₹6,000 annual financial assistance to farmers was credited to their Jan Dhan accounts. A series of regular meetings followed the next day as Modi kept up the pretence of normalcy. But under the calm exterior, anxiety was reportedly mounting: Modi would stay awake all night, one eye on the computer screen, the other on the phone. He had taken a big gamble, one that could make or break his prime-ministerial tenure. It was only around 4 a.m. that Modi was informed of the mission's successful completion and he could finally relax a bit. His early morning yoga routine was going to be particularly energizing. By 11.30 a.m., the then foreign secretary Vijay Gokhale officially acknowledged the strikes inside Pakistan as part of a 'non-military, pre-emptive strike', claiming that a number of fidayeen and terror trainers had been killed. 'I think Balakot was a strategy of measured escalation that was proportionate to the Pakistani provocation and deserves to be applauded,' says G. Parthasarathy, former Indian high commissioner to Pakistan. Islamabad's 'nuclear blackmail' threat had been responded to in a decisive manner. The world was standing by India's action as was most of the country.

This was the moment Prime Minister Modi had been waiting for from the day he moved to 7 Lok Kalyan Marg. His complex persona is riven by a desire to be both feared and embraced. The 'fear factor' had been established domestically early enough; now, the world was ready to accept him as a true global figure. Not since the 1971 war, when Indira Gandhi was prime minister, had the Indian air force penetrated so deep into Pakistani airspace and inflicted damage on the 'enemy'. Although he might not admit it publicly, Indira Gandhi is a politician whom Modi admires, even if he often describes the Emergency as a 'dark chapter' in democracy. 'Modi often attacks Nehru but despite the Emergency, you will rarely see him condemn Indira. I think he secretly approves of her autocratic, centralizing tendencies in spirit if not in letter,' says Nilanjan Mukhopadhyaya, a Modi biographer. Balakot, at least in the shaping of Modi's larger-than-life image, was his version of 1971, proof of decisive leadership.

This 'strongman' image would soon be further enhanced. Just a day after the Balakot strike, the very next morning, Pakistani fighter jets came rushing into Indian airspace in broad daylight over J&K's Rajouri and Naushera sectors and dropped bombs in uninhabited areas. India believes Pakistan's intention was to target ammunition points and army bases. Indian jets immediately gave chase, a dogfight ensued and an Indian Air Force pilot, Wing Commander Abhinandan Varthaman, was captured after Pakistani jets shot down his MiG-21. Videos released by Pakistani authorities showed the strapping Abhinandan being interrogated while being tied and blindfolded, his face and gun-slinger-like moustache all bloodied. 'That was the one moment when we felt that maybe we could be losing control over events,' admits a government official. And yet, just a day later, on 28 February, Imran Khan announced at a joint sitting of the Pakistani parliament that his government was releasing Abhinandan as a 'gesture of peace'. It marked perhaps the final capitulation by a beleaguered Pakistani leadership, already under pressure to deliver on anti-terror operations or face blacklisting under the stringent financial action task force norms. Top government sources reveal that Abhinandan's swift release followed sustained diplomatic pressure in which both the US and Saudi Arabia were involved. 'Both Washington and Riyadh played a major role behind the scenes in ensuring that Islamabad got the message,' claims a senior government official.

Typically, Abhinandan's release became another media 'event' for the Modi government to artfully exploit. Addressing a political rally on the day of the release, Modi dubbed the pilot a 'national hero'. 'The nation is proud of your exemplary courage and valour,' declared the prime minister. The incessant TV coverage meant that Abhinandan's fearsome handlebar moustache was 'trending' across the country within twenty-four hours. Dairy giant Amul even produced a video featuring a little girl wearing an Abhinandan-style moustache! The BJP propaganda machine too was quick to act: posters suddenly appeared at all party offices featuring Modi and the wing commander together.

The military operation inside Pakistan was over; now the political campaign at home would begin. At the heart of it was a media blitz that would see Modi being projected as a political 'superman'. On TV, the BJP's spokespersons went into overdrive, likening the prime minister to Bahubali, the fantasy film hero who would destroy all evil in his path. Memes and videos – some with Prime Minister Modi dressed in army fatigues – were quickly produced by the party's tech support teams and spread across thousands of WhatsApp groups and on social media. Information and Broadcasting (I&B) minister Rajyavardhan Rathore and chief BJP spokesperson Anil Baluni reportedly telephoned news channels, asking them to hold 'national security summits' where the BJP's cabinet ministers would be lined up to speak on the Modi government's achievements. A series of day-long conclaves were organized across news channels where government ministers kept eulogizing the prime minister's 'fearless' decision-making. 'What's wrong in publicizing a victory when we would have faced flak if things had gone wrong in Balakot?' asks a senior Modi minister. Even serving generals were encouraged to praise the political leadership, revealing a potentially dangerous blurring of lines between the netas and the men in uniform.

And yet, a few knotty questions remained. Should Balakot really be seen as a 'warlike' triumph? What of the intelligence failure in Pulwama that had resulted in the loss of forty jawans? What of the shooting down of an Indian Mi-17 chopper, allegedly by an IAF missile, in which six servicemen were killed? (The IAF would admit to this 'mistake' only in October 2019 when a new chief took over.) Should the government not have provided some 'proof' of the 'success' of Operation Bandar? The last question would prove politically contentious as 'government sources' were busy leaking 'information' that at least 300 terrorists had been killed in Balakot. While the air force was cautious in putting a figure to the casualties, ministers were calling up journalists to 'confirm' the death toll. Credible Western media outlets like the *New York Times* and the *Guardian*, meanwhile, reported that eyewitness accounts suggested that only a few trees had been felled and there were no signs of mass deaths. Senior Pakistani TV journalist Hamid Mir, who works for the country's leading news network Geo, put out a video which shows him allegedly in Balakot, claiming that all he has found is a dead crow; the video went viral within hours. When I contacted Mir and asked him if he was parroting the Pakistani army line, he retorted sharply: 'Why would we not report the story accurately? Weren't we the channel which also broke the story that Ajmal Kasab was a Pakistani after the 26/11 Mumbai terror attack?'

The debate over whether the Modi government should have provided more 'proof' of the Balakot strikes acquired a distinct election-driven edge when BJP president Amit Shah boasted at a rally in Gujarat: 'Under

Modi's leadership, the government carried out an air strike and killed more than 250 terrorists.' The Congress reaction was immediate, with party leaders accusing the BJP of milking the air strikes for political gain. The Congress response was met with familiar counter-accusations by the BJP, questioning the opposition's 'patriotism'. 'The entire media narrative in the country was horribly one-sided,' Congress leader Kapil Sibal tells me. 'The BJP leadership claims that 300 people died in Balakot, not us. The world media is questioning the exact damage, not us. So who is politicizing Balakot and how do I become anti-national suddenly?'

Sibal's angst is understandable: the national media was playing cheerleader to the BJP's drumbeat. But maybe the Congress-led opposition could have at least put up a more cohesive post-Balakot strategy to combat the BJP's offensive, rather than speak out in multiple voices. Punjab Chief Minister Captain Amarinder Singh, for example, could well have been the person to present the Congress stand more effectively on national security: a former military officer and war historian, he enjoyed a well-deserved reputation as a blunt, tough-talking politician on strategic affairs. Yet, the captain was barely used by the party during the entire election campaign; the Congress chose instead to project Amarinder Singh's local 'rival', Navjot Sidhu, as a 'star' speaker for sheer crowd-pulling entertainment value. I recall meeting Amarinder later during the Punjab campaign and asking him why he hadn't spoken out more strongly on Balakot. 'Well, I did speak but I live in Chandigarh and the national media seems obsessed with only what happens in and around Delhi,' he countered.

With the opposition floundering, the political momentum was now firmly with Prime Minister Modi. He had once again shown an unbridled appetite for risk-taking which had paid off: after all, giving the go-ahead to a strike inside Pakistan was a tough executive decision that required courage and firm leadership. Modi had shown both and was deservedly basking in his success. A day after Abhinandan's release, the prime minister spoke at the annual *India Today* conclave, one of the more prestigious media conclaves in the country. He was the last speaker at the two-day summit and a full house was waiting to greet him. As he strode confidently into the Durbar Hall of the Taj Palace Hotel, the audience rose in unison and broke out into prolonged applause, almost as if greeting a conquering hero – the kind of euphoric reception usually reserved for a film star.

That Modi was on a roll is best illustrated by a story related by ace *India Today* photographer Bandeep Singh. Before Modi could walk on to the stage, Singh was doing a quick photo shoot with the prime minister in the waiting room next to the main hall. 'I will need a few more pictures, sir, can I get some time from you for a more extended photo shoot?' asked Singh. Modi, ever-obliging before the camera, laughed. 'Sure, but let us plan to do it after my swearing-in is over in May!'

The words may have been spoken in jest but they reflected the growing self-belief of a consummate politician who was riding the crest of popularity. 'I have been shooting with Modi for nearly twenty years, but that day he looked like an absolute winner, no doubt about it,' says the veteran lensman. The Balakot effect was evident.

Were the Balakot air strikes really the turning point of the 2019 elections as is often advocated? Yes and no. The large survey done by the BJP in August–September 2018 which gave the BJP 300-plus seats would suggest that the prime minister was in the driver's seat even before Balakot happened. People-centric welfarism like building toilets and providing LPG gas connections were seen as Modi's vote-catching achievements and he remained well ahead of his rivals in the leadership stakes. And yet, the Congress's triple triumph in December 2018 indicated a closer race in the build-up to the general elections with issues like falling farm incomes and lack of jobs being highlighted and Rahul Gandhi suddenly being taken more seriously.

Balakot though shifted the narrative decisively away from the opposition and reinforced the prime minister's 'mazboot neta' (strong leader) image. In a sense, it ensured that the 2019 elections would be presidential in nature, a 'Modi versus who' battle in which there would be only one winner. Psephologist-turned-politician Yogendra Yadav explains, 'What Balakot did was foreground the issue of leadership and the key question of kaun banega pradhan mantri [who will become prime minister]. It forced people to once again confront the question: if not Modi, do you really want someone like Rahul Gandhi as prime minister?' Significantly, as a Centre for the Study of Developing Societies pre-poll survey in March 2019 shows, those who had heard of Balakot were more inclined to vote for the BJP by a substantial margin (46 per cent of those who had heard of the Balakot preferred Modi as PM versus 32 per cent amongst those who had not heard of it). This became what journalists called the 'Balakot bump' or the sharp uptick in Modi's approval ratings.

Balakot gave the BJP a compelling narrative to take to the voter: 'muscular nationalism' as embodied in the Modi persona, the party strategized, was enough to push a weak and divided opposition on the defensive. The post-Balakot contrast between a 'warrior-like' Modi figure and his predecessor, the scholarly, 'accidental' prime minister, Dr Singh, could not have been starker. A public rally in Ahmedabad, just a week after the Balakot strikes, defined the narrative. 'Yeh naya Bharat hai. Aatank ke saamne kabhi nahin jhukega, chun chun kar badla lega. Aur zaroorat padi toh dushman ke ghar jaakar bhi hisaab chukta karega!' (This is a new India. It will never bow before terrorism. We will take revenge. And if need be, go into enemy territory and do so!) he roared. His home audience in Gujarat clamoured 'Modi, Modi!' approvingly. Before Balakot, the '56-inch-chest' analogy was often used to lampoon the prime minister; now, he was cast as an avenging superhero. Modi's teeth-clenched open threat – 'Yeh hamara siddhant hai, hum ghar mein ghus ke marenge' (This is our stand, we will enter your home and hit you) – became a new high for aggressive nationalism. The weak-kneed pussy-footedness of past leaders had been replaced by an altogether new level of public bellicosity from the 'bahubali' PM. What may have been thought of as impossible in previous decades, was now possible.

The slightly filmi dialogue even gave the BJP's advertising campaign, spearheaded by the redoubtable Piyush Pande, the executive chairman of Ogilvy India, a fresh tag line that would resonate almost as widely as the 'Achhe din' slogan of 2014: 'Modi hai toh mumkin hai' (Nothing is impossible with Modi) became the pithy one-liner around which Team Modi now sought to build a pro-incumbency wave. 'In 2014 we were making a promise of better days or achhe din, now we were talking of performance and in that context, Balakot was one of a basket of issues around which we could create an effective campaign,' says Pande, whose trademark handlebar moustache could give fair competition to Abhinandan's.

The highly emotive post-Balakot narrative of anti-Pakistan 'nationalism' or 'rashtrawaad' also fitted in well with the RSS's core Hindutva identity and its vision of an 'Akhand Bharat'. As authors Walter Andersen and Shridhar Damle write in their book, *The RSS: A View to the Inside*, 'The essence of Hindutva is loyalty to the nation. The rationale for the formation of the RSS in 1925 was to train a cadre of men who would, motivated by a training in character-building, use diverse cultural elements to forge a loyalty to a unified Indian state.'

This notion of 'cultural nationalism' though is not always benign and inclusive: it involves a relentless search for an 'enemy' or 'hate figure' with ideological opponents being branded as 'anti-nationals'. Strident Hindutva nationalism, as the saffron brotherhood's core identity, has been primarily directed at the Indian Muslim: it was, after all, the Ram mandir movement and the subsequent demolition of the Babri Masjid in the early 1990s that transformed the BJP from a marginal party into a serious contender for power. Shrill slogans like 'Saugandh Ram ki khaate hai, mandir wahin banayenge' (In the name of Lord Ram, we swear to build a temple on that spot) and 'Jo Hindu hit ki baat karega wahi desh pe raaj karega' (Those who speak in favour of Hindus will rule the country) were part of the sant-sadhu-samaj political drumbeat. The post-Ayodhya riots led to a scarring of Hindu–Muslim relations and a consolidation of the Hindu vote bank. Modi himself was a political beneficiary of this period of intense communal conflict and his rise in Gujarat owed much to the post-2002 Hindu vote consolidation in the state. There's no space for reconciliation or consensus in the politics of Hindutva nationalism, which relies, instead, on constant confrontation. Since ideology is so dominant, there is a perpetual search for enemies, not only to galvanize the core of storm troopers and cadres, but also to keep the ideological pot churning and attract new fired-up converts. The enemy is the rallying point for political Hindus.

If, in 2002, it was the Godhra Muslims and their alleged Pakistani handlers who were the 'enemy', in 2019 it was the Kashmir-based terror groups and their Pakistani masterminds who were the obvious target of ire. The Jaish and its leader, Masood Azhar, had given the BJP leadership an emotive issue of 'muscular' religious nationalism to take to the people.

To understand how this notion of Hindutva nationalism operated in the realm of electoral politics in 2019, I met with the RSS's joint general secretary, Krishna Gopal, a key mediator between the various Sangh affiliates. Like many of his colleagues, the bright-eyed Gopal lives an ascetic-like life in a small single room near the RSS headquarters on a congested street in Jhandewalan, central Delhi. The room is sparsely furnished, a few books and newspapers are strewn around and portraits of Hindu deities smile down from a wall calendar. Initially, Gopal attempted to steer the conversation away from party politics but admitted that the RSS strongly endorsed Modi in the 2014 and 2019 elections because the prime minister, once a pracharak himself, was furthering the RSS's 'nation-building' ideological beliefs. 'Our swayamsevaks must have taken over five lakh voter education meetings in the months leading up to the general elections,' he tells me. The RSS itself has a loyal cadre of around 12 lakh swayamsevaks who participate in the daily early morning exercises in approximately 60,000 shakhas across the country (add the weekly / monthly shakhas and the number goes to 40 lakh swayamsevaks). They form a well-trained 'saffron army' network which canvasses for the BJP at election time: the pretence of being apolitical has been truly buried in the Modi era with RSS sarsanghchalak Mohan Bhagwat having worked out a strong personal equation with the prime minister.

I then asked Gopal the prickly question of where Muslims figured in the RSS's definition of a Hindu Rashtra. 'We are not against our Muslim brothers so long as they respect the cultural traditions of the country,' Gopal replied smoothly. 'If Jains, Buddhists, Sikhs can assimilate into this land, why can't Muslims? You can't break our temples, declare non-Muslims kafirs, and then expect us to embrace you,' he stresses. Although he didn't say it directly, it was apparent that in Gopal's world view, Muslims needed to prove their 'loyalty' to the nation.

I was reminded of this conversation when I was travelling through Kashmir on a shoot during the 2019 elections. On a glorious spring morning, we drove through the picturesque hilly countryside towards Pulwama, crossing the very spot along the highway where the jawans had been killed just months earlier. As we sat down for an adda in the local market, the crowd that slowly gathered around us didn't seem too pleased by our presence. 'Aap Dilli se yahan kyon aaye hain? Aap sab log toh TV mein har Kashmiri ko aantankwaadi dikhate hain!' (Why have you come here from Delhi? You people portray every Kashmiri as a terrorist!) an elderly man shouted. We managed to quell tempers a bit but it wasn't easy. In the Kashmir valley, the media, especially the so-called 'national' TV channels, are the new 'enemy'. The anti-TV sentiment mirrors a deeper disquiet towards India, a barely concealed desire for 'azaadi', freedom, from anyone who is seen to be connected to the Indian state. I asked the group if they condemned the suicide attack in Pulwama. 'Aapko bas Pulwama ka hamla dikhta hai. Hamare saath toh daily zulm hota hai. Aap apne Modiji ko kaho, humko na terrorist se kuch lena hai, na Pakistan se, na India se' (You only see the Pulwama attack, but we suffer on a daily basis. You tell Modi, we want to have nothing to do with terrorism, Pakistan or India), was the emphatic response. I left the place soon after, a little shaken but not surprised: the tormented voice of the Kashmiri Muslim, angry, alienated and trapped in a mindset of permanent victimhood, has echoed in my ears for years now.

Just a few days after my Kashmir visit, I was watching an evening 'debate' show on a Hindi news channel. With India Gate as the impressive backdrop, the almost ritual 'tu tu main main' catfight had broken out amongst the participants. Balakot was being discussed yet again and as the decibel levels rose on stage, the audience became more raucous. 'Modiji ne Pakistan aur yeh Kashmir mein baithe deshdrohi Musalmano ko achha sabak sikhaya hai' (Modi has taught a lesson to Pakistan and the unpatriotic Muslims in Kashmir), shrieked an audience member to loud applause. As the news anchor tried to control the crowd, boisterous cries of 'Bharat Mata ki Jai' rent the air. Maybe, the Kashmiris in Pulwama were right after all: the TV camera is truly their enemy, a potent medium today being expertly and strategically deployed to stir religious divides and promote manic hyper-nationalism. Cunningly creating daily enemies on prime time, pushing the majority community into furious Islamophobia through slanted debates, using the power of TV to systematically target those speaking up for minority rights or pluralism as 'enemies of the nation' – most of Indian TV is indeed the public ally of majoritarian nationalism. It is also a formidable weapon for garnering votes as Team Modi would so cleverly and ruthlessly demonstrate right through the 2019 election campaign.

SEVEN

'Prime-time' Prime Minister

NEW Year's Day is usually a relatively soporific day in most newsrooms, the overnight revelry taking its hungover toll on the news flow. Journalists often saunter in late to duty and most news channels choose light feature programming and year-end specials as their staple content. However, 1 January 2019 was very different. At the start of what promised to be an action-packed election year, it was always likely that there would be some news break, especially when you have a leader who likes to repeatedly set the news agenda. On the last day of 2018, while large parts of India were getting ready to party, Narendra Modi had recorded a ninety-minute interview with Asian News International (ANI) editor Smita Prakash. It was a well-considered choice. ANI is a virtual monopoly in the TV news syndication business: more than 300 channels across the country subscribe to ANI's news feed and its tie-up with global agency Reuters extends to over 180 countries. Also, news agencies by their very nature tend to be proximate to whoever is in power and are conscious of avoiding any adversarial or hostile cross-questioning: ANI, in that sense, was the perfect platform for the prime minister to express himself without fear of being ambushed by any tricky questions. By doing the year's first interview with a news agency, Modi was assured that he would dominate the headlines in the new year. Sure enough, every news channel in the country carried Modi's comments at prime time as their first headline, the interview getting several repeat telecasts too. 'We got our scoop and the prime minister got a lot of play in every channel, I guess it was a win–win for all,' says Prakash.

It was. But only up to a point.

Just a day after the interview was telecast, at a press conference at the Congress headquarters, Rahul Gandhi drew attention to it, accusing the interviewer of 'stage-managing' the question-and-answer session. 'He [Modi] does not have the guts to come and sit in front of you. I am coming here ... you can ask me any question. I come here once in seven–ten days, and you saw the prime minister's interview yesterday ... matlab "pliable" journalist, woh question bhi kar rahi thi, pradhan mantri ka answer bhi de rahi thi side mein [she was asking questions as well as prompting the answers].'

Prakash was incensed, describing Rahul's attack as a 'cheap shot'. 'You want to attack Mr Modi, go ahead, but downright absurd to ridicule me. Not expected of the oldest political party in the country,' she tweeted. News organizations mostly supported the journalist, accusing the Congress president of unfairly dragging the media into a political fight. 'I don't think Rahul Gandhi had even seen the interview when he made those remarks. Does anyone who remotely knows Mr Modi think that he would need prompting during an interview? It is totally crazy,' Prakash tells me. She admits that the PMO did ask for a list of 'general' questions in advance, as it often does, but did not veto any question or choreograph the interview in any manner. A list of more than thirty questions was lined up over the ninety minutes. 'We are a news agency, not a TRP-driven or anchor-centric channel. We are not here to build my persona as an interviewer but only to ensure that our clients get sufficient newsy material which I think the interview did manage to generate,' argues Prakash.

More than even the news headlines, the interview spawned a controversy that would get amplified right through the 2019 election battle: was the Indian media, especially news TV, 'pliant', a 'godi' (lapdog) media, doing the bidding of the ruling party as the opposition repeatedly alleged? It's a question which polarized opinion like so much else in a surcharged election atmosphere. 'A large part of the Indian news media as an independent entity that dares to tell truth to power has ceased to exist, its dead,' says Randeep Surjewala, the Congress's chief spokesperson. 'The Congress party and its leadership should stop shooting the messenger and reflect instead on the failure of their fake message which does not entitle them to any coverage beyond a press conference,' counters the BJP spokesperson, Nalin Kohli.

Beyond the inevitable political rhetoric, here are the facts gleaned from TV viewership monitoring agency Broadcast Audience Research Council (BARC) based on its study of eleven Hindi news channels.

During the peak election period, 1–28 April 2019, Narendra Modi received about three times more TV airtime than Rahul Gandhi. Modi was shown by TV news channels for more than 722 hours during this period while Rahul was shown for a little less than 252 hours during the same period. This, despite the fact that Rahul actually addressed one more rally than Modi in this month.

In the four weeks leading up to the election, Modi got about 26 per cent of the total channel airtime, twice as much as anyone else.

Modi's interviews on Hindi news channels reached an audience of 129 million, again far exceeding that of the competition.

The cold statistics don't reveal the full story, though. True, Modi was tracked with a sense of breathless excitement, his every major rally and roadshow covered 'live', his every interview telecast several times over. But more than the incessant coverage of the prime minister, it is the *manner* in which he was positioned that is revelatory. Every appearance was craftily packaged in a style that suggested a regal air of an invincible political heavyweight. Take, for example, the interview that India TV's popular anchor and editor Rajat Sharma did with Modi just ahead of the fifth phase of voting in early May. The programme was titled *Salaam India*, and filmed inside the gigantic Jawaharlal Nehru Stadium auditorium. A crowd of over 2,000 people had packed into the venue, with several BJP leaders and spokespersons occupying the front rows. Modi arrived on the stage like a conquering hero; the audience gave him a standing ovation, whistling and cheering him with chants of 'Modi, Modi' and 'Bharat Mata ki Jai'. By the sound of it, it could have been a rock concert or a film awards night, only it was a politician who had taken centre stage as the iconic star of the event. It wasn't just a news show: this was a theatrical performance being enacted against the backdrop of a decisive election.

Sharma, a staunch ABVP activist in his college days, denies the charge that the show was 'fixed' in any manner. 'I don't really care for the views of 300–400 opinion-makers who have nothing better to do than criticize. I have always done audience-based shows that reflect the views of people – that is my strength. It was entirely our idea to do the show in a grand manner in a stadium because we felt that it would break with the news clutter of other interviews the prime minister had done until then. The prime minister didn't suggest a single question in advance and I asked him all the tough questions, including on the charge that he had benefited Anil Ambani in the Rafale deal. If Mr Modi is able to connect with the audience and viewers, why should we be blamed for it?' contends the veteran TV personality who is also the president of the News Broadcasters Association. (During the 2014 elections, Sharma had done an interview with Modi which had attracted similar charges of being orchestrated. One of his senior news editors had even quit in protest.)

Sharma enjoys a long-standing relationship of mutual trust and friendship with the prime minister that stretches back several decades and the comfort factor between the two is obvious. During the interview, Modi was often praised for the Balakot strike and there was a euphoric air that marked the eighty-five-minute show, almost as if the re-election was a mere formality. Sample this: the sharp-suited Sharma started the programme by reading out laudatory SMSs which he claimed were received from viewers, one of which said: 'Modi ne kar diya ailaan, kaan khol kar sun lo, Imran, kehta saara Hindustan, ab nahin bachega Pakistan!' (Modi has declared, listen carefully, Imran, now the entire India says that Pakistan won't survive!) The audience was in raptures as Sharma asked

Modi almost reverentially, 'Did you ever think you would get so much love from Indians?' Modi blushed and called Sharma a true 'janata ka patrakar' (people's journalist) before wondering how the words 'Modi, Modi' had become a national rage. More claps. More chanting. More gushing. It was love-fest being played out on TV.

The interview not only garnered high TRPs but also was retelecast on voting days in the fifth, sixth and seventh rounds of polling when, as per EC guidelines, news channels are not supposed to show any material that could conceivably influence the electorate. 'I don't think that is a valid criticism at all; every channel will promote and play up an interview in which there is high viewer interest as often as possible,' argues Sharma.

Interestingly, Sharma claims that he made every attempt to organize a similar news event with Rahul Gandhi and Priyanka Gandhi Vadra to ensure a level playing field. 'I sent them so many letters, spoke to several Congress leaders, even contacted Robert Vadra to try and convince either Rahul or Priyanka to come on the channel. And yet, I didn't get a response, not even an acknowledgement of my letters,' he reveals.

The India TV boss's gripe is an all-too-familiar one. Over the years, many news channels and anchors have tried to get Rahul to interact with them, attend media conclaves, do special programmes, only to be greeted with silence. ANI's Prakash too claims to have written several formal mails and letters seeking an interview with Rahul but, again, not even getting the courtesy of a response. My own experience has been disconcertingly similar. For several years now, I have requested an audience with the Congress leader, only to be rebuffed without even a one-line reply to my umpteen mails. In February 2019, ahead of the *India Today* marquee annual conclave, we invited Rahul to address the gathering. We made several attempts through his media team to convince Rahul, who only months earlier had been chosen by the magazine as 'Newsmaker of the Year', to participate in the high-profile speaker-fest. Prime Minister Modi had agreed to attend so we thought it only appropriate that Rahul, as the main opposition leader, be given equal billing. I met Sam Pitroda, one of Rahul's closest advisers, hoping that he could swing it for us. 'We can discuss the format and issues that Rahul wants to focus upon in advance and address any queries he might have suitably,' I told Pitroda. The media-savvy Pitroda seemed positive: 'Yes, it's a great platform for Rahul to express himself. Don't worry, I will speak to him and get this done!' Feeling reassured, I informed the office to be prepared to showcase Rahul as a star speaker.

Yet, the final go-ahead never came from the Congress leader's office. 'Rahul is not comfortable in these media gatherings, it's not really his kind of scene,' a member of Team Rahul later explained to me. I was a little perplexed. Only a year earlier, Sonia Gandhi had attended the *India Today* conclave and made a distinct impact with her interaction. Now, in this crucial election period, Rahul had missed an opportunity to be heard at one of India's largest media events. Modi, not surprisingly, stole the show with his closing address at the conclave.

During the campaign, I once again frantically tried to get a Rahul interview with the sole intent of giving the Congress leader prime-time space and ensuring a level playing field. Finally, we received confirmation that Rahul would do his first TV interview of the campaign with us in Jaipur where a Congress rally was being held the next day. Extensive arrangements were made, multiple camera crews and production teams were lined up to travel for the shoot. The night before I was to leave for Jaipur, I got a call around 11 p.m. from one of Rahul's media advisers. 'Sorry, we are going to have to call off the interview,' was the brusque message. I was taken aback. What's the problem, I asked anxiously. 'We can't do this interview unless you change the cover photo of Rahul in your magazine!' was the blunt take-it-or-leave-it ultimatum. Apparently, *India Today* magazine had just interviewed Rahul and had planned a big cover splash. 'Rahul loves the interview he's done with them but isn't happy with the cover photo; it shows him looking way too angry!' I was told. The magazine had already gone into print and the cover picture couldn't be changed. Rahul and his team were adamant: there would be no TV interview the next day. Right through his election campaign, Rahul did a number of interviews with a variety of media houses but was not seen on India's biggest news TV platform that includes Aaj Tak, the country's largest Hindi news channel by some distance.

Frankly, I was terribly disappointed not so much for losing out on an exclusive with the opposition leader, but by the message which his last-minute rejection sent. Here was one news network that, in a difficult and polarized news whirl, was consistently pushing the concept of a 'democratic newsroom' and attempting to give every political viewpoint an equal chance to be heard, only to be told that the Congress president would not speak to us because of a cover picture that the Gandhi family did not like. It seemed to be a case of gross overreaction, one that need not have resulted in a sudden communication breakdown. Ironically, just the day before this unfortunate contretemps, I had interviewed Priyanka – typically charming and sound-bite conscious – on the road in Amethi. Her interview dominated the news agenda that day on both our Hindi and English channels. The contrast between the mistrustful, camera-wary brother and his welcoming, camera-friendly sister, or indeed even father, Rajiv Gandhi, who as prime minister was easily accessible and reportedly even took a keen interest in camera angles and shooting frames, could not have been more stark.

Team Rahul, as always, has an explanation for their leader's wariness. 'Just look at the way the media, especially TV, has portrayed Rahul. The news channels keep ridiculing him and the Congress in every debate and then expect him to make himself available whenever the media wants,' argues a Rahul aide. At one level, the argument is not without merit. There is little doubt that the projection of Rahul has been terribly unfair: the media narrative, especially on the screechy, so-called 'nationalist' channels is designed to stridently mock the Congress leader and his party at every possible opportunity, at times in a manner which defied any logic but was only aimed at pushing a pro-BJP agenda. Every little misstep was magnified. Even a harmless act like going to a movie theatre became an occasion to berate him.

As news TV increasingly transitions almost wholly to a debate format, noise has replaced news; shrill, high-pitched discussions on sharply polarizing issues like religious identity now garner the maximum ratings even if the argument is often in the nature of a 'fixed' match. News TV's prime-time warriors are in perpetual search of a 'hate' figure to scorn: for many, Rahul is a soft target, as is the opposition in general. On pro-Modi, right-wing channels like Republic (which was initially part-owned by BJP MP Rajeev Chandrashekhar) and Zee (owned by Subhash Goyal who became a Rajya Sabha MP with BJP support), the daily agenda in the run-up to the 2019 elections was relentless Congress-bashing. Other popular channels like Times Now took the cue: a business model was fostered over hyper-nationalism and a majoritarian outlook. Pawan Khera, Congress spokesperson, says that sitting in a TV debate during the elections, he almost felt 'stupid' at times. 'The anchor, the audience, the questions, the narrative being spun had only one goal: make the opposition look foolish and Modi look great. It really was a futile exercise,' he insists. (In June 2019, the Congress party formally decided not to send any of its official spokespersons to TV debates as a mark of protest against TV media bias.)

I wondered if Rahul was still affected by the interview he had done with anchor Arnab Goswami ahead of the 2014 elections on Times Now. The conversation had exposed Rahul's limitations as a public speaker, revealing him to be embarrassingly short of answers on key issues. In the five years since, Rahul had shown more signs of confidence in front of the camera. With his St. Stephen's College mate Nikhil Alva carefully curating his media interactions, Rahul was slowly emerging from the shadows of vagueness and presenting a more self-assured persona on screen. Alva, the son of veteran Congress leader Margaret Alva at least recognized the importance of the medium in image-building. Those who attended some of Rahul's closed-door, off-the-record meetings with journalists in 2018 admit to be struck by his willingness to take every question thrown at him with a measure of poise. 'Rahul has done so many press conferences, has Modi done even one in five years?' asks an irate Surjewala. It is a justifiable comparison, one which reflects the growing marginalization of the news media in the Modi universe.

Yet, somehow, his public interventions have never quite taken Rahul to the next level as a political communicator. Even the several interviews he finally did on the campaign trail appeared to give the impression of a leader trying too hard to overcome his natural diffidence before the camera, almost as if he was being made to perform an unpleasant chore. Many of them were done literally on the move: near a public rally stage, or on a charpoy, without the frills or multi-cam razzmatazz that accompanies the prime minister's TV appearances. 'That's the way RG likes it. He wants to show the contrast between himself as just another leader and Modi as a VVIP,' insists a media aide.

It was a strategy that was doomed to fail, especially when matched against Modi's consummate media skills. Modi has always been a 'performer' in front of the camera, a talent that goes back to his school-days when, as an old school friend from Vadnagar recalls, 'He was a shy boy who came alive during the school drama competition.' It's a talent which served him well in the 1990s when he was a BJP spokesperson and private news networks were slowly opening up in the country; Modi was rarely at a loss for words in TV debates. That flair for the theatrical is in evidence as prime minister too: his Independence Day speeches from the Red Fort, for example, are as much about dramatic delivery as they are about content.

But the Modi media interface is not only about on-camera drama. While Modi is the on-screen presence, there is a strong back-room team in the PMO that handles his TV 'image management', choreographing the finer details of his appearances for maximum impact. The core team is led by his communications and IT head in the PMO, Hiren Joshi, an electronics engineer from Rajasthan who had worked as an assistant professor in Bhilwara before being hand-picked by Modi in 2008 to handle his digital presence as Gujarat chief minister. Modi's brief to Joshi and his young assistants – most of them are in their twenties and thirties – was simple: ensure that the media narrative is fully controlled. While Joshi focused on the PM's TV and social media engagements, senior PMO officials and media-savvy union ministers would reportedly often call up news channel heads and owners, gently 'advising' them on prime-ministerial coverage. Previous governments often had veteran journalists playing this role; that Modi chose not to have a professional journalist in his core media relations team reflects a shift in approach. 'Modi doesn't trust journalists; he is much more comfortable with young technocrats, especially those who've worked with him in Gujarat,' is the explanation given by a government official.

Team Modi follows a structured corporate-like media strategy for the prime minister similar to what might be adhered to for the CEO of a multinational company, every move consciously micro-managed. Any major national address was mostly timed for after 8 p.m. to ensure prime-time 'domination', in sharp contrast to Rahul whose interjections, on Rafale for example, would sometimes be in the forenoon, giving his opponents enough time to hit back. A strong research team in the PMO led by Pratik Doshi, who had also been part of the chief minister's office in Gujarat, would provide the prime minister with a detailed briefing of relevant issues. While Rahul would often arrive unshaven for a public interaction, Modi was always immaculately dressed, not a hair out of place, not a crease on the kurta. He was even fastidious about camera angles. For example, when Atal Bihari Vajpayee died, a three-cam unit with a switcher recorded the prime minister's tribute to the BJP patriarch: close-up shots zoomed in on Modi's teary eyes. It was melodramatic but effective.

Team Modi's overarching media philosophy of 'command and control' also meant restricted access to the prime minister and his bureaucrats. During his five years in office, Modi has given only a handful of interviews to select journalists and taken no press conferences. He also discontinued the practice of taking journalists aboard Air India One on his foreign trips. Since the wide-bodied aircraft has enough empty seats to accommodate them, past prime ministers always took a thirty- or forty-member media contingent with them. While the journalists were expected to pay for their hotel stay and local expenses, the MEA did ensure the mediapersons were well looked after – food and liquor flowed quite freely. 'Yeh sab band karna hai' (All this has to stop), was Modi's strict instruction to MEA officials soon after taking over. The official reason given was that this was a needless extravagance: why should the taxpayer be expected to contribute to the alcohol intake of journalists out on a junket? It was an expertly spun explanation which put the media on the defensive by caricaturing the journalist as a freeloader who deserves no special benefits. Targeting journalists as enemies of the Modi revolution is a familiar tack with the establishment, meant to strike a populist note.

Keeping news crews off the prime-ministerial plane enabled the PMO to deny the media privileged access to the prime minister and his key officials. I have travelled with both Atal Bihari Vajpayee and Manmohan Singh and have been journalistically enriched by the many discussions with PMO officials on major national issues during long flights. The icing on the cake was the prime minister's on-board press conference at the end of every trip. A wide range of questions could be asked of the prime minister at such informal interactions. I recall one conversation with Vajpayee stretching on for almost an hour till a prime-ministerial aide finally intervened and suggested we allow the BJP leader some rest. Even the otherwise reticent Dr Singh would often open up at such press meets. Modi, on the other hand, clearly didn't want pesky journalists asking him any awkward questions in mid-air which might embarrass him on the ground. 'Arre, tum logon ka agenda hota hai!' (All of you have an agenda!), a Modi aide told me once dismissively when I asked why a large section of the media was not being allowed to engage with the prime minister. It seemed that Modi wanted to freeze the media out in a manner that ensured his supreme executive authority wasn't questioned at any stage.

I sometimes wonder if his experience post the 2002 Gujarat riots hasn't scarred Modi forever: an unrelenting focus on his failure to prevent the ferocious communal violence was a significant feature of the TV coverage at the time. The pre-2002 Modi had been open, accessible and media friendly, but in his post-2002 avatar, he was cagey and distrustful, reluctant to open himself up to any scrutiny. Before 2002, where Modi and I would regularly communicate, in the years since, the conversations have become increasingly infrequent. We would still speak on the phone occasionally: when my father passed away in 2007, Modi was among the first to call me up to condole. In the lead-up to the 2014 elections, when Modi still wasn't certain of making the great leap from Gandhinagar to Delhi, he would often call me to get feedback. But once he became prime minister, I came to be seen in some quarters of the government as a marked man. When Union minister Arun Jaitley, one of Modi's chief media managers, hosted a series of dinners for journalists with the prime minister soon after he took charge, I was not invited. When I asked Jaitley if I was now persona non grata, he laughed: 'Not quite, but you know Narendrabhai, he still hasn't forgotten the Gujarat riots coverage!'

This 'targeting' of individual journalists was driven home to me when, while sipping coffee at the India International Centre one day, a bright-eyed young man came up to me, looking a little anxious. 'Sir, I am an admirer of your journalism but I have a confession to make. I do some freelance work for Rajya Sabha TV but I am also part of a media monitoring group which has to prepare a detailed brief every day for the I&B ministry on which news anchor took what line and on which subject. I have been assigned to follow your debates and tweets. It's not something I am happy about but I need the job and the money,' he admitted. I was taken aback but not entirely surprised: in a hyper-polarized media eco-system, Big Brother was watching. When I narrated the story to a senior government official, he laughed it off. 'In this government, they don't care what you say on English news TV, only Hindi and regional channels matter!'

That the Modi government was determined to get influential sections of the mainstream media to fall in line was obvious when, in March 2017, the prime minister opted out at the last minute of a high-profile summit being organized by a leading business newspaper because the PMO was reportedly 'unhappy' with the paper's coverage of the UP assembly elections. Union ministers scheduled to attend the event also pulled out as did the lead sponsor, the TDP-led Andhra Pradesh government which was then an NDA ally. A despairing newspaper owner sought BJP president Amit Shah's intervention to resolve the impasse. 'I can't do anything, my party and leadership are angry, change your editorial stance first,' was Shah's blunt message. A detailed dossier of articles, cartoons, even tweets critical of the government was placed before the owner.

Another leading newspaper editor was suddenly forced to resign because the PMO was reportedly displeased with a 'hate tracker' where the daily was documenting cases of communally linked mob violence. A popular Hindi anchor was removed from his prime-time show and eventually made to resign after the BJP decided to 'boycott' the channel in protest against a story disparaging of the Modi government. In another instance, a Union minister reportedly even rang up private companies asking them to withdraw ads to an 'anti-national' channel which was accused of running anti-government stories. When I mentioned these examples of media bullying to Jaitley, his response was combative. 'Tell me, how many stories were done against the Gandhis when the UPA was in power? If false stories are done against us, why should we not respond?' he shot back. I was surprised. If even the supposedly more accommodative face of the Modi government, who often passionately espoused the cause of media freedom and had been jailed in the Emergency years, was now playing to a different beat, then the space for an independent media was clearly shrinking even further.

Just ahead of the 2019 elections though, Team Modi reluctantly opened the forbidding gates of 7 Lok Kalyan Marg to the media. They had an election to win. Modi embarked on a series of TV interviews during the campaign. Each interview – he did around ten for national TV channels alone, in addition to several print interviews – was carefully scheduled and choreographed by his team. They were mostly recorded on a Thursday or Friday and telecast at a time when they would garner the most attention, and then retelecast several times over the weekend. From making tea for the news anchors in one interview, if only to own his chaiwallah image, to taking a boatride on the Ganga in his home constituency of Varanasi in another, Modi was on a charm offensive designed to portray him with a prime-ministerial halo. If Rahul, with his 'Chowkidar chor hai' slogan, was the angry young man of 2019, Modi was now the pro-incumbent who was talking of lofty issues of governance and leadership, a well-sculpted strategy to enable him to rise above the din of competitive politics and be seen as much more than just another power-hungry neta seeking re-election. He was the problem solver, the keeper of promises to an electorate weary of broken vows. The constant supply of superhero imagery fostered a collective closing of the eyes to uncomfortable realities, keeping the belief in the individual intact.

Perhaps the best example of this 'soft focus' Modi branding was the prime minister's much discussed interview with film star Akshay Kumar. Team Modi was keen to take a break from the routine news interviews which they felt were getting a tad repetitive. 'We wanted something "hatke", something that would strike a chord with a much wider audience than just those who watch news, which in any case is only a small fraction of the overall TV-viewing universe,' expounds a Team Modi strategist. Several names were considered. Although he had been spotted with Modi ahead of the 2014 elections at the kite-flying Uttarayan festival in Ahmedabad, Salman Khan was deemed far too controversial for a prime-ministerial encounter. Sachin Tendulkar was reportedly on the shortlist: he is, after all, a Bharat Ratna and a former nominated Rajya Sabha MP, but his interview skills were untested. Karan Johar was an option – his *Koffee with Karan* is a very popular show – but he was eventually ruled out as perhaps being too flippant.

Akshay Kumar, by contrast, fit the bill: a big star with a wide appeal who was a self-confessed admirer of the prime minister. More significantly, he had a 'nationalist' image: he had started a 'Bharat ke Veer' initiative to provide financial assistance to the families of armed forces martyrs. His hit film *Kesari*, a rousing patriotic film where he plays a Sikh solider who takes on Pashtun invaders, had just been released in March 2019. His film *Toilet: Ek Prem Katha* (2017) was based on the prime minister's Swachh Bharat initiative and another film, *Padman* (2018), spread social awareness about menstruation and the need for low-cost sanitary napkins, issues which gelled well with the Modi narrative. 'His status as a popular film star with a macho patriotic image whose stardom is not based on family lineage made him the perfect fit for us,' explains a Team Modi strategist.

The interview was meticulously planned. A multi-cam shoot, it was filmed like a high-quality production. While ANI provided the basic cameras and a switcher, a professional jib camera unit was hired for a high-angle view to give the shoot a sense of grandeur. Akshay was dressed in a casual white shirt and light pink trousers while the prime minister was a tad more formal in his long-flowing kurta and churidar with a blue unbuttoned Modi jacket. The tone and setting – the two took a stroll across the verdant lawns of the prime minister's residence and then sat down to converse – was designed to create a sense of personal camaraderie between star and politician. The answers were just as calculated: Modi, the poor boy from Vadnagar who was untouched by the trappings of power. We were told how Modi played gilli-danda in his village, how he used to wash clothes near the village pond, how his mother gave him 'sawaa' rupee (Rs 1.25) as pocket money and how he loved plucking mangoes from trees and eating them. A suitably deferential and awestruck Akshay asks Modi, 'How do you sleep for just three and a half hours?' The prime minister's reply was just as deliberate: 'When I met President Obama, he also asked me, "Don't you sleep ..." But my body cycle is such that I don't sleep for longer than three to four hours.' The humble workaholic, the karmayogi neta found the perfect foil in the admiring film star. Akshay Kumar was visibly impressed, and the viewer was also encouraged to be. It was the perfect promotional video.

Even the timing of the interview was planned with a firm eye on the elections. Aired on 24 April, just five days before the fourth round of polling when the battle was slowly shifting from the south to Mumbai, north India and the Hindi heartland. An interview with a top Bollywood star just before this phase of voting was ideal publicity, especially when every major national news channel telecast the interview several times over. The opposition and even a section of the media criticized the interview for being a pre-scripted attempt to deflect from real issues like jobs and agrarian distress but for Team Modi the goal had been achieved: the prime minister's personality was once again the central talking point. 'Like it or not, it was a PR coup,' contends a BJP leader. 'Who stopped Rahul Gandhi from being interviewed by an Aamir or a Shah Rukh Khan?'

Shrewd political marketing and continual 'headline management' that is driven by an obsessive desire to get the optics right has always been an integral part of the Modi communication strategy. In his Gandhinagar years, the American lobbying firm APCO was paid top dollar to help 'sell' Modi's 'Gujarat model' to the world, while organizing flashy business summits like Vibrant Gujarat. Now that he was the prime minister, Team Modi was even more fixated on showy image-building events. Every anniversary of the Modi government was celebrated like a grand birthday, with songs, catchy slogans, media conclaves. On the third anniversary in 2017, the slogan used was 'Mera desh badal raha hai' (My country is changing), accompanied by a song composed by adman Piyush Pandey and his Team Ogilvy who had also worked on the 2014 BJP election campaign. 'We dealt with ministers Jaitley and Piyush Goyal on each campaign theme but the final approval for the idea would come from the prime minister himself,' Pandey tells me. The song mandatorily became the caller tune of most BJP leaders and ministers. It was almost as if the Modi government was in constant campaign mode, parading its achievements and promising even more. In this cycle of upbeat messaging, there was no time to press the pause button, listen to naysayers or introspect. The voter literally had no time to breathe: barely would one news event end than another would be inaugurated with equal fanfare. By the fourth anniversary in 2018, the slogan was changed to 'Saaf niyat, sahi vikas' (Good intent, right development), accompanied yet again by more professionally produced glitzy videos. Even if there was creeping fatigue with the sloganeering, it wasn't allowed to settle into any form of anger against failed promises.

TV media, in particular, was being led into a blissful Modi-transfixed news universe where there was almost no space for negativism or interrogation of the leadership. Every time a potentially adverse story was broadcast, the narrative would be cleverly diverted. I recall one instance in January 2019 when a NSSO report revealed that unemployment was at a forty-five-year high. The story was flashed for a while before suddenly a fresh 'breaking news' was put out: 'Sources say government still considering an ordinance on Ram Temple in Ayodhya'. There was no verification of this story and yet it became a prime-time debate on many channels. The parlous state of the economy, not for the first time, had lost out to a potentially emotive and divisive religious issue. Divert and rule was the government's extremely effective tool to capture the media's attention.

This unremitting brand-building exercise is not just driven from the PMO: Team Modi has created a parallel ecosystem in which many individuals and groups are involved in designing Brand Modi. For example, a 'not-for-profit' company called BlueKraft Digital Foundation, has brought out several books revolving around Prime Minister Modi while tying up with major publishers. One of them, the bestselling *Exam Warriors*, is 'authored' by the prime minister to help children fight exam stress. Another book is on Modi's monthly radio broadcast, 'Mann ki Baat', a show hyped as a 'social revolution on radio'. Both books are aimed at projecting Modi as an avuncular feel-good guru, someone who inspires the youth in particular, a critical demographic in Modi's outreach. Started in 2016, BlueKraft positions itself as a 'knowledge and technology' partner in such exercises but most of its founder members are connected to Team Modi and the BJP. One of them, Hitesh Jain, a Mumbai-based lawyer and BJP spokesperson, tells me, 'Our aim is to sell the "new India" dream as embodied in the strong persona of Mr Modi.'

The 'Mann ki Baat' radio show, in fact, is a great example of how the Modi model of unending communication works like a seamless exercise across multiple platforms, creating a continuous reverberation in the public mind. Started on Vijayadashami in October 2014, 'Mann ki Baat' became a half-hour monthly show, aired at 11 a.m. every last Sunday of the month. Broadcast in Hindi on the government-owned All India Radio, it was also paired with relevant pictures and shown on state-controlled Doordarshan. Additionally, it was translated into eighteen languages, and made available on the NaMo App, BJP websites and across social media. Even private news channels would often cut live to it. A tech-savvy politician was embracing a medium which was considered outdated simply by creating a new style of direct, cross-media, scaled-up messaging that would eliminate the traditional politician–journalist interface.

An entire back room of researchers in PMO-backed organizations like BlueKraft were tasked with identifying 'positive' stories of hope and change which the prime minister could speak about every month. Citizens were also encouraged to send in their inspirational stories through MyGov.in, the Modi government's citizen engagement platform. 'Our target was clear: maximize public participation and motivate people beyond narrow political talk,' explains a Team Modi member. The content was not strictly political – the prime minister would speak on a variety of issues ranging from yoga to drug abuse – but the goal clearly was: position Modi as not just another powerful political leader but as a transformational figure who could guide students one day, and usher in social reform for women the next. Almost every aspect of citizens' personal lives was being drawn in under the prime minister's benevolent aegis.

The conscious and unceasing push for 'Brand Modi' may seem narcissistic but it also holds up a mirror to an age of personality-driven politics in which a voter is made to feel 'connected' with the 'Supreme Leader'. This is where TV has played a key role, offering a ready platform for a canny political communicator to exploit. Rather than speaking the truth to those in power, there is a growing inclination to 'follow the leader' with an uncritical, unquestioning gaze, almost as if mainstream media has been co-opted into a permanent embrace with the ruling elite. It has doubtlessly happened with previous governments too – most notably in the Indira years in the 1970s – but not quite with the sheer impudence of the times in which we now live.

In 1995, TV viewers across India became fascinated by images of a Ganesha idol that apparently began to 'drink milk', later revealed as capillary action of fluid absorption by stone surfaces. Whatever the explanation, TV relayed this modern-day 'miracle' and created an unprecedented display of blind faith even among educated professionals; media images can create a situation where rationality is suspended and belief has the upper hand, never mind what common sense dictates. Recall the slew of remarks made by Modi and other prominent leaders to emphasize the supremacy of ancient India in the realm of science and technology, many of them inaccurate and often downright bizarre: from claiming that Lord Ganesha's elephant head must have been a case of plastic surgery to linking the birth of Karna to genetic engineering to even suggesting that the Balakot strike was successful because a heavy cloud cover prevented Pakistani radars from detecting Indian fighter jets. Rarely have such claims been challenged; it is almost as if belief in the individual has to be preserved, even at the cost of scientific temper. In the Modi era, the media's collusion with the political executive has touched such unprecedented heights that the reality checks that the press is supposed to provide on the claims of those in power simply do not exist. When loyal courtiers echo a monarch, the truth tends not to matter.

In November 2014, in what is a telling example of this collusion, the BJP organized a Diwali Milan for mediapersons at its party office. There was obvious excitement amongst journalists because the prime minister was slated to make an appearance, his first press interaction since his May 2014 triumph. Sure enough, there was a loud chorus of applause as Modi arrived on the stage. He spoke for a couple of minutes and offered Diwali wishes before stepping down to meet and greet the waiting crowd. What followed was utter pandemonium as editors and reporters alike literally clambered over each other to take selfies with the prime minister. Not a single question was asked about pressing national issues. Not a single fact that might put the prime minister and his government in the dock was raised. In his five years in power, Modi did not address a single press conference. Perhaps he didn't feel the necessity: after all, when a fawning media is already 'in your pocket' (in a manner of speaking) why open yourself to scrutiny in an unscripted press meet that can't be controlled as easily?

We in the media may not all be as 'pliable' as Rahul Gandhi alleges, but we certainly need to rediscover a spine or else be pushed into growing irrelevance. As it is, there is a new beast stomping around in the 'media jungle': the rise of social media and digital mobile technology has changed the rules of the game. Not surprisingly, the hydra-headed multimedia enterprise that is Team Modi has remained ahead in this game too in 2019.

'If he were not a politician, he would make a pretty good digital entrepreneur. Narendrabhai loves gadgets,' observes an old associate of the prime minister from Gujarat. In the 1990s, at a time when a notebook was still the norm, Modi used an electronic diary to scribble phone numbers. (He once claimed in an interview that he used a digital camera in 1988 but that seems a bit far-fetched since the digicam came to India much later.) Not surprisingly, Modi, then Gujarat chief minister, was one of the first politicians in the country to have accounts on Twitter and Facebook in 2009. The opportunity to directly communicate and control the narrative through his vast social media 'army' without any outside editorial intervention was part of the attraction: Modi was convinced that mainstream media had been unfair to him in the aftermath of the 2002 riots. While Modi's 2014 election campaign made full use of social media platforms like Twitter and Facebook, it was TV that remained his primary platform of mass engagement. It was only once he became prime minister that the balance seemed to shift inexorably towards an even deeper social media focus. 'No leader probably anywhere in the world is as obsessed with social media as Modi is, he even gets a detailed list of which social influencer has tweeted what about him every evening,' claims a former government official.

Every prime-ministerial tweet is vetted by more than one individual before being officially 'cleared', each tweet is aimed at shoring up Modi's stature as the country's tallest leader. As Gujarat chief minister, he would often tweet angrily against the Manmohan Singh government: for example, when the rupee was falling in 2013, he tweeted, 'UPA government and the Rupee seem to be in a competition with each other on who will tumble down more.' But once he was prime minister, the tweets revolved almost entirely around his achievements or the rituals of high office, like birthday greetings to his political rivals. 'We don't do anything off the cuff on Twitter or Facebook like a Donald Trump might, each tweet is carefully planned,' claims a Team Modi member.

By April 2019, on the eve of the general elections, Modi was by some distance the most popular leader on Facebook, with over 43.5 million 'likes' on his personal page and 13.7 million on his official page. On Twitter, he had over 45 million followers, making him the second most followed leader in the world, next only to Donald Trump. He has over 100 playlist videos on YouTube, and a LinkedIn account. As of October 2019, Modi has more than 30 million followers on Instagram, the preferred platform for millennials. 'Modi has been at the forefront of the intersection of politics and technology like no other Indian leader before or since,' says Professor Joyojeet Pal, an expert in the relationship between social media and politics.

And it isn't just Modi. Every senior BJP leader and member of his cabinet is expected to have an 'engaged' social media presence, carefully monitored by the PMO. Most cabinet ministers have their own social media teams in their offices and their personal assistants stay in constant touch with each other through WhatsApp groups, sharing tweets and videos to be uploaded. 'We have a very well-organized system where any tweet from the prime minister is immediately liked and retweeted, any video he puts out is immediately shared,' claims a Union minister.

This systems-driven approach was tested on 17 March 2019, just weeks ahead of the Lok Sabha elections, when the prime minister changed his personal Twitter username to 'Chowkidar Narendra Modi' a day after launching the '#MainBhiChowkidar' campaign on the service. It was a calculated response to Rahul Gandhi's 'Chowkidar chor hai' jibe that the Congress was convinced was resonating with the voter. 'Your chowkidar is standing firm and serving the nation. But I am not alone. Everyone who is fighting corruption, dirt, social evils is a chowkidar. Everyone working hard for the progress of India is a chowkidar. Today, every Indian is saying: #MainBhiChowkidar,' tweeted Modi. Within minutes, every cabinet minister and BJP leader had affixed 'Chowkidar' to their usernames. In another tweet, Modi uploaded a three-minute video to his personal Facebook and Twitter pages, urging his supporters to take a 'Main bhi chowkidar' pledge. The video was also made available on the NaMo app which has around 1.5 crore downloads. On 31 March, Modi interacted with a live audience of 'chowkidars' in more than 500 locations across the country from Delhi's Talkatora Stadium via video-conferencing. 'I don't think there has ever been a bigger social media event in Indian politics,' exults a Team Modi member.

The 'Chowkidar' campaign was designed by the social media team at the PMO and executed by Gurugram-based ABM, the political consultancy linked to BJP president Amit Shah and reportedly functioning as his personal election unit. What Prashant Kishor's event management skills had done for the Modi campaign in 2014 with innovative concepts like 'Chai pe Charcha', ABM was hoping to achieve in 2019 with the 'Chowkidar' idea. Only, ABM was much more secretive and under the radar, which is exactly how Shah wanted them to function. Astonishingly, the 31 March Chowkidar event was broadcast on Doordarshan even though the model code of conduct was in place. The lines between government and party, not for the first time, had become completely blurred.

The outreach didn't stop there. Half a dozen 'Main bhi chowkidar' videos and a theme song were released for TV and social media: the videos were the creation of Manish Bardia, the head of Moving Pixels, a small Ahmedabad-based advertising agency which has worked with Modi's political campaigns since 2002. 'Main bhi chowkidar' merchandise

– caps, T-shirts, wristbands – were also sold through the NaMo app. The 'Chowkidar' campaign went viral almost immediately. The timing was perfect. In the first six weeks of 2019, it was the Congress which was trending more than the BJP on Twitter, its popularity driven by the high decibel 'Chowkidar chor hai' slogan. Then, on 14 February, the Pulwama terror attack happened and the political agenda shifted from corruption to national security. Within a fortnight, post-Balakot, Modi went from form 'chowkidar chor', a symbol of thievery, to 'chowkidar', the valiant defender of national interests. 'The big difference between the Modi social media campaigns of 2014 and 2019 is just how much more finessed their messaging now is. Modi's team knows just how to make something go viral in the shortest possible time,' observes Professor Pal.

In 2014, India had around 250 million internet users; in 2019, that number had more than doubled. The number of smartphone users – 155 million in the 2014 election – had tripled in five years to 450 million in 2019. With more than 300 million WhatsApp users and an almost equal number of Facebook accounts at the start of the new election cycle, Team Modi was convinced that the 2019 elections would be fought on smartphones, especially amongst the younger, more urbanized demographic. 'This is India's first truly social media-driven election, fought on WhatsApp with much greater intensity than in a TV studio,' says Amit Malviya, convenor of the BJP's IT and social media cell.

The slickly groomed Malviya, seen on TV in button-down collar shirts, was a corporate banker with the Bank of America and HSBC before formally joining the party in July 2015 as one of Amit Shah's back-room boys. The task before him was to integrate and consolidate the BJP's digital assets. Working with a small team of around twenty-five people from the party headquarters in the national capital, Malviya eventually began travelling across the country and holding social media workshops for party workers and volunteers. 'From the centre, we went right down to the booth level. In each of our booth committees, we now have at least five people who are tech-savvy and equipped with smartphones,' claims Malviya. The sheer scale of the BJP's social media outreach is mind-boggling. 'When I started, our domain name BJP4India had 17 lakh followers on twitter, we now have 11.6 million. Our Facebook followers were 7. 2 million, now the number is close to 16 million. We have 12 lakh registered social media volunteers. It's a purely organic growth that has enabled us to mobilize people on an unimaginable scale,' he asserts. At the heart of this mobilization drive are the lakhs of WhatsApp groups which BJP members and supporters have set up in the last five years, each group constantly interacting and sharing information with the other, making the app the ideal pipeline for unremitting political propaganda.

West Bengal is a classic case study in how the BJP used WhatsApp as a political 'weapon' in 2019. Ujjwal Pareek, an IT professional, helped set up the BJP's Bengal unit IT cell in 2012 before taking a break to work abroad. He returned in January 2018 after a stint in the United Kingdom because he was driven, he says, by a 'fierce ideological passion' to work for the BJP and defeat the Mamata Banerjee government. In the course of the twelve months leading up to the 2019 elections, Pareek supervised the party's digital outreach, travelling to district headquarters across the state to create an 'army of digital soldiers'. By January 2019, he had assembled a team of 10,000 social media volunteers and created 50,000 WhatsApp and ShareChat groups, all connected from the booth level to the state headquarters in Kolkata through a distinct chain of command. 'There are 65 million voters in Bengal and 30 million smartphones; what better way to reach out to the voter than share videos in real time with almost half the voting population through WhatsApp?' says Pareek.

This WhatsApp-driven model of political campaigning was in evidence on 4 May 2019 as a highly charged Bengal campaign entered the final stretch. Pareek was having a relatively restful day in his office when he suddenly received a fifteen-second video of Mamata Banerjee confronting a group of BJP supporters in West Midnapore district and accusing them of abusing her, when in fact they were shouting 'Jai Shri Ram' slogans. Pareek and his team got to work right away: the video was sent out on WhatsApp, ShareChat and Facebook with the headline 'Joi Shri Ram Kono Gaala-Gaali Nai' (Jai Shri Ram is not an abuse) in Bengali, and a scroll at the bottom that asked, 'Joi Shri Ram e Didi'r ato raag kano?' (Why is Didi so upset over a Jai Shri Ram slogan?) It was quickly subtitled in English and put out on Twitter to reach out to a wider national audience. Within minutes, the video had gone viral and become a prime-time talking point across news channels and everyday conversation in Bengal. 'We managed to amplify the political message in real time with just one video and reach more people than a political rally ever can,' says Pareek gleefully. In just one month of electioneering, the BJP4Bengal claims to have engaged with 20 million people on Facebook, many of them young voters, crucial to the BJP's ascent in the state.

But is the outreach infiltrated at times by false and malicious content? On Twitter, Mamata Banerjee is often called 'Mumtaz Begum', a reference to her alleged pro-minority politics. 'We aren't responsible for this abusive name-calling, no such tweet or message has ever gone from the official Bengal handle, we can't be held responsible for what individuals say,' argues Pareek. The combative Malviya, a familiar presence on TV debates, is also insistent that the party does not endorse 'fake news' in any form. Ironically, he was once accused of posting photos on social media of Jawaharlal Nehru with a number of different women friends, suggesting that the country's first prime minister was a philanderer. Many of the pictures are in fact of Nehru sharing affectionate moments with his family members, sister and niece. Despite being called out for misleading people, Malviya is unapologetic. 'I maintain Nehru was a womanizer,' he insists. The anti-Nehru campaign is no surprise: social media is full of derogatory statements about and morphed pictures of the former prime minister being obsessively circulated by BJP supporters.

Interestingly, Amit Shah was once caught on tape boasting that his party workers were capable of making any message go viral among people, regardless of whether it was true or false. While addressing the BJP social media volunteers in Kota in September 2018, Shah spoke glowingly of harnessing the power of the lakhs of BJP WhatsApp groups as a propaganda weapon. Referring to a message claiming that Akhilesh

Yadav had slapped his father, uploaded during the UP elections by a party volunteer, Shah admitted that it was fake news. 'One should not do such things, but in a way a mahaul was created. This is something worth doing, but don't do it,' he advised amidst much laughter.

The truth is, the digital universe functions in a normless black hole of moral ambiguity in which there are no rules to be followed, no code of conduct to be observed. In electoral politics, in particular, character assassination through social media is now fair game. Thousands of anonymous pages on Facebook and fake Twitter accounts have been created with the sole purpose of pushing false, often toxic, narratives. Congress leader Rahul Gandhi has frequently been the target of a concerted campaign by right-wing groups out to completely destroy his reputation, a systematic vilification programme from which he has struggled to recover. While covering the 2018 election campaign in Karnataka, I was shown a meme of Rahul praying before a mosque with three female devotees by his side. It was headlined: 'Muslim premi Rahul aur unki teen biwiyaan' (Muslim-lover Rahul and his three wives). The fake picture was one of many such communally venomous photos and videos shared through WhatsApp to polarize the electorate. Another fake news post, shared through a Google Plus group called 'Narendra Damodar Das Modi', reads: 'Of the total 40,000 rape cases in India in the last ten years, 39,000 had a Muslim rapist. Still Congress and Rahul Gandhi say Hindus are rapists and terrorists.'

Ahead of the Lok Sabha polls, a young BJP social media volunteer admitted to me that boosting Modi's image and 'taking down' Rahul and the Congress were the prime objectives of the right-wing 'ecosystem' which included Twitter handles, Facebook pages, websites, TV channels, all acting in tandem. He showed me messages on a GooglePlus group sent by a BJP IT cell member giving the exact times when anti-Rahul tweets and hashtags would be posted and re-posted online so that they could quickly 'trend'. Ominously, the same hashtags were also aired on prime-time debates on pro-BJP channels and the messages retweeted and shared by the party's pool of social media influencers.

'We are like an army working together to propagate content that will go viral,' he admitted.

The volunteer also shared with me several videos that his team had created in Hindi across different Facebook pages and for TikTok, the fast-growing social media video app. In many of them, Rahul is shown as a buffoon who can never measure up to 'Hindu Sant' Modi. One of the Facebook videos has a twenty-second video clip of Rahul's remark during a rally in the 2017 Gujarat campaign, claiming that he will instal a machine in which 'Iss side se aloo ghusega, uss side se sona niklega' (If fed a potato from one side, gold will come out from the other). The video, which sparked off several Rahul jokes on social media, was actually an edited version of a speech where Rahul was making the 'aloo-sona' reference in the context of the promises that Modi had made to farmers. 'We edited the clip to ensure that Rahul looks like a fool, that is our mandate.' The social media volunteer was unapologetic, perfectly aware that the clip was a lie and yet totally unrepentant about propagating it and other untruths. When I raised this with Malviya, his response was dismissive: 'We don't need to make fun of Rahul, he does it all on his own.'

Unlike Modi, Rahul Gandhi did not enter the social media space enthusiastically, or even voluntarily. During the 2014 elections, Rahul was not on Twitter or Facebook because, apparently, he wanted to communicate 'face to face' with the general populace. Abstaining from using social media's enormous reach to woo potential voters seemed counterintuitive, as well as reflective of a certain reluctance to change with the times. Stuck in the belief that the Congress was the champion of the poor, Rahul saw social media as an elite distraction rather than an emerging political necessity. Rahul finally got a Twitter account in April 2015, six years behind Modi, and created a Facebook page two years later. In March 2018, his 'OfficeofRG' Twitter handle became 'Rahul Gandhi', an important landmark in his social media evolution, a sign that he was finally coming to terms with the need to open up to a new, younger, hyperconnected, less officious world.

Rahul's 'discovery' of this new universe also coincided with a change in leadership in the Congress's social media team. The party's social media cell was initially handled by Deepinder Hooda, a young MP from Rohtak. 'We had a shoestring budget and a very small operation at the time that was going nowhere because of typical Congress bureaucracy. We were even asked to once take a paper print out of our website for approval by the higher-ups!' a cell member recalls. In May 2017, Divya Spandana, a successful film star and Congress politician from Karnataka was drafted in to replace Hooda because Rahul was reportedly impressed with her spunky willingness to challenge the BJP head-on. The actor didn't have much of a political base – she had once won a by-election from the Vokkaliga heartland of Mandya in south Karnataka – but brought some much-needed energy and zing to the Congress's otherwise staid social media outreach. Divya moved from Bengaluru to Delhi, rented a flat in the posh south Delhi enclave of Jor Bagh, assembled an enthusiastic young team, mainly women in their twenties, some straight out of college, and for a time made a valiant attempt to disrupt old-fashioned, stuck-in-the-groove, hierarchical Congress systems. 'She shook things up for sure and at least marketed our social media outreach effectively,' claims one of her team members.

That she had direct access to Rahul didn't hurt at all. Suddenly, the Congress leader was far more aggressive on social media, especially Twitter, taking the 'battle' to the Modi camp. In 2018, Rahul actually 'outperformed' Modi on Twitter in terms of median retweets even as his follower count began to steadily climb (he had more than 10 million followers by mid-2019). 'Rahul was direct, he was sarcastic, he was making a real news buzz; he was actually doing to Modi what the BJP leaders had done to him in 2014 by being so hard-hitting in his tweets,' says Professor Pal, who tracked both leaders closely on social media. For example, Rahul repeatedly referred to Amit Shah's son, Jay, as 'Shah-zada', a spin on Modi's allusion to the Congress leader as 'Shehzada' or prince. Another combative tweet said: 'If BJP had a film franchise, it would be called Lie Hard #BJPLieHard.' The Congress, it seems, had finally recognized the power of a hashtag!

The spunkiness of the keyboard warrior didn't always work though. When Divya tweeted 'Is that a bird-dropping?' with a photograph of the prime minister at the foot of the Sardar Patel statue in a white kurta, from her personal account, senior Congress leaders agreed that the tweet was 'in poor taste' and pushed to rein in the party's social media star. Soon, Rahul's low-profile college senior, Nikhil Alva was tasked with handling his social media profile while Divya (nicknamed 'Diva Divya' by her critics) was asked to focus on the party site. 'You must understand that in the Congress nothing remains the same for long – the power equations keep changing based on access to the top leadership,' a former Congress MP reminds me.

In the end, the Congress lost out to the BJP in the high-profile social media game, quite simply because its creaking, dilapidated organization structure was roundly defeated by the latter's tightly run communication systems; a more visible presence online could never compensate for the weak and scattered Congress ground game. 'When Narendra Modi tweets, the entire BJP machine right down to the booth level gets galvanized in minutes but if Rahul Gandhi tweets, not everyone responds because we are still far too decentralized and, dare I say, democratic, to follow any orders,' suggests a Congress leader by way of comparison. A 'cultural disconnect' between the old and new guard may be a better way to explain the Congress's predicament with new-age communication. While the Modi–Shah duo have embraced technology as an essential tool in politics and passed the message all the way down the line to their cadres, the Congress continues to operate in silos. 'We have young leaders who are only interested in their Facebook profiles and taking selfies at protest meets, and we have older leaders who are still wary of using Facebook for political messaging,' moans a Congress MP.

The other, more predictable, grouse is that the Congress simply didn't have the funds to match the BJP's social media onslaught. 'The BJP has "paid" WhatsApp administrators to manage their groups; we don't,' argues a Congress social media team member. It's an allegation which the BJP vehemently denies. That the BJP has a huge cash advantage over its rivals is now increasingly apparent, even though social media doesn't always need big money as much as creativity for successful outcomes. Official figures show that the BJP spent ₹4.23 crore on 2500 ads on Facebook while the Congress spent ₹1.46 crore on 3686 ads. On Google, again, the BJP was the highest spender with ₹17 crore, followed by the DMK with ₹4.1 crore, and the Congress limping behind with ₹2.71 crore.

More than the money spent, it is the manner in which the BJP has built its vast network of affiliates and supporting groups that is striking. Multiple sources have confirmed that the Shah-sponsored ABM manages Facebook pages like My First Vote For Modi, Main Bhi Chowkidar and Nation with NaMo and uploads videos and memes that go viral across millions of followers. On the day the Pulwama attack took place, the Nation with NaMo page immediately shared videos of Congress leader Navjot Singh Sidhu hugging Pakistan army chief General Asif Bajwa. The next day, the page had pictures of Rahul checking his cell phone while the bodies of the martyred jawans lay at the airport, the tricolour over them. Between February and April 2019, the BJP's official page and the fan pages of Prime Minister Modi managed by ABM were the top spenders on Facebook ads. 'Pages like Nation with NaMo are nothing but disguised advertising for the BJP,' says Samarth Bansal, a young journalist who has tracked ABM's journey.

Nor is ABM the only BJP-backed company operating in the social media space. The Ahmedabad-based Silver Touch Technologies which set up the NaMo app has received over ₹60 crore in government contracts. It also runs verified accounts on the app like 'The India Eye' with 1.9 million followers. Bansal's research shows that India Eye was used to spread misinformation about the opposition parties. This includes claims that the Congress is the fourth most corrupt party in the world according to the BBC, and that Sonia Gandhi is the fourth richest woman in the world – fake posts that were widely shared. In April 2019, Facebook took down India Eye along with over 700 other political pages and accounts for engaging in 'coordinated inauthentic behaviour'. While the 687 pro-Congress pages taken down had 206,000 followers, the 15 pro-BJP pages were all linked to Silver Touch and had more than 2.6 million followers.

The NaMo app, launched in June 2015, is a good example of how the lines between government and party, between business and politics are blurred. Writes Bansal in a January 2019 article in the Huffington Post: 'State governments and business entities such as mobile phone companies are now bundling the NaMo app into their offerings: the app came pre-installed in free smartphones distributed by the Chhattisgarh government when the BJP was ruling the state. It comes pre-installed in the low-cost phones made by Reliance Jio.'

In the build-up to the 2019 elections, Modi put the NaMo app to good use to scale up his outreach. He would routinely interact with various interest groups through the app: if it was Ujwala beneficiaries one day, it was self-help groups the next and BJP booth workers on the third. A personal, intimate connection was being cemented between the leader and lakhs of his followers; the artful use of technology was slicing through traditional methods of communication. 'The app is a campaign tool which has made one leader central to the political discourse. The obvious concern is, what impact will it have on the ability of other political parties to have a level playing field in their campaign outreach,' says Professor Pal.

These concerns were highlighted when NaMo TV was launched on 31 March 2019, just two weeks before the elections, to coincide with the 'Chowkidar' campaign. The BJP claimed that the channel would capture the 'real-time excitement' of the prime minister's bid for re-election. The opposition argued that the channel, with the prime minister's logo displayed prominently on the screen, was nothing but another advertisement platform for the prime minister. 'NaMo TV is only part of the NaMo app ecosystem. The video content that you get on the app was now on TV so I am not sure what the fuss was all about,' argues Malviya. Meanwhile, direct-to-home (DTH) and cable service providers rushed to allocate prime slots for the channel which became operational without requiring official permission from the I&B ministry, normally imperative for channels to begin broadcasting. The ever-obliging ministry backed the BJP's contention: NaMo TV is not a licensed channel but a DTH advertisement platform that doesn't require approval for broadcast. Clearly, the BJP was exploiting a regulatory void to maximize political advantage.

As if all this was not enough, the release of a biopic on the prime minister, *PM Narendra Modi* was slated to coincide with the elections until the EC stepped in and deferred its release till after the polls were completed. The lead actor in the film, Vivek Oberoi, is an unabashed Modi supporter. When I asked him about the film's timing, he retorted, 'The constitution guarantees me the freedom to show this film when I want and in the manner I choose to do it. If the judiciary has no problem with the biopic, why do you have an issue? Tomorrow, I could argue that your daily TV show is also influencing the elections.' The confrontational, point-scoring ready-for-a-fight disposition of the Modi cheerleaders is often both impressive and disconcerting, an audacity of intent and ruthlessness in action that has little space for self-doubt or criticism, where the magnetic appeal of an individual triumphs over rules and rationality. It is a form of political hypnosis, an unquestioning cultist zeal that leads to subversion of norms, and is tough to combat.

The Modi biopic was just another cog in the sleek and well-organized political machine whose ever-widening sphere of influence went beyond just one election. The making of Brand Modi was, in fact, a gigantic commercial enterprise with its tentacles all over the place. I realized this when I was told that Tajinder Singh Bagga, a Delhi BJP spokesperson, is manufacturing Modi T-shirts for sale. I knew Bagga as an internet-savvy 'troll army' mobilizer who would often target any critic of the government in an unseemly manner. He gained notoriety when he physically attacked senior lawyer and activist Prashant Bhushan in his Supreme Court chambers in 2011. He even later gloated about it on Twitter: 'He try to break my nation, I try to break his head. Hisab Chukta, Congrats to all: operation Prashant Bhushan successful.' Later, in 2014,

Bagga put up posters near our Noida office calling me a 'deshdrohi' after my much discussed tangle with Modi supporters in New York's Madison Square Garden. In 2015, he was one of the 150-odd social media influencers whom Prime Minister Modi met and feted at his residence. Once the self-styled head of the Bhagat Singh Kranti Sena, he formally became a BJP spokesperson in 2017. That the ruling political party had chosen a thuggish lout as its spokesperson only demonstrated how rapidly the rules of the political game had changed: being a social media 'influencer', however controversial, was now a ticket to getting access to the power corridors. In fact, the prime minister was accused of following many abusive Twitterati, one of whom, Nikhil Dadhich, a Surat-based textile trader, actually 'celebrated' the killing of journalist Gauri Lankesh on the microblogging site with the disgusting tweet: 'A bitch died a dog's death and now all the puppies are wailing in the same tune.'

Bagga claims to have started his clothes manufacturing unit in Delhi in 2016. 'I sell products with a patriotic touch,' he asserts. His collection includes brightly coloured T-shirts with personalized messages and slogans like 'Main Bhi Chowkidar', 'Modi Hai to Mumkin Hai', 'My PM Works Till AM' printed on them. 'You can also buy one, it's our hottest selling item,' he tells me. I didn't bite the bait. But the brisk sale of Modi merchandise only confirmed my growing belief that in the build up to the 2019 elections, Brand Modi was literally everywhere: TV, radio, mobile, online, movies, books, billboards and, yes, even at a store near you. What chance did the systematically lampooned and cunningly marginalized opposition really have in the face of this 360-degree media blitzkrieg revolving around a total 'capture' of voter mindspace with one man's persona? The year 2019 would truly be India's first multimedia 'convergence' election.

EIGHT

Modi Hai Toh Mumkin Hai

THE bugle for the 2019 elections was officially sounded on 10 March but not without a certain amount of controversy. For over a week, the media was kept waiting, amidst speculation about why the EC was delaying the announcement. With Prime Minister Modi on an endless whirl of poll-related engagements where he was happily declaring a slew of last-minute welfare schemes, the Congress party's leader Ahmed Patel tweeted: 'Is the Election Commission waiting for the Prime Minister's "official" travel programs to conclude before announcing dates for General Elections?' The sarcasm was impossible to miss: the opposition was convinced that the BJP was dictating terms to the EC. A few days later, the commission refuted the criticism. 'We don't operate as per PM's schedule, we have our own schedule,' commission sources told journalists.

However, the sharp response couldn't mask the fact that the EC's reputation was on the line: an institution which had built its standing during the T.N. Seshan years in the mid-1990s for being a watchdog to curb political excesses at election time was now being censured for going 'soft' on the ruling party. In one particularly rancorous exchange with the commission, TMC leader Derek O'Brien reportedly raised his voice and confronted the commission members. 'You are "cheats" who are acting on behalf of your "masters",' he screeched. The TMC MP was incensed at the manner in which the commission was transferring police officers in Bengal. When I met CEC Sunil Arora to discuss the many controversies swirling around the commission, he didn't appear too fazed. 'My conscience is clear and I will stick to my guns and follow the model code of conduct,' he said firmly.

The silver-haired former secretary was, in the words of a colleague, a 'purana khiladi' (old player), an experienced bureaucrat who knew how to deal with the political system. A Rajasthan cadre officer, he had served as principal secretary to BJP chief ministers Bhairon Singh Shekhawat and Vasundhara Raje. He was also chairperson at Indian Airlines during the Vajpayee government and was widely credited for engineering the airline's turnaround at the time. In 2004, following a change in government, he found himself at loggerheads with the UPA's civil aviation minister, Praful Patel, when he accused the minister of deliberately allowing the national carrier to collapse. His name also surfaced in the notorious Niira Radia tapes controversy in which he is heard discussing, among other things, corruption in the judiciary and alleged 'fixing' of judgements with the well-networked lobbyist. No-nonsense bureaucrat or political 'yes-man' – the jury was still out on Arora when he took over as CEC in December 2018, just months ahead of the general elections.

What was immediately apparent though was that Arora was no Seshan-style combatant who would stoutly position himself against the political executive. 'I am here to organize an election, not get into a wrestling match,' is his defence. He claims that he had given every political party a chance to be heard in the 93 meetings that were held between March and May 2019: 20 with the BJP, 28 with the Congress and 45 with other smaller parties. The opposition parties were particularly concerned over the possible tampering of the electronic voting machines (EVMs). 'We have conducted more than 120 elections in the country with EVMs, no one had a problem then. Now suddenly they are blaming the EVM,' is the CEC's rejoinder. Arora has a point: the EC had completed a successful state election exercise in November–December 2018 and there had been minimal complaints of malfunctioning EVMs. Credible experts too doubted that the EVMs could be tampered with. In their book, *The Verdict*, which maps electoral patterns over the years, Dr Prannoy Roy and Dorab Sopariwala write: 'In our experience with EVMs over the years, the fundamental and unique feature of each machine being stand-alone, not connected to the Internet, Wi-Fi or Bluetooth, has convinced us that they are impossible to be hacked.'

But what of the alleged violations of the model code of conduct by the ruling party? Not only was NaMo TV, the BJP's 'advertising' channel, allowed to remain on air right through the poll schedule, it even telecast Modi's speeches during the 48-hour 'silent period' before polling. 'We asked all the content to be vetted and certified by the common certification regime, that is all we can do. The rest you must ask the I&B ministry,' says Arora, pleading helplessness in the matter.

In the run-up to the elections, the political rhetoric was ratcheted up several notches. Prime Minister Modi and BJP president Amit Shah took every opportunity to make the Balakot strike a prime election point. In a speech in Latur, Maharashtra, the prime minister declared, 'I want to tell first-time voters: can you dedicate your first vote to the brave soldiers who carried out the air strike on Balakot in Pakistan? Can you dedicate your vote to the brave martyrs of Pulwama?' Meanwhile, in rousing speeches in Maharashtra and Bengal, Shah alleged that when the prime minister sent '*his* air force' and decimated the terror camps in Balakot, the act was mourned in Pakistan and by the Rahul Gandhi–led Congress and Mamata Banerjee's office. The opposition parties lodged a formal complaint, alleging that the armed forces were being wrongly used for political propaganda. Despite the fact that a 'general advisory' issued by the commission on 25 March 2019 notes that 'campaigners should desist, as part of their election campaigning, from indulging in any political propaganda involving activities of the Defence Forces', the three-member EC gave Modi–Shah a clean chit. In addition, it overruled the dissenting note put up by Ashok Lavasa, one of the three commissioners. (The dissent note, which called for the BJP leadership to 'cooperate' with the election rules, was not even placed on record because the commission was not deemed to be a 'quasi-judicial' body. Lavasa's family would, in September 2019, be subject to an income tax inquiry, raising troubling questions yet again of allegedly vindictive executive action.) Weren't the speeches by Modi and Shah glaring infringements of the EC's advisory, I asked Arora. 'It is not so simple, we need to clearly define political propaganda,' was his somewhat peculiar justification for the commission's inaction against the top BJP leadership.

Interestingly, the commission did act against other senior politicians: UP Chief Minister Yogi Adityanath, BSP chief Mayawati, SP leader Azam Khan and the Congress's Navjot Sidhu were all censured and banned from campaigning from forty-eight to seventy-two hours for alleged communal remarks that violated the poll code. 'We even acted against Rajasthan governor Kalyan Singh for calling himself a BJP karyakarta. We didn't allow the Modi biopic to be shown till after the elections were over. Why don't you look at what we did instead of only focusing on what we didn't do?' asks Arora irritably.

In April 2019, a group of retired senior civil servants wrote to President Kovind questioning the EC's 'crisis of credibility'. 'I was hurt, I am human after all,' admits Arora. Did the EC do enough to allay the fears of its critics? With a 90-crore-plus electorate and more than 10 lakh booths, there will always be the odd controversy during election time. Under Article 324 of the Constitution, the commission has enough powers to act tough, but somehow the impression persists that the commission is reluctant to take on the Modi government beyond a point. A commonly voiced derisive comment heard is that the Election Commission has turned into an Election Omission. Is another institution now being brought under the ever-widening ambit of political power? My mind goes back to a brief conversation I once had with the South African anti-apartheid revolutionary politician, late Nelson Mandela, in the 1990s. I had asked Mandela what it was about India that he was most impressed by. 'Well, Gandhi and his message of non-violent protest, of course. But also the way you conduct free and fair elections every five years – the world should learn from India,' he had pronounced. Would the great Mandela have viewed the 2019 election as a truly level playing field supervised by a 'neutral' umpire, I wonder.

'Narendra Modi and Amit Shah relish elections like merit-list students who enjoy competitive exams,' a BJP leader who has worked with them in Gujarat tells me. And like those who consistently make it to the list of toppers, the Modi–Shah duo too realize that extensive preparations hold the key to success. A former executive with ABM – the BJP's election management private agency – recalls preparing a 132-slide PowerPoint presentation one year ahead of the 2018 Karnataka assembly elections in which every district was mapped. 'We made the presentation to the prime minister and BJP president at 6 p.m. and finished in the wee hours of the morning. They rigorously went through every detail with us before signing off. It was like preparing for a major brand launch with a top corporate,' the executive reveals.

Not surprisingly, Shah began planning for the 2019 general elections from 2014 itself, soon after taking over as BJP president. Poring over India's political map, he gauged that the BJP faced a mighty challenge in replicating its 2014 success. Of the 282 seats which the party had won then, as many as 241 had come from a north-west arc of just twelve states. 'We knew we had maxed out in many of these states and needed to ensure that not only did we minimize our losses here but also looked for new frontiers to conquer,' says Bhupendra Yadav, the BJP MP and general secretary who has rapidly emerged as a key lieutenant to the BJP president.

Typically, Shah set a rather ambitious target for his team: Mission 400. 'Let us identify 400 seats where the NDA has a good chance of winning,' was his directive. This included around 120 seats which the BJP had lost in 2014 but which were now seen as 'potentially winnable': the seats were divided into 25 clusters, each under a state or Union minister, and a strategy devised to expand the BJP's footprint. 'Most people would think that the BJP has no chance in certain parts of the country but with Amitbhai, nothing is seen as impossible,' avers Yadav. (The BJP would eventually contest 82 of these 120 seats, and win 56 of them, many for the first time in states like Telangana, Bengal, Odisha and the North-east.)

Not everything was initially going according to plan, though, especially south of the Vindhyas. For twelve months, the BJP had worked on superstar Rajinikanth and tried to convince him to become the 'face' of the party in Tamil Nadu. Party leaders involved in the negotiations claim that Rajinikanth had almost agreed – he even set an auspicious date for the announcement – before suddenly backing out. The actor was never fully committed to public life, unwilling to abandon cushy film star comforts for the daily grind of politics. The party's Plan B of remote-controlling a badly factionalized All India Anna Dravida Munnetra Kazhagam after the death of Jayalalithaa in December 2016 had also not quite worked out. The DMK, meanwhile, was skilfully reviving itself by accusing the Modi government of being 'anti-Tamil Nadu'. It was the one state where, every time he visited, Modi would be greeted with black flags and a well-orchestrated #ModiGoBack campaign across social media. 'Every time anything went wrong in our state, be it a cyclone or even the NEET exam suicides, we immediately blamed the Centre for it!' remarks a DMK political strategist. The original Dravidian political identity had been built on an anti-Centre, anti-New Delhi sentiment which still resonates in Tamil Nadu: somehow, the BJP's Hindi–Hindu–Hindustan identity politics has been unable to find a toehold in the southern state, where the Dravidian identity has been proof against the north Indian 'Aryan' imperialist inclinations of those wanting to subdue Tamil pride.

Shah made a determined push in Kerala too, a state where the BJP had never won a Lok Sabha seat, in the firm belief that this was a potential growth area for the future. 'We will be a true national party only when we win from Kerala to Bengal,' he once told his colleagues. In the 2016 assembly elections, the BJP increased its vote share from 6 to 15 per cent in Kerala. In October 2017, Shah embarked on a Jan Raksha Yatra (People's Protection Yatra) to protest the killing of RSS–BJP workers under CPI(M) government rule. Shah had hoped for a gradual consolidation of the Kerala Hindu vote while projecting both the left and the Congress as soft towards Islamist and Christian groups. But breaking into the entrenched left–Congress duopoly was not going to be easy, especially in a state where the BJP's core Hindutva agenda on issues like cow slaughter would not find too many takers. The party was hoping that the Sabarimala temple controversy would give it a boost: a Supreme Court verdict in October 2018 ruled that women have the right to enter the temple dedicated to the eternally celibate Lord Ayyappa, sparking off protests in the state which were led by party workers. The BJP identified three seats where felt had half a chance to make a breakthrough, but in the end the party would draw a blank. 'I guess it was the Congress and not us who got the major chunk of the post-Sabarimala anti-left vote which we were hoping would come to us,' says Rajeev Chandrashekhar, a BJP Rajya Sabha MP. Another feature of Kerala that makes the BJP's prospects in the state difficult is the highly competitive politics. Over the years, alternating spells of the left and Congress in power has ensured that both outfits retain strong cadres that won't easily cede space. Moreover, the pressure on local governments to constantly deliver tangible welfare to citizens – Kerala ranks high on most social indicators – makes it difficult for a third player to easily break in.

In Andhra Pradesh, the BJP was on the wrong side of a regional battleground. For Andhra chief minister and TDP leader Chandrababu Naidu, his principal rival was YSR Congress leader Jaganmohan Reddy, an ambitious young man determined to carry forward his late father Y.S. Rajasekhar Reddy's political legacy. In November 2017, Jagan embarked on a 3,500 kilometre yatra, which gradually gathered traction. He even hired Prashant Kishor as a political consultant to create a buzz around his campaign: at one stage, Kishor had a 400-plus team working in the field in the state. A worried Naidu decided to revive the issue of 'special status' for Andhra to counter Jagan but found that the BJP wasn't willing to oblige. A despairing Naidu quit the BJP-led NDA at the Centre in April 2018, making Andhra 'pride' his calling card. It was too late for him to stop Jagan's march, but he was still able to dent the BJP's prospects in the state.

All this southern discomfort meant that Shah's 'Mission 400' was now looking like a pipedream. Suddenly, ensuring that the NDA did not split any further became a priority for the BJP president. Two large states were key to the BJP's alliance arithmetic: Maharashtra and Bihar. In 2014, the NDA had won 73 of the 88 seats in these two states but since then its alliances had been in a state of flux. In Maharashtra, in particular, the Shiv Sena was routinely sniping at the BJP leadership. In December 2018, in the wake of the BJP's assembly poll defeat, Shiv Sena chief Uddhav Thackeray went so far as to virtually appropriate Rahul Gandhi's 'Chowkidar chor hai' jibe in the context of the Rafale deal. 'Today, security persons have themselves become thieves,' thundered Thackeray at a party rally. At a book event in the national capital, Sena MP Sanjay Raut added to the sense of unease when he told me, 'We want a revival of Vajpayee's BJP which knows how to run an alliance government.'

A section of the BJP was incensed enough to suggest breaking the thirty-year-old alliance. 'We don't need them if they can't control their tongue,' an irate senior central minister told the BJP president. Shah, though, was playing it cool. 'Chunaav ke pehle yeh sab hota hai' (These things happen before elections), was his calm response. Shah had no love lost for the Sena leadership but he knew that snapping the alliance at this stage would only help the rival Congress–NCP. Hoping to quickly seal a deal, Shah took the initiative of travelling to Mumbai and meeting Uddhav at his Matoshree residence. It was only his second visit to the Sena leader's home since 2014: he had gone in 2017 to seek support for the presidential election. The Shah who met the Sena chief was a different man. Gone was the anger and truculence of the past. Warm and gentle, he insisted on a one-on-one meeting with Uddhav over typically Maharashtrian fare of wadas and sabudana khichdi. 'I don't think I have ever seen Amitji like this. He was smiling all the time and treating us like a long-lost friend,' remarks Raut. The ice was broken. A mutually beneficial seat-sharing deal was announced for both the Lok Sabha and assembly elections.

Bihar was a little more complicated since there wasn't just one ally who needed to be placated here. Union minister Ram Vilas Paswan was getting restive and exploring options with the opposition Congress–RJD alliance. Paswan is the archetypal neta of the coalition age, astutely switching sides every few years, depending on which way the political breeze is blowing. 'Mausam-vaigyanik' (weather expert) was his moniker in political and journalistic circles. Soon after the December 2018 assembly elections, Paswan established contact with the Congress, sensing that the BJP's fortunes were on the decline.

Shaktisinh Gohil, the Congress general secretary for Bihar, and Paswan shook hands on a plane ride from Patna to Delhi and reportedly agreed to finalize an alliance. Upon his arrival in Delhi, though, Paswan found that Bhupendra Yadav, the BJP leader in charge of Bihar, was waiting to meet him. Shah had heard of Paswan's imminent departure from the NDA and asked Yadav to convince him not to quit. Paswan's vote base may have been shrinking, but he was still Bihar's most prominent Dalit face. The BJP offered him as many as six Lok Sabha seats and, importantly, a guarantee of a Rajya Sabha nomination. It was enough to seal an election pact. 'I guess we just moved quickly,' smiles Yadav. 'He used us to get a better deal from the BJP,' sighs Gohil. The political weather expert had done it again.

Paswan was easy enough in the end for the BJP to retain in the alliance. A more difficult partner was Nitish Kumar, the chief minister of Bihar. The canny politician had surprised everyone when he returned to the NDA in July 2017 after having fought a long, acrimonious – and rather personal – battle with Prime Minister Modi for several years. He, along with Lalu Prasad and the Congress, had given the Modi–Shah combine a bloody nose in the 2015 Bihar elections before suddenly dumping Lalu in July 2017, allegedly because he was 'sick and tired' of his partner's corruption stain and interference in governance. Now, as the 2019 elections approached, a restless Nitish, annoyed by the prime minister's refusal to give him more political space at the Centre, was reportedly ready to test the water again. He even re-established contact with

Rahul Gandhi and travelled to Delhi to meet him and work out another political realignment. 'We waited for almost a week, several SMSs were exchanged, but Rahul did not meet us,' says Prashant Kishor, who was playing mediator. 'How do you trust someone who switches sides so often,' counters the Congress's Gohil.

Shah, in contrast, was more than willing to meet the Bihar chief minister halfway. In the 2014 elections, the BJP and Nitish had fought separately: the BJP winning as many as twenty-one seats; Nitish's JD(U) just two. Now, Nitish wanted an equal number of seats as the BJP. Surprisingly, Shah agreed to the proposal almost immediately even though it meant fighting for fewer seats than the party had actually won in 2014. The two sides would fight seventeen seats each, and Paswan would get the remaining six of Bihar's forty seats. It was clever politics by Shah: losing a little with an eye on gaining a lot more, a tactic not usually preferred by India's big political egos. 'I think the BJP's move was tactical and well calculated. They were not only looking at the Lok Sabha elections of 2019 but also at the Vidhan Sabha polls of 2020 where they hope to become the main player in the state,' says Sankarshan Thakur, senior journalist and chronicler of Bihar's politics.

The seat-sharing deals in Bihar and Maharashtra sent out an unequivocal message to the entire political ecosystem: the BJP was willing to make short-term compromises for electoral gain. Bihar and Maharashtra were large states, but even in the relatively smaller ones the BJP seemed amenable to make the odd sacrifice. In Assam, in early January 2019, for instance, the union cabinet cleared the contentious Citizenship Amendment Bill that would offer a path to citizenship for minority groups from neighbouring countries, including Bengali Hindus from Bangladesh, on grounds of religious persecution. Hindus, Jains, Sikhs, Buddhists and Parsis from neighbouring countries could get Indian citizenship; Muslims had been conspicuously left out. It was a clear attempt to play the communal card and win the Hindu migrant vote, especially in the bordering state of Bengal. The nativist Asom Gana Parishad (AGP), an ally of the BJP, objected on the grounds that it was a violation of the Assam Accord that had set 1971 as the cut-off date for all migrants to be granted citizenship. The AGP ministers resigned from the BJP-led government and other North-east allies too joined the protests. Caught in a complex tangle of ethnic and religious politics, Ram Madhav, the BJP's general secretary for the region, sought Shah's advice. 'Don't do anything, don't accept any resignation, don't react in anger at all,' he was told. Eventually, the AGP patched up with the BJP and fought the Lok Sabha polls together. 'The AGP may be a small party today with a single-digit vote share but for Amitbhai every seat mattered,' observes Madhav. The BJP won nine of the fourteen seats in Assam, getting votes from both Assamese- and Bengali-speaking Hindus.

Another telling illustration of the BJP's willingness to walk the extra mile to win even one additional seat is the 'deal' the party struck with the relatively unknown Rashtriya Loktantrik Party (RLP) in Rajasthan. The RLP is essentially a one-man party headed by Hanuman Beniwal, a rough-talking, sturdy Jat leader who was once the president of the Rajasthan University Students' Union. Beniwal was extremely keen to fight from his Jat bastion of Nagaur and was in talks with Chief Minister Ashok Gehlot of the Congress. The two had almost shaken hands on it, when Gehlot was explicitly told by the party high command: 'The Nagaur seat is reserved for Jyoti Mirdha.' (Jyoti, who had won the 2009 Lok Sabha elections from Nagaur but lost the seat in 2014, comes from a family of several generations of Congress loyalists.) A spurned Beniwal immediately contacted the BJP leadership. Within twenty-four hours, he was offered the Nagaur seat and the alliance was sealed. 'Rajasthan ka poora Jat vote maine BJP ki taraf kiya' (I got the entire Jat vote to swing towards the BJP), he now claims. The BJP would end up repeating its 2014 success of sweeping all twenty-five seats in the state – a remarkable achievement when you consider that the party had just lost in the assembly elections in December 2018.

An even bigger challenge awaited the BJP in UP: the SP–BSP alliance meant that replicating the party's 2014 success, where the BJP had won seventy-one of the eighty seats, would be almost impossible. The BJP with its ally, the Apna Dal, had got around 43 per cent of the vote in UP in 2014; the SP–BSP vote when counted together had similar figures. A simple addition of the 2014 SP and BSP vote share would reduce the NDA tally from 73 to 37 seats in the state, a loss of almost half the seats. Most political observers felt that the BJP would be lucky to reach that figure in 2019. 'I must confess that no one was giving the BJP more than 40 seats in UP,' admits veteran Lucknow-based journalist Sharat Pradhan.

No one except those close to Shah that is. At a closed-door meeting in Lucknow in 2018, Shah told his core UP team to treat the election as a 'Panipat-like war', one where it would be 'BJP versus the rest'. 'We need to get 51 per cent of the popular vote at all costs,' he affirmed. For Sunil Bansal, the UP BJP's all-powerful campaign chief, this was now a fresh challenge. 'We were talking about an 8 to 9 per cent increase in vote share. We knew that it was going to be a struggle but also felt that we now had a better election machine than our opponents,' says Bansal.

Once again, the BJP had a head start in its preparations. In 2018, Bansal organized twenty-eight state-level sammelans in Lucknow, primarily for non-Jatav SC and non-Yadav OBC communities as part of the BJP's strategy of an artful 'social re-engineering' of UP's traditional caste blocs. In early 2019, five smaller meetings were held in each of UP's eighty Lok Sabha constituencies for SC, OBC, farmer, women and youth groups. It didn't end there: the party's ambitious membership drive meant that Bansal had built what he cheerfully calls a 'chalees lakh ki fauj' (40-lakh-strong army) of full-time political workers who would criss-cross India's most populous state through the year. The BJP had even identified five young bikers – party workers on motorbikes to round up voters – per polling booth in the state, a total of almost 8 lakh bikers across UP. In every Vidhan Sabha segment, a 'Kamal Sandesh' bike rally was organized in the lead-up to the elections, a practice that was followed in other states too. Stickers and flags were put up at the home of every BJP worker with the slogan 'Mera parivar, Bhajpa parivar' to create a community spirit.

Another innovative move was to initiate a 'Kamal Deepavali' programme in October 2018 where one crore lamps were lit over the festive season in the homes of 'labhartis' or beneficiaries of central government schemes. Labharti sampark pramukhs were appointed – on an average, one for every eight to ten booths – and tasked with engaging with the beneficiaries, taking photos and videos with them and posting these on social media sites. The citizen was no longer just an anonymous voter but a 'labharti': the sarkar and sangathan were one – government and party structure seamlessly merged – united by the notion of a 'Bhajpa parivar' with Modi as the paterfamilias. 'The maximum number of people who have gained from schemes like Ujwala and Swachh Bharat are in UP, almost 3.4 crore. This is where we got most of our additional votes from in this election,' asserts Bansal. If you were the beneficiary of a government scheme, you were also duty-bound to be a voter of the ruling party was the subliminal message.

Voter mobilization and caste arithmetic is only one aspect of the BJP's UP success story. The other is Shah's morally questionable 'jugaad' politics where the means don't matter, only the ends do. The BJP was reportedly funding Akhilesh Yadav's estranged uncle Shivpal Yadav who was travelling across the state in a gleaming helicopter with a single-point agenda: giving his nephew a bloody nose. In the run-up to the elections, the BJP lured a number of SP and BSP second-line leaders to switch sides. Praveen Nishad, a leader from the influential Nishad community of eastern UP, is one such leader. In 2018, Nishad contested and won a by-election from Gorakhpur on an SP ticket, striking a big blow on Chief Minister Yogi Adityanath's home turf. It had been a shocking setback to the ruling party's winning streak in UP, a rare TV moment when channels had headlined a BJP failure. Now Shah moved in, offered Nishad a Lok Sabha seat and worked out a last-minute deal. The BSP was even more vulnerable to poaching. Three of the BJP candidates in SC-reserved seats were from Mayawati's party who switched to the BJP just before the elections: all three won. 'The BJP was throwing money for fun in this election,' insists Akhilesh. 'Everyone wants to be on the winning side, what's wrong with that?' contends a UP BJP leader. In UP, the BJP went for broke. Up against a formidable caste alliance, the saffron party left no stone, or seat, unturned.

In the ultimate analysis, though, this was a UP and, arguably, a national election where candidates scarcely seemed to matter, only the leader did. As many as eighteen of the BJP's candidates in UP were first-timers, and twenty-four of the seventy-one sitting MPs were dropped. Nationally, the BJP fielded 204 debutantes, denying tickets to 113 out of the 282 sitting MPs who won in 2014. In Chhattisgarh, for example, all ten sitting BJP MPs were replaced with fresh faces which proved to be a winning formula: nine of them won. 'You must understand the philosophy of the Modi–Shah combine. Right from their Gujarat days, in every election, they drop at least 30 to 40 per cent of the sitting MLAs/ MPs. They believe the leader wins an election, not the candidate,' a BJP union minister tells me.

Indeed, across the country, and in UP in particular, the persona of the prime minister was pitched as the BJP's ultimate calling card to offset any local anti-incumbency. State units were specifically told to ensure that Modi's image towered above that of the regional leader in their publicity campaigns. When the rage and anguish of UP farmers over the Yogi government's misplaced cow vigilantism – which resulted in stray cattle being let loose, causing damage to crops and public mayhem – could not be contained, the narrative was quickly shifted from Yogi to Modi Raj. This election, the party claimed, was not about UP, it was about who should rule at the Centre; it was about 'desh' (nation), not 'gaon' (village). Once again, playing the triple role of 'vikas purush', OBC leader and 'Hindu hriday samrat', Modi on the campaign trail in UP was the BJP's unwavering mascot, addressing twenty-nine rallies and roadshows in the final stretch, the most he did in any part of the country. 'There was a silent undercurrent for Modi which we all missed,' confesses Pradhan.

The sharply focused cohesiveness in the BJP campaign was in marked contrast to the complete disconnect in the BSP–SP 'mahagathbandhan'. I travelled on the campaign trail with Akhilesh Yadav on a day when he was addressing two joint rallies with Mayawati. It seemed like the perfect time to get an exclusive interview with the two allies together, but I was firmly told that 'Behenji does her own thing'. In fact, near each rally venue, a separate room, painted in traditional BSP blue, had been 'reserved' for Mayawati. She only emerged from her room and met Akhilesh when the rally was about to start. Until then, there was almost no communication between the two partners. This was an alliance relying on pure caste arithmetic with near-zero personal chemistry. Mayawati remained an imperious presence, a yesteryear messiah who appeared disdainfully unmindful, even unconcerned about her thinning credibility. Akhilesh played 'bhatija' to her 'bua', yet his speeches seemed stagey and bombastic, unable to overcome decades of Dalit–Yadav mistrust on the ground. Still battling a Yadav intra-family turf war, the junior Yadav was reportedly improving his tennis game in Lucknow while 'Dalit ki beti' Mayawati whose grassroots plebeian identity had once been her great strength was now someone whose homes had been raided by the Income Tax Department and was seen parading her young nephew on stage as her heir. The mass connect was somehow missing. Not surprisingly, in a number of seats, the BSP vote just did not transfer to the SP and vice versa. The limitations of caste-based politics were cruelly exposed, especially when the leaders themselves were faced with a serious credibility deficit. 'We had a story to tell in UP, our opponents had nothing but a negative anti-Modi agenda,' affirms Bansal.

When the results were declared, the BJP had won sixty-two seats in UP, its ally the Apna Dal two seats. Significantly, the alliance poll percentage crossed 50 per cent, a clear sign of a 'wave' election. The BJP vote share, in fact, increased in as many as seventy-six of the eighty constituencies in the state, a reflection of its growing cross-caste appeal and ability to cut through the rural–urban divide as well. The UP verdict was a triumph of the BJP's strategy, its organization, messaging and leadership, a case study in how to win an election where the odds are stacked against you. The never-say-die attitude of the 'new' BJP leadership, a point-blank pugnacious refusal to give up or concede any losses whatsoever had paid off. But even the UP elections of 2019 were not a patch on what would prove to be the biggest battle of the year: the fight for West Bengal.

'Mark my words, in 2019 the lotus will bloom from the east, whatever seats we lose in north and west India, we will make up in the east.' That was the firm assertion of the BJP's North-east election manager, Himanta Biswa Sarma, at the *India Today* (east) conclave in Kolkata in November 2018. The BJP's determined 'Look East' politics – a clever mix of regional alliances, defections and, in the case of Tripura, a stunning election turnaround – had helped them conquer state after state in the North-east. The party was eyeing Odisha too, where the failing health of the long-serving chief minister, Naveen Patnaik, had presented it with an opening. But the ultimate prize remained West Bengal, a state with forty-two seats, the third largest in terms of Lok Sabha seats after UP and Maharashtra. 'We will conquer Bengal also, just you wait and see,' insisted Sarma when I expressed my scepticism.

In the audience at the conclave, listening intently, was TMC leader and Rajya Sabha MP Derek O'Brien. The media-savvy, urbane O'Brien was a bit of an oddity in West Bengal's rapidly transforming political milieu. Hailing from Kolkata's small but dynamic Anglo-Indian community, he is a cheery, anglicized presence, a link to Bengal's genteel 'bhadralok' culture, who seems more likely to be spotted at one of the city's clubs and gymkhanas with a drink in hand than with a political symbol on his shirt. In a previous avatar, he was the host of a highly successful TV quiz show before he switched to politics and emerged as a close confidant of Chief Minister Mamata Banerjee. As always, the chatty and gregarious O'Brien had a quick-witted response to the BJP's claim of 'conquering' Bengal. 'Tell them, Bengal is not Gujarat. Here, the Modi–Shah style dangal politics won't work, here our Didi is the Boss, the dada!' he claimed.

O'Brien had reason to feel supremely confident. Under Mamata Banerjee's leadership, the TMC had emerged as the dominant party in West Bengal, leagues ahead of the competition. From the moment Mamata breached the seemingly impregnable fortress of the Left Front in 2012, she had gone from strength to strength, making West Bengal her fiefdom. By contrast, the BJP was a marginal player in the state: in fifteen previous Lok Sabha elections, the party had won just seven seats, including two in its Jana Sangh avatar in 1952 with Dr Syama Prasad Mukherjee at the helm. In the 2014 elections, the BJP won two seats, including Darjeeling with the support of the local Gurkha parties; the TMC, in comparison, swept the state by winning thirty-four of the forty-two seats. Beneath Mamata Banerjee's quixotic persona is a highly astute politician with her finger firmly on the public pulse. Under her guidance, the TMC became almost as entrenched a force as the left had once been, both in civil society and on Bengal's volatile political ground. 'I guess if you told anyone that we would be competing on level terms with Mamata in 2019, they would think we were mad,' admits Babul Supriyo, Union minister, who first won on a BJP ticket from Asansol in 2014.

But there was a method to Amit Shah's 'madness' in Bengal, a plan which was crafted in 2015–16 and carefully scripted and executed over a four-year period. He projected Bengal as the next frontier for the BJP; 'Mission 22', Shah's plan for capturing at least half the Lok Sabha seats on offer, initially seemed like an empty boast. But the BJP president would lead from the front in this battle, at times making it a grinding, bitterly personal match between him and Mamata. Post the 2014 general elections, the BJP president travelled almost every month to West Bengal, a clear sign of his appetite for the challenge. 'I think no state has obsessed Amitbhai in the last five years as much as West Bengal. Whenever we speak, the conversation invariably comes down to winning Bengal,' Sarma tells me now.

In late 2015, Shah appointed the party's Indore strongman Kailash Vijayvargiya as the BJP general secretary for West Bengal, asking him to get the party battle-ready to combat Mamata. A few weeks later, Vijayvargiya returned despondent: 'Amitbhai, we don't have the feet on the ground or the organization to take on Mamata; it will take us at least ten years to build the party.' Shah, however, was determined to give it a go. 'Aap bas koshish kariye, kuch bhi ho sakta hai!' (You just give it a shot, anything can happen!), was his directive.

The choice of Vijayvargiya was an interesting one. A staunch hardline Hindutva mobilizer who plays unabashed religious politics and takes a strident line against Muslims, the former Indore mayor has always flaunted his Hinduness. His two-storeyed house on a bustling Indore street is filled with images of Hindu gods and goddesses, and he himself has often participated in religious functions dressed as Krishna and Vishnu. He is never seen in public without the trademark vermilion tilak slashed across his forehead. 'He is a "kattar" [fierce], unapologetic Hindutvawadi,' is how a local Indore journalist describes the six-time MLA who once trolled superstar Shah Rukh Khan, comparing him to Dawood Ibrahim and branding him a Pakistani at heart. The deceptively soft-spoken leader insists that the perception of him as an anti-Muslim muscleman politician has been 'cooked up' by his detractors. 'I am a man of peace, who only eats "satvik" food – no onion or garlic also, only vegetables. I would never harm anyone,' he insists.

As Shah's hand-picked lieutenant in West Bengal, Vijayvargiya was expected to demonstrate his prowess at winning elections while carving a distinct 'Hindu' identity for the BJP. It is perhaps no coincidence that in a state which had seen relative communal peace during the previous left government rule, a series of religious conflicts suddenly erupted in different parts of West Bengal from 2016 onwards as the BJP slowly began making its presence felt in the state. In the border district of Malda, riots broke out when a Muslim mob protesting remarks made by a Hindu Mahasabha leader against the Prophet turned violent and vandalized public property. In Basirhat, a Muslim-majority district, rioting was triggered when a Hindu teenager allegedly posted a meme on the Prophet. In Asansol, four people died when a Ram Navami procession ended in violent clashes. In Bengal, where Durga Puja dominates the holy calendar, Ram Navami celebrations have traditionally been mostly low-key. But now, BJP district units were told to organize Ram Navami processions in a more elaborate fashion, with little children wielding swords amidst raucous parades that wended their way through Muslim-dominated mohallas. 'Kya Ram Navami ka karyakram koi paap hai?' (Is it a crime to hold a Ram Navami programme?), asks an aggressive Vijayvargiya. In time, public demonstrations of Hindutva combined with high-pitched Hindu victimhood would become integral to the BJP's Bengal mobilization.

The BJP's game plan was apparent: build a vote bank around Hindu revivalism while 'exposing' Mamata as a Muslim-appeasing neta. Pictures of the West Bengal chief minister offering namaz with her head covered in traditional Islamic garb were constantly pushed on social media sites and WhatsApp messenger groups. 'Mamata Banerjee is really Mumtaz Begum,' screeched BJP supporters. Every time, Mamata announced a scheme for minority groups – for example, a monthly stipend given to imams and muezzins – the BJP would immediately raise a red flag. In September 2017, when Mamata decided that the immersion of the idols of on Vijayadashami would be postponed so as not to coincide with the Muharram procession, the BJP accused her of appeasement once more, claiming that Hindus were 'victims' in Mamata's rule. 'Do you know that I attend dozens of Durga Puja pandals every day? Who are these RSS–BJP types to tell me how to celebrate Pujo, what do they know of our traditions? Hum sabko saath lekar chalta hai [We take everyone along], not like your Narendra Modi or Amit Shah!' she told me at the time.

In that brief conversation in 2017 during one of her rare visits to Delhi, I sensed that Didi was rattled by the high-decibel BJP campaign against her. I have known Mamata for years. She is a tempestuous politician; warm and friendly one moment, irritable and enraged the next. I was accustomed to her mood swings but now sensed a creeping insecurity, one that hinted at a loss of nerve. She would not take calls, answer messages or agree to be interviewed – not at all like in her first tenure as chief minister. 'All of you national media has been bought by Modi and Shah, tum lok sab bik gaya hai [You have all sold out]!' she blurted angrily. I tried to placate her but to no avail. The mental make-up of many of our leaders is one in which supreme power breeds hyper-anxiety bordering on acute paranoia. Mamata seemed convinced that she was a lonely warrior, fighting an 'evil' Centre that was about to snatch away her 'kingdom'. Herself a 'strongman' leader, she viewed any challenge as a mortal threat. In this, both Mamata and Narendra Modi are similar: neither can tolerate any opposition.

This conviction that the BJP posed an existential threat was further strengthened when her right-hand man, Mukul Roy, left her in November 2017 to join the BJP. The bustling, short-statured Roy had been Didi's man for all seasons, helping build up the TMC across the state by a mix of muscle power and back-room deals. The rise of Mamata's young, go-getter nephew Abhishek Banerjee had reportedly relegated Roy to the margins, so he began exploring options. 'The problem with Mamata is that she trusts no one, she is a one-woman show,' is Roy's defence for switching sides. He claims to have been in touch with BJP leader Arun Jaitley as far back as 2014, before finally taking the plunge three years later.

The timing, though, was suspicious. Roy was being questioned in the Saradha chit fund scam and was named in an FIR in the Narada sting operation in which several TMC politicians, including Roy, were caught on camera accepting cash bribes in exchange for favours to a fictitious company. The moment he joined the BJP, Roy's interrogation came to a halt and the investigation slowed down. 'That is the BJP under Shah you see: you are corrupt when you are in the opposition but once you join the BJP you get "purified",' observes a TMC MP. Roy, of course, claims he is innocent of all the charges against him. The BJP wasn't complaining: they now had someone on their side who knew the TMC election machine inside out and who would be invaluable in exposing the party's weakest links to the saffron party.

That the conquest of Bengal was firmly on the BJP's Mission 2019 became apparent when, in April 2017, Shah chose the Naxalbari block, the epicentre of the Naxal movement in Bengal in the 1970s, to launch the Deendayal Upadhyaya Vistarak Yojana, a year-long national campaign by which the party's 'vistaraks' (expansionists) were expected to visit booths across the country and connect with BJP booth workers. The launch from Bengal was a symbolic gesture, one designed to convince the BJP's state organization that the party leadership was serious about expanding its footprint in the eastern frontier.

The real turning point in the battle for West Bengal came in the state's panchayat polls of 2018. Like in other states, in Bengal too the panchayat system is at the heart of political power at the grassroots, a platform for distributing government funds and cementing local support through state patronage. For thirty years, the left had controlled Bengal's panchayats through unbridled cadre power until Mamata's takeover, when one 'army' took over from another. The steady rise of the BJP, which announced its intention to fight the panchayat polls with all its might, seemed to unnerve her. A firman was reportedly issued to the local TMC leaders to ensure 'a win at all costs' in maximum panchayats. What followed was mayhem: around fifty people were killed and hundreds injured in a bloody summer of polling. In more than a third of the seats, the TMC's intimidatory tactics meant that none of the opposition parties even put up candidates. 'Dar ke aage jeet hai' (There is victory beyond fear), says Vijayvargiya. 'They tried to scare us but it also strengthened the resolve of our workers and the ordinary people to teach Mamata a lesson.' Today, even senior TMC leaders admit that Mamata went 'too far' in managing the panchayat polls. 'It's not as if the BJP has not followed similar tactics in Tripura or the left hasn't resorted to bloodletting in the past in Bengal, but yes, we went overboard,' is the belated admission. Here was another example of Bengal's illiberal secularism in action, in which the left and TMC, both 'secular' regimes, exercised their writ through the politics of violence, instilling and perpetuating fear among citizens and stamping out their freedoms. When so-called secularism is expressed through force, the scene is set for a rival gang of toughs to barge in and practice their own form of strong-arm tactics.

In 2011, Mamata had ridden to power in West Bengal on an emotional pitch of 'Ma, Mati, Manush' – Mother, Motherland, People – targeting the left's land acquisition policies as anti-people. Her own people-centric, populist protest set her up as a mass agitationist, and her war cry of 'poriborton' (change) became a rallying point for all anti-left sentiment in the state. In 2018, seven years later, the trappings of power threatened to consume her government, allegations of corruption and extortion having chipped away at her original appeal of being a 'simple' leader committed to transforming the life of the common Bengali. The politics of 'poriborton' appeared to have reached exhaustion point, especially among Bengal's restless youth. The TMC's cadres on the ground had begun to be feared, just as CPI(M) workers once were.

In the panchayat polls, the BJP's vote share grew exponentially, from 1 per cent in 2013 to 18 per cent in 2018, the first sign that the party was now the main opposition force in West Bengal. As the 2019 elections approached, the BJP stepped on the accelerator, speedily expanding its footprint across the state. The state's forty-two seats were divided into four clusters, each assigned to a national leader six months before the elections. Party cadres from neighbouring Jharkhand were pushed into the tribal belt of Bengal. In western Bengal, RSS–VHP and the even more militant Bajrang Dal youth were used to spread the message of Hindu revivalism. In north Bengal, in areas bordering Bangladesh, the fear of rising 'Muslim infiltration' was used as a propaganda weapon to cement the Hindu vote. In urban pockets, Mamata's alleged minority appeasement became a talking point among middle-class voters. Roy, the original TMC organizer, began weaning away local TMC 'gang-leaders' by offering them inducements to switch. The booth committee network was strengthened amidst allegations that volunteers were being paid a hefty daily allowance to work for the BJP. 'In 2014, we had proper booth-level workers in 10 to 15 per cent of the seats; by 2019 we had covered 65 to 70 per cent of the state,' claims Vijayvargiya who was now almost a permanent resident of the state. When the EC announced a seven-phase poll for Bengal, ostensibly to ensure maximum presence of central forces in every constituency, another of Mamata's strengths was nullified: TMC supporters would not be able to bulldoze these paramilitary troops the way they might have the local police.

The TMC still believed it had one advantage: Mamata's regional connect which it was confident no state BJP leader could match. As she invoked Bengali subnationalism ('Jai Bangla, Jai Hind') to counter the 'Jai Shri Ram' slogan, the BJP realized that it had to make this a 'Modi versus Mamata' battle. The prime minister was a hugely popular figure in Bengal, his rallies attracting the kind of hysterical crowds usually seen only in the Hindi heartland and Gujarat. Modi's first-ever rally at Brigade Parade Ground – a historic and politically surcharged venue, site of the Bangladesh liberation rally in 1972, the place where the left once held its most gigantic, roaring public meetings – drew an immense, ecstatic crowd. For the first time the sprawling open-air ground was entirely covered with makeshift hangars to accommodate the lakhs of people who turned up despite the scorching heat. 'We would book a ground with a capacity of one lakh and twice that number would land up,' enthuses Vijayvargiya. Not surprisingly, Modi made the maximum trips to West Bengal outside of UP right through the key election period: seventeen rallies over the seven phases, each raising the stakes even higher. In what would literally become a quote-a-day battle, Modi launched a vicious attack on the Mamata government: 'From permission to admission, people have to shell out money … you will now find it tough to survive as chief minister.' He even appeared to hold out an open invite for horse-trading: 'Didi, on 23 May, the day of the results, the lotus will bloom everywhere and your MLAs will leave you and run. Even today, Didi, forty of your MLAs are in touch with me.' The jibes were highly personal: 'Speed-breaker Didi' is how he disparagingly referred to his rival, an attempt to blame her for not coordinating with the Centre when a cyclone hit Bengal in the middle of electioneering. Modi even turned a popular slogan that Mamata had once used against the left to target her this time: 'Chup chap phule chhap' (Stay silent and vote for the flower), he urged the crowds, exhorting them not to be afraid of the TMC's muscle power. The original TMC symbol is two flowers and grass, only this time the prime minister was seeking votes for the BJP's 'kamal' (lotus) flower!

The constant taunts were designed to get under Mamata's skin, to force her to react with her trademark impetuosity. 'When Modi comes to Bengal and calls us extortionists, I feel like giving him one tight slap of democracy,' she hit back in anger. Despite having been in politics for several decades, Mamata still often acts on impulse rather than careful calculation. She relishes a street fight even if it means abandoning the protocol of a government functionary. This is precisely what seems to have happened in May 2019 when, in the middle of a heated campaign, a group of BJP supporters in West Midnapore district chanted 'Jai Shri Ram' slogans while her convoy was passing by. Any other chief minister might have ignored the sloganeering, but Mamata is sui generis. She stopped the car, alighted in a rage and stomping over to them, demanded to know why the young men were abusing ('gaala-gaali') her. Within minutes, the video had gone viral, deliberately spread like wildfire by the BJP's WhatsApp army. Mamata was ambushed, accused once again of being anti-Hindu, of going off the deep end just because the slogan 'Jai Shri Ram' was raised. A damaging joke began to circulate: 'In other states the police arrest you if you commit a crime, in Bengal they arrest you if you chant "Jai Shri Ram".' Politically, it was terrible optics. 'Yes, we made a mistake, we fell into a BJP trap,' admits a TMC leader.

Just days after the incident, I tracked Mamata on the campaign trail. I had taken an early morning flight to Kolkata to catch a Mamata rally in the sweltering heat of Midnapore, and hopefully interview her, but I was subject to her typically whimsical behaviour. As a merciless midday sun beat down on the red dust of south Bengal, drenching us in sweat, the crew and I pleaded with her for time. But it seems the angry heat of the day and of election politics had got to her. She seemed ill at ease and frantic to get to her next venue and brushed us off. 'Not today, I won't talk to you today, meet me tomorrow on my padyatra,' she said dismissively. The next day, I drove another two hours, hoping that Didi would be in a better mood. Well, not quite. 'I will speak to you, but only for ten minutes, not more,' she stated. I was left with little choice but to fall into step with Mamata on her padyatra, mic in hand, my well-built cameraman being jostled around by the chief minister's security. Now, Mamata on a padyatra in her customary white sari and rubber chappals doesn't 'walk', but literally runs from one spot to another. The heat was excruciating as was the pace being set by our champion political walker. As the sun climbed higher, she seemed to walk even faster, indefatigable in the inferno-like conditions. Between breaths, I managed to sneak in my questions. But the moment I raised the contentious 'Jai Shri Ram' issue, Mamata flared up again: 'Please don't ask me about all that ... all you national media is sold to Modi–Shah ... sab bik gaya hai ...' I was flabbergasted: here I was, virtually collapsing in the oppressive, maddening heat of a May afternoon in Bengal after pleading with her for an interview, only to be told that I was an agent of the BJP's power couple! I sensed that day just how the pressure of a high-voltage political battle can get to even seasoned netas. A foul-tempered Mamata was clearly in trouble.

The concluding act of the Bengal drama would play out in the heart of Kolkata. In a final push ahead of the seventh and last phase of polling, the BJP decided to take out a roadshow led by Amit Shah in north Kolkata, one of the most crowded areas in the city. In a show of strength, the BJP had roped in cadres not just from Bengal but from neighbouring states as well. The procession was making its way near Calcutta University when 'black flags' were waved at Shah by TMC youth members. The BJP claims that the procession was pelted with stones, allegedly from the direction of the hostel of the nearby Vidyasagar College. In the violence that broke out right after, bikes were set on fire and a mob vandalized the college hostel and smashed the 200-year-old statue of the iconic nineteenth-century educationist and social reformer Ishwar Chandra Vidyasagar, one of Bengal's most revered figures. *India Today*'s Manogya Loiwal witnessed the bedlam first-hand. 'The fact is, there weren't enough police personnel along the entire stretch of the roadshow, just around fifty policemen along the entire route who were clearly ill-equipped to control the situation,' she notes.

In the blame game that followed, Mamata shrewdly played the nativist card, painting the BJP as a party of 'outsiders' unaware of Bengali culture and ethos. In the fog of allegations made by both sides, no one is quite certain who damaged the statue of Vidyasagar. But images of the broken statue at Amit Shah's roadshow began to make the rounds, sending shock waves through the city's educated electorate, and in the final round TMC swept the nine seats in and around Kolkata.

Despite the BJP's unwitting 'self-goal' in the roadshow, it became increasingly apparent that the party was now a force to reckon with in West Bengal. The TMC, though, was still in denial over the shifting mood. When the India Today Axis My India exit poll reported that the BJP could get 19 to 23 seats in Bengal, a furious Derek O'Brien rang me up late at night and scoffed at the poll findings. 'You have got it badly wrong, my friend, for every seat more than ten that the BJP gets in Bengal, I will buy you dinner!' he said dismissively. Four days later, when the final results were out, the BJP had won eighteen seats in West Bengal, the TMC twenty-two. A humbled O'Brien conceded that he had misread the voting patterns. He pointed out, however, that while the BJP vote share went up by an incredible 23 per cent (from 17 to 40 per cent), the TMC vote also rose from 40 to 44 per cent. 'We lost out only because the left vote crashed from 31 per cent to 7 per cent and swung almost entirely to the BJP.' O'Brien isn't wrong in pure psephological terms: Bengal did become a bipolar contest and the BJP was a major gainer from the collapse of the left vote. As the pithy phrase went: Bengal had gone from Vam (left) to Ram. But the number game can't take away from the scale of the BJP's achievement in what was once a distant outpost. The perceptive Sarma was right after all: in 2019, the lotus was blooming across eastern India.

Incidentally, O'Brien still hasn't bought me the dinners he promised. He has offered an excuse though. 'In Bengal, we had the bigger heart but they had the thicker wallet. In truth, the BJP simply outspent us with an unimaginable budget the likes of which the state has never seen,' he maintains, even colourfully tweeting that the BJP's supply of money came to Bengal as if through a streaming endless firehose.

Ah! Money: the inescapable reality of Indian politics.

Is the BJP the most formidable election machine in the history of Indian elections? It's a question worth reflecting upon while analysing the scale of the mobilization effort which marks the party's 2019 election campaign. For five years, from 2014 onwards, the BJP systematically built up its organization structure by launching ambitious membership drives and then ensuring sustained year-round communication with lakhs of booth workers across the country. This level of continual engagement between a party leadership and a grassroots structure is unprecedented in Indian politics and is the engine that drives the BJP juggernaut.

From panna pramukhs in every booth who were tasked with contacting sixty to seventy voters on an average on a single electoral roll page to the top leadership, the BJP remained in constant 'mission' mode. In May 2018, nearly a year ahead of the general elections, the party initiated a 'Sampark for Samarthan' (Contact for Support) drive wherein every BJP member was expected to contact at least ten people to propagate the achievements of the Modi government on its fourth anniversary. I was taken slightly aback when one morning I got a call from the BJP's media incharge, Anil Baluni, saying that he wanted to come and see me at my residence. Not being on the BJP's list of most favoured journalists, I wondered what the sudden visit was all about. Sure enough, Baluni – an ever-smiling, sweet-talking former journalist-turned-Rajya Sabha MP from Uttarakhand – was at my doorstep at the appointed time with a glossy pamphlet detailing the PM's achievements. 'We want to establish contact with as many people as possible, irrespective of whether they support the BJP or not,' he pointed out. We chatted a bit over chai and then, as he was preparing to leave, Baluni insisted on taking a picture with me. 'You see, I need to have photo evidence that I have met at least ten mediapersons!' he laughed. I was, I'm quite sure, pretty low on the BJP's 'must contact' list. Party president Shah was busy getting clicked with a range of celebrities from Madhuri Dixit to Kapil Dev. Prime

Minister Modi too found his own unique way of establishing 'sampark' with the voters. He would interact with beneficiaries of the Pradhan Mantri Ujwala Yojana and the Mudra Yojana via video-conference. He even initiated a survey on the popular NaMo app – by February 2019 it had more than one crore downloads on the Google Play Store alone – by asking people to rate the performance of his government and that of individual MPs and MLAs. 'It is your vote that counts!' tweeted Modi, while inviting people to participate in the survey. Just ahead of the elections, the prime minister interacted over videoconference with more than one crore party workers and volunteers under the 'Mera booth sabse mazboot' initiative, again via the NaMo app. 'We were using technology to directly connect with workers and galvanize them into action. What could be better!' affirms a Team Modi member.

The 'sampark' (communication) wouldn't end just with the leaders. About six months before the elections, in October 2018, the BJP set up 161 round-the-clock call centres (or sampark kendras) across the country (on an average one for every three Lok Sabha seats) where the staff were given a pointed brief: establish direct communication with each and every one of the over 8.6 lakh BJP booth committees and ensure regular feedback. Their task didn't end there: the call centres were provided a detailed list of all the 22 crore 'beneficiaries' of government programmes and asked to contact them via SMS, WhatsApp, email and even make personal visits to remind them of how the Modi government was transforming their lives.

The call centres were supervised by state-level BJP leaders with a nodal centre established at the BJP's 11 Ashoka Road office in Delhi. Up to 100 people, working round the clock in two shifts, were deployed in every call centre. 'It was a massive operation; we had more than 15,000 tele-callers manning these centres across the country,' reveals a BJP leader. Many of these tele-callers were 'paid' employees on a short-term contract, earning between ₹8,000 and ₹15,000 per month.

The sheer scale of this unique tech-driven operation meant that at least part of the task was outsourced. A Mumbai-based private company called Jarvis Technology and Strategic Consulting, which had worked closely with Chief Minister Devendra Fadnavis in Maharashtra, was contracted to aid the BJP in this specific assignment. On its website, Jarvis claims to 'leverage cutting-edge technology and advance data sciences to create scalable solutions to complex problems for government agencies and political parties'. One of those 'scalable' solutions it devised for the BJP in 2019 was to set up and connect with government programme 'beneficiaries' through WhatsApp groups and call centres. Jarvis, whose management did not respond to repeated attempts to contact them, is reportedly funded by builder-turned-Mumbai BJP chief Mangal Prabhat Lodha. He, however, denies having financed the venture. What is undeniable, however, is the huge potential impact such direct, hyper-personalized telemarketing must have had. 'With one phone call or SMS or WhatsApp message to a beneficiary of a gas connection or a toilet or bank loan, we were creating a personal bond between the voter and the prime minister,' is how a BJP core group member puts it.

The outreach was innovative but was it entirely above board? A private agency contracted by the party was being provided access to the personal data of beneficiaries of Modi government schemes. Whether through Aadhaar cards or by accessing details available with concerned ministries, a political party was now able to effectively track down citizens through big data mapping and use their personal information available with state agencies to enhance the efficacy of its election campaign. The lines between government and party were being completely blurred as a result; a classic case of 'sarkar' and 'sangathan' working in unison. The potential for misusing Aadhaar data is what right-to-privacy activists have been complaining about for a long time while expressing the fear that such data could be exploited for commercial or political gains. In August 2017, in a landmark judgement, the Supreme Court ruled that there is a fundamental right to privacy under the Indian Constitution. 'Technically, if my personal data is being used by a political party for its election agenda without my consent it would constitute a violation of the right to privacy. But this is precisely why you need a data protection legislation to make these rights real,' argues Arghya Sengupta, legal scholar. There are shades here of the Cambridge Analytica exposé and the scandal that erupted in 2018 when a media house showed that the political consultancy organization had been using citizens' personal data from Facebook to design political campaigns.

The BJP leadership, though, didn't seem too concerned over such legal niceties: there was a major election to be won. In the first week of February 2019, the BJP took its mass outreach programme to another level with the launch of 'Bharat ke Mann ki Baat', a multimedia platform which the party claimed would ensure citizens' participation in framing the election manifesto. The five-star Ashoka Hotel was the venue for another big-bang announcement with slickly produced videos of Prime Minister Modi being looped on a large screen. Three hundred raths (chariot-like vans) would travel 100 kilometres per day, or 9 lakh kilometres in a month, with the ostensible aim of collecting public feedback. The BJP's own in-house election consultancy ABM was handling the event management and amplifying the message over social media platforms like Facebook. 'Our aim was simple: keep the buzz going around the prime minister at all times,' a party organizer tells me.

There was one question which continued to gnaw at me: how was the BJP able to run, and sustain, a series of nationwide mobilization campaigns at such a high pitch over an extended period? More specifically, where were the resources to organize a constant stream of glitzy events, poll surveys, mass contact programmes coming from? On record, the BJP insists that the party was running a 'value for money' campaign without any excess or extravagant spending. 'We even encouraged micro-donations from our supporters of sums as low as ₹5 through the NaMo app just to create a sense of greater public participation and ownership in the campaign,' a BJP leader remarks.

The truth is that in 2019 the BJP was not just the largest, but also easily the most cash-rich party in the history of Indian elections, with a cash flow which fuelled its unmatched propaganda machine. A June 2019 Centre for Media Studies report claims that the BJP spent a record

₹27,000 crore on the elections, which was around 45 per cent of the ₹60,000 crore (approximately) total expenditure incurred. It is impossible to verify these figures but the fact that many scaled-up election management tasks like the nationwide call centre operations were at least partly outsourced to professionals reveals the rapid transition of the BJP from a purely volunteer-driven force to a more businesslike political enterprise. Here is another telling fact: more than 3000 BJP vistaraks were out in the field for two years, staying at the houses of karyakartas (workers) to coordinate with booth committees at different levels. During this two-year period, apart from their daily expenses, the vistaraks' mobile and petrol bills were also covered by the party. In some instances, the local party unit provided them with bikes and mobile phones/tablets. A freely flowing 'kosh' (treasure chest) and motivated karyakartas (workers) can be a deadly combination. In 2019 the BJP had what no other political party in India has ever managed: a business model for electioneering.

The contrast, especially with the Congress, could not have been more stark with the party asking many of its candidates to fend for themselves. Ranajit Mukherjee, a young, first-time Bengal Congress candidate from Durgapur, for example, claims to have received just ₹25 lakh from the party funds, and being compelled to raise a few more lakhs from 'donations' from family and friends. 'I think my BJP rival S.S. Ahluwalia must have exhausted the amount I spent on an entire campaign on just one roadshow,' he laughs. Kirti Azad, the cricketer turned politician, who switched from the BJP to the Congress just ahead of the 2019 elections, claims that there is no comparison between the two major national parties in terms of resource mobilization. 'I got just ₹50 lakh from the Congress to fight the 2019 elections whereas the BJP election budget in 2014 itself ran into a few crore per candidate,' he reveals. Rohan Gupta, who was involved in the Congress's media campaign, claims that the BJP had an average of 300–400 outdoor hoardings per Lok Sabha constituency, where the Congress had merely 30 to 40. 'Both in volume and total ad spend, they outspent us ten to one, maybe more,' he says. Sam Balsara, chairman of Madison Advertising, which handled the BJP's media outlay, insists that the party spent less in 2019 than it did in 2014 on print and TV advertising. 'Our campaign was less intense this time but perhaps wider and deeper. We did focus a lot on regional channels but the frequency was less than five years ago; much more controlled expenditure,' he asserts.

The final numbers might be disputed but what is undeniable is the fact that the BJP, as the party in power, not only had access to the levers of state authority but was clearly well funded; no BJP candidate has complained of a cash shortage even while the fund utilization is tightly controlled and supervised by the party's central leadership (no BJP candidate was willing to come on record to divulge exact amounts spent but the average figure for a ruling party candidate runs into several crore). In contrast, almost every Congress candidate I spoke to said they were struggling for funds (the maximum the party reportedly gave its 'A' category candidates in exceptional cases was ₹2 crore). 'We were in power for so many years but can you imagine my party now tells me that we are bankrupt!' one of them told me rather nonchalantly. 'Wealthy individuals in a "poor" party' is a popular Congress refrain: it almost seems as if a run-down second-hand Maruti was being forced to take on a sleek Mercedes! Or, as Arundhati Roy puts it, the battle between the BJP and the Congress was a race between a Ferrari and a bicycle.

The hard numbers gathered by the election watchdog Association of Democratic Rights (ADR) only confirm the widening disparities. While the BJP received as much as ₹400 crore or 92 per cent of the total corporate donations made to all political parties in financial year 2017–18, the Congress got just ₹19 crore: in other words, the BJP tapped twenty-one times more corporate donations than its closest rival. In terms of the total donations received in the same period, based on their tax returns, the Congress raised about ₹199 crore while the BJP raised as much as ₹1,027 crore. The by no means transparent system of electoral bonds introduced by the Modi government in 2017, by which corporates and anonymous individual donors can purchase banking instruments for funding eligible parties without any obligation of public disclosure, reveals a further windfall for the BJP: of the ₹215 crore received through this route in 2017–18, the ruling party got ₹210 crore and the opposition just ₹5 crore. An RTI response shows that the State Bank of India sold bonds worth ₹1,056.73 crore in 2018 but sold bonds worth as much as ₹1,716.05 crore in just the first three months of 2019 – a quantum jump right before the general elections, with the BJP again the biggest beneficiary by some distance (and remember, none of these figures account for the large clandestine cash payments made to parties during elections). 'There is no level playing field in Indian elections, be it between an individual citizen and the political system or between the political parties themselves,' laments Professor Tarlochan Sastry, founder chairperson of ADR. One of India's most visionary leaders and founder of the Swatantra Party, C. Rajagopalachari often remarked that rampant money power, if not checked, had the potential to destroy the fragile Indian democracy.

Rajaji has proven prescient: money is now an increasingly critical, near-decisive factor in Indian elections. Ahead of the 2019 elections, an ADR report showed that of the 521 MPs analysed, 430 or 83 per cent were crorepatis and the average assets per sitting MP in the 2014 elections amounted to ₹14.72 crore. Cross-checking with several MPs across party lines, the amounts cited to fight a Lok Sabha election today are staggering, ranging from ₹5 crore to ₹50 crore, with southern states like Andhra, Tamil Nadu and Karnataka being labelled as the 'most expensive' states for electioneering. The 'official' EC ceiling for these states is ₹70 lakh which seems like a cruel joke. As former CEC, Dr S.Y. Quraishi admits, 'We have singularly failed to check the flow of money at election time.'

That candid admission is a pointer to the fact that elections in contemporary India are now, as one senior politician describes it, a 'cash and carry game', one which the well-oiled BJP machine was singularly better positioned nationally to take advantage of. But what made it easier for the BJP to stay well ahead in the race was the chaotic nature of the campaign being run by its main opponents, especially the Congress.

In mid-May just ahead of the final phase of polling, the Congress core committee met at the party's 'war room' at 15 Gurdwara Rakabganj Road in Delhi. The white-painted Lutyens-style bungalow with its gates usually firmly shut to prying media eyes is the hub for Congress's brainstorming sessions. Once again some of the party's seniormost leaders gathered, almost all of them former Union ministers and multiple-time MPs. Between them they had almost 300 years of cumulative political experience in the war room. The near-unanimous verdict emerging from their meeting was that the Congress was in a 'good position' to play a crucial role in the next government formation. 'The BJP is not crossing 180 to 200 and we should be around 115 to 125, maybe even a little more,' was the conclusion. 'This is like 1999 all over again but Vajpayee could form a government then because he had strong allies with him, this time the regional parties won't go with Modi, but with us,' was another optimistic assessment.

How did the Congress party, the most seasoned political outfit in the country, get the 2019 election so terribly wrong? Several core committee members pin the blame on Praveen Chakravarty, the party's data analytics team head. A former investment banker and managing director at Banque National de Paris, the Wharton-educated Chakravarty was drafted into the Congress in February 2018 by Rahul Gandhi. Rahul was reportedly impressed with Chakravarty's strong economics and research background and wanted him to give the Congress a more solid foundation in big data management. 'I want our party to start using data to make informed political choices,' was reportedly the brief given by Rahul to Chakravarty, who had also worked on the Aadhaar project kick-started by Nandan Nilekani. Inducting lateral entrants such as Chakravarty from the corporate world was part of what Rahul, who had just taken over as party president, saw as an attempt to 'transform and professionalize' the Congress. One of Chakravarty's first projects was to devise a data platform that would be called Shakti, a verified database with a web–mobile application which would allow Congress workers and volunteers to connect easily with the party leadership. By the onset of the 2019 elections, Shakti had reportedly created a database of over 60 lakh Congress members. Rahul was extremely impressed. 'If the BJP can embrace big data, why can't we,' was his mantra. A buzzing room at the AICC headquarters in its Akbar Road office became the nerve centre for the Congress's data analytics team, an upgrade from the poky computer cell which the party would earlier function from.

And yet, unsurprisingly, there was resistance from within the grand old party, marked by an element of envy too stemming from the direct access Chakravarty had to the party leadership. 'The problem with Rahul is that he gets carried away too easily by smooth talkers, especially those with foreign degrees. This project Shakti is all very well but can it really be a substitute for having a strong cadre base on the ground and will an app decide who should be our candidates?' asks a veteran Congress leader. 'Praveen is throwing numbers at us all the time, but is anyone verifying whether those numbers are accurate?' asks another senior leader. The battle between the 'old guard' and the 'new blood' in the Congress was still being fought, hardly the ideal situation when fighting the rock-solid BJP election machine, attuned to a direct chain of command.

Was the soft-spoken, academically inclined Chakravarty made a fall guy when it became clear that the Congress was not doing as well as predicted? Or had he indeed made an unforgivable blunder when he'd dismissed the post-Balakot Modi wave that was slowly but surely sweeping the country? In party meetings, Chakravarty, who had famously called the 2014 verdict a unique 'black swan' moment – a rare event unlikely to be replicated – would reportedly keep insisting that there was no visible wave and 2019 was a case of 'highly localized' 543 constituency-wise battles: 'We are fighting twenty-nine different state elections,' was his considered analysis. He was also working closely with Priyanka Gandhi Vadra on the Congress's UP game plan with candidates chosen with the sole purpose of dividing the BJP's upper-caste vote. As Priyanka would later tell me in an interview, 'I have personally looked into the selection of candidates for UP. We have chosen them very carefully so that they cut into the BJP votes and benefit the BSP–SP alliance wherever the gathbandhan is strong.' The strategy failed: in eight seats in UP, the winning margins of the BJP were less than the votes polled by the Congress candidates. The party won just the lone seat of Sonia Gandhi in Rae Bareli and lost its deposit in sixty-three of the sixty-seven seats it contested in UP with a paltry 6 per cent vote share.

Nevertheless, to blame an individual for a collective failure seems grossly unfair. The truth is, the Congress was increasingly functioning like an echo chamber where leaders told each other only what their high command wished to hear. A few sample messages exchanged between senior party leaders reveal a make-believe world in which the Congress was living: 'Don't worry, at least six to eight seats in Gujarat are assured', 'In Jharkhand we will get ten seats guaranteed', 'Party is doing very well in Vidarbha and rural Maharashtra', 'Madhya Pradesh–Chhattisgarh is looking really good' was some of the feedback being shared. With sycophancy having been proved a virtue for political careerists, echo chambers are known to exist in almost every party in the country. And yet, in a badly factionalized party like the Congress, with a weakening central leadership, the 'echo effect' resulted in the party being cut off from ground realities.

In Rajasthan, for example, where the Congress formed a government in December 2018 after squeaking home in the assembly elections, the victory did not end the embarrassing public feuding for the top post between Ashok Gehlot and Sachin Pilot, two leaders representing a generational clash within the party. As Rahul prevaricated over taking a decision, he commissioned a poll through the Shakti app to find out whom the party workers would prefer as their chief minister. Gehlot won out, but only after a group of senior Congress leaders met Rahul and warned him: 'If you don't make Ashokji the chief minister, we won't win many seats in Rajasthan in the Lok Sabha!' Virtually bullied into making Gehlot the chief minister, Rahul requested a peeved Pilot to bide his time and accept the role of deputy chief minister. Pilot was initially reluctant but agreed only after he was promised that the situation would be reviewed after the Lok Sabha polls. 'We have a crazy situation in Rajasthan where our top two leaders openly bad-mouth each other. How can a party function like this?' a long-serving Rajasthan Congress leader tells me. The vertical divide was one contributory factor in ensuring the BJP swept all twenty-five seats in the state. Gehlot spent a week parked in his home constituency of Jodhpur but even that was not enough to save his son, Vaibhav, from defeat. 'I think Ashokji spent more time campaigning in Jodhpur then he did in the rest of Rajasthan!' moans another Congress leader. 'Son-stroke' is another common failing across Indian political parties but almost endemic in the Congress. Leaders become obsessively focused on furthering the family business in politics often at the cost of the party; when an empire begins to crumble, it's every man – or every local chieftain – for himself.

Rajasthan wasn't an exception; in almost every state, the Congress was in disorder ahead of the elections. Mumbai, a megapolis which has become the bellwether for voting patterns in recent general elections, witnessed a bizarre two-year-long tussle for control of the city unit between Mumbai Congress president Sanjay Nirupam and former minister Milind Deora. If Gehlot and Pilot were caught in a generational conflict, Deora and Nirupam were hostage to a socio-cultural war. The urbane Deora is the son of the city's long-standing Congress boss Murli Deora, and represented the South Mumbai business elite which had once controlled the city's politics. As an English-speaking, rock guitar-strumming, America-educated dynast, he formed an instant rapport with Rahul, who saw Deora as one of his closest friends in the Congress, amongst the few he could easily bond with. Nirupam, though, had adopted an entirely different route to the top: hailing from Bihar, this one-time Shiv Sena MP and editor of the Sena's Hindi newspaper, the firebrand leader embodied the ascent of the north Indian migrant – lacking sophistication in language but always spoiling for a good fight – in Mumbai society. Despite growing demands to replace him as the city chief for openly playing north Indian identity politics in a cosmopolitan milieu, Nirupam hung on to his post till suddenly, just a fortnight before the polls, Deora was appointed in his place to avoid further dissonance. 'If you want to replace someone, do it two years before the elections, not two weeks before it's for god, sake!' argues a Mumbai Congress leader. The last-minute change in guard in Mumbai was a mirror to a muddled mindset. As it is one of the party's articulate young spokespersons, Priyanka Chaturvedi, had quit and joined the Shiv Sena, reportedly disgruntled over being denied a ticket. Actor Urmila Matondkar had been drafted by Nirupam to contest from Mumbai North and lend some much-needed glamour to the Congress campaign but she failed to score despite a camera-friendly campaign. A confused Congress was unable to put up even the semblance of a fight in the maximum city and the BJP–Sena alliance won all six Mumbai seats by an impressive margin.

Nevertheless, the high-level of disarray in Mumbai pales in comparison to the mess in the Congress's strategy for Delhi, another bellwether city and as the national capital, politically significant. For months before the 2019 elections, there was talk of a possible alliance between the Congress and AAP in Delhi, possibly even extending to Punjab, Haryana, Chandigarh and Goa, a total of thirty-three seats. Arvind Kejriwal, AAP chief and Delhi chief minister, was desperate for a tie-up which he felt would both raise his national profile once again and give a genuine fight to the BJP. NCP leader Sharad Pawar even hosted a tea for all the opposition leaders in February, where an AAP–Congress alliance was discussed. Pawar, who had a strong rapport with Rahul, asked the Congress leader to initiate the alliance talks with their 'common goal' of defeating the BJP. 'I am sorry but my local party unit doesn't want any alliance; we think we can win at least three seats on our own,' was Rahul's blunt response. Kejriwal retorted: 'If you win even one seat in Delhi, I will give up politics!' It was left to Pawar and Chandrababu Naidu to try and cool down fraying tempers and persuade Rahul to give the alliance a chance.

After prolonged back and forth, another attempt was made. Back-room negotiations to work out a deal were initiated once again with the concurrence of Rahul: Ahmed Patel and Ghulam Nabi Azad were acting on his behalf while AAP MP Sanjay Singh represented Kejriwal. But the Congress was unwilling to accept a wider alliance beyond Delhi. A despairing AAP leadership then proposed a 5–2 seat-sharing formula for the seven seats in the national capital but the Congress insisted on a 4–3 arrangement (AAP would get one extra seat). 'Everything was almost final, we even planned to make a big joint announcement and then, suddenly, we were told the deal was off. I don't think the Congress was ever serious about the alliance,' says a miffed Singh. Apparently, the late Sheila Dikshit, three-time chief minister of Delhi, who had just taken over as Delhi Congress chief, put her foot down and told Rahul that she would quit her post if the party tied up with Kejriwal who had once accused her of corruption.

What followed was even more inexplicable and only reveals the mutual mistrust and complete disorder in the opposition ranks. Instead of quietly attempting to resolve the impasse, Rahul and Kejriwal engaged in an acrimonious Twitter 'war', each side blaming the other for the breakdown. Two leaders, who hours before were negotiating an alliance, were now warring publicly with each other on social media like adolescents: the contrast with the flexibility shown by the BJP in its poll tie-ups could not have been more stark. Like in Mumbai, the BJP took all of Delhi's seven seats. The collapse of the Congress–AAP alliance in Delhi might not have made a difference to the eventual result since the BJP won more than 50 per cent of the votes in all seven seats, but it is a pointer to the scrambled state of mind of Team Rahul. The leadership was clearly divided between strengthening the Congress's base and ceding space to potential allies. Perhaps, still unable to reconcile itself to losing its pre-eminent national status, the Congress was reluctant to truly embrace the concept of a 'mahagathbandhan' or grand alliance. Maybe, after its December state election triumphs, the Congress thought that it could dictate terms to the regional parties. It would prove to be another costly error of judgement. The Congress's inability to move quickly and nimbly, to recognize the cut-throat realities of BJP-dominated politics and mount a no-holds-barred challenge was glaringly evident.

The losses due to the Congress's inflexibility and superiority complex were not limited merely to AAP. Vanchit Bahujan Aghadi leader Prakash Ambedkar, banking on a rising Dalit–Bahujan assertion in Maharashtra, pushed for an alliance with the Congress. He was asking for twelve seats, perhaps only as a bargaining ploy. The Congress leadership refused to even meet him. 'We were convinced that he was being propped up by Amit Shah only to divide and confuse the anti-BJP vote,' a Team Rahul member contends. It's a charge which Ambedkar rejects. 'Do you think the grandson of Babasaheb Ambedkar can't rustle up the money for one chopper? I am not a ghulam of the Congress,' he argues. Spurned by the Congress, an embittered Ambedkar went ahead and tied up with Asaduddin Owaisi's All India Majlis-e-Ittehadul Muslimeen in an attempt to carve out a Dalit–Bahujan–Muslim alliance in Maharashtra. When I asked Owaisi if this alliance was the result of Shah's prodding, he was enraged: 'Yes, we struck a deal in your house, Rajdeepbhai, don't you remember!' Whether as a BJP-backed 'Third Front' or unintentionally, the Ambedkar–Owaisi alliance damaged the Congress–NCP in as many as ten seats in Maharashtra. In the state where Congress chiefs like Y.B. Chavan, Vasantdada Patil and Sharad Pawar had once exercised unbroken dominance for decades, the party won just one out of forty-eight seats, and even that was a Shiv Sena defector who was given a ticket just before nominations closed.

To blame Rahul alone for the party's failure to stitch alliances would be unfair: the pulls and pressures in a large organization like the Congress make alliance-building notoriously difficult. Even in Karnataka where the Congress had a tie-up with Deve Gowda's Janata Dal (Secular) (JD[S]), the party cadres on the ground refused to honour an alliance which was crafted in Delhi in a desperate bid to keep the BJP at bay. 'Pure arithmetic calculation with zero chemistry never works. In almost every constituency, JD(S) workers tried to defeat us and vice versa,' admits a senior Karnataka Congress leader. The Congress and JD(S) have traditionally fought each other, especially in the southern Karnataka region: former Congress chief minister Siddaramaiah and the Deve

Gowda family are staunch adversaries. When Siddaramaiah pushed for an early decision on seat-sharing, Deve Gowda reportedly shot back, 'I will discuss these matters only with Rahul Gandhi and not with "local" leaders.' The final seat allocation was worked out just a week before nomination day. Once more, in the midst of a Modi wave, the Congress managed to win just one of the twenty-eight seats in Karnataka, another state where the party had once dominated in its pomp.

But Rahul can't escape responsibility for some of the choices he did make which reveal a measure of political naivete and reluctance to step out from his comfort zone. For instance, he replaced Gehlot in the crucial post of general secretary (organization) with K.C. Venugopal, a Congress MP from Kerala who just didn't have any connect with the party units outside southern India. 'Gehlot going back to Rajasthan just months before a major general election was a big loss to us in Delhi. Venugopal could never replace someone of Ashokji's experience in such a short time,' admits a Team Rahul member.

There were more signs of an inexperienced Congress leadership taking ad hoc decisions in the poll build-up. Congress spokesperson Randeep Singh Surjewala was coerced at the very last moment into contesting a Haryana assembly by-election from Jind even though he was already a sitting MLA. 'My rivals in the party want to finish me but how do I turn down Rahulji's request,' a peeved Surjewala told an aide. He would eventually finish a poor third in the race. Former Delhi chief minister Sheila Dikshit had been unwell for some time and was reluctant to contest a Lok Sabha poll. Rahul reportedly sent her a private message, reminding her of their strong family ties. 'You must do this for me,' he implored. An unenthusiastic and ailing Dikshit was forced into the battle. In Punjab, Rahul initially vetoed former Union minister Manish Tewari's candidature, claiming that Tewari had failed the party by opting out of contesting the 2014 elections. It required doughty Punjab Chief Minister Captain Amarinder Singh to step in and insist on Tewari being given a ticket in one of the few states where the Congress holds its own. In UP, Rahul confidant Jitin Prasada threatened to withdraw from the election fray, claiming that he had not been consulted on candidate selection in his neighbouring constituencies. There were even reports that he might switch over to the BJP. It required a last-minute personal appeal by Rahul while they drove together to the airport to stave off a high-profile exit. It almost seemed as if the Congress was lurching from one crisis to another, its general unable to galvanize either the troops or the local commanders in the battlefield.

In another strange selection, the Chicago-based Sam Pitroda, Rahul's mentor of sorts and an intimate friend of the Gandhi family, was tasked with being a key point person for coordinating the Congress's publicity campaign. By enlisting Pitroda into his election team, Rahul was only creating another power centre within a party machine that already operated in silos. 'We all like and respect Sam, but do you really expect someone who spends most of the year in America to suddenly come to India and take on the Modi–Shah duo? It just doesn't happen like that,' says a senior Congress leader. Staying in a Lutyens' Delhi bungalow allotted to TMC MP Dinesh Trivedi, Pitroda would take long meetings to review and ideate on the Congress's strategy. 'I was only trying to help because I felt that democracy was being hijacked, lies were being spread, the idea of India was under assault. I was doing all this to help the Congress work as a team, not to seek power for myself,' Pitroda responds angrily.

As Pitroda would soon find out, an Indian election is no picnic for well-meaning technocrats. Seemingly unaware of just what a minefield politics is in times of bristling hyper-nationalism and hungry social media cells ready to pounce, he made a public gaffe. In an interview to ANI, he asked for proof of the death toll in the Balakot strike. 'If they [the IAF] killed 300, that is okay. All I am saying is can you give me more facts to prove it,' he said. In a thirty-minute interview, Pitroda spoke on a variety of issues, even clarifying that his Balakot comments were his personal views and not those of the Congress party. It was too late: the single sound bite was enough to spark a political storm. The prime minister was among the first to hit back with a tweet: 'Loyal courtier of Congress's royal dynasty admits what the nation already knew – Congress was unwilling to respond to forces of terror.' A series of prime-time debates followed, some even questioning Pitroda's patriotism. A livid Pitroda rang me up to complain: 'I have given the best years of my life to India without charging a bloody dime and this is what you media guys do to me!' I empathized with him but maybe I should have warned him to be more careful in the future. I felt it was time 'experts' from the easy-going 1980s, however distinguished, became much more aware of how the media, social media and a super-competitive political environment demanded entirely new rules of engagement.

Just weeks later, Pitroda found himself in a spot again: this time, he had responded to a TV reporter's query on the role of Rajiv Gandhi's government in the 1984 anti-Sikh riots, by putting up a counter-question: 'What is with 1984? Why don't we speak about what happened in the last five years? It happened in 1984, so what, hua to hua!' (If it happened, it happened.) The last three words sounded terribly insensitive, and when further twisted and made viral by the BJP's propaganda machine, became ideal political fodder for his critics. With the Delhi and Punjab elections just days away, Rahul Gandhi was forced to step in and do damage control. 'Sam Pitroda is wrong, he should be ashamed and must apologize to the nation,' he declared. It was perhaps the final blow to the ardent family loyalist, trapped in a manic news whirl he was clearly not cut out for. Rahul's public rebuke was misjudged too, sounding like an imperious rebuff to a genuine supporter. Just before he left the country days before the results were to be announced, I met Pitroda. 'What can I say, your one-sided media just lies all the time!' he cribbed. And then graciously offered me a glass of red wine. Somehow, Pitroda's 2019 misfortunes were more evidence of the divide between an anglicized, Nehruvian elite and the 'new', saffronized India.

Nothing quite exemplifies the Congress's flailing about for a cohesive strategy to combat the BJP than the confusion over its core campaign plank of Nyay, Nyuntam Aay Yojana (Minimum Income Guarantee Scheme, or MIG). It was in late January 2019, at a victory rally in

Chhattisgarh that Rahul first promised a nationwide minimum income scheme for the poor if the Congress was elected to power at the Centre. Riding on the wave of his assembly poll wins, Rahul was hoping to firmly shift the narrative away from the BJP's 'mazboot neta' (strong leader) catchphrase to a more inclusive, pro-poor agenda. He seemed convinced that Modi's Achilles heel remained his 'suit-boot ki sarkar' image, one that a well-planned MIG scheme might once again highlight. No substantial details of the scheme were announced at the rally. When I pestered former finance minister P. Chidambaram for a response, he advised patience. 'We are working on it, why are you in such a hurry?' was the answer. Over the next month, Chidambaram, as the head of the Congress manifesto committee, along with Praveen Chakravarty of the data team, would get inputs from several renowned economists from India and the world on what an ideal MIG should look like. 'From Raghuram Rajan to Abhijit Banerjee to Thomas Piketty, we consulted several experts on the issue. We even got Dr Manmohan Singh on board to endorse the idea,' says a member of Team Rahul.

And yet, for weeks after the original announcement, there was little forward movement on how to amplify the MIG concept. When, in February 2019, Pulwama and then Balakot happened, the storyline changed dramatically. National security and the BJP's 'muscular nationalism' became the party's calling card and the Congress was thrown into bewilderment and uncertainty on how to combat the new ultra-nationalism. When advertising agencies were called in to pitch for the Congress's campaign, they were perplexed with the indecision within the party on the way forward. Team Rahul reportedly still wanted the 'Chowkidar chor hai' slogan even though it was clearly losing momentum. Other campaign themes were 'Congress hai na', a positive campaign intended to highlight the previous UPA government's achievements, and 'Vote nahi maafi maango', a negative campaign aimed at exposing the Modi government's alleged failures. 'Every Congress leader at our meetings seemed to have a different idea on what should be the campaign focus; there was simply no clarity,' laments a leading advertising company head. 'We had planned multiple campaigns on themes ranging from jobs to agriculture and then Balakot happens and suddenly every poll plank gets lost in the noise of national security,' counters a Congress publicity committee member.

The confusion only exemplifies how the Congress finds itself particularly helpless in the face of the BJP's 'muscular nationalism' thrust. Where Indira Gandhi once stood forth as the embodiment of national pride, heroine of the 1971 war, the Congress's drift to the left, towards university campus radicals and civil society NGOs has led to an abandonment of a no-nonsense patriotism exemplified by leaders like Punjab Chief Minister Captain Amarinder Singh or even former prime minister Manmohan Singh; a centrist nationalism based on merging Indian national interests with democratic values as a counter to the BJP version has not been given as much emphasis in Congress vision statements as much as pro-poor initiatives and welfarism.

Rahul finally unveiled his MIG scheme only on 25 March, promising ₹72,000 per annum to the poorest 20 per cent of India's population: it was nearly two months after his original promise, and less than twenty days before the first round of polling was to begin. By then, the BJP had already distributed cheques for the first tranche of its ₹6,000 per annum Kisan Samman Nidhi Yojana for small and marginal farmers. Suddenly, the Congress was faced with the challenge of spreading the Nyay message within a very short period of time. Nikhil Alva, Rahul's media incharge, was now entrusted with putting together an effective ad campaign on Nyay (the word was reportedly coined when the party top brass realized that Nyuntam Aay Yojana was a real tongue-twister). Alva roped in his Bengaluru-based sister-in-law, ad woman and author Anuja Chauhan, film director Nikhil Advani and noted lyricist–writer Javed Akhtar to design the campaign. The 'Ab hoga nyay' (Now there will be justice) campaign was formally launched on 7 April, just four days before the election cycle was to kick off. 'It was crazy, many of us in the publicity committee didn't even know about the campaign till the last moment, even the creatives were not ready when we did the formal launch,' claims a senior Congress leader.

A CSDS pre-poll survey shows that just 48 per cent of respondents had heard of Nyay. Awareness was even lower among those who stood to benefit from it (around 39 per cent). Interestingly, the gap between Rahul and Modi as choice for prime minister was narrower among low-income groups who had heard of the scheme than those who had not. Unfortunately, in a political ecosystem where messaging is key, the Congress had missed another trick: Nyay would be drowned out in the cacophony over Balakot. Even manifesto chief Chidambaram now reluctantly admits that the Nyay promise may not have reached some parts of the country. 'In Tamil Nadu and Kerala, we succeeded in spreading the message. As to why it didn't reach north and central India, you must ask the party organization there,' he observes.

In reality, the Congress was faced with a familiar problem: good intentions but no cohesion, a disconnected high command leading a dispirited rank and file. With decision-making resting with a small group, a number of Congress leaders didn't seem as actively involved in the 2019 campaign as they perhaps should have been. Team Rahul was trying hard to drive the party forward but lacked the political bandwidth to challenge the BJP's micro-managed, high-decibel presidential-style campaign. An inexperienced leader operating out of an echo chamber, a party system working in silos, well-meaning experts crafting schemes without a strong enough or solid enough game plan – the Congress was, as one former MP puts it, 'a shipwreck waiting to happen!'

It was not just the main national opposition party which was living in delusion. Just two days ahead of the results when I met Sharad Pawar at his Delhi residence, he predicted that the Congress–NCP would get an equal share of the seats in Maharashtra: the alliance ended up with just five of the forty-eight seats. With his own grand-nephew being defeated, it was apparent that even in their western Maharashtra heartland the Pawars were under siege. In Bihar, Tejaswi Yadav claimed that the RJD-led alliance would be the 'new force' in state politics: the alliance won one of forty seats. Tejaswi, once an IPL cricketer and lacking his father's natural political charisma, was squabbling with his allies over almost every seat, and was proving to be yet another entitled dynast overestimating his appeal. But perhaps the biggest fantasy universe was that of Telangana Chief Minister K. Chandrashekhar Rao. The TRS leader was somehow convinced that the BJP would not cross 200 seats and he would be one of the kingmakers in a hung parliament. 'Main Dilli aa raha hoon [I am coming to Delhi]. Let's meet soon,' he told me forty-eight hours before counting day. As it turned out, the TRS leader had to abort his Delhi trip and stay back in his farmhouse outside Hyderabad. Even his daughter, K. Kavitha, lost her seat.

The 2019 TsuNamo had drowned nearly the entire opposition. Yet some of India's biggest leaders had, for some unfathomable reason, just not seen it coming.

Around 120 kilometres from Lucknow is Amethi, one of the most significant constituencies in the country. It is a nondescript place, bumpy dirt tracks and thatched-roof villages existing cheek by jowl with meagre semi-urban stretches with the odd yellow-painted office block and ramshackle stores. Since 1980, Amethi has been a Gandhi stronghold and for decades was considered a sure-shot seat for the Congress's first family. With its privileged status came a whiff of change, especially in the years when Rajiv Gandhi was prime minister: a number of public sector units were set up in this dusty UP district. Post-Rajiv, development appeared to visibly slow down as the Congress found its dominance being challenged by new political forces in UP. In 2004, when Rahul Gandhi first fought from here, the locals felt confident that good times would return: he was elected with a 66 per cent vote share that year which rose further to an even more impressive 71 per cent five years later. Rahul promised to transform Amethi's fortunes and make it a model for self-help groups: since 2004, more than 10,000 women in the district have benefited from this vision.

And yet, all too soon hope transformed into disenchantment. Many of the planned large projects didn't take off and the condition of basic amenities – village roads, schools and health centres – remained sub-par. Every time I travelled over the dirt tracks of rural Amethi I was reminded of the sharp contrast with Sharad Pawar's pocket borough of Baramati near Pune which had, in two decades, gone from a sleepy village into a bustling, enriched district, with spanking roads and gleaming street lights, and was a shining example of how sustained political investment can spur social and economic change. 'Yeh UP hai, sir, yahan vikas ko aage badhana aasan nahin, Rahulji ne bahut koshish ki' (This is UP, sir, it is not easy to push development here. Rahul tried his best), laments Akhilesh Singh, UP Congress spokesperson and staunch Gandhi family loyalist.

By 2014, it was apparent that the Gandhi family's hold over Amethi was weakening. The BJP under Modi–Shah's leadership decided to take the battle to the Gandhi bastion. Less than a month before the elections, they pitted former TV star-turned-MP Smriti Irani against Rahul. A charismatic, aggressively combative, and slightly controversial public figure, Smriti was relishing her enlarged profile as a potential giant-slayer. The stakes were suddenly raised. 'Until then, no one had dared to take on the Gandhis in Amethi, but we changed the rules of the game,' says the feisty Smriti. She polled more than 3 lakh votes, and brought Rahul's winning margin down to just over 1 lakh.

Five years later, Smriti was back, only this time she and the BJP were better prepared. In the 2017 assembly elections, the BJP had won from four of the five Amethi segments, a clear indication of the shifting public mood. Soon after their 2017 UP victory, Shah reportedly told his team, 'Jo bhi ho, Amethi mein Congress ko 2019 mein harana hai!' (Whatever happens, we have to defeat the Congress in 2019 in Amethi!) Over the next 24 months, the BJP prepared an elaborate plan for Amethi: its MLAs were energized, Congress workers were weaned away, district officials were put on notice, and central government programmes were closely monitored in the district. 'Bahut paisa daala hai BJP ne Amethi mein, kai adhikariyon aur gram pradhan ko dhamkaya' (The BJP put a lot of money in Amethi, they intimidated many officials and village heads), insists Akhilesh Singh.

Smriti though dismisses the charges of misusing state power, pointing instead to the arduous effort that she and the BJP cadres put into the district. Despite her ministerial duties, she would travel at least once every month to the constituency in a relentless attempt to shore up her base. 'Are you aware that I have covered each and every one of the 830 panchayats in Amethi and have actually gone to every booth in the district?' she says. She also cites the case of Piprigaon, a village which was suffering from soil erosion and where the villagers had been agitating for years to have an embankment built. 'The Gandhis didn't do anything for the village in seventy years; we built an embankment in 2018,' she claims.

In contrast, since Rahul was criss-crossing the country as Congress president, Amethi was no longer his top focus. When he did come on short two- or three-day trips, the tight SPG security cordon around him meant that not many people could meet him. The disillusionment was growing: 'Rahulji ko milna bahut mushkil hai' (It is very difficult to meet Rahul), was a common complaint. As the 2019 campaign was taking off, it was apparent that Rahul was in trouble on the home turf. Feedback from the ground suggested that Amethi was no longer a safe seat. Family nostalgia was no longer a guaranteed vote-catcher. For years, the Gandhis' relationship with Amethi was driven by a sense of noblesse oblige; now, an aspirational generation wanted more than just handouts.

A worried Team Rahul felt that a Plan B was needed. His organization secretary and Kerala MP K.C. Venugopal mooted the idea of contesting from verdant Wayanad in Kerala as an additional seat. With its large Muslim and Christian population, Wayanad was a relatively safe seat for the Congress. When the announcement finally came, it proved to be a double-edged sword: the news was greeted with enthusiasm by the Congress's Kerala unit but it also exposed the party's pitiable situation in UP, apart from angering the ruling left in Kerala. Fulminated the CPI(M)'s Brinda Karat: 'What signal is the Congress president sending to secular forces when he comes to Kerala to fight against a potential ally, the left?'

For the BJP, Rahul's decision was a portent of imminent nationwide victory. 'I think the day Rahul "ran away" from Amethi and decided to contest from Wayanad, we knew this election was over,' said Arun Jaitley, 'The only reason he chose Wayanad is that it has a large minority population, basically he was acknowledging what we have been saying from the beginning: the Congress is now a minorities-only party!'

In a rally in Wardha in Maharashtra, Modi echoed this line: 'Those who were called terrorists have now woken up. We [Hindus] consider the whole world as one family and they insulted us [by calling us terrorists]. They are now afraid of the majority and the punishment given by Hindu terrorists has forced them to take refuge in a place where the majority has become a minority.' The prime minister's provocative remarks appeared to be a deliberate attempt to play the Hindu–Muslim card: despite a formal complaint from the Congress, the EC took no action against Modi, and eventually gave him a clean chit.

Interestingly, just a few days later, the BJP announced the candidature of Pragya Singh Thakur, better known as Sadhvi Pragya, from the prestigious Bhopal seat. The saffron-robed, rabble-rousing leader had been charged as a co-conspirator in the 2008 Malegaon bombings in which six people were killed and over a hundred injured. While the National Investigation Agency withdrew the charges under the anti-terrorism MCOCA Maharashtra Control of Organised Crime Act against her in 2017, she was still under trial for multiple charges under the Unlawful Activities Prevention Act and was out on bail on health grounds. A pattern was discernible where all those accused of 'saffron terror' were being systematically let off by the courts since the BJP came to power in 2014.

That the BJP had chosen someone who was still facing terror charges for a Lok Sabha seat reveals an unabashed disregard for the rule of law, quite apart from a conscious attempt to stoke communal divisions. 'A fake case has been made out in the name of Hindu terror,' snarled Amit Shah, defending Pragya's candidature. She was Shah's personal choice, disregarding stray contrary voices within the party. 'Yes, I don't think we should have given Pragya a ticket, it sends out the wrong message, especially to our middle-class voter,' Jaitley would later tell me. Shah though had his own reasoning. The Congress, fresh from its assembly election win, had chosen two-time chief minister Digvijaya Singh for the contest. The moment Digvijaya's name was announced, Shah's political antennae shot up. Digvijaya Singh was one of the Congress leaders he disliked intensely, viewing him as part of a 'lobby' that had conspired against him and the hard-line Hindutva groups. Pragya, he felt, was the right nominee to 'expose' the Congress's alleged 'anti-Hindu' bias. The prospect of political benefit through heightened communal polarization was clearly on his mind.

When the results were declared Pragya had won the Bhopal seat by over 3 lakh votes. In Amethi, Smriti Irani had defeated Rahul in a stunning upset by over 55,000 votes. Rahul did win Wayanad by a huge 4 lakh margin. Dynasty politics had been conquered. A shrinking southern outpost was now the last refuge of the once-mighty Congress. The political map of India and its power equations had been well and truly altered. Hard Hindutva had triumphed.

Narendra Modi drove into Varanasi like an ancient Hindu king on a modern-day SUV chariot. It was 25 April and Modi had been on the road non-stop for almost a month, traversing the country, often addressing four to five rallies a day (his eventual tally of public appearances was 142 rallies plus four roadshows in a 51-day 2019 blitzkrieg). But Varanasi was special: this was where five years ago he had firmly stamped his arrival on the national stage by filing his nomination from the banks of the Ganga, holy river of Hindus and symbol of India's ancient civilization. Then he had been the contender, now he was the incumbent; then he had been the challenger, now he was the prime minister; then Varanasi and large parts of India hadn't quite known of him, now he was the most trusted 'face' of Indian politics. 'I think there was a novelty factor in 2014 which led to a more frenzied public response; this time, the crowds who lined up were coming to greet Modi more in the nature of a homecoming of their favourite son,' says India Today's Rahul Shrivastava who covered both the 2014 and 2019 Varanasi campaigns.

All Modi roadshows are choreographed right down to the last detail, and this one was no exception. Dressed in a saffron kurta and white pyjama with an angavastram draped around his shoulders, the prime minister took two and a half hours to cover the 7-kilometre-long route, garlanding the statue of Banaras Hindu University founder Madan Mohan Malaviya, before wending his way through the narrow lanes of the ageless city. Thousands had lined up to greet him, showering rose petals on him from building roofs and balconies as he enthusiastically waved from his gleaming black SUV's sunroof. He drove through the localities of Hindu sari-shop owners and the weaver colonies with a substantial Muslim population. Over one hundred specially created displays highlighting various government schemes were put up along the route with Modi posters, flags and hoardings dominating the skyline. It was, as one local BJP leader put it, a 'Namotsav' (Modi festival) where an entire city was taken over by the cult of personality. The final act was at the fully lit up Dhasasvamedh Ghat where, well after sundown, Modi performed the Ganga-aarti with Amit Shah by his side, a religious ritual which he unfailingly carries out after a major public event in Varanasi. Every move was captured by a multi-cam production unit with drone cameras hired by the BJP being used to track the ceremony from mid-air. 'We have a separate team that works on such mega events for the prime minister,' I was told later by a BJP leader. Event management has always been Modi's forte since the time he first organized L.K. Advani's rath yatra on its Gujarat leg in 1990. The spectacularly arranged event designed for maximum camera exposure transforms every media outlet for at least a couple of hours into an uncritical disseminator of this political rock concert, subtly converting voters into awestruck spectators.

As I watched the roadshow, I wondered at the expense involved in pulling off such a large-scale razzle-dazzle political spectacle. Wasn't the prime minister exceeding his ₹70 lakh per candidate limit in just one roadshow? A close aide of Modi's, who was handling his back-office work in Varanasi, refutes the charge of excess expenditure. 'All the monies for such roadshows come from the party coffers. A candidate's individual expenses only start from the filing of nomination so our meter starts ticking only then,' he points out. 'Do you know we made only digital payments to all our vendors in Varanasi? One vendor was too scared to accept a cheque with the prime minister's signature, so we had to do it through RTGS!' The division between 'party money' and 'individual expenses' is craftily used by our top netas to get around EC norms.

Big money show or not, this was definitely a show of strength. The next morning, when Modi went to the Varanasi district collectorate to file his nomination, he was accompanied by the entire galaxy of BJP and NDA allies, many of whom had flown in the night before in private chartered planes. From foe-turned-ally Nitish Kumar to restive Shiv Sena partner Uddhav Thackeray to Akali Dal patriarch Prakash Singh Badal, every leader lined up dutifully behind the prime minister. 'We will create history in this election, you are witnessing a pro-incumbency wave,' he told BJP workers as they cheered him with raucous chants of 'Modi, Modi'.

Unlike 2014, this time the Varanasi seat appeared less like a truly competitive fight. Over five years, Modi had impressively nursed the constituency. From cleaning up the river ghats to constructing a 17.5-kilometre-long four-lane highway linking the airport to the city to initiating an underground cabling system, there was a visible attempt to overhaul the ancient city's crumbling infrastructure. Just two days before the election dates were announced, the prime minister laid the foundation for the Kashi Vishwanath temple corridor which would replace the serpentine maze of narrow alleys and connect the ancient Shiva mandir with the main ghats along the Ganga. The same firm of architects that developed the Sabarmati waterfront in Ahmedabad was handling the ambitious project aimed at decongesting an area which sees lakhs of people daily. It wasn't quite yet Kyoto as the prime minister once promised but funds were clearly pouring in. A city of antiquity was now aspiring for modernity, even though some Varanasi locals continue to lament the loss of precious heritage for the sake of soulless progress.

Varanasi doesn't need to become Kyoto; its ancient features like its homes and streets need to be preserved rather than obliterated, observes Varanasi's long-time chronicler–academic Amitabha Bhattacharyya. Yet for the BJP, the drive for development is key to its political ambitions. 'We have announced more than 300 projects for the city. The PM through his work has made it impossible for anyone other than the BJP to win this seat,' says Sunil Oza, a former BJP MLA from Gujarat who is supervising Varanasi's development.

Oza may be right, at least for now. Unlike in Amethi, where the BJP was confronting Rahul Gandhi head-on, in Varanasi, the opposition had given up without putting up even a semblance of a fight. In 2014, at least AAP leader Arvind Kejriwal had created a flutter by challenging Modi from Varanasi and positioning himself bang in the middle of a David versus Goliath battle. Now, Kejriwal was struggling to retain his base in Delhi while the Congress was trying to manage a campaign that was like a chaotic performance without a script or actors. For weeks, there was feverish speculation that Priyanka Gandhi Vadra would 'take on' Modi from Varanasi, adding a truly spicy edge to the contest. Priyanka had parked herself in eastern UP for a month, even undertaking a 'Ganga yatra' by boat along the river. Each time journalists asked her whether she was ready to fight the election from Varanasi, Priyanka would smile mischievously. 'Why just me, even you can contest an election if you want to. I will do whatever the party and the Congress president decide.'

On the campaign trail in Amethi–Rae Bareli where Priyanka would eventually spend much of her time trying to protect the family bastion, I asked her whether she had backed off from contesting Varanasi because she feared losing to Modi. Her answer was combative: 'Jis din Priyanka Gandhi Vadra ko dar lagega, woh ghar baith jayegi. UP mein main ladne aayi hoon!' (The day Priyanka is scared, she will stay at home. I have come to UP to fight!) Defiant words but scarcely enough to translate into a winning formula.

In the highly secretive world of the Congress first family we will perhaps never know the real story behind the formal announcement that

Priyanka would not contest, but its timing could not have been worse. It was made on the very morning of the Modi roadshow in Varanasi. What had been billed as a potential heavyweight fight which the media was getting ready to showcase, suddenly suffered a bathos-filled anticlimax with one high-profile contender suddenly deciding to drop out from the ring. It was yet another defining moment in the 2019 elections: the BJP was on a high; the Congress workers were further demoralized. The so-called Priyanka 'brahmastra' (ultimate weapon) which the Congress was counting on had been withdrawn from the battlefield even before it could be unleashed, revealing the limitations of the party's strategy. Perhaps the Congress, which for years had banked on Priyanka's charisma to lead a turnaround, was finally waking up to a harsh reality: eyeballs do not get votes in the absence of a solid organizational set-up. Priyanka captured TV time and radiated charisma, but she had parachuted into the election at the last minute when there were no local teams to back her up. Yes, she made headlines but it is also true that she failed to deliver any significant impact. She would have been much more effective if she had spent five years working in UP's grassroots; without a ground game or a history of local toil, the Priyanka phenomenon became overwhelmed by too many expectations. The TIMO (There Is Modi Only) factor was overriding all else in Varanasi and beyond.

In the last stretch of the 2019 election, unlike in 2014, Modi did not even bother to return to Varanasi to campaign, so sure was he of victory. Instead Modi chose to pull off another typical last-day surprise. Campaign over and just a day before Varanasi was to vote, he embarked on a Kedarnath 'yatra'. It wasn't quite the rigorous trek to the mountain shrine, rather a VVIP darshan instead. Yet again, the omnipresent cameras followed Modi like bees to a honeypot: images of the prime minister in a grey jubba, a long customary woollen dress worn by Garhwali men, striding along a red carpet towards the holy shrine of Lord Shiva at snow-bound Kedarnath flooded TV screens and the internet. The final image was the most striking: the prime minister sitting cross-legged in a cave upon a white bed, leaning against pillows, his body draped in a bright saffron shawl, eyes closed in meditation. Only in this instance the ubiquitous camera was part of the meditative photo-op. Yet another 'shock and awe' event had been created around Modi's persona, an obvious attempt to reinforce his dual image: devout Hindu and political karmayogi. It was another masterclass in imagery to round off the campaign: the prime minister seated amid lofty mountains in solitary splendour, far above the squabbling lesser mortals who were his political opponents. Varanasi was to vote the next day as was Bengal. The TMC protested before the EC, calling the photograph a 'media event' aimed at influencing voters. The EC gave the green signal to the Kedarnath foray even though the model code of conduct was in force. Not for the first time, Team Modi had managed to circumvent the election campaign rules through canny planning. 'Our opponents crib too much. This is sharp competitive politics we are engaged in, not a joyride,' was Jaitley's response to criticism of the Kedarnath 'tamasha'.

Modi would win Varanasi by a huge margin of more than 4.7 lakh votes; the SP–BSP 'mahagathbandhan' candidate Shalini Yadav was a distant second. The Congress's Ajay Rai lost his deposit for a second consecutive election. It was literally a walkover: game, set and match. For centuries, Varanasi has been at the confluence of India's great spiritual traditions: now, it was at the heart of a twenty-first-century political empire.

By 7 p.m. on 23 May, the BJP headquarters on 6A Pandit Deendayal Upadhyaya Marg in central Delhi was lit up like a midsummer Diwali celebration. The NDA had not quite achieved its 'Mission 400' but with 353 seats, including 303 for the BJP alone, it had pulled off an astounding victory. Ministers and party leaders were hugging each other, smiling broadly. Young men and women with Modi tattoos and T-shirts were dancing in delight. Laddoos were being distributed in bulk and crackers were being burst by overexcited supporters. 'We have created history, pro-incumbency has won,' a beaming Union minister Prakash Javadekar kept repeating before the large assemblage of TV cameras. He was right in a way: no incumbent prime minister since Indira Gandhi at her peak in 1970 had won two consecutive parliamentary majorities.

Just one final triumphal act remained to be performed. Shortly after 6 p.m., BJP president Amit Shah entered the party office in a saffron kurta, white pyjama and black sleeveless jacket, accepting greetings from a flock of admirers clustering around him. An hour later, the prime-ministerial cavalcade was spotted. The moment he emerged from his BMW in his beige kurta and dark jacket, the cries of 'Modi, Modi' were taken up once again amidst flashing bulbs. But right at that moment, the skies opened up and it began to pour. Security men rushed out with umbrellas. Shah bowed before his leader, greeted him with a bouquet of yellow flowers, before the duo walked together, arms triumphantly raised and showing off the 'V' sign as the adoring crowd showered them with rose petals. It was an unusual frame: Modi was sharing the glory with his chief lieutenant. It was a symbolic reminder that the 2019 success belonged as much to the indefatigable campaigner as it did to a finely tuned organizational machine. A makeshift stage, glowing in saffron, had been erected from where first Shah, then Modi, once Gujarat's 'Jodi Number One', and now the ruling power couple of the BJP and the country, would address the gathering.

Modi's voice sounded hoarse after a long campaign but he would, as always, have the last word: 'People are chanting "Modi, Modi". But this is not a victory of Modi, it is the victory of the people who are desperate for honesty in the system. I will not do anything for myself. I will devote every moment of my time and every fibre of my being for my countrymen ... You have filled this fakir's bag with a lot of hope. All your hopes, dreams, ambitions are dependent on it.' While accusing the opposition of 'wearing a false mask of secularism', he struck a conciliatory note too: 'We have to move ahead, we have to take everyone with us, even our opponents ... there are only two castes which will remain in the country, the poor and those contributing to alleviating poverty.' A parallel from the Mahabharata was drawn: 'Krishna was asked after the war which side he supported and he answered that he stood for Hastinapur. Now, people have spoken in the elections that they stand for India.' With every punchline the crowd would get even more hysterical in their chanting.

Poverty and garib-kisan, nation-building and nationalism – familiar themes in a long and controversial 2019 campaign, one in which the BJP had clearly changed the rules of the game by orchestrating a near-total 'capture' of the state machinery and the public mindspace. The dominant image till the very end was that of the ascetic–strongman Modi himself, the supreme communicator who had succeeded in completely rendering the feeble and divided opposition invisible. His larger-than-life image, hypnotically alluring to some and terrifyingly divisive to others, had won the day. In the newsroom, I was taking copious notes from the speech when one of my colleagues, flush with excitement, turned to me with a huge smile. 'Aaj toh bol dijiye, sir, Modi hai toh Mumkin hai.' (At least today, sir, say it: 'Anything is possible if Modi is there.) I smiled back faintly. Like it or not, 2019 was, after all, the Modi election.

Afterword

1 September 2020

IF a week is a long time in Indian politics, a year can be an eternity. The first anniversary celebrations of the Narendra Modi 2.0 government in May 2020 had none of the 'band, baaja, baarat' razzmatazz that is such an intrinsic part of the Modi style of political marketing. India was in lockdown mode and the rising cases of Covid-19 across the country meant that public celebrations would not be possible. Instead, Prime Minister Modi was forced to acknowledge that the pomp and pageantry had to give way to the demands imposed by the pandemic and ensure his supporters stayed indoors. The prime minister therefore chose to write an open letter to his 'fellow-Indians' on the occasion, stating: 'During normal times, I would have been in your midst. However, present circumstances do not permit that. That is why I seek your blessings through this letter.'

Typically, the letter was drafted in a manner to showcase a chief executive in complete control of the situation, a strongman leader seeking to demonstrate that he would not allow a virus to interrupt the 'rising' India story in uncertain times. Consummate political communicator that he is, Modi converted the lockdown into a national mission, exploiting the opportunity for the archetypal Hindu right nationalist leader to once again invoke a feeling of 'Bharatiya' nationalism driven by a mix of populist fervor and artful event management. Said the prime minister in the letter:

> Many feared that India will become a problem for the world when Corona hits India. But today, through sheer confidence and resilience, you have transformed the way the world looks at us. You have proven that the collective strength and potential of India is unparalleled compared even to the powerful and prosperous of the world. Be it clapping and lighting a lamp to the honouring of Corona warriors by India's armed forces, Janta curfew or by faithful adherence to rules during a nationwide lockdown, on every occasion you have shown that Ek Bharat is the guarantee for Shrestha Bharat.

Lost in the upbeat narrative was the harsh reality of those living on the margins who had been pushed to the brink. The national lockdown, imposed at just four hours' notice, had resulted in considerable social and economic disruption in millions of lives and livelihoods. Images of thousands of migrant labourers being forced to return to their villages from the big cities – many of them walking hundreds of kilometres in the oppressive summer heat in the absence of means of transportation – had finally awakened the country to the plight of the urban poor. The sense of utter despair was symbolized by the news headline on 8 May 2020: '16 migrant workers run over by goods train near Aurangabad'. Exhausted, the labourers had fallen asleep on the tracks after walking for hours. The decision to completely shut down the country's public transport system – especially the railways – for several weeks seemed to have been taken in haste and with scant regard for its consequences. There were more reports during the lockdown of horrific accidents involving overcrowded trucks and buses in which dozens were killed. A particularly harrowing image of the unprecedented suffering was of a toddler scurrying about on a railway platform, attempting in vain to awaken his dead mother.

The poor handling of the migrant crisis would have badly bruised and shaken up most governments. But here it appeared to be just a blip. The Modi first anniversary letter did refer briefly to the predicament of the impoverished masses –

In a crisis of this magnitude, it can certainly not be claimed that no one suffered any inconvenience or discomfort. Our labourers, migrant workers, artisan and craftsmen in small scale industries, hawkers and such fellow countrymen have undergone tremendous suffering. We are working in a united and determined way to alleviate their troubles.

– but there was no acceptance of any moral or political failure, much less an apology at the unfolding human tragedy in which millions had suffered.

A Centre for Monitoring Indian Economy (CMIE) report claimed that 12.2 crore Indians (about 122 million), majority of them daily wage labourers, lost their jobs in April 2020 alone. The unemployment rate shot up to 27.1 per cent, the highest ever, in the first week of May. While the numbers improved in June – driven largely by greater rural employment under the National Rural Employment Guarantee Scheme – the job crisis caused by the lockdown was undeniable (CMIE claims 5 million salaried people lost their jobs in July 2020). It was obvious that an already slowing pre-lockdown economy was now facing a dramatic recessionary slump. Most global rating agencies predicted a sharp economic downturn, some even forecasting a negative growth rate in the fiscal year 2020–21. The government's economic managers, led by Finance Minister Nirmala Sitharaman, insisted the situation wasn't as dire as prophesied. Sitharaman announced a Rs 20 lakh crore stimulus, claiming it would revive the economic engine. But the much-hyped booster dose failed to address the fundamental demand side crisis: shrinking incomes and declining consumption needed direct cash support which was missing.

The prime minister spoke of converting this crisis into opportunity, throwing up a new catchy slogan of an 'Atma-Nirbhar' (self-reliant) Bharat while pushing ahead with a slew of reforms. Some of the structural changes, especially in the agriculture sector, are much delayed steps in the right direction. And yet, for the stressed small and micro businesses, in the vast informal sector in particular, the prime minister's fine words were no balm: the coronavirus pandemic and forced lockdowns have broken supply chains that will take time to restore. In an unprecedented time when each day was full of grinding hardship, personal tragedy and emotional trauma, the declaration of high policy with little relief on the ground struck a jarring, unsympathetic note. Few were genuinely reassured. In private, many business leaders admit that the Modi government needs to urgently address the sense of economic drift but few are willing to speak out. One of those who did was industrialist Rajiv Bajaj who claimed that the economy had been 'decimated'. 'We have flattened the wrong curve,' he tersely remarked.

It wasn't just the economic stagnation that was disconcerting. In June 2020, India found itself in a messy border tangle with China in eastern Ladakh. On 15 June, twenty Indian soldiers were killed in a flare-up while patrolling along the disputed Line of Actual Control between the two countries. While the prime minister insisted that 'no one is inside our territory nor is any of our posts captured', the on-ground evidence suggested a massive Chinese build-up in the Galwan Valley and Pangong Tso Lake region of eastern Ladakh, including areas where Indian troops normally patrol. The fact that this expanded Chinese presence in the region went unnoticed for weeks suggests an obvious intelligence failure, one that the government seems hesitant to acknowledge. Till a few months before the border incident, Prime Minister Modi claimed to enjoy a personal rapport with Chinese president Xi Jinping while hosting him at high-profile summits in Ahmedabad and Mamallapuram. Now, however, the warmth of the Sino-Indian 'hug-fest' seemed to have frozen over in the icy climes of Ladakh. The 'personality-driven' foreign policy had unravelled but no one was willing to admit to the botch-up.

Instead the Modi government tried to invoke national pride while ordering the banning of fifty-nine Chinese apps, including the popular short video app Tik Tok. The call for boycotting Chinese goods couldn't take away from the ground reality: this was not just another routine border intrusion as was initially portrayed. While both sides have since agreed to de-escalate tensions, the process of forcing the Chinese to pull back and restore the status quo ante is likely to be a long and cumbersome one. As Shivshankar Menon, a former national security adviser, warns, 'The danger with the Chinese is that they take two steps forward and then negotiate one step back and present you with a fait accompli.'

More worrying though was the 'war' against the coronavirus, the deadly contagion that was spreading rapidly across the world and wreaking havoc in its wake. A well-equipped Indian army could possibly combat the Chinese People's Liberation Army, but how could a weak healthcare infrastructure cope with a respiratory disease that was infecting millions? The answer was a severe lockdown that would provide respite to an over-burdened hospital care system. In a speech in March 2020 to his constituents in Varanasi, the prime minister invoked the Mahabharata, affirming that while that famed battle was won in eighteen days, the war against the coronavirus – he hoped – would see victory in twenty-one days.

As it turns out, a virus knows no timelines. By the end of August, the total Covid-19 cases in the country had gone well past the 30 lakh (3 million) mark, with more than 70,000 new cases being detected every day. In a tally, which no one really wanted to be in, let alone top, India was now in third place, behind only the United States and Brazil. Its only solace: the cases per million population and, most crucially, the mortality rates were lower than countries in a similar predicament. As cities and states were forced into a continual cycle of lockdowns, un-lockdowns and re-lockdowns, it was apparent that the virus wasn't going anywhere. From 'chase the virus' to 'live with the virus', the Union home ministry used its emergency powers under the National Disaster Management Act (2005) to unilaterally issue hundreds of notifications aimed at directing the states on how to contain the spread of the disease. And yet, in the terribly congested lanes and bylanes of a vast country like India, it was never going to be easy to control a virus by central government firman alone. The limits of the cult of the Big Boss leader and a highly centralizing policy framework were being exposed by the unpredictable trajectory of the pandemic: even Home Minister Amit Shah and several other VVIPs were felled by the virus.

But even when faced with the prospect of a 'three front' war – Covid 19, China and the economy – Prime Minister Modi's personal popularity appears undimmed. Most opinion polls conducted during the lockdown period show high approval ratings for his leadership. It is almost as if nothing has changed since the 2019 election victory despite the mounting health, economic and national security concerns. The virus may have revealed the frailty of human existence but the Supreme Leader seems somehow invincible. This paradox of societal disruption but a seemingly indestructible leadership has been a recurrent theme of the 2019 election book, demonstrating just why Modi could achieve what no Indian politician since Indira Gandhi in 1971 has been able to accomplish while winning two successive electoral majorities.

Modi's seeming ability to tide over any crisis – for example, the ill-conceived policy choice of demonetization in 2016 – is due to a variety of factors: from astute headline management to the lack of an effective opposition. At the core of his appeal lies a personality cult that goes well beyond 'normal' political behaviour, the kind of irrational admiration enjoyed by populist authoritarian leaders across the globe who have yoked religion and nationalism to their aura. He may be a deeply polarizing figure, but the truth is Prime Minister Modi has successfully built a durable relationship of trust with a large section of the voting population, an influence that goes well beyond the ordinary connect between a leader and the citizenry. The average Modi supporter is not just a pro-BJP or anti-Congress voter; they belong to a 'religio-political cult' where the Supreme Leader is projected as a near messianic figure who promises to transform the country into not just a global superpower but also a Hindutva haven, one where religious identity and the development narrative are intertwined. The bond with his adulatory audience is cemented more as an emotional connect than the transactional appeal of the more traditional politician. Modi is not just endorsed by public opinion; armed with careful media management, he also 'manufactures' public opinion in his favour through the enormously impactful mass media. Modi can shock and awe, but also inspire fear, which quells any questioning and promotes widespread hero worship.

This might explain why Modi's passionate appeals to the public during the Covid crisis – be it his 'diya jalao' or 'taali-thali bajao' campaigns – attract such instantaneous and euphoric, if illogical, behaviour. His is the appeal of a Pied Piper-like mass hypnotist, someone who knows exactly who his core constituency is, and then inexorably draws them into his circle of influence by touching an emotional chord. As a close Modi associate once told me, 'The more he is criticized by the liberal elite and all you journalists and opinion makers, the stronger he becomes amongst his supporters.' A menacing figure for his critics is transformed into a macho symbol of a 'new' aspirational India for his obedient followers.

In a fascinating article, Asim Ali, a researcher with the Centre for Policy Research, goes a step further while likening Modi to the Iranian Supreme Leader Ali Khamenei. Asim Ali writes, 'Modi confounds normal political analysis because his appeal isn't merely political. The appeal is quasi-religious ... he is the self-described "fakir", unattached to family and material possessions, who is here to lead India not just politically, but also socially, morally and spiritually. This is why he generates not mere following, but devotion. And this devotion is immune to the performance of the government he leads.'

This leads us to another critical question prompted by Modi's electoral triumphs and post-election behaviour: Are we well and truly in the age of the elected autocrat, a single person rule of a larger than life figure who has 'captured' power through the ballot box and seeks to exercise that power in the manner of a despotic ruler with little regard for democratic institutions?

Certainly, in the first year of Modi 2.0, there has been ample evidence of an increasingly authoritarian, vindictive regime that appears to be contemptuous of the institutional checks and balances of a parliamentary democracy. Take, for example, the manner in which all potential rivals have been downsized and opposition-ruled governments toppled in states like Karnataka and Madhya Pradesh, the latter even as the country was about to enter a Covid-19–induced lockdown. In each instance, the storyline has followed a familiar script: A section of MLAs is persuaded to switch sides, taken to resorts for 'protection' and given ministerial posts, while those opposing the Centre are selectively targeted by punitive enforcement agencies. It isn't as if horse-trading hasn't taken place in previous governments, but the sheer brazenness with which it is carried out now is what sets the present ruling arrangement apart. If the CBI seemed like a caged parrot in the UPA era, the ED is a Rottweiler in Modi 2.0. As a despairing opposition politician puts it, 'The Modi government's best ally at the moment is the ED!'

Even the pretence of political morality has been swept aside by unabashedly ruthless power games. In Goa, for example, two-third of the Congress legislature party defected in July 2019: one of the MLAs, whom the BJP had accused of corruption, was made the deputy chief minister while another, against whom the BJP had previously levelled rape allegations, was also accommodated. When the BJP tried to bring down a Congress-led government in Rajasthan in July 2020, historian Ramachandra Guha accused Modi and his lieutenant, Home Minister Amit Shah, of having 'gutted' democracy through money power. Writes Guha, 'These transactions raise a more fundamental question still: if legislators can be bought and sold at any time, what is the purpose of holding elections in the first place? Does not this nullify entirely the democratic will of millions of Indians who voted in the assembly elections in these states? If the money power of the BJP can so effectively override the outcome of a supposedly free and fair election, can India even call itself an "election-only" democracy?'

In particular, electoral bonds are now seen as contributing to a grossly unequal contest, one where the ruling party has access to a bulk of political donations. Since the bond system remains prima facie opaque – the identity of the bond donor is kept anonymous to all except the government – there can be little scrutiny of any potential quid pro quo dealings. What is troubling is that the issue remains unresolved despite several investigative reports, RTI queries and petitions before the Supreme Court: the power elite, it seems, will not bite the hand that feeds them.

Meanwhile, any political opposition to the BJP has almost evaporated. Still struggling to deal with the scale of its 2019 loss, the Congress party exemplifies the predicament of a beleaguered and dispirited opposition. Within days of the May election defeat, Rahul Gandhi, in a moment of pique, announced during a CWC meeting that he was resigning from his post as party president. If Rahul was hoping that his decision would trigger a spate of resignations and enforce an element of accountability within the grand old party, he was clearly mistaken. Rahul spoke of how several senior Congress leaders had chosen to put the interests of their children ahead of the party, a reference presumably to the likes of Rajasthan Chief Minister Ashok Gehlot, who had allegedly spent much of the election campaign canvassing for his son who was eventually soundly defeated. Rahul's sister, Priyanka Gandhi Vadra was reportedly even more scathing, accusing the party of abandoning Rahul and leaving him to virtually fight on his own. 'Party sangathan ke kaatil sab yahin hain … (The killers of the party organization are here). All those who are responsible for the party's defeat are sitting in this room,' she pointedly remarked. A few Congress leaders blamed EVMs for their defeat while some others simply chose to stay silent. No one was willing to confront the elephant in the room: a poorly led, ideologically weakened, organizationally decrepit Congress had run a badly managed campaign that was pitted against the BJP's well-trained, highly motivated and resource-rich political machine. 'Rahul and Priyanka blamed everyone but themselves for the debacle. It is the height of entitlement,' an angry CWC member told me later. In what seems to be a fitting parallel, the Netflix series The Last Czars poignantly captures the plight of Russia's ruling family – the deluded Romanovs who clung to their belief in their 'sacred bond' with the people even as the Bolshevik revolution raged through their lives and finally consumed them.

While a sulking Rahul stuck by his decision, it was not till mid-August 2019 that the Congress was finally ready to make a change in guard. After prolonged deliberations, it was announced that Sonia Gandhi would be the 'interim' Congress president. Sonia was reportedly reluctant to take charge: after nineteen years at the helm of the party as its longest-serving president, she had told close friends that she was 'tired and almost retired'. And yet, the failure of Rahul's leadership meant that the party was in a spot: chained to its First Family, it now needed Sonia's reassuring presence to at least do a holding job. 'The Gandhis are the glue that binds us, get in any other leader and we will break up into bits,' is how one veteran Congressman rationalizes the party decision.

In truth, this is classic status quo-ism at play where the more things change, the more they remain the same. The dynasty has enfeebled the Congress and prevented the emergence of mass-based leaders, while remaining the fulcrum for the party's survival. Even as the Modi–Shah combine is relentlessly driving the BJP juggernaut forward, the Congress is trapped in feudal loyalties of an ancient regime. Rahul has resigned but is still the party's 'face'; Sonia wants to 'retire' but is still chairperson emeritus; Priyanka is in politics but still not a 24x7 politician on the ground. I asked a senior Congress leader how, in these circumstances, they were planning to combat the Modi–Shah-led BJP. 'Strategy is for later, first we need to exist,' was his candid response.

It is precisely an existential crisis that is staring the Congress in the face. In March 2020, Jyotiraditya Scindia, once a part of Rahul Gandhi's inner circle, who 'could walk into [Rahul's] house at any time', quit the party and joined the BJP, aiding and abetting in the fall of the Congress government in Madhya Pradesh. In July, another poster boy of the Congress's gen-next, Sachin Pilot, also 'rebelled' in Rajasthan while demanding the chief minister's post for himself. Vaulting personal ambition may well have driven the Scindia–Pilot duo to consider life beyond the Congress, but the party's failure to manage the internal conflicts is also reflective of an extremely weak Congress high command that can neither compel the next-gen leaders to toe the line nor accommodate their desires.

In the midst of turbulence, there is the periodic chant from Rahul loyalists for their leader to return as Congress president. An attempted image make-over by his media managers which has seen the release of several short videos in which Rahul asks searching questions of the Modi government on issues ranging from Covid to China to the economy is being projected as a sign that he is ready for a comeback. But a cyberspace re-invention cannot really compete with a solid ground game. If Rahul Gandhi is indeed keen to fight an ideological war against the Sangh Parivar as his acolytes claim, or emerge as a self-styled 'moral' force of change, then he must be willing to forsake the 'work from home' attitude and do the hard yards in rebuilding a comatose party organization. This painstaking exercise must go well beyond clever tweets and viral videos on social media. In private conversation, several Congress leaders – old and young – admit that Rahul's whimsical working style is perhaps ill-suited to reviving the struggling party, yet few are willing to openly push for a non-Nehru–Gandhi family member to lead the change. When a group of twenty-three Congresspersons wrote a letter in August 2020 calling for sweeping organizational changes and stressing the need for a more 'visible' 'full-time' leadership, they were instantly targeted as potential rebels while the party closed ranks around the Gandhi family. The leaking of the letter to the media ahead of a CWC meeting may have embarrassed the Congress leadership, but few could quarrel with its contents. A political party in desperate need of a nuts and bolts overhaul like the Congress demands a hands-on, energetic and accessible leadership that is willing to break out of the cocoon of privilege and actually take the 'war' to the 'enemy camp'.

Perhaps the Congress could take a leaf out of the political playbook of the ageing Maratha war-horse and NCP leader Sharad Pawar, who somehow managed to cobble together an unlikely Shiv Sena–NCP–Congress alliance in Maharashtra and kept the BJP out of power in the state in November 2019. That a seventy-nine-year-old could campaign with such vigour – the sight of the unflagging septuagenarian addressing a rally in Satara in pouring rain was a defining image of the Maharashtra assembly election – and then manage to outmanoeuvre the BJP leadership in a well-calculated post-poll chess game suggests that what the opposition desperately needs is a few more political grandmasters with an ear to the ground and the fire in the belly to win at all costs. Even if the Maharashtra alliance smacks of opportunism and ideological compromise, it reveals that power politics in the Modi era is not for the gentle and squeamish: it is truly a no holds barred fight to the finish.

In fact, the results of the assembly elections of late 2019, held within months of the Lok Sabha elections, are a pointer to the fickle nature of Indian politics. In all three states – Maharashtra, Haryana and Jharkhand – the BJP's vote share sharply declined from its general election high point. The BJP lost power in Maharashtra and Jharkhand and was forced into a coalition government in Haryana. A more localized state election revealed the limitations of the Modi-centric campaign that had been the BJP's calling card in the larger, presidential-style national election. To that extent, a highly competitive multiparty democracy at the state level offers a counterpoint to the 'One Nation, One Party, One Leader' drumbeat of the Modi brigade and should serve as a reality check for the BJP's fanciful dreams of an 'opposition-mukt' Bharat.

But beyond the tumult of election politics and a weakened opposition, there is a reason why the Modi brand of leadership and governance has sparked off fears of a creeping 'elected autocracy'. In particular, it is the hollowing out of the institutions that are the bedrock of democracy and are designed to check any excess of executive power that lies at the root of the deeper crisis of constitutional values confronting our nation. Parliament, for example – once the scene of democratic argument and legislation – has been reduced to a notice board, designed to merely endorse executive action. I was in Parliament that dramatic August 2019 morning when the government pushed through the decision to revoke the special status granted to J&K under Article 370. I had met the home minister in Parliament's central hall a few days earlier and sought an explanation for the heavy troop presence in the state. The buzz, I said, was that the Modi government intended to scrap Article 35 A that conferred special rights and privileges to the 'permanent residents' of J&K. The pugnacious Shah, surrounded by a group of fawning BJP MPs, stared at me grumpily. 'Dekhiye agar hum chahe toh Article 35 ko ek minute mein khatm kar sakte hain ... lekin aisa koi plan bana nahi hai. Lagta hai aap logon ke paas aur koi khabar nahi hai,' (If we want, we can do away with Article 35 within a moment's notice, but there is no such plan right now. Looks like all of you have no other news today), was his dismissive answer. The troop deployment, he insisted, was 'routine' with Independence Day fast approaching.

I wasn't the only one groping for answers. The opposition was clearly in the dark. When Parliament convened at 11 a.m., Shah was spotted striding purposefully into the Rajya Sabha. The leader of the opposition in the Rajya Sabha and former chief minister of J&K, Ghulam Nabi Azad, looked anxious. 'Can we be told what is happening in Kashmir? You have spread so much fear and uncertainty, soldiers are everywhere, phone lines are being cut, what is going on?' he asked. Amidst the commotion, the chairman of the house and Vice President Venkaiah Naidu, assured the restless opposition that Shah was there to answer all queries. The legislative business of the house had listed the J&K reservation bill on the agenda, a fairly innocuous enactment that wouldn't need much debate or discussion. But Shah had far weightier issues on his mind as was amply clear minutes into his speech. 'I am presenting the resolution (sankalp patra) on Article 370 in J&K. The resolution has been sent to the President for signature and the moment it is notified in the official gazette, the provisions of Article 370 will no longer apply.'

Article 370 grants special status to J&K and was the cornerstone of the state's accession to India in 1947. For Kashmiris, Article 370 carried universally profound psychological attachments even though over time, the article as a law had become more honoured in the breach than in observance. The BJP, and its original avatar of the Jan Sangh, had long protested against Article 370, claiming it had prevented the 'integration' of J&K with the rest of the country. And yet, previous governments had refrained from touching a contentious constitutional provision which was seen as a tinderbox in an explosive Valley. Now, on a defining Monday morning, the Modi government had just ended seventy-two years of prevarication and shattered the status quo by pulling off a constitutional coup. India's only Muslim-majority state had been reduced to a union territory by executive firman, and Parliament, the supreme legislative body of the Republic, was now a mere notice board.

The opposition was stunned. For a few seconds, there was deathly silence in the House. As soon as the implications of what the home minister had just pronounced began to register, opposition MPs got to their feet in protest. They kept trying to interrupt Shah's speech, but the home minister was having none of it; he was on a roll. Not only would Article 370 be rendered inoperative, so would Article 35A. By another legislative amendment, the minister announced the 'reorganization' of the state of J&K into two separate Union territories: J&K, and Ladakh. With every announcement, the treasury benches were exultant, cheering and thumping the tables. Two Valley-based PDP MPs marched into the well of the house, tore copies of the Constitution and had to be bodily lifted and removed by the Rajya Sabha marshals. Ghulam Nabi Azad was struggling to be heard. By the time he could make an intervention, there was near-total pandemonium. 'Shut up!' Azad screamed then, in an uncharacteristic show of temper, but his voice was drowned out in the uproar. 'You have murdered the Constitution by removing a historic legislation,' he warned. Shah, though, was unbending. 'I will not go into the history of Article 370, but yes, the bill which I have brought today will create history!' he claimed in an increasingly aggressive tone. Within the next twenty-four hours, the resolutions had been passed in both houses of Parliament with several opposition parties like the TRS, BJD and BSP supporting the government stand. The Congress and its allies were isolated, clearly taken by surprise by the swiftness with which the government had moved.

On the ground in Kashmir, a near-total lockdown came into place. Politicians from the Valley, including three former chief ministers – Farooq Abdullah, Omar Abdullah and Mehbooba Mufti – were placed under house arrest/detention. All mobile phone services were suspended and internet connectivity was blocked. Security was heightened across the state. Citizen movement was restricted and schools closed. Eid was just days away but this time it would be a festival spent under the shadow of the gun and iron barricades. 'Would you ever do something like this during Diwali, or are we Kashmiris going to be treated with suspicion and as potential terrorists all our lives,' a Delhi-based Kashmiri friend asked me indignantly. I didn't quite know how to respond.

I recall asking a cabinet minister whether they had been aware of the move to annul Article 370. He smiled, 'Kya Rajdeep bhai, which world are you living in? In this government, only two and a half people really know what is going on!' The 'half' in this instance was National Security Adviser Ajit Doval who was seen as the chief executioner of the Modi government's Mission Kashmir operation. Perhaps, the defining photo-op in Parliament was when Modi stretched his hand to congratulate Shah after the bill was successfully passed while the home minister bent down obsequiously before his 'Saheb'. The Supreme Leader blessed his key lieutenant for a job well done; the chosen heir had served up fare that was applauded from the very top. Gujarat's 'jodi number one' had done it again: much like with demonetization in 2016, a major, hugely disruptive move had been made without any wider consultation or discussion with key stakeholders, but with a single-minded determination to browbeat the opposition into submission, an essential characteristic of the Modi–Shah style of leadership. An election majority may have just been won but the appetite for risk-taking was clearly intact. From demonetization to the abolition of article 370, Modi and Shah choose to put citizens through major invasive surgery without blood tests or anaesthesia. Legislation by stealth and governance by diktat – typical of a regime that viewed the 2019 mandate as voter affirmation for its core ideological agenda. Or as one BJP backbencher MP tells me, 'Please understand, with Modi-Shah it is always a case of "Yeh dil maange more!"'

A year later, the state remains trapped in its bloodied turbulence with little sign of the 'terror-free' 'Naya' Kashmir transformation that was promised. The revocation of Article 370 may have led to celebrations among BJP supporters but it has only widened the mistrust on the ground, and deepened the fear that the Modi government wants to fundamentally alter the Valley's uneasy equation with Delhi by imposing its will on the people of Kashmir. 'They want us to be subjects of a Hindu Rashtra not citizens of India,' is how a local Kashmiri journalist explains the sense of continued alienation in the valley. 'Do you really think we are more Indian today than we were yesterday?' an emotional Farooq Abdullah asked me after having spent several months under house arrest. Interestingly, Home Minister Amit Shah had told Parliament in August 2019 that Abdullah was not under detention, a barefaced lie as it turned out.

The contentious Citizenship Amendment Act (CAA), also piloted by Shah, has followed a similar pattern of being bulldozed through with a sneering disdain for any criticism. While the legislation claims to provide protection and fast-track citizenship to minority groups being discriminated in neighbouring countries (primarily Pakistan and Bangladesh), it explicitly makes a distinction between non-Muslim and Muslim migrants. In effect, religion has been made a defining marker for citizenship, contrary to the country's secular, constitutional ethos. The Modi government was unperturbed by the protests against the new law, claiming instead that the legislation was an election manifesto promise – as was the revocation of Article 370. It is almost as if the massive 2019 election victory validated the BJP's long-held core beliefs which had been kept on the backburner because of the compulsions of coalition politics. Now, unfettered by any pesky alliances, Modi 2.0 appears to carry the conviction of a political-ideological force, of a saffron brotherhood that believes its time has come: the lip-service to notions of 'sarva dharma sambhav' (all religions are equal) can now be openly jettisoned.

Those who oppose this assault on the Constitution are vociferously attacked and lampooned as 'urban Naxals', the 'tukde-tukde gang', the 'Khan market gang', 'libtards' – each term carefully chosen to portray a hateful figure, an 'enemy' who can be charged not just for being anti-BJP or anti-Modi but 'anti-national' or 'desh-drohi' as well, thereby shrinking the space for legitimate dissent. Any difference of opinion with the government is in danger of being criminalized. When, for example, a group of women decided to organize an anti-CAA dharna in a predominantly Muslim locality of Shaheen Bagh in Delhi, the instant reaction was to target the protestors as part of a wider anti-India 'Muslim conspiracy' to weaken the Indian state. That many of the protestors were elderly homemakers braving the harsh Delhi winter on the streets didn't seem to matter. The 'Muslim as anti-national' propaganda is now so deeply ingrained into the narrative of the 'new' India that dissenters of Shaheen Bagh, and the students of the nearby Jamia university who joined the anti-CAA protests, were easy targets for the state machinery. The violent clashes between the Jamia students and the Delhi police in December 2019 are reflective of a deepening anger and mistrust between minority youth and the men in khakhi.

In the highly polarized Delhi assembly election campaign that followed, characterized by hate speech, Union Minister Anurag Thakur was seen exhorting a crowd to shoot the 'treacherous' protestors, a clear reference to the Shaheen Bagh protests. (The minister can be seen on tape, screaming, 'Desh ke gaddaron ko,' while the excitable crowd shouts back, 'Goli maaro saalon ko!'). Home Minister Amit Shah too was accused of stirring the communal pot when he told a political rally to 'press the voting button with such anger that Shaheen Bagh feels the current'. Such was the nature of the ominous religious divide on the ground that incumbent Delhi Chief Minister Arvind Kejriwal could not even challenge the home minister on the Shaheen Bagh issue for fear of losing the 'Hindu vote'.

The social and political discontent in the capital, and indeed the nation, was a combustible mix waiting to explode. Which is exactly what happened in north-east Delhi in February 2020. Even as Prime Minister Modi was preparing to roll out the red carpet for US President Donald Trump, barely a few kilometres away from the seat of power the streets were aflame with violent communal clashes. With mixed neighbourhoods in congested areas as the epicentre of the targeted violence the state was pushed back into its gory past.

A Delhi police charge sheet of the violence draws a link between the anti-CAA protests and the rioting, almost blaming the protestors for inciting the feud. But the report has little to say on the deplorable role of the political class or indeed on the serious allegations of one-sided police behaviour. A Delhi Minorities Commission report later claimed that the violence was 'planned and targeted' with an aim of 'changing public perception by attributing the riots to CAA protestors in general and Muslims in particular. This reflects injustice and partisan bias in the system which is neither good for a democratic system nor for our nation as a whole.' The truth is, the violence wasn't a one-sided pogrom but a riot in which criminal elements from both communities were involved. Most of the fifty-three people who died in the clashes were Muslims, yet the police charge sheet gives the impression that it was the minority community that was the primary aggressor.

As social cleavages continue to widen and state action reveals a dangerously bigoted mindset, galloping religious majoritarianism, witnessed in the run-up to the 2019 elections, only seems to have been consolidated. Which once again raises disconcerting questions over the role of institutions that are expected to safeguard constitutional rights. A large section of mainstream media seems to have been further compromised, having blindly bought into the narrative of 'Nation First' – where the lines between 'nation' and government are indistinguishable. Obsequious news channels in particular have become an extension of the government's propaganda machine: even at the height of the migrant crisis and economic distress during the Covid-19 pandemic, the storyline was deliberately slanted to avoid any harsh scrutiny of the ruling party at the Centre. 'Our mantra has changed from telling truth to power to bending the truth before power!' is a telling comment in a WhatsApp group comprising of senior journalists.

The Supreme Court is just as culpable in jeopardizing democracy, whether it is in choosing to prevaricate over petitions challenging the erosion of fundamental rights – be it in Kashmir on Article 370, in protecting migrant worker rights, in the context of the CAA legislation, or in the manner in which highly regarded human rights activists like lawyer and trade unionist Sudha Bhardwaj and even student activists are arrested under the draconian Unlawful Activities Prevention Act and then are routinely denied bail. In a trenchant critique, legal scholar Gautam Bhatia reflects upon how the Supreme Court under Chief Justice Ranjan Gogoi has overseen a drift from a Rights Court to an Executive Court. Bhatia writes, 'The Supreme Court has gone from being an institution that – for all its patchy history – was at least formally committed to the protection of individual rights as its primary task, to an institution that speaks the language of the executive, and has become indistinguishable from the executive.'

This perception of a pliant judiciary unable to stand up to a tough executive was strengthened when, in the weeks before his retirement, Justice Gogoi ruled in favour of the Centre in the Rafale defence deal, giving a clean chit to the Modi government over allegations of irregularities in the purchase of the jet planes. It was a case that had dominated the political discourse in the lead up to the 2019 elections. Justice Gogoi was then nominated to the Rajya Sabha less than six months after retirement, a sinecure that smacks of government largesse to a key judicial functionary. Another Supreme Court sitting judge Justice Arun Mishra described Prime Minister Modi as a 'versatile genius', raising more grave questions over judicial independence.

November 2019 saw another signal victory for the BJP with the long-awaited judgement in the Babri Masjid–Ram Janmabhoomi dispute in Ayodhya – incidentally, also presided over by Justice Gogoi. While decreeing that the contentious land be given to the deity 'Ram Lalla', the apex court cleared the way for constructing a Ram Mandir in Ayodhya, thereby bringing to an end a turbulent political issue that had simmered for decades. Not surprisingly, the Sangh Parivar was jubilant: the revival of the Ram Janmabhoomi agitation in the 1980s and the demolition of the mosque by a large mob of kar-sewaks in 1992 had been central to the ascent of the BJP as the country's premier national political force. That the dispute has been 'settled' in the year when the BJP under Modi had scored its second major general election victory is a telling reminder of just how much the political landscape of the country has changed in the intervening three decades. Calling for peace and harmony, the prime minister described the verdict as signifying a 'new dawn'. 'Many generations may have been affected by the dispute, but we must resolve that we make a new start for a New India ... anyone holding on to any bitterness, I request that they too give it up,' said Modi in a televised address to the nation.

Those fine words are not without irony. Way back in 1990, BJP leader L.K. Advani had set off on a Ram rath yatra from Somnath to Ayodhya with a symbolic bow and arrow in an attempt to capture a mood of Hindu revivalism across the country. While Advani was pitched as the ideological mascot of a resurgent BJP, Modi was chosen to organize the first leg of the journey across Gujarat. It was the first big break for the young, ambitious pracharak–politician. The yatra – literally a political chariot of fire – culminated in the debris of the Babri Masjid, sparking off riots across the country in which hundreds of people were killed, and opening the doors of the Delhi durbar for the BJP.

Now, Advani is in lonely retirement and his one-time protégé rules the country with an iron fist as India's most powerful prime minister since Indira Gandhi in the 1970s. Then, the cries of 'Jai Shri Ram' had been a rousing political battle cry that ignited communal passions; now, it is a symbol of the ultimate triumph of the political idea of Hindutva. Then, religious identity politics was a fringe phenomenon; now, it is mainstream. Then, Modi was a mere foot-soldier in the cause; now he is the undisputed General. At the Ram temple bhumi pujan in Ayodhya on 5 August 2020, hundreds of TV news cameras were fixed on the prime minister's every move. Dressed in dhoti-kurta with a well-manicured grey beard giving him a sage-like air, Modi offered sashtang pranam (prostration) before the Ram Lalla idol. An image captured for posterity, it marked his ascent into the pantheon of political gods. The 'secular' divide between personal belief and political power was erased by a prime minister proudly wearing his Hindu religious identity on his flowing shawl. No other cabinet minister was there to share the moment of saffron 'splendour' with the Supremo. On stage with Modi were the RSS sarsanghchalak Mohan Bhagwat and monk-turned-politician Yogi Adityanath. Addressing the sadhu-sant samaj, the prime minister even likened the moment to the pre-1947 freedom struggle, conveniently forgetting that the mandir nirman could not be de-hyphenated from the 1992 masjid demolition, a violent, criminal and extra-Constitutional act.

In 1992, I was a twenty-seven-year-old journalist reporting the horrors of the post-Ayodhya Mumbai riots. Now, in 2020, I was watching a victory ceremony of those who had once ridden the chariot of militant majoritarianism. The wheel has come full circle. Unapologetic and aggressive use of state power in the pursuit of political Hindutva is here to stay. Modi 2.0 is determined to fulfil the Sangh Parivar's long-held dream of a Hindu Rashtra. And construct a 'new' Republic.

Acknowledgements

ELECTIONS have always engaged and fascinated me. The fervour of an Indian voter reminds me of my other abiding passion, the cricket field, where victory and defeat remain unshakeable companions. My journey in chronicling elections through books began with the historic 2014 general elections. That I have chosen to narrate the story of an equally extraordinary verdict in 2019 is principally because of the persistence shown by Ananth Padmanabhan and Udayan Mitra at HarperCollins. Over several sumptuous breakfasts, we discovered a meeting of minds. In the quietly efficient Shatarupa Ghoshal, I have been lucky to have an editor who has worked on the manuscript with great diligence. My thanks also to other members of the HarperCollins team for the interest they have shown in this endeavour.

Writing a book amidst the mad rush of being a TV news professional isn't easy. I am grateful to the unstinting support from the India Today group, especially Kalli Purie who has given me the space and freedom to practice journalism without fear or favour. My data and research colleagues Praveen Shekhar and Nikhil Rampal have been very helpful at all times as has been my assistant Surinder Nagar. Bandeep Singh is an ace photographer who can make anyone look good! Special thanks to Shreyas Sardesai and Sanjay Kumar at CSDS for sharing their detailed post-poll study which is a goldmine of information. Rahul Verma, fellow at Centre for Policy Research, was kind enough to offer his valuable insights. Throughout the book, I have quoted several fellow journalists and politicians: I am grateful to all of them. In particular, my gratitude to the late Arun Jaitley, who, despite being gravely ill, was generous with his time and wisdom. I will miss him.

Writing a book is a solitary task that can be all-consuming. My wonderful children, Ishan and Tarini, have been a source of endless good cheer and support. This year marks not only my twenty-fifth year in TV journalism but also the twenty-fifth year since my bachelorhood ended. Sagarika Ghose has been my best friend and companion as well as an invaluable editor and guide on book writing. For thirty-one years as a newsman, I have had a privileged ringside view to Indian politics: I wish to acknowledge all those who have contributed to this journey. The voyage of life continues.

APPENDIX 1

Results Data

Table 1: Seats won and votes polled by political parties and party alliances in the seventeenth Lok Sabha election

Total Seats: 542*
Total electorate: 908722153
Total votes polled: 613136854
Voter turnout: 67.47%

Alliances and Parties	Seats Contested	Seats Won	Seat Change compared to 2014	Vote %	Vote Change compared to 2014 (% points)
NDA: National Democratic Alliance	541	352	0	44.87	5.59
BJP: Bharatiya Janata Party	436	303	21	37.36	6.37
AGP: Asom Gana Parishad (Assam)	3	0	0	0.24	0.14
BPF: Bodoland People's Front (Assam)	1	0	0	0.07	0.01

Alliances and Parties	Seats Contested	Seats Won	Seat Change compared to 2014	Vote %	Vote Change compared to 2014 (% points)
JD (U): Janata Dal (United) (Bihar)	17	16	14	1.45	0.43
LJP: Lok Janshakti Party (Bihar)	6	6	0	0.52	0.10
BJDS: Bharat Dharma Jana Sena (Kerala)	4	0	0	0.06	0.06
KEC (T): Kerala Congress (Thomas) (Kerala)	1	0	0	0.03	-
SHS: Shiv Sena (Maharashtra)	23	18	0	2.05	0.23
NDPP: National Democratic Progressive Party (Nagaland)	1	1	1	0.08	0.08
SAD: Shiromani Akali Dal (Punjab)	10	2	-2	0.62	-0.04
RLP: Rashtriya Loktantrik Party (Rajasthan)	1	1	1	0.11	0.11
AIADMK: All India Anna Dravida Munnetra Kazhagam (Tamil Nadu)	21	1	-35	1.28	-1.90
PMK: Pattali Makkal Katchi (Tamil Nadu)	7	0	-1	0.37	0.04
DMDK: Desiya Murpokku Dravida Kazhagam (Tamil Nadu)	4	0	0	0.15	-0.23
TMC: Tamil Maanila Congress (Tamil Nadu)	1	0	0	0.04	0.04

Alliances and Parties	Seats Contested	Seats Won	Seat Change compared to 2014	Vote %	Vote Change compared to 2014 (% points)
AD (S): Apna Dal (Sonelal) (Uttar Pradesh)	2	2	0	0.17	0.02
AINRC:All India Namathu Rajiyam Congress (Puducherry)	1	0	-1	0.05	0.00
AJSUP: All Jharkhand Students Union Party (Jharkhand)	1	1	1	0.11	0.02
BJP-supported Independent (Mandya-Karnataka)	1	1	1	0.11	0.11
UPA: United Progressive Alliance	525	91	27	26.74	0.91
INC: Indian National Congress	421	52	8	19.49	0.15
RJD: Rashtriya Janata Dal (Bihar and Jharkhand)	21	0	-4	1.08	-0.27
RLSP: Rashtriya Lok Samta Party (Bihar)	5	0	-3	0.24	0.04
HAM: Hindustan Awam Morcha (Bihar)	3	0	0	0.16	0.16
VIP: Vikassheel Insaan Party (Bihar)	4	0	0	0.11	0.11
JD (S): Janata Dal (Secular) (Karnataka)	7	1	-1	0.55	-0.07
IUML: Indian Union Muslim League (Kerala and Tamil Nadu)	3	3	1	0.26	0.11

Alliances and Parties	Seats Contested	Seats Won	Seat Change compared to 2014	Vote %	Vote Change compared to 2014 (% points)
KCM: Kerala Congress (M) (Kerala)	1	1	0	0.07	-0.01
RSP: Revolutionary Socialist Party (Kerala)	1	1	0	0.08	0.01
BVA: Bahujan Vikas Aaghadi (Maharashtra)	1	0	0	0.08	0.03
NCP: Nationalist Congress Party (Maharashtra)	19	4	0	1.37	-0.04
SWP: Swabhimani Paksha (Maharashtra)	2	0	-1	0.14	-0.06
DMK: Dravida Munnetra Kazhagam (Tamil Nadu)	23	23	23	2.26	0.53
CPI: Communist Party of India (Odisha and Tamil Nadu)	3	2	2	0.18	0.13
CPI (M): Communist Party of India (Marxist) (Odisha and Tamil Nadu)	3	2	2	0.17	0.12
VCK: Viduthalai Chiruthaigal Katchi (Tamil Nadu)	1	1	1	0.08	0.08
JMM: Jharkhand Mukti Morcha (Jharkhand)	5	1	-1	0.30	0.05
JVM: Jharkhand Vikas Morcha (Jharkhand)	2	0	0	0.12	-0.16
BSP alliance (Mahagathbandhan)	428	15	10	6.49	-1.03

Alliances and Parties	Seats Contested	Seats Won	Seat Change compared to 2014	Vote %	Vote Change compared to 2014 (% points)
BSP: Bahujan Samaj Party	383	10	10	3.63	-0.52
SP: Samajwadi Party	37	5	0	2.53	-0.72
RLD: Rashtriya Lok Dal (Uttar Pradesh)	3	0	0	0.24	0.12
LSP: Loktantra Suraksha Party (Haryana)	2	0	0	0.01	0.01
LIP: Lok Insaaf Party (Punjab)	3	0	0	0.08	0.08
Left Front	159	6	-5	2.5	-2.05
CPI: Communist Party of India	49	2**	1	0.58	-0.20
CPI (M): Communist Party of India (Marxist)	69	3**	-6	1.75	-1.50
RSP: Revolutionary Party of India	6	1	0	0.12	-0.18
AIFB: All India Forward Bloc	35	0	0	0.05	-0.17
Non-aligned parties					
YSRCP: Yuvajana Sramika Ryuthu Congress Party (Andhra Pradesh)	25	22	13	2.53	0.00
TDP: Telugu Desam Party (Andhra Pradesh)	25	3	-13	1.39	-1.16
BJD: Biju Janata Dal (Odisha)	21	12	-8	1.66	-0.05

Alliances and Parties	Seats Contested	Seats Won	Seat Change compared to 2014	Vote %	Vote Change compared to 2014 (% points)
TRS: Telangana Rashtra Samiti (Telangana)	17	9	-2	1.26	0.04
AIMIM: All India Majlis-e-Ittehadul Muslimeen (Telangana)	3	2	1	0.20	0.08
AAP: Aam Aadmi Party (Punjab, Delhi, Bihar, Haryana, etc.)	35	1	-3	0.44	-1.61
JKNC: Jammu & Kashmir National Conference	3	3	3	0.05	-0.02
JKPDP: Jammu & Kashmir Peoples Democratic Party	2	0	-3	0.01	-0.12
AITC: All India Trinamool Congress (Bengal, Odisha, Assam, etc.)	62	22	-12	4.07	0.13
AIUDF: All India United Democratic Front (Assam)	3	1	-2	0.23	-0.19
NPP: National People's Party (in Assam and Northeast)	11	1	0	0.07	-0.03
NPF: Naga People's Front (Manipur)	1	1	0	0.06	-0.12
MNF: Mizo National Front (Mizoram)	1	1	1	0.04	0.04

Alliances and Parties	Seats Contested	Seats Won	Seat Change compared to 2014	Vote %	Vote Change compared to 2014 (% points)
SKM: Sikkim Krantikari Morcha (Sikkim)	1	1	1	0.03	0.01
Other small and minor parties	2732	0	0	4.09	-0.47
Independents	3441	3	2	2.59	-0.13
NOTA	542	0	0	1.06	-0.02

*Excludes Vellore parliamentary constituency where elections were cancelled and held in August

**Includes seats won by CPI and CPI (M) as part of UPA in Tamil Nadu and Odisha

Note: Total seats won exceeds 542 and total vote percentage exceeds 100 since seats won and vote share secured by CPI and CPI (M) as part of the UPA alliance have also been shown again under 'Left Front'.

Table 2: Lok Sabha election 2019: State-wise result for major national parties and their allies

S. No.	States	Total Seats	Turnout %	Congress		Congress allies		BJP		BJP allies		BSP+		Others	
				Won	Vote%	Won	Vote %	Won	Vote%	Won	Vote%	Won	Vote%	Won	Vote%
1	Andhra Pradesh	25	79.70	0	1.29	0	0.00	0	0.96	0	0.00	0	0.26	25	97.49
2	Arunachal Pradesh	2	78.47	0	20.87	0	0.00	2	58.25	0	0.00	0	0.00	0	20.88
3	Assam	14	81.51	3	35.44	0	0.00	9	36.05	0	10.72	0	0.00	2	17.79
4	Bihar	40	57.26	1	7.70	0	22.91	17	23.58	22	29.67	0	1.67	0	14.47
5	Goa	2	74.94	1	42.92	0	0.00	1	51.18	0	0.00	0	0.00	0	5.90
6	Gujarat	26	64.11	0	32.11	0	0.00	26	62.21	0	0.00	0	0.86	0	4.82
7	Haryana	10	70.34	0	28.42	0	0.00	10	58.02	0	0.00	0	4.07	0	9.49
8	Himachal Pradesh	4	70.22	0	27.30	0	0.00	4	69.11	0	0.00	0	0.85	0	2.74
9	Jammu & Kashmir	6	44.63	0	28.47	0	0.00	3	46.39	0	0.00	0	0.87	3	24.27
10	Karnataka	28	68.64	1	31.88	1	9.67	25	51.38	1	0.11	0	1.17	0	5.79
11	Kerala	20	77.67	15	37.27	4	9.97	0	12.93	0	1.87	0	0.25	1	37.71

S. No.	States	Total Seats	Turnout %	Congress		Congress allies		BJP		BJP allies		BSP+		Others	
				Won	Vote%	Won	Vote %	Won	Vote%	Won	Vote%	Won	Vote%	Won	Vote%
12	Madhya Pradesh	29	71.10	1	34.50	0	0.00	28	58.00	0	0.00	0	2.38	0	5.12
13	Maharashtra	48	60.79	1	16.27	4	16.43	23	27.59	18	23.29	0	0.86	2	15.56
14	Manipur	2	82.78	0	24.63	0	0.00	1	34.22	0	0.00	0	0.00	1	41.15
15	Meghalaya	2	71.43	1	48.28	0	0.00	0	7.93	0	0.00	0	0.00	1	43.79
16	Mizoram	1	63.12	0	0.00	0	0.00	0	5.75	0	0.00	0	0.00	1	94.25
17	Nagaland	1	83.09	0	48.11	0	0.00	0	0.00	1	49.73	0	0.00	0	2.16
18	Odisha	21	73.06	1	13.81	0	0.92	8	38.37	0	0.00	0	0.76	12	46.14
19	Punjab	13	65.96	8	40.12	0	0.00	2	9.63	2	27.45	0	3.49	1	19.31
20	Rajasthan	25	66.07	0	34.24	0	0.00	24	58.47	1	2.03	0	1.07	0	4.19
21	Sikkim	1	78.81	0	1.13	0	0.00	0	4.71	0	0.00	0	0.00	1	94.16
22	Tamil Nadu	38	72.02	8	12.76	29	39.88	0	3.66	1	26.62	0	0.38	0	16.70
23	Tripura	2	83.20	0	25.34	0	0.00	2	49.03	0	0.00	0	0.00	0	25.63
24	Uttar Pradesh	80	57.37	1	6.31	0	0.00	62	49.56	2	1.20	15	38.90	0	4.03
25	West Bengal	42	81.69	2	5.61	0	0.00	18	40.25	0	0.00	0	0.39	22	53.75
26	A.& N. Islands	1	65.08	1	45.98	0	0.00	0	45.30	0	0.00	0	1.20	0	7.52

S. No.	States	Total Seats	Turnout %	Congress		Congress allies		BJP		BJP allies		BSP+		Others	
				Won	Vote%	Won	Vote %	Won	Vote%	Won	Vote%	Won	Vote%	Won	Vote%
27	Chandigarh	1	70.62	0	40.35	0	0.00	1	50.64	0	0.00	0	1.62	0	7.39
28	Dadra & Nagar Haveli	1	79.59	0	4.33	0	0.00	0	40.92	0	0.00	0	0.48	1	54.27
29	Daman & Diu	1	71.83	0	31.62	0	0.00	1	42.98	0	0.00	0	0.91	0	24.49
30	Delhi	7	60.51	0	22.51	0	0.00	7	56.56	0	0.00	0	1.08	0	19.85
31	Lakshadweep	1	84.96	0	46.86	0	0.00	0	0.27	0	0.00	0	0.00	1	52.87
32	Puducherry	1	81.21	1	56.27	0	0.00	0	0.00	0	31.36	0	0.34	0	12.03
33	Jharkhand	14	63.49	1	15.63	1	18.95	11	50.96	1	4.33	0	1.11	0	9.02
34	Chhattisgarh	11	71.48	2	40.91	0	0.00	9	50.70	0	0.00	0	2.30	0	6.09
35	Uttarakhand	5	61.48	0	31.40	0	0.00	5	61.01	0	0.00	0	4.48	0	3.11
36	Telangana	17	62.71	3	29.48	0	0.00	4	19.45	0	0.00	0	0.24	10	50.83
	Overall	542	67.47	52	19.49	39	7.25	303	37.36	49	7.51	15	6.49	84*	21.90*

*'Others' column excludes seats won and vote share secured by CPI and CPI (M) in Tamil Nadu and Odisha as part of the UPA alliance. Those seats and votes have been shown under Congress allies.

Table 3: BJP's vote share was highest in big cities followed by villages; UPA's success rate was better in small towns than in villages and cities

Locality	Total Seats	Congress		Congress allies		BJP		BJP allies		BSP+		Others	
		Won	Vote (%)	Won	Vote (%)	Won	Vote (%)	Won	Vote (%)	Won	Vote (%)	Won	Vote (%)
Rural	342	29	18.13	16	7.02	198	38.10	35	6.91	11	7.56	53	22.28
Semi Urban	143	20	21.95	17	7.73	70	33.75	8	8.73	4	5.66	24	22.18
Urban	57	3	21.14	6	7.33	35	42.47	6	7.62	0	2.22	7	19.22
Overall	542	52	19.49	39	7.25	303	37.36	49	7.51	15	6.49	84	21.90

Note: Classification based on Census 2011 data. Rural means urban population below 25%; Semi Urban means urban population between 25% and 75%; Urban means urban population >75%;

Source: ECI results and CSDS Data Unit

Table 4: BJP's success rate was greatest in reserved ST constituencies

Reserved Categories	Total Seats	Congress		Congress allies		BJP		BJP allies		BSP+		Others	
		Won	Vote (%)	Won	Vote (%)	Won	Vote (%)	Won	Vote (%)	Won	Vote (%)	Won	Vote (%)
Reserved (SC)	84	6	16.74	6	5.35	46	35.34	8	8.97	2	9.43	16	24.17
Reserved (ST)	47	4	28.67	1	3.78	31	42.68	1	2.00	0	0.97	10	21.90
General	411	42	19.05	32	8.03	226	37.20	40	7.78	13	6.48	58	21.46
Overall	542	52	19.49	39	7.25	303	37.36	49	7.51	15	6.49	84	21.90

Source: ECI results

Table 5: BJP vote share was higher than average in constituencies with sizeable Scheduled Tribe population

ST Population	Total Seats	Congress		Congress allies		BJP		BJP allies		BSP+		Others	
		Won	Vote (%)	Won	Vote (%)	Won	Vote (%)	Won	Vote (%)	Won	Vote (%)	Won	Vote (%)
Below 10%	418	43	17.07	38	8.44	212	34.90	41	8.56	15	8.02	69	23.01
10-29.9%	72	3	25.88	0	2.18	57	46.70	6	5.03	0	1.48	6	18.73
30-49.9%	21	2	26.95	1	8.67	15	45.96	1	2.31	0	1.06	2	15.05
50% and above	31	4	33.36	0	0.47	19	42.24	1	1.72	0	0.98	7	21.23
Overall	542	52	19.49	39	7.25	303	37.36	49	7.51	15	6.49	84	21.90

Note: Classification by ST population based on Census 2011 data.

Source: ECI results and CSDS Data Unit

Table 6: BJP's vote share was lower than average in constituencies with high Scheduled Caste population

SC Population	Total Seats	Congress		Congress allies		BJP		BJP allies		BSP+		Others	
		Won	Vote (%)	Won	Vote (%)	Won	Vote (%)	Won	Vote (%)	Won	Vote (%)	Won	Vote (%)
Below 10%	124	17	26.76	9	6.63	68	38.13	9	7.07	0	0.80	21	20.61
10-19.9%	273	24	18.95	18	8.31	152	37.30	31	7.68	7	5.71	41	22.05
20-29.9%	117	6	15.28	10	5.91	68	37.69	7	6.70	8	12.72	18	21.70
30% and above	28	5	13.38	2	3.70	15	33.56	2	10.33	0	10.79	4	28.24
Overall	542	52	19.49	39	7.25	303	37.36	49	7.51	15	6.49	84	21.90

Note: Classification by SC population based on Census 2011 data.

Source: ECI results and CSDS Data Unit

Table 7: BJP secured the highest proportion of votes in constituencies where Muslims are present in sizeable numbers (20-40% of total population) but aren't the majority, indicating the possibility of Hindu consolidation on such seats

Muslim Population	Total Seats	Congress		Congress allies		BJP		BJP allies		BSP+		Others	
		Won	Vote (%)	Won	Vote (%)	Won	Vote (%)	Won	Vote (%)	Won	Vote (%)	Won	Vote (%)
Less than 10%	287	33	22.34	33	9.14	154	35.60	24	8.86	1	3.13	42	20.93
10-19.9%	167	7	15.89	3	6.52	106	39.64	23	7.27	6	8.48	22	22.20
20-39.9%	64	7	16.34	1	1.89	38	43.26	2	3.47	5	14.65	11	20.39
40% and above	24	5	19.71	2	4.64	5	24.24	0	3.39	3	9.77	9	38.25
Overall	542	52	19.49	39	7.25	303	37.36	49	7.51	15	6.49	84	21.90

Note: Classification by Muslim population based on Census 2011 data.

Source: ECI results and CSDS Data Unit

Table 8: Nearly half the seats that the BJP won were won by margins of over 20 percentage points; BJP was the only party to win seats by a 50% point plus margin

Victory margin *(difference between vote % secured by winner and runner-up)*	BJP		Congress		Others	
	Seats won	% of total won	Seats won	% of total won	Seats won	% of total won
>50% points	3*	0.9	0	0	0	0
40-49.99% points	20	6.6	1	1.9	2	1
30-39.99% points	49	16.2	3	5.8	14	7.5
20-29.99% points	79	26.1	4	7.7	38	20.3
10-19.99% points	69	22.8	13	25	62	33.2
5-9.99% points	42	13.9	12	23.1	35	18.7
<5% points	41	13.5	19	36.5	36	19.3
	303	100	52	100	187	100

* The three seats are: Navsari (victory margin of 52.73% points), Surat (51.31% points) and Karnal (50.44% points)

Source: ECI results and CSDS Data Unit

Table 9: Nearly three of every four seats that the BJP won were won by margins of over 1 lakh votes; BJP won 15 seats by 5 lakh plus margins

Victory margin *(difference between votes secured by winner and runner-up)*	BJP		Congress		Others	
	Seats won	% of total won	Seats won	% of total won	Seats won	% of total won
>5 lakh	15	5.0	0	0.0	2	1.1
4 to 4.99 lakh	29	9.6	3	5.8	3	1.6
3 to 3.99 lakh	61	20.1	2	3.8	16	8.6
2 to 2.99 lakh	59	19.5	4	7.7	42	22.5
1 to 1.99 lakh	62	20.5	12	23.1	60	32.1
50k-99.9k	37	12.2	12	23.1	30	16.0
<50k	40	13.2	19	36.5	34	18.2
	303	**100**	**52**	**100**	**187**	**100**

Source: ECI results and CSDS Data Unit

Table 10: BJP polled more than 50% votes in 224 of 436 constituencies it contested; in 2014 this figure had been 136 of 428.

Percentage of votes polled	BJP contested seats 2009	BJP contested seats 2014	BJP contested seats 2019
< 10%	134	31	41
10-20%	52	43	15
20-30%	52	38	11
30-40%	80	67	43
40-50%	86	113	102
> 50%	29	136	224
Total contested	433	428	436

Source: ECI results and CSDS Data Unit

APPENDIX 2

Making Sense of the 2019 Verdict Through Select Sample Survey Data

1. MODI EFFECT/LEADERSHIP

Table 1: People's choice for PM - Modi's popularity scaled new heights; unlike 2014 his favorability rating was higher than NDA overall vote share

	2014 %	2019 %
Narendra Modi	36	47
Rahul Gandhi	14	23
Other leaders	21	10
No response/Can't say	29	20

Source: National Election Studies (NES) 2014 and 2019 by Lokniti-CSDS
Question asked: After this election who would you prefer as the next Prime Minister of India?
The question was open-ended and no names were offered to the respondent

Table 2: One in four voters of Left and State parties also wanted Modi to be PM

	Preferred Narendra Modi as PM %
Overall	47
BJP voters	88
BJP allies' voters	77
Congress voters	7
Congress' allies' voters	8
BSP+ voters	11
Left voters	23
Others' voters	29

Source: NES 2019

Question asked: After this election who would you prefer as the next Prime Minister of India?

Table 3: PM choice: Narendra Modi's advantage over his nearest rival Rahul Gandhi had narrowed in May 2018 before widening again

	Narendra Modi's lead over Rahul Gandhi
April-May 2014	22% points
May 2017	35% points
January 2018	17% points
May 2018	10% points
March 2019	19% points
April-May 2019	24% points

Source: NES 2014 and NES 2019 (Pre and Post Polls), and Mood of the Nation Surveys (MOTN) 2017-18

Note: Figures show difference between proportion of those who wanted Narendra Modi as PM and those who wanted Rahul Gandhi as PM

Table 4: States where over one-fourth BJP voters would not have voted for BJP had Modi not been PM candidate

2014	2019
Assam	Andhra Pradesh
Bihar	Bihar
Gujarat	Goa
Haryana	Gujarat
Karnataka	Haryana
Odisha	Himachal Pradesh
Rajasthan	Jammu-Kashmir (Jammu Region Only)
Tamil Nadu	Karnataka
West Bengal	Madhya Pradesh
Delhi	Maharashtra
Jharkhand	Odisha
	Rajasthan
	Tamil Nadu
	Uttar Pradesh
	West Bengal
	Delhi
	Chhattisgarh
	Jharkhand

Source: NES 2014 and 2019

Table 5: BJP voters were least likely to have considered the Candidate while voting; nearly one-third voted for BJP thinking of Modi and said so spontaneously

	Party mattered more than candidate (%)	Candidate mattered more than party (%)	Neither party nor candidate, but PM candidate mattered most (%)*
Overall	43	31	17
Cong voters	52	36	7
Cong allies voters	46	43	7
BJP voters	39	27	30
BJP allies' voters	35	30	31
BSP+ voters	52	30	11

	Party mattered more than candidate (%)	Candidate mattered more than party (%)	Neither party nor candidate, but PM candidate mattered most (%)*
Left voters	57	25	14
Others' voters	47	35	8

Source: NES 2019
Question asked: People have different considerations when they go out to vote. What was the most important consideration for you when you voted in the Lok Sabha election - party or candidate?
Note: The rest of the respondents either said 'neither of the two' or did not respond to the question
*Spontaneous response that was not read out while asking the question

Table 6: Economic issues didn't matter much to voters as was widely presumed; nearly one in five couldn't tell which issue had mattered to them the most

Single most important voting issue for voters	(%)
Economic issues *(Economy, unemployment, price rise, poverty, GST, demonetization)*	25
Development and Government performance *(Development generally; water, roads, electricity, education, health etc. specifically)*	25
Vote for a party/leader/candidate/government	6
Corruption	4
Emotive issues *(communalism, Hindutva, Ayodhya, Kashmir issue, SC-ST Act etc.)*	4
Farming-related issues	3
Welfare policies	1
Balakot air strikes/national security/terrorism/nationalism	1
Other issues (<1% each)	13
No response	18

Source: NES 2019
Question asked: What was the most important issue for you while voting in this election? The question was open-ended and options were not offered to the respondent. All answers given were spontaneous.

Table 7: The effect of Balakot strikes in blunting the impact of key voting issues: half of those who saw economic issues and development as the biggest voting issues and were at the same time aware of the Balakot strikes voted for the NDA. Balakot may not have been a top of mind issue as shown in Table 16 but it seems to have played a role at a sub-conscious level

	Voted UPA (%)	Voted NDA (%)
ECONOMIC ISSUES		
Those for whom economic issues were the biggest voting issues and had **not heard** of India's air strike on terrorist training camps in Pakistan	42	36
Those for whom economic issues were the biggest voting issues but had **heard** of India's air strike on terrorist training camps in Pakistan	31	47
DEVELOPMENT		
Those for whom development was the biggest voting issue and had **not heard** of India's air strike on terrorist training camps in Pakistan	31	39
Those for whom development was the biggest voting issue but had **heard** of India's air strike on terrorist training camps in Pakistan	23	52

Source: NES 2019

3. RAFALE ISSUE DIDN'T CLICK FOR CONGRESS

Table 8: Importance of corruption as an issue for voters consistently declined between 2017 and 2019

	(%)
Corruption as country's biggest problem in May 2017	13
Corruption as country's biggest problem in January 2018	9
Corruption as country's biggest problem in May 2018	6
Corruption as most important voting issue March 2019 (Pre Poll)	5
Corruption as most important voting issue April-May 2019 (Post Poll)	4

Source: Mood of the Nation Surveys (MOTN) 2017-18 and NES 2019 (Pre and Post Polls)
Question asked in 2017 and 2018: What is the single biggest problem facing the country today? (Open-ended question, no options were offered)
Question asked in 2019: What was the most important issue for you while voting in this election? (Open-ended question, no option was offered)

Table 9: Awareness about Rafale deal: only half the voters were aware of it

	(%)
Heard about Rafale deal controversy	50
Not heard about Rafale deal controversy	50

Source: NES 2019
Question asked: Have you heard of the controversy surrounding the Rafale aircraft deal?

4. NO NYAY EFFECT

Table 10: Those supposed to benefit from NYAY were least aware about it; Congress campaign on NYAY it seems did not reach the poorest

	Heard about NYAY (%)
Overall	58
Monthly household income up to Rs. 3,000	47
Monthly household income Rs. 3,001 to 5,000	50
Monthly household income Rs. 5,001 to 10,000	54
Monthly household income Rs. 10,001 to 15,000	64
Monthly household income Rs. 15,001 to 20,000	66
Monthly household income over Rs. 20,000	74

Source: NES 2019
Question asked: Have you heard of the Congress's promise of Minimum Income Guarantee *(Nyunatam Aay Yojana/NYAY)* for poor households if it gets elected to power?

Table 11: PM-KISAN may have worked in the Government's favour. 7 of 10 farmers who said they had received money from the Central government in month prior to election wanted the government to return to power

	Modi Government should get another chance (%)	Modi Government should not get another chance (%)	No response (%)
All farmers	49	34	17
Farmers who said they had received money from Central government in month before election (42%)	71	22	7
Farmers who said they had received money from State government in month before election (34%)	36	29	35
Farmers who said they had received money from Both governments in month before election (12%)	71	13	16
Farmers who said they had received money from government in month before election but didn't know which government sent the money (12%)	41	24	35

Source: NES 2019

Questions cross tabulated: 1. In the last month, have you or your family members received any money from the government? 1a. (If Yes) From which government did you receive the money - state government or central government? 2. Should the BJP-led NDA government get another chance?

5. RELIGIOUS DIVIDE IN VOTING PREFERENCES

Table 12: Hindu support for BJP went up by 8 percentage points; main minorities largely stayed away from it

	Vote for BJP (NDA) %		Vote for Cong (UPA) %	
	2014	2019	2014	2019
Hindus	36 (43)	44 (52)	16 (19)	17 (23)
Muslims	8 (9)	8 (9)	38 (45)	33 (45)
Christians	7 (17)	11 (16)	29 (31)	39 (45)
Sikhs	16 (49)	11 (31)	21 (22)	38 (39)

Note: Figures in parentheses are vote shares of NDA and UPA; Voting preferences of voters belonging to other religions not given due to inadequate/low sample size.
Source: NES 2014 and 2019

Table 13: Support for BJP rose across all Hindu castes and communities compared to 2014

	Vote for BJP (NDA) %		Vote for Cong (UPA) %	
	2014	2019	2014	2019
Upper Caste	47 (56)	52 (59)	13 (16)	12 (18)
Upper OBC	30 (39)	41 (52)	15 (20)	15 (25)
Lower OBC	42 (50)	48 (58)	16 (17)	15 (19)
SC	24 (30)	34 (41)	18 (20)	20 (25)
ST	37 (40)	44 (46)	28 (31)	31 (37)

Note: Figures in parentheses are vote shares of NDA and UPA; Voting preferences of voters belonging to other religions not given due to inadequate sample.
Source: NES 2014 and 2019

Table 14: Most Hindus were in favour of giving the Modi government another chance; most Muslims, Christians and Sikhs however were against it

	Modi government should get another chance (%)	Modi government shouldn't get another chance (%)
Hindus	54	29
Muslims	15	64
Christians	17	55
Sikhs	29	55

Source: NES 2019

Question asked: Should the BJP-led NDA government get another chance?

6. YOUTH VOTE

Table 15: Even as young voters preferred BJP more than voters from other age groups, the gains made by the BJP among first time voters compared to the 2014 elections were the least

Age groups	Voted for .....(%)				
	Congress	Congress allies	BJP	BJP allies	Other parties
18-22 years	20 (+3)	5 (+3)	41 (+4)	7 (0)	27 (-10)
23-27 years	18 (-2)	6 (+3)	40 (+8)	7 (0)	29 (-9)
28-35 years	19 (0)	7 (+4)	39 (+6)	7 (0)	28 (-10)
36-45 years	20 (+2)	7 (+4)	37 (+7)	7 (0)	29 (-13)
46-55 years	20 (0)	8 (+5)	36 (+6)	7 (+1)	29 (-12)
56 years and above	19 (-1)	8 (+3)	35 (+7)	7 (-1)	31(-8)

Note: Figures in parentheses indicate vote shift/change from 2014. Figures have been rounded off.

Source: NES 2014 and 2019

Table 16: BJP emerged as the most favored party among youth (18-25-year-olds) cutting across different Hindu communities; youth from religious minorities however were less likely to vote for BJP compared to 2014 elections

	Voted for BJP		
	2014 (%)	2019 (%)	Change since 2014 (% points)
Upper caste youth	53	56	+3
Upper OBC youth	36	45	+9
Lower OBC youth	44	58	+14
Dalit youth	28	35	+7
Adivasi youth	37	46	+9
Muslim youth	8	7	-1
Youth from other religious minorities	22	11	-11

Source: NES 2014 and 2019

Table 17: BJP was most favored by the youth (18-25-year-olds) living in towns

	Voted for BJP		
	2014 (%)	2019 (%)	Change since 2014 (% points)
Youth living in villages	34	40	+6
Youth living in towns	35	44	+9
Youth living in cities	34	38	+4

Source: NES 2014 and 2019

Table 18: Younger voters (18-27 year olds) were nine percentage points more likely to want Modi as PM than eldest voters (56+ years)

	Want Modi as PM 2014 (%)	Want Modi as PM 2019 (%)	Change since 2014 (% points)
18-22 yrs	43	51	+8
23-27 yrs	40	51	+11
28-35 yrs	38	48	+10
36-45 yrs	36	47	+11
46-55 yrs	33	46	+13
56 yrs and above	30	42	+12
Overall	36	47	+11

Source: NES 2014 and 2019

7. WOMEN'S VOTE

Table 19: Women's support for BJP in the 2019 election was 3 percentage points less than that of men

	Voted Congress (%)	Voted Congress allies (%)	Voted BJP (%)	Voted BJP allies (%)	Voted BSP+ (%)	Voted Left (%)	Voted Others (%)
Women	20	7	36	7	6	2	22
Men	19	7	39	7	7	2	20

Source: NES 2019

Table 20: BJP has always had a gender disadvantage among women (NES 1996-19)

Election years	Women's vote share minus men's vote share for Congress (% points)	Women's vote share minus men's vote share for BJP (% points)
1996	+1	-3
1998	+3	-5
1999	+5	-3

Election years	Women's vote share minus men's vote share for Congress (% points)	Women's vote share minus men's vote share for BJP (% points)
2004	+1	-1
2009	+1	-2
2014	0	-4
2019	1	-3

Source: National Election Studies

Table 21: BJP's gender disadvantage seen across social categories in 2019

	Women who voted for BJP (%)	Men who voted for BJP (%)	Women's vote for BJP minus Men's vote for it (%)
Rural	36	38	-2
Urban	37	41	-4
Poor	34	38	-4
Lower	35	36	-1
Middle	37	39	-2
Rich	43	45	-2
Non Literate	34	35	-1
Up to Primary	33	37	-4
Up to Matric	36	39	-3
College and above	41	42	-1
Dalits	32	35	-3
Adivasis	41	46	-5
OBC	43	44	-1
Upper Caste	50	55	-5
Muslims	8	8	0
18–25years	40	41	-1
26- 35years	38	40	-2
36- 45years	36	39	-3
46- 55years	35	36	-1
56 years and above	32	37	-5
Average	36	39	-3

Source: NES 2019

Table 22: Men were more likely to want Modi as PM than women in 2019; that said, Modi's favorability went up the most among women than men

	Want Modi as PM 2014 (%)	Want Modi as PM 2019 (%)	Change since 2014 (% points)
Men	40	49	+9
Women	30	44	+14

Source: NES 2019

Question asked: After this election who would you prefer as the next Prime Minister of India?

The question was open-ended and no names were offered to the respondent

8. MEDIA EXPOSURE EFFECT

Table 23: TV emerged as the voters' main source of political news by a wide margin; social media, internet and mobile phones were main sources for only 7%

	Main source of obtaining political news %
Television	49
Friends/neighbors/people	11
Newspaper	10
Social media	3
Internet	2
Mobile phone	2
Radio	1
No response	22

Source: NES 2019

Question asked: From where or which medium do you mostly get news on politics?

The question was open ended and no options were offered to the respondent

Table 24: At the time of the 2019 election, overall social media usage was still lagging traditional media usage

	Daily %	Sometimes/ Weekly %	Monthly/ Rarely %	Never/no response %	*Overall usage/ consumption (Daily, Sometimes and Rarely combined) %*
Watch TV News	35	28	10	27	73
Read newspaper	18	16	11	55	45
Use WhatsApp	30	2	2	66	34
Use Facebook	23	4	5	68	32
Use YouTube	25	3	3	69	31
Use Instagram	9	2	4	85	15
Use Twitter	4	2	6	88	12

Source: NES 2019

Questions asked: Traditional media - How regularly do you do the following – daily, sometimes, rarely or never? a/ Watch News on TV b. Read the newspaper Social media questions - How often do you use the following - many times a day, once or twice a day, some days a week, some days a month, very rarely or never?

Table 25: BJP/NDA's vote share among those who never watch TV news was nearly as high as those who watch TV News regularly

	Voted Congress (%)	Voted Cong allies (%)	Voted BJP (%)	Voted BJP allies (%)	Voted BSP+ (%)	Voted Left (%)	Voted Others (%)
Watch TV News daily	18	8	39	7	7	2	19
Watch TV News sometimes	21	6	39	7	5	2	20
Watch TV News rarely	21	6	32	7	5	3	25

	Voted Congress (%)	Voted Cong allies (%)	Voted BJP (%)	Voted BJP allies (%)	Voted BSP+ (%)	Voted Left (%)	Voted Others (%)
Never watch TV News	19	7	37	8	8	2	20
No response	19	2	32	9	11	2	25

Source: NES 2019

Note: Figures may not add up to 100 due to rounding.

Table 26: Higher the frequency of newspaper reading, greater was the BJP's vote share

	Voted Congress (%)	Voted Cong allies (%)	Voted BJP (%)	Voted BJP allies (%)	Voted BSP+ (%)	Voted Left (%)	Voted Others (%)
Read newspaper daily	19	5	43	5	9	3	17
Read newspaper sometimes	21	6	41	5	8	2	18
Read newspaper rarely	20	9	35	7	5	1	23
Never read newspaper	19	8	35	9	5	2	22
No response	20	5	35	7	9	2	23

Source: NES 2019

Note: Figures may not add up to 100 due to rounding.

Table 27: No neat correlation between regularity of social media usage and vote for BJP/NDA

	Voted Congress (%)	Voted Cong allies (%)	Voted BJP (%)	Voted BJP allies (%)	Voted BSP+ (%)	Voted Left (%)	Voted Others (%)
Facebook							
Daily users	20	7	41	7	6	1	19

	Voted Congress (%)	Voted Cong allies (%)	Voted BJP (%)	Voted BJP allies (%)	Voted BSP+ (%)	Voted Left (%)	Voted Others (%)
Weekly	19	7	38	8	7	2	20
Monthly/ rarely	19	8	35	9	11	1	18
Never used	20	7	36	7	6	2	22
Twitter							
Daily users	15	12	38	9	7	1	18
Weekly	19	8	52	5	3	<1	12
Monthly/ rarely	19	7	38	6	12	1	18
Never used	20	7	37	7	6	2	21
WhatsApp							
Daily users	20	7	41	7	6	1	20
Weekly	21	8	39	8	4	2	18
Monthly/ rarely	19	7	33	7	16	1	18
Never used	19	7	36	7	6	2	22
Instagram							
Daily users	20	7	42	7	6	1	17
Weekly	24	5	43	5	6	2	15
Monthly/ rarely	16	8	42	8	8	1	19
Never used	20	7	37	7	6	2	21
YouTube							
Daily users	20	7	39	8	6	1	20
Weekly	19	6	44	7	5	2	16
Monthly/ rarely	22	5	37	6	8	2	20
Never used	19	7	36	7	7	2	21

Source: NES 2019

Note: Figures may not add up to 100 due to rounding.

NOTE

Survey data shown in Appendix 2 is from National Election Studies (NES) 2019, 2014, 2009, 2004, 1999, 1998, 1996 and Mood of the Nation (MOTN) Surveys May 2017, January 2018 and May 2018. All surveys were conducted by the Lokniti programme of the Centre for the Study of Developing Societies, Delhi.

The sample size and coverage details of the surveys are as follows:

NES 2019: Sample size (N) - 24,236; Coverage - 26 States, 208 Parliamentary Constituencies
NES 2019 Pre Poll: N - 10,010; Coverage - 19 States, 101 Parliamentary Constituencies
MOTN May 2018: N - 15,859; Coverage - 19 States, 175 Parliamentary Constituencies
MOTN January 2018: N - 14,336; Coverage - 19 States, 175 Parliamentary Constituencies
MOTN May 2017: N - 11,373; Coverage - 19 States, 146 Parliamentary Constituencies
NES 2014: N - 22,295; Coverage - 26 States, 306 Parliamentary Constituencies
NES 2014 Pre Poll: N - 20,957; Coverage - 21 States, 301 Parliamentary Constituencies
NES 2009: N - 36,169; Coverage - 29 States and Union Territories; 536 Parliamentary Constituencies
NES 2004: N - 27,189; Coverage - 31 States and Union Territories; 420 Parliamentary Constituencies
NES 1999: N - 9,418; Coverage - 21 States, 108 Parliamentary Constituencies
NES 1998: N - 8,133; Coverage - 19 States, 112 Parliamentary Constituencies
NES 1996: N - 9,614; Coverage - 21 States, 114 Parliamentary Constituencies

For detailed methodology and sampling method adopted, visit www.lokniti.org

Index

About the Author

Rajdeep Sardesai is a senior journalist, author, columnist and news presenter with more than thirty years' experience in print and television news. Having begun his career with the *Times of India* in 1988, Rajdeep moved to NDTV in 1994. He was the founder–editor of the IBN18 Network, which started news channels like CNN-IBN. He is currently a consulting editor with the TV Today Network and anchors a flagship prime-time show.

Rajdeep has won several awards for journalistic excellence including the Ramnath Goenka award, the International Broadcasters prize, the Asian TV award and the Prem Bhatia Political Journalism award (in 2019, for his general election coverage). He received the Padma Shri in 2008.

He is the author of three previous books: *2014: The Election that Changed India*; *Democracy's XI: The Great Indian Cricket Story*; and *Newsman: Tracking India in the Modi Era*. He lives in New Delhi.